CW00406567

UNDER EMERALD SKY

A novel

Copyright © Juliane Weber 2020

All rights reserved. This book or any portion thereof may not be reproduced or used in any manner whatsoever without the express written permission of the publisher, except for the use of brief quotations in a book review.

Portions of this book are works of fiction. Any references to historical events, real people, or real places are used fictitiously. Other names, characters, places and events are products of the author's imagination, and any resemblances to actual events or places or persons, living or dead, are entirely coincidental.

ISBN 979-8-5528-3374-0

Cover design by White Rabbit Arts

www.julianeweber.com

For my husband, who encouraged me to write the first words.

Ireland
June 1843

1.

I CAN PINPOINT the moment my brother started losing his mind.

It was the day after father's funeral.

I had awoken with swollen eyes and a heavy heart. Kieran and I had held each other at the graveside, supporting each other as we faced a new and unknown world—one that didn't include either of our parents to guide us. Sharing our common grief, I'd felt connected again with a brother who'd been my closest friend when we were children. I had hoped we could be that close again, that we could help each other through the sadness that engulfed us.

Instead, Kieran had turned away from me.

"I've decided that I will be in charge of Talamh na Niall's ledgers from now on," he'd announced the moment he'd seen me, referring to the family farm.

I was taken aback.

Kieran had never had a head for numbers and had never shown the slightest interest in the farm's finances. I'd been assisting father with the ledgers almost since I'd learnt how to count and had assumed I would take over the job now that he was gone, being a woman notwithstanding.

I gaped at Kieran, at a loss for words.

"It's man's work," he declared haughtily, sticking his nose up in the air.

This statement made me puff up in indignation. He'd shared some of his thoughts on the apparent inferiority of women before, but this was the last straw.

"Is that so?" I said, trying not to shout. "And what does that make you? You've never done such work a day in your life!"

"It wasn't needed of me before." He dropped his gaze briefly before looking pompously back up at me. "Now that I'm the *man* of the house, I shall be solely in charge of the farm and run things accordingly.—As I please!"

"You'll run the farm into the ground, that's what you'll do!" I yelled. "You never took any interest in the farm's business while father was alive, and now you want to run it yourself? You're mad!"

We stared at each other, the closeness we'd felt the day before forgotten.

"Don't you speak to me that way! Show some respect!" Kieran's cheeks and ears turned pink as he continued to stick his nose into the air in an exaggerated gesture.

"Why should I?" I demanded, unimpressed with his act. "You don't have the slightest clue what you're doing. I'd be surprised if you even know how to use a spade, much less when to plant which crops or how to work out the labourers' pay."

Kieran narrowed his eyes at me. I narrowed my own and glared back.

"Father let you get away with far too much," he said finally. "You've forgotten your place—and how the world works. Women do as they are told—get used to it!"

With this, he had turned on his heel and walked out.

I had at first tried to excuse his behaviour, as was my natural inclination when it came to Kieran's bad habits, always wanting to believe the best in him. His conduct could be explained because he was grieving and confused, I told myself. Surely, he would come around, I thought.

Only he hadn't.

He had made good on his threats, refusing to let me participate in anything he considered *man's work*—which included absolutely everything of interest to me—informing me self-importantly that there'd be nothing whatsoever preventing him from throwing me out if I didn't follow his orders.

And why shouldn't he throw me out if he were so inclined? It was a man's world after all.

Unlike many girls, I'd had the good fortune that my father had believed in a thorough education for both of his children and had treated Kieran and me as equals. In contrast to me, though, my brother had never shown much interest in the farm's business, a fact that had driven a wedge between the two of them, as my father despaired at Kieran's ability to manage the estate after his death.

Fortunately, my father's fears and my own prediction that Kieran would run the farm into the ground hadn't come true.

This was largely because the overseer, Mr Smith, did know how to run a farm, and Kieran was at least smart enough to take his advice. Despite his lofty aspirations to be in charge himself, over time, Kieran had given Mr Smith more and more responsibilities, until the overseer was in fact the one running Niall—

as we affectionately called the farm for short—although Kieran would never admit it.

I had tried to resign myself to my fate—after all, it was the fate of almost every other woman in Britain to play second fiddle to men.

To begin with, I had attempted to keep myself busy by assisting in the management of the household, but it quickly became apparent that our cook, Mrs O'Sullivan, and the other servants under her care had things well under control and required no assistance, most certainly not from me, being better versed in wage disputes and market values than the planning of menus and the like. And so, I had surrendered the household to Mrs O'Sullivan and was eventually left with little else to do all day but while away my time in father's library. Although this was an occupation I would otherwise have enjoyed, doing nothing else left me feeling empty, unfulfilled, like a beautiful vase stashed away at the back of the cupboard, gathering dust.

"It's time I arrange a husband for you," Kieran said to me now, reiterating an opinion he'd been expressing ever more frequently in recent times. "Hopefully, you'll be of more use to him than you are to me here," he added with a small frown.

"And whose fault is that?" I snapped, bristling at the insult, although the effect seemed largely lost on Kieran.

"You are twenty-two after all," he went on, ignoring me while he buttered his bread, light brown curls bent over his breakfast. "Perhaps one of the O'Malley brothers?"

"Why do you hate me, Kieran?"

He looked up at me across the dining table, with a seemingly genuine expression of astonishment on his face. "I don't hate you, Alannah."

"For two years, you have let me do nothing but pick the tableware for dinner parties, and yet you complain that I am idle. I can help you. I can read receipts and orders, work out budgets, calculate taxes and so much more.—I did all these things before, when father was still alive."

I looked at Kieran intently, wanting him to remember a time when we'd been closer. He held my eyes for a moment, memories flashing across his face. I wanted to reach out to him, to cross the distance that had come between us, but before I could say anything, he swallowed heavily and pointedly lifted his chin.

9

"He is gone now," he said in a cold voice as his face hardened, all traces of sentimentality vanished. He got up abruptly. "I am the head of this household now and you will do as I tell you...and marry whom I say! It's about time you had a husband and children to take care of...it'll keep you out of mischief!"

He glared at me arrogantly, compressing his lips stubbornly.

I stared back silently until he stormed out, leaving me to contemplate what excitement I might be able to dredge up on what promised to be yet another dull day.

I WAS ENGROSSED in an outdated copy of *The Lancet*, which my former tutor Mr Henderson had sent me from London.

Having nothing in the way of farm or other work to do did have its advantages, I reflected.

I was an avid reader and was especially fascinated by all things scholastic in nature, devouring any academic publications I could get my hands on—which were, unfortunately, few and far between. The issue I held now was therefore a welcome treasure—old though it was—and I paged through it reverently, wishing I could conduct my own research and have it published in such a journal, to be seen by the most influential minds of the time.

All of which are men, I thought sullenly, but was distracted by the title on the page I had just turned.

DESCRIPTION OF THE ARTERIES ENGAGED IN THE ERECTION OF THE PENIS, jumped out at me in capital letters, and I leaned closer to learn more about this fascinating topic. The promised description ensued, leaving me captivated.

"These erectile branches are most easily discovered in man," I read. Well, more likely so than in women, I mused...how unfortunate there aren't any pictures.

"There's an Englishman come to Glaslearg."

I jumped, dropping the journal, and blushing furiously. Kieran narrowed his eyes at me but didn't say anything.

"Um...an Englishman, you say? The landlord, I presume?"

"The landlord's son, I heard. Come to cause more trouble, no doubt. That's all the English have ever been good for."

He left as speedily as he'd arrived, leaving me wondering about what he'd said.

Glaslearg was our closest neighbouring farm, which dealt mostly in the export of food crops, with some of the land leased to local tenant farmers. By all accounts it hadn't been doing very well in recent seasons. Glaslearg was customarily run by a steward while the owner resided in England, as was the case on many Irish farms.

This particular owner hadn't set foot on the farm for the past decade at least, and yet he had sent his son to see to his affairs now.

I wondered what the man's appearance would mean for us.

2.

QUIN LOOKED AROUND the sparsely furnished study—if such a word could be used to describe the place, which contained a single wooden table parading as a desk and a lone matching chair—trying to remember what on God's green Earth had possessed him to take on this task.

Not only was the house itself scarcely liveable, there were only two servants, both old and barely functioning, with fewer words of English between them than teeth. How was he supposed to communicate his most basic needs, much less instruct them on the finer points of sustainable agriculture and business aplomb?

And what would the point of such instruction be, in any case?

The entire estate looked like it was about to be reclaimed by the wilderness. Had anybody grown anything here in the past decade, he wondered? It certainly didn't look like it at the moment. No doubt it had looked rather different the last, and only, time father was here, Quin thought.

Then again, perhaps not.

Wilfred Ernest Cecil Williams, more formerly known as The Baron Williams of Wadlow, was a man with pecuniary interests that were not easily swayed by circumstance. He was concerned with making a profit, not nursing the feelings of those he might crush in the process. As far as Glaslearg was concerned, he obsessed about the estate's income and took great pains to collect his tenants' rents but had never shown the slightest interest in the estate or the residents themselves, much less the tenants' wellbeing. As far as he was concerned, they could do what they liked, as long as they paid up. And if they didn't, they were simply evicted—the moment they were in arrears.

Quin's father didn't much believe in second chances, and he knew he could easily replace unpaying tenants with other Irishmen looking to make a living on the land of their British proprietors—a state of affairs that didn't bother him in the least.

Quin sighed and shook his head. "Things just don't change."

While a former soldier of the British Army himself, the oppression of other peoples had never sat entirely well with him. Surely, we're all just people, he thought, and should be able to live our lives in reasonable peace and happiness, whether we're English, Irish, French or anything else.

Such thoroughly un-English thoughts would infuriate his father, who believed England was the centre of the world and that all other nations were there to do Her bidding. That other nations might be opposed to doing so never occurred to him. They simply would do what the English wanted voluntarily or be forced into it, so his father thought.

How a man with such opinions could ever have found happiness with his mother was still a mystery to Quin.

He smiled, remembering how his mother had told him stories when he was a boy, about the ancient Greeks and Egyptians, and the Chinese who lived half a world away, always ending her tales with a light touch on his stubby little nose, saying, "that could have been you, if you'd been born in another place or another time," making him feel connected in some way to people he would never see.

If his father had had any objections to his mother's bedtime tales, he never said anything. Nor did he object to her frequently reminding Quin of the biblical instruction to love your neighbour like yourself, which, she informed him repeatedly, meant all mankind, not just your literal neighbour. The latter was usually accompanied by a wink at Quin's father when he was present, as his mother was fully aware of his views on the non-English.

Fortunately for Quin, his mother's more tolerant views had ingrained themselves in him more heavily than his father's rigid opinions.

"Or perhaps it isn't fortunate after all," Quin groaned.

As it was, it was these humanitarian thoughts that had landed him in his current predicament—and of his own making!

One month earlier, he'd been comfortably ensconced in his London house on a rainy afternoon, going through some receipts, when his father had stormed in and informed him without preliminaries—or removing his top hat—that the Irish were going to the Devil. Fed up with the non-existent profit his Irish estate Glaslearg was making, compounded by the latest tenant who couldn't pay the rent—and the lack of a trustworthy agent to collect it—his father had flown into a rage about Irish ineptitude and stupidity, surmising they weren't even good enough to polish his boots and that the whole lot of them should be thrown off their damned island so it could be rightfully claimed by the English. He had emphasised the latter point by thumping his walking stick onto the edge of

Quin's desk. The desk being made of sturdy oak, the stick had cracked clean in half, which did nothing to improve his father's temper. Thus further infuriated, he had declared he would set sail for Ireland himself and personally evict every last tenant on his land, whether they had paid their rent or not, and God help them if they showed any resistance.

Having observed this tirade from the other side of his abused desk, Quin had slowly gotten up, gently removed the remains of the walking stick from his father's hand and found himself promising to go to Ireland in his father's stead to see if there was ought to be done about the state of Glaslearg and its tenants, in order to improve productivity and income, as well as ensure the happiness of its inhabitants without having to throw anybody out—all the while wondering why he was offering to do any such thing, knowing his father's rage would likely have blown over by morning.

Morning had come and gone, though, and here he was, standing at a much less sturdy desk, contemplating the prospect before him.

"THIS ISN'T A good start at all," Quin muttered, exasperated.

Rupert, his valet who'd travelled with him from London, looked around the crowded room with big eyes, taking in the unfamiliar sights. Having never been outside of London before, he was bursting with excitement at his Irish adventure.

Quin was not nearly so excited himself.

He had lined up before him the two ancient servants and fifty or so tenants, all of whom looked utterly wretched, with their ragged clothing and downtrodden expressions. He'd hoped to be able to discuss with them his concerns about the estate, but it was looking less and less likely anything of the sort would be achieved.

While the men had been reasonably civil when he'd introduced himself, all subsequent attempts at communication had been met with wary stares, interrupted only by the occasional nod and the odd muttered comment he could barely understand.

He was fully aware he was dealing with uneducated peasants who'd probably seen nothing of the world except the small tracts of land they farmed, which, among other things, resulted in a general lack of linguistic accoutrements, being mostly restricted to the barbarous Gaelic tongue. However, he'd been under the impression that a large portion of the Irish peasantry was able to speak at least some English, the British having gone to considerable trouble to root out the Irish language, which they believed to be a sign of disloyalty and contagion.

And so, he couldn't quite work out whether it was a complete lack of understanding of English speech or a natural reservation about talking to an Englishman that had made his current Irish audience largely mute. He knew the servants understood at least a few words of English, but even they were currently pretending otherwise.

"All right," he said. "I shall simply have to find another way of getting through to you."

He gave the men a broad smile, ensuring them in his most formal manner that he was there to assist them, not interfere with their lives. He ended with the assurance that he would do all he could to improve their conditions and secure their livelihoods. He then bowed formally to them en masse and bade them farewell, all the while contemplating how best to go about the business of honouring the promises he had just made.

"This place needs a complete overhaul," he grumbled to himself later, while contemplating the dinner he had been served. This consisted of a rather tough-looking saddle of mutton and a heap of boiled potatoes, the latter having made an appearance in one form or another in all four meals he'd been served thus far. He knew the Irish had a penchant for potatoes—they were the predominant crop on this very farm—but he found this evidence thereof to be rather excessive.

"Even potatoes won't be growing here for much longer."

The difficulty was one of management, he thought, of the opinion that organisation and planning could solve most problems.

Like most estates, Glaslearg—which supposedly meant green hillside in Gaelic, or so he'd been informed—was one large estate split into several plots. On Glaslearg, the largest of these were used to farm crops and raise a small quantity of livestock meant for export, while the smaller plots were leased out to tenant farmers, his father being of the opinion that one should never rely on a single source of income.

"So how do we go about improving the estate's productivity?" Quin asked himself with a frown. "And improving the tenants' situation to boot?" he added, remembering the sad state of the men he'd met that morning.

"Well, it will be difficult, won't it, unless we find a way to talk to them in the first place," he muttered, simultaneously wondering who he meant by *we* and why he was talking to himself. "Because there isn't anybody else to bloody talk to, that's why!" Defiantly, he finally tucked into his dinner, which he found to be reasonably palatable.

Returning to his earlier thoughts, he mused that the linguistic trouble he seemed to be experiencing might be one of the reasons why many English landlords tended to be absent from their Irish estates, the inability to communicate with mostly Gaelic-speaking, illiterate Irishmen making the prospect of permanent residence look rather bleak. Then again, a good number of English landowners had been living in Ireland for generations and considered it home; besides, Quin thought cynically, most landowners were unlikely to spend much time speaking to their tenants or labourers in the first place, English-speaking or not. The absence of landowners from some estates was more likely to be caused by the fact that many landlords owned not one but several plots of land and thus inevitably had to be absent from at least one of them at any given time, even if all their estates were in Ireland.

Quin looked out the window at the alien Irish landscape and suddenly felt a longing for his comfortable London house and the feeling of the city around him.

Not that the Irish countryside wasn't beautiful, he thought. In fact, riding through the gently rolling hills on his way to the estate, the sight of the luscious green scenery had taken his breath away.

"A trustworthy, bilingual factor might be the answer," he decided, returning to the present.

But where to find such a person, he wondered, looking around for inspiration and finding nothing but an empty sideboard. His father had faced the same difficulty, not once but repeatedly. Uninterested in setting foot on Glaslearg himself after he'd purchased it, he'd gone through a number of stewards, who he'd hired to oversee the running of the estate and manage the tenants, and all of whom he'd found to be cheats and liars.

With some reason, Quin thought, having discovered that the last steward, Mr Brennan, had run off with the previous season's rents before Quin had even set foot in Ireland. Quin presumed Mr Brennan had taken pre-emptive measures, under the assumption he would be dismissed forthwith. This was, of course, entirely correct; however, Quin had hoped to have someone to assist him, at least initially.

He shrugged. "I suppose I'm on my own for now."

It might be useful to meet the neighbours, though, he thought a moment later—an opportunity might present itself. Besides, he mused, it would be good to find out what local society there is to be had here, if there is such a thing...

With this plan of action, trifling though it was, he asked Rupert, who had fortuitously appeared, to call Denis, the very elderly butler whose previous foray into speaking with Quin had given the latter a substantial headache, ending with him being none the wiser as to the answer to his question, which he'd forgotten in the process in any case. A similar tableau ensued, but repeated finger-pointing and wild gesticulating finally led Quin to believe the nearest farm to the east belonged to someone called O'Neill.

Evidently one of the few local landlords left in Ireland, Quin thought as he rubbed his head, wondering whether this would be a good thing or a bad thing.

He decided to pay them a visit in the morning.

3.

QUIN LOOKED UP at the O'Neills' white-harled, two-storeyed farmhouse and smoothed the legs of his striped, grey trousers. Tugging on the tails of his black morning coat he wondered how his Irish neighbours might greet him. Did they feel any resentment toward the English, who had deprived so many of the Irish of their land?

"Best get on with it," he said.

With a final adjustment to the collar of his cream-coloured waistcoat, he knocked at the door.

A diminutive maidservant answered.

"Yes, sir?" came a mousy voice with an Irish lilt.

"Good morning, miss," Quin greeted her with a smile. "I am Mr Williams, the acting landlord from the adjoining estate. I wondered if I could perhaps have a word with the owner of this homestead?"

"I'm sorry, sir, the master is out," the maidservant whispered, looking mortified at having to deliver such ghastly news.

"I see, and when might I be able to call again?"

"I'm afraid I really can't say, sir," the little maid answered, looking even more distraught.

And just about ready to burst into tears, Quin thought with trepidation. Just as he was contemplating how best to extricate himself from the situation, he heard another woman speak.

"What is it, Margaret?"

This voice wasn't mousy at all, but strong and sure, with a soft Irish lilt.

Before Margaret could answer, the other woman was at the door, giving Quin a questioning look.

"Madam." Quin gave her a bow. "I am Mr Williams. My father owns the adjoining land and I have come as his proxy to oversee its further running."

"I know who you are," the woman said before he could continue. "What is it that you want from us?"

"I..." Quin floundered, somewhat taken aback by the note of resentment in her tone, as well as the observation that she was a most striking woman. Tall, standing straight and proud, she had vivid blue eyes, smooth ivory skin and black hair that fell in shiny ringlets down her back.

She raised one elegant black eyebrow expectantly.

Pulling himself together, Quin drew himself up to his own not inconsiderable height and explained that he'd simply come to meet his neighbours.

The woman continued to look at him askance for a moment before slowly opening the door. "Do come in," she said with the barest of smiles and a cock of the head.

Quin shrugged his shoulders and followed her into the house. The woman sent the maid in search of refreshments and led Quin to a small parlour, where she invited him to sit. Having waited for her to do so first, Quin wondered whether it would be socially inappropriate to ask her who exactly she was.

"I haven't introduced myself yet," she said suddenly, as if divining his thoughts. "I'm Miss O'Neill. My brother owns this land."

"I'm honoured to make your acquaintance, Miss O'Neill."

She inclined her head toward him in acknowledgement. "So Mr Williams, you've come to take over the running of your father's estate, you say?"

"I have." Quin nodded, wondering whether he could say anything that would make her laugh.

"And how have you found things thus far?"

"Aside from the general disarray of the estate as a whole and the widespread disinterest of my tenants...splendid!"

This remark did, in fact, result in the slight lifting of one side of her mouth. "Are your tenants giving you trouble, then?" she asked with a hint of mockery.

"The *trouble*, as it were," Quin began slowly, ignoring her tone, "appears to be mostly a matter of a language barrier. While I had assumed at least some of the tenants to be able to speak passable English, they seem by-and-large to speak only the Gaelic. And with me speaking none, there's a slight discord in our methods of communication, as I'm sure you can imagine, which will make it all the more difficult to achieve my goals."

Miss O'Neill gave him a deep blue look. "And what might those goals be?"

"The successful running of the estate, allowing my father to make a decent profit whilst also enabling the tenants to live with reasonable comfort off the land they work."

"The latter is a noble goal indeed, one not many landowners in these parts would place much value on, most of them being quite uninterested in who occupies or works their land, as long as their pockets are lined."

"I believe in equality for all men."

"Do you indeed? And what about equality for women? Is that next on your agenda of impossible feats to achieve?"

"I shall endeavour to address this very issue the moment the present situation at Glaslearg has been resolved, Miss O'Neill," Quin answered with a tinge of sarcasm, refusing to be baited into a trap.

The young woman's stern expression dissolved at his response, and she gave a small laugh, which quite transformed her features.

Quin breathed a sigh of relief, having felt rather put out by her scrutiny of his motives—although nevertheless pleased he had, in fact, managed to make her laugh.

At this opportune moment, Margaret the maid arrived with a tray bearing a silver tea set. She placed this on the low table between them and proceeded to make each of them a cup of tea.

"You're saying it wrong," Miss O'Neill said suddenly once the maid had finished her ministrations.

"I beg your pardon?" Quin looked at her in some confusion, teacup hovering in mid-air.

"The name of your estate." Her voice was soft, and a becoming blush crept into her cheeks. She cleared her throat and looked down, seeming suddenly embarrassed.

"I see," Quin said, feeling not the least bit offended by her criticism, but smiling to himself at her evident disconcertment. "It's a Gaelic name, is it not?" he asked with interest as he replaced his cup on the saucer.

"It is. It means green hillside."

He nodded at the familiar explanation. "And would you care to enlighten me on its proper pronunciation?" He had been calling the estate *Glasleer*, which was the way his father had always said the name.

"It's pronounced Glass-la-rrugg," she said slowly, enunciating each syllable carefully while looking at him intently.

"Glaslarug," he repeated, trying to roll the r the way she'd done and coming reasonably close, or so he thought. He looked at her expectantly, raising one brow.

"Better," she said with a small smile, making him grin, feeling ridiculously pleased with himself.

"I suppose I have a lot to learn," he murmured to himself in some amusement as he picked up his cup once more.

He glanced back at Miss O'Neill, who was eyeing him with an unreadable expression on her face, although one corner of her mouth was turned slightly up.

"Well, Mr Williams," she said with a glint of humour in her eyes, "now that you've discovered what your estate is called...perhaps you're ready to deal with the issues at hand."

"Indeed." He wrinkled his brow. "I don't suppose you know of an overseer seeking employment? Someone who could assist me in talking to my tenants, at the very least?"

"We do have an excellent overseer who runs things for us here at Niall, but I'm afraid competent overseers without current employment are not exactly thick on the ground.—So I'm afraid I can't recommend anyone to you at present." She paused briefly before adding, almost as an afterthought, "You could of course ask my brother once he has returned. He may be able to assist you further."

"Perhaps I shall do that, thank you," Quin said. He got the feeling, though, that Mr O'Neill was unlikely to tell him anything different, based on his sister's attitude.

"Although," Miss O'Neill's voice cut in on Quin's thoughts, "if a lack of communication is your primary concern, perhaps..." She hesitated before going on tentatively. "Perhaps...I could assist you myself. I am fluent in both English and Gaelic after all."

"Oh. That would be most kind of you, Miss O'Neill. But...are you not kept busy on your own estate?"

To Quin's surprise, the young woman's expectant expression hardened into one of discontent. She looked down at her hands in her lap and was quiet for a moment before turning back toward him.

"I'm afraid my brother doesn't have much use for me here," she said softly. "Unlike you, he does not believe in equality for all men, and certainly not women." She compressed her lips momentarily before going on, giving him a frank blue look. "But let us work on one problem at a time.—Tell me what I can do to help."

CLOSING THE DOOR on my visitor I was quite perplexed as to what to make of him—and not a little astounded at my own willingness to assist him even so. While he had been friendly, polite and forthcoming, I'd nevertheless found myself to be somewhat wary of him—at least initially—which I could only attribute to the fact that he was an Englishman.

"Not his fault," I muttered to myself, "just Kieran's bad influence."

For even greater than his growing belief that women were incapable of anything much except bearing children and performing menial tasks, was Kieran's hatred of the English and his conviction that Ireland would only prosper once free of English rule.

Not that he didn't have a point.

English interference with the Irish people had been going on for aeons, even long before Henry VIII finally stamped his authority over the island by having himself declared its king. But more centuries of bloodshed followed, as English and Irish battled for dominance, with the latter most often coming out on the losing side.

In an attempt to civilise the unruly inhabitants during the sixteenth and seventeenth centuries, the English crown had ordered countless Irish Catholic landowners to be replaced with better behaved Protestant Englishmen and Scots.

In fact, I reflected, the only reason my own family still owned any land was that my many times great grandfather, Cathal O'Neill, had switched sides. Seeing the handling of his rebellious Catholic peers, he'd promptly declared his allegiance to the English and announced his conversion to Protestantism, thus making himself an ally to the Crown and preventing seizure of his land.

While most of his descendants had seemed content with this arrangement, Kieran felt only contempt toward his ancestor, who he believed had displayed nothing more than traitorous cowardice.

"He should have fought for the Irish instead of hiding behind lies," he'd declared on one of the numerous occasions he'd brought up the topic.

"And died with all the rest?" I countered, for history told a sad tale of Irish rebellion, with thousands upon thousands of lives lost in the attempt to oust English rule.

"He might have made a difference!" he insisted.

"Or he might have been run through in his first battle, thereby sparing us the tediousness of the present conversation by preventing our existence with his own demise," I said, exasperated. "Why can't you just accept the past and move on? Make something of yourself and your life? Instead of continuously fretting about what might have been."

This was met with a cold blue glare, his eyes a reflection of my own, but filled with scorn.

"You're nothing but a silly woman who doesn't understand the workings of men." Kieran lifted his chin self-importantly. "Once I've found a husband for you, you'll be too busy to stick your nose into my affairs.—I will tell you this, dear sister, Ireland *will* be free! I'll devote my life to the cause!"

And that, I thought, summed up precisely how my brother saw the world.

Women, to him, were little more than tools to achieve his own gains, which were centred on the liberation of the Irish people from their English oppressors. History had taught him nothing and he saw the world as black and white—you were either against the English or you were against Ireland.

This narrow-minded viewpoint made me ponder the wisdom of breaking the news to Kieran that his sister had declared herself willing and able to assist one supposedly tyrannical English landlord in the further subjugation of his Irish tenants by providing linguistic assistance.

"Well, then I just won't tell him," I said to myself and marched up the stairs to my quarters.

4.

I WAS CLIMBING the three broad steps to the grand house of Glaslearg—which was beautiful in design but rather in disrepair—debating the wisdom of showing up at Williams' estate. Kieran wasn't likely to be best pleased with his wayward sister, whether I was here out of the goodness of my heart or out of spite for his treatment of me—a question I was still debating myself.

And what could I conceivably achieve here in any case?

It was unlikely the lives of the tenants would be much improved, no matter what Williams said. Equality for all men? Surely, he knew such a thing was impossible. Yes, there were some landlords who did care a great deal about their tenants, treating them more like family than paying residents, but the fact remained that the vast majority of Irish people were landless labourers or poor peasants who rented tiny plots of land for vast sums, often living in appalling conditions and surviving from day to day. And most people with any sort of social standing simply didn't care, especially the rich landlords on whom the poor were entirely dependent.

What were the odds of this particular landlord—who was an Englishman to boot—going to any lengths to improve the hardships of the Irish families on his land? Or rather, his father's land, I reminded myself, wondering why exactly Williams had come here.

"Certainly not to become a farmer," I said to myself, remembering his pristine appearance at our previous meeting.

Standing in front of the door, I glanced back briefly across the courtyard in the direction of the stable, where I'd left my horse in the company of an ancient groom. He'd offered to accompany me to the house, but I'd declined, unsure whether his aged legs were up to the task.

I smiled at the thought and knocked.

After waiting for what seemed like ages, the door was opened by another old man, this one wearing thoroughly decrepit-looking clothes that had perhaps once been a butler's uniform. He stared at me short-sightedly, his dark eyes almost invisible in their wrinkly beds.

"*Dia duit, a bhean uasal,*" the man greeted me in Gaelic in an ancient, cracked voice. "*An féidir liom cabhrú leat?*" *Good day, madam. How can I assist you?*

Feeling that I really ought to be the one who should be assisting him—to his bed, at once—I explained that I'd come to see the master of the house.

Having ensured me this personage was indeed present, he led me to the reception room at the front of the house and went in search of Williams in his study. Considering the length of time it had taken us to take the ten steps from the door to the reception room, I estimated I had a good half an hour at least before the Englishman would make his appearance.

While waiting, I wandered about the room, inspecting the sparse furnishings, which consisted of nothing but three simple wooden chairs and a single wooden chest. By the looks of it, the latter appeared to be frugally used as writing surface, tea table or any other contrivance necessary.

"Poorer than he looks or too frugal with his riches?" I wondered out loud, picturing Williams' well-tailored and expensive-looking attire.

"Neither one," came his voice from behind me.

I whirled around, feeling heat rush to my cheeks. I stammered an apology, but Williams brushed it off.

"Think nothing of it, Miss O'Neill. I am the first to admit this place is in a ghastly state." He shook his head. "Unfortunately, my father only cares about the estate as a source of income. He's been here only once, fifteen years ago when he acquired the place, and made it clear to all concerned that minimal expenses were to be used in the estate's upkeep." Williams shrugged. "I suppose he hasn't enquired about the state of the house and its grounds since then, because he simply doesn't care—typical of his demeanour, really. And when you have as little as these folks here, ornate furnishings and satisfying the trappings of the rich are certain to be rather low on your list of priorities, especially when your employer has given specific instructions against such expenditures. Thus, the miserly preparations for my coming, no doubt. Nevertheless, Miss O'Neill"—he spread his arms in an expansive manner—"I welcome you to my humble home."

"Thank you, Mr Williams," I replied slowly, somewhat taken aback by his frankness about his father's affairs. I thought it best to remind him of the purpose of my visit. "Er...Mr Williams, you had said you were in need of a translator?"

"Yes, thank you, Miss O'Neill. I am greatly indebted to you for offering your services," he said and gave me a low bow.

Rising, his eyes met mine and I saw they were a startling green, fringed with long, dark lashes, captivating in their intensity. I held his gaze far longer than social etiquette allowed before finally tearing my eyes away, only to find myself looking down at the tops of his polished black shoes, feeling the blood rise to my cheeks for the second time that afternoon.

Completely flustered, I waited the space of a few heartbeats before looking back at his face, which was showing no signs of having been at all disconcerted by the recent exchange, instead bearing a smile almost as captivating as the eyes above. I noticed he had a small dimple in his left cheek, this being cleanly shaven, contrary to the style of the times.

Williams, entirely composed, returned to our conversation with ease.

"I must admit I have been feeling rather perplexed as to how to run this place effectively with no useful means of communicating with most of its people, particularly as I hadn't expected the difficulty to be quite this pronounced.—But if you are indeed willing to assist, I had hoped we might start with the house servants and then address the tenants, to open the lines of communication as a start..."

He looked at me expectantly.

"Yes...yes, of course," I said, pulling myself together at last. "I am happy to be of assistance. It's a far more appealing prospect than drowning in boredom on my family's farm." I shut my mouth abruptly, surprised at my own bluntness.

"Ah, yes, you had mentioned your brother hasn't been able to find you suitable occupation."

"It's more a matter of him not believing I'm capable of anything," I said, unable to stop myself from correcting Williams, "being of the opinion that women in general, and I in particular, are blessed with brains that are no use for anything except the bearing of children."

Astonished at the vehemence with which I'd said this I turned away to inspect the bare mantelpiece above the fireplace. Although I'd long since known it to be the truth, this was the first time I'd ever voiced it to another living soul. The depth of feeling, and indeed resentment, the speaking had evoked was rather unnerving.

"I would venture to say you have far more to offer than that."

"And what would you know about it?" I demanded, suddenly annoyed, turning to face Williams.

"I offer no disrespect, Miss O'Neill. I simply meant to divulge an opinion based on the observation of our brief acquaintance that you are well spoken, witty and clearly blessed with sufficient intellect as to enable you to take on any number of tasks required on a homestead."

I gaped at him, my rancour somewhat chastened by his evident sincerity, but not completely appeased.

"In fact," he went on, "I had pondered how you came to be as educated as you evidently are, it being rather an uncommon practise in these parts to spend much time and effort on educating girls."

I had narrowed my eyes at this statement and now blew out my breath slowly through my nose to maintain my composure before answering.

"Well, Mr Williams," I finally managed, "I will have you know there is a school at Knockany and another at Lisgonnell that caters for both boys *and* girls.—And I can assure you I myself can not only read and write, but do sums to boot, as well as discuss philosophy, the arts and science, and a number of other topics, making me quite capable of far more than running a homestead." I took a deep breath and glared at him. "As to how I came to be so inappropriately educated, my father, unlike my backward-thinking brother, firmly believed a thorough education was the basis for progress, and that it was never wasted, even on girls."

I abruptly stopped speaking, being suddenly overcome with such longing for my father I felt tears prickling at the corners of my eyes. I quickly averted my gaze until I could get myself under control again.

"I never said educating girls was inappropriate, only that it was not common practise to do so...certainly not past the most basic of schooling." Williams paused for a moment. "I can see I have upset you. That was not my intention. Please accept my apologies."

He took a step toward me, and I looked up at him.

About a head taller than I, he cut an imposing figure. Broad shouldered, strong and handsome, he also had on his face a look of such regret that the anger went out of me all at once.

"There's nothing to apologise for." I sighed. "It's not you that I'm upset with. It's only that all I do is abide by my brother's wishes while waiting for him to marry me off to whomever provides the best prospect, when I feel I have so much more to offer, could be doing so much more." I shrugged. "Kieran doesn't

27

like me to have such opinions or any opinions really, for that matter, preferring me to play the meek bride to a rich man from whom he could profit. My father indulged my unladylike ideas, but Kieran is in no way so inclined."

And if I didn't abide by his rules, he could simply throw me out if he so chose. The reality was Kieran could and would do whatever he liked with me. Women were nothing more than property, and my brother being my sole living relative, he could command me as he liked.

Williams' gentle throat-clearing broke in on my reverie. He came to stand before me and extended his hand toward me. Without conscious thought I placed my own hand in his.

"Miss O'Neill, I deeply regret your circumstances and the unwitting role I have played in making you recount your hardships this afternoon. I had no such intentions and wished only to converse with you, whom I find to be most intriguing.—I hope perhaps to find a way of being of assistance to you in whatever capacity is in my power."

Williams had been holding my hand throughout this gallant speech, and my grasp involuntarily tightened in his.

"I mean it," he said, giving my hand a gentle squeeze in return. "But perhaps," he added with a grin that made his green eyes sparkle, "we could choose a more pleasant topic of conversation upon the occasion of our next encounter."

RIDING HOME LATER, I found myself contemplating the afternoon's events.

I was quite astonished—and not a little embarrassed—about how forthcoming I'd been with Williams, a virtual stranger, and an Englishman to boot! Yet I'd felt so comfortable with him that I'd borne my soul in a way I hadn't done in years— ever, really, if I was being honest with myself.

"And I forgot all about why I went there!" I remembered suddenly, having just realised my interpreter skills hadn't been tested once.

I suppose I'll have to go back again tomorrow, I thought, experiencing an unmistakable thrill at the idea of seeing the Englishman again.

"Don't be ridiculous!" I said to myself.

And yet, I couldn't pretend I hadn't enjoyed spending the afternoon with someone who let me speak my mind, without having to worry about the consequences.

"And he's not unpleasant to look at either," I continued my monologue.

My brown mare, Milly, twitched her ears, which I took to be a sign of agreement. But while Williams' looks were certainly a point in his favour, it was the way he'd made me feel about myself that occupied my mind now. For possibly the first time in my life—except in the presence of my father—I'd been able to be myself completely, without having to make any excuses for it.

After the precarious start to our conversation, Williams had asked me about my schooling, showing nothing but genuine interest.

"Well," I began tentatively, "as I mentioned, my father believed in the importance of schooling, being an educated man himself. Not only did he impart a great amount of knowledge to us himself, but he also arranged a tutor for my brother and me." I paused. "Come to think of it, the tutor was English, which is perhaps why my brother was never enamoured by him, nor the idea of learning in general.—He isn't overly fond of the English," I explained apologetically.

"I wouldn't imagine so," Williams said, surprisingly. I stared at him for a moment in amazement. "That being the case, though," he continued with a small smile, "it does surprise me that he's allowing his sister to visit a dastardly Englishman without a proper chaperone."

I looked down to hide my face.

Kieran *hadn't* allowed me to visit Williams without a chaperone, because he hadn't allowed me to visit him at all. I'd stuck to my resolve not to tell my brother about my extracurricular activities, for fear he would forbid me from going, and had waited for him to be about his business before sneaking out of the house.

I risked a peek at Williams, expecting him to press me for a response. But he only inclined his head and said, "Do go on, Miss O'Neill."

"Er, yes… The tutor, as I mentioned, was English. Only the good Lord knows how he came to find himself in the middle of Ireland, but regardless, his tutoring was of excellent quality. He also was not averse to teaching girls, as might have been the case, and seeing my inexhaustible thirst for learning, he was happy to oblige me by teaching me everything he knew."

I smiled in remembrance, recalling Mr Henderson's untiring devotion to answering my never-ending questions.

"I quizzed him relentlessly about every imaginable topic. We spoke for hours about Greek philosophers, Roman architecture, and ancient Egyptians and their scrolls. I was fascinated by everything to do with the natural world and couldn't spend enough time discussing the newest discoveries."

I paused for breath and Williams gave me a smile that made my heart skip a beat.

"When Mr Henderson taught me to read, he opened up a whole new world to me, and I devoured every book I could find, begging my father to buy me more. Mr Henderson himself wrote to his London acquaintances for further reading material and so I got to study the latest medical papers alongside the works of Plato.—I dreamt of going to university and envisioned becoming a famous scientist myself, making wondrous discoveries and travelling the world." I sighed at the recollection of the disillusioned girl I'd been. "My brother was only too eager to enlighten me that women were not allowed to attend university and that, indeed, they were far too stupid to even try. Being completely uninterested in academia himself, he nevertheless would not permit me to experience even the limited joys that were available to me.—But I told him firmly there will come a day when women can choose their own path and have equal opportunities to men."

I had said this with some conviction and looked at Williams to see whether he would be shocked at the notion, but he only gave me a wry smile.

"My mother would have liked you very much," he said, catching me completely off guard. I stared at him in bewilderment.

"She was also a lover of books and of knowledge and believed all people should be given equal opportunities," he explained, with a tender expression on his face at the recollection. "An utterly shocking concept to most Englishmen, of course," he added with a grin.

That explained rather a lot, I thought now.

For one thing, it made it clear to me that Williams genuinely seemed to be interested in making the lives of his tenants a little more bearable, perhaps as a tithe to his mother, who would have wanted him to do so.

"Then I shall do my best to assist him," I declared and spurred Milly on home.

5.

THE FOLLOWING MORNING, I again found myself in Williams' reception room, awaiting his arrival. My heart began to beat faster as he came toward me and gave me a bow.

"Miss O'Neill, I am delighted to see you again," he said, with every evidence of sincerity.

"I left yesterday without assisting you with your tenants," I blurted out, embarrassed in retrospect.

"Yes, I had noticed something of the sort. But never fear, the estate hasn't yet fallen down around my ears, so we're likely safe for a few more days." His green eyes twinkled with mischief, and I couldn't help but smile in return.

Having sent someone to gather the tenants for the supposed interview, Williams gave me a tour of the house and grounds.

Although Glaslearg was small in comparison to some of the enormous estates owned by single landlords in Ulster province, which could measure upwards of ten-thousand acres, it was nevertheless a good-sized farm that was considerably larger than Niall. The land on the four-hundred-acre holding clearly wasn't being fully utilised, though. From what I saw, some parts showed orderly rows of vegetation, while large plots had evidently been left to the wild, growing haphazardly, resulting in no usable produce—rather a waste of good land, I thought.

And good land it was. On a gentle slope, with good drainage and lush soil, with the small river that also crossed Niall running through it, the estate should have been yielding plentiful bounty, enough to provide an ample income for Williams' father and the tenants. But as it was, the estate—and the tenants—were barely surviving.

According to Williams, this all came down to bad management.

"We don't have enough labourers working the arable land," he said to me as we observed the farmland spread out before us. Situated on a slight rise, the manor house was surrounded by a small park, or demesne, which contained a haphazard array of foliage that straggled across what presumably was once a pristine lawn, down to the stream, across from which lay the fields and beyond this, the tenants' land.

"It's clear large tracts of land have fallen into disuse. It's no wonder the estate's income has been so poor in recent years. And from what I've seen of them, the tenants aren't faring any better.—It's hardly surprising with the small plots of land my father saw fit to lease, but even so…" He glanced at me. "They need somebody to guide them, to show them a better way of doing things…to support them. And I need them to work this land, to increase its productivity, which I believe can be of mutual benefit if we come to the right agreement."

I looked out across the land before me and saw its potential, and felt the determination of the man beside me.

"I'll help you," I said, and our eyes locked for an instant.

Despite the fact that I hardly knew him, I felt myself being drawn to him, overcome with the urge to touch him, to place my hand on his cheek and run my fingers through his hair, to stand on tiptoe and kiss his lips. I thought I could see the same impulse reflected in the depths of his eyes, which shimmered like dark green pools in the sunlight.

But instead, after a long moment, he offered me his arm and led me back to the manor.

Having regained my composure somewhat by the time we got there, I declared myself delighted at the prospect of a tour of the house. Wandering through the rooms, though, I found I was so distracted that I doubted I would remember anything he said. This was limited in any case, there being very little worth seeing inside.

Although the estate's former steward had evidently lived in the house, the furnishings tended to be restricted to the bare necessities, made in the simplest of styles. I suddenly wondered if Williams' bedroom looked the same and blushed furiously at the thought.

"Are you all right, Miss O'Neill?"

"Yes, certainly, thank you," I stammered. "I do wonder if the tenants have arrived though?"

In fact, they had. And what a sad sight they were, huddled together in the large drawing room that opened onto the portico at the back of the house, the demesne spreading out along the grounds beyond. Dressed virtually in rags—in stark contrast to their opulent surroundings, even diminished though these were—their eyes spoke of a lifetime filled with unimaginable hardships and little hope of improvement.

Living in Ireland, a land where poverty was as common as dirt, I'd seen my share of desperate souls, but something shifted in me at the sight of these men; men who had toiled and laboured their entire lives to be able to rent a tiny patch of farmland for their families, and who still looked as wretched as the poorest labourer with no ground to his name.

I vowed then and there I would do everything I could to improve the lives of these men and their families, whom destiny had thrown in my path. At last, I had found a purpose, one far greater than the scholarly life I'd dreamt of, which was closed to me in any case.

For what greater purpose was there than to improve the lives of others?

Once Quin had welcomed the tenants in English, I greeted the assembly in Gaelic and gave the men a warm smile. *"Dia duit, uaisle,"* I said. *"Ba mhaith liom fáilte a chur romhaibh ar fad inniu."* Good day, gentlemen. I'd like to welcome you all here today.

They stared back at me, looking rather dumbstruck at my formal manner, but returned the greeting—although clearly wondering who I was and what I was doing there. I explained that Williams had asked me to act as translator so he could converse with them about their tenancy and the running of the estate.

A few eyes narrowed at this. They were clearly expecting the worst—it wouldn't be entirely unheard of for a landlord to simply evict anyone he was unhappy with.

"Er, what exactly is it you would like me to say to them?" I asked Williams, looking askance at the forlorn faces.

"That I am here to improve the running of the estate, which I hope to be able to achieve to their and my satisfaction."

This statement received further sceptical looks, even before I'd finished translating, indicating that several of the men did understand at least some English. They eyed Williams and me warily as I continued to relay what he said.

Williams explained he wished to offer each of the men a written agreement of tenure, which would secure their tenancy on Glaslearg for the next five years, with an extension of said contract possible—and indeed desirable—after this time. The tenants' eyes widened at this, and they began murmuring excitedly amongst themselves. Tenants-at-will and yearly tenants often had no leases, which could leave them without any legal protection should their landlord choose to evict them.

Williams raised his voice to be heard above the commotion as he continued to outline his plan. In addition to the written contract, he would offer the tenants the opportunity to earn a stipend for working on the estate's main plots, where crops were grown for export, with the possibility of a small share of the profit made on these crops. The men's speculative murmurs rose again at this, but Williams went on. He explained he would also offer his assistance, where possible, in the upkeep and working of their own four-acre plots, in order to ensure the wellbeing of the tenant families residing on the estate.

"*Ceithre acra*?" one of the men bellowed, as further expostulations erupted around the room, this time in anger and confusion. "*Nach bhfuil againn ceithre acra!*"

"What is he saying?" Williams asked me, unable to understand the reason for the men's dismay.

"He's saying the tenants weren't given four acres of land to farm."

"But that's what my father agreed to!" Williams said, surprised. "What is the meaning of this?"

Through a convoluted discussion that involved fifteen or so men shouting at the same time—often in an unintelligible mixture of Gaelic and broken English I tried to decipher and translate as quickly as I could—it finally emerged that instead of the four acres of farmland Williams' father had apparently set out to lease, each tenant and his family instead lived on plots that were half that size. This trickery, it seemed, had been orchestrated by the estate's last steward, Mr Brennan, who'd overseen all the current tenants' arrivals on the estate, replacing previous tenants who'd supposedly been unable to pay the rent and were thus evicted.

"He probably planned it that way all along! Get rid of the old tenants so he could swindle the new ones." Williams was fuming. "No doubt he also increased their rent without my father's knowledge and considered the extra money to be his personal commission on a job well done."

Evidently, this was precisely what Mr Brennan had done, as became clear by the discovery that the rent the tenants were required to pay twice a year was considerably higher than what Williams' father had agreed to.

Williams was so enraged he began pacing around the room, spitting with anger.

"But..." he said suddenly, turning toward me, "if twenty-five families are leasing two acres each, what's being done with the remaining tenure land? There were one-hundred acres in total."

It was becoming quite clear to me—and by his expression, to Williams as well—exactly what was being done with the remaining land. My supposition was borne out when a tall, emaciated-looking fellow with straggly, dirty blonde hair informed us with a sour expression that there were in fact fifty tenant families on Glaslearg, not twenty-five.

"Fifty families?"

Stunned, Williams stared at the assemblage, evidently realising the men before him must be the heads of the fifty households inhabiting the estate, with only a few stragglers-on. It seemed the enterprising Mr Brennan had not only increased the amount of rent to be paid but had also halved the tenants' farmlands and doubled their numbers, without informing his landlord of either, thereby providing himself with a sizeable income nobody would miss.

"No wonder the bastard took off the moment he heard I was coming!" Williams said, visibly fuming.

He shook his head in disgust and let out his breath in a puff of anger. He turned to the men, making an obvious effort to be civil, while his eyes burned with green fury.

If left to his own devices, I thought he might hunt down the absent Mr Brennan and force him to answer for his crimes.

As it was, he contented himself with apologising to the tenants and their families, promising to try his utmost to correct the wrongs done to them—an act I found spoke volumes about his character, considering he was under no obligation to do so.

With this, the meeting came to an end and the tenants started filing out of the room. When the last of the men had left, Williams sent Denis the butler in search of refreshments and leaned heavily against the mantelpiece. His valet, Rupert, hovered in the corner awaiting instructions.

"I can't believe what's been going on here without my father or I knowing about it!" he said, in continued astonishment. "I always thought four acres of farmland were vastly insufficient. In fact, I argued vociferously with my father about the inadequacy of the size of the plots he was leasing, insisting he should give the tenants at least six. But two?—It's hardly better than leasing a patch of land as conacre for a season, aside from the benefit that the tenants don't have to leave once the season is over...assuming they can pay the rent. It's no wonder nobody can quite explain the difference between a smallholder and a cottier or a labourer...there's no recognisable distinction between them!" He looked at me, green eyes intent. "How do these people survive with two acres of land to farm for their livelihoods and their own sustenance, and with rent to pay?" He shook his head, clearly not expecting a response to this rhetorical question, having seen the state of the tenants himself.

"Unfortunately, what Mr Brennan did isn't all that uncommon," I said softly. "With many landlords absent from their estates, middlemen and land agents have become invaluable for managing their affairs. While some landlords take great care to hire honest men and make sure their tenants aren't exploited, many landowners are only interested in making a profit—as long as the money is coming in, they don't ask too many questions. An agreeable situation to someone like your former overseer, who would benefit from increasing the number of tenants paying rent, as he's the one collecting it with nobody here to report to."

I stopped talking as I suddenly realised what I was saying might be offensive to Williams, his father being the landlord in this case. But he seemed only genuinely outraged at what was sadly a not uncommon practise in Ireland—the exploitation of people already so poor it left them completely destitute.

Perhaps his opinion of his father was such that even behaviour of this nature wouldn't have surprised him.

"I'm sorry I couldn't be of more help," I said, feeling somehow—absurdly—that his predicament was my fault.

"Not at all, Miss O'Neill." Williams came to stand in front of me. "I cannot thank you enough for your assistance. Without your linguistic skills—and excellent people skills, I must add—the tenants and I would still have been staring at one another ten years hence, having made no progress whatsoever." He smiled. "Now at least we know where the problems are and can address them."

"Alannah. Please, call me Alannah.—And you're welcome."

"Alannah. That's a beautiful name." Williams gave me a look that made my heart beat faster. "In that case, you can call me Quin."

"Quin, short for Quinton?" I asked, struggling to maintain my composure, which I was losing ever more frequently in his presence, to my extreme agitation.

"It is indeed.—Quinton Fletcher Philbert Williams, at your service, ma'am," he declared and bowed. "My parents felt it necessary to burden me with the greatest number of dreadful names they could come up with."

"Oh, it's not so bad. It sounds…well…very English," I ended lamely and laughed.

"I do admit it could have been worse. I might have been called Goddard or Cuthbert, or, heaven forbid, Wilberforce, like one of my uncles." He shuddered, in mock horror.

"I think Quin suits you. And…whatever your name, I think you're going to make a big difference to these people," I said, looking up at him. Feeling suddenly that I would get lost in his eyes if I looked for too long, I dropped my gaze.

"I thank you for the kind words, my lady," Quin responded softly, making me lift my eyes once more. "And I thank you for granting me the pleasure of your company on this fine day."

He smiled at me, showing the small dimple in his left cheek, and I smiled back up at him.

And I knew with certainty our lives would be entwined from that day on.

6.

THE FOLLOWING MORNING, I could hardly wait to return to Glaslearg—not least of all to see Mr Williams, or rather, Quin, I reminded myself with a slight thrill, admitting to myself I was very much looking forward to being in his presence once more—but also to assist him in his self-appointed task of bettering the lives of the people living on his estate. I wasn't sure how far my own efforts could possibly extend, as I was only the interpreter and any changes were solely dependent on Quin himself, but I'd promised him my help and that I would deliver.

Besides, I thought irritably, it's not as if I have anything better to do.

When I came down to breakfast, Kieran was just leaving the dining room, evidently in a foul mood.

"It's about time you got out of bed!" he snapped the moment he saw me. "Do you expect me to do everything around here while you laze about all day?"

"I hadn't realised eight o'clock was considered midday," I countered. "Besides, you won't let me get involved in the running of the farm, although you're perfectly aware I'm more than capable of doing so. It's your own fault I have nothing to do all day but laze about, as you say."

I glared at him. He stared back at me, a look of extreme annoyance on his face as he stuck out his chin.

"You are overstepping your boundaries, Alannah."

"Oh, and what boundaries are those?" I asked sarcastically. "Am I not allowed to tell my pig-headed brother when he's being an ass?"

Kieran compressed his lips while his cheeks turned red at the insult. "Don't test me!" he growled. "You are a woman, and you will do as I say, and nothing else. It's best you accept that as your lot in life, *dear sister*." The emphasis on the address that was usually used as a term of endearment made it clear he felt very little such affection for me. "You should use your time to rehearse your ladylike behaviour—God knows you need the practice if you are to be a good wife that doesn't bring me shame."

I opened my mouth to respond, but before I could say anything, Kieran suddenly took a step toward me, blue eyes boring into mine.

"Don't bother wasting your breath complaining. You *will* do as you're told, and you *will* marry whom I say."

With this, he turned his back on me and stormed out the door, disappearing before I'd said another word.

I let out the breath I hadn't realised I'd been holding.

"Bloody ass," I muttered to myself. "If anyone needs to practice better behaviour, it's him."

Unsettled by Kieran's outburst, I ate without tasting my food, trying to dismiss him from my mind, but finding it difficult to do so.

He was my brother. We had played together as children, gotten up to mischief and rolled in the dirt, and I loved him. We had once been close, but the differences that had seen us start drifting apart in our youth were becoming more and more apparent.

Kieran's opinions about women were hardly unique, of course—in a male-dominated society that masqueraded behind superficial chivalry, prejudiced beliefs about women's naiveté and their excessive sensitivity were easily excused, if not actively encouraged. While many men genuinely seemed to love their female relations, a good number of these same men nevertheless recoiled at the thought of giving women more freedom.

I'd come to the conclusion this was in all likelihood based on the preposterous fear that women wouldn't be able to handle such freedom and would end up getting themselves into trouble—as simple-minded as we were, of course—although I suspected some men were simply worried about being outdone by women if they were given the chance.

In Kieran's case, though, I thought it was something else.

While he'd made some disparaging remarks about women early in his youth, such talk was never encouraged by my parents. But our mother had died when he was fifteen and, not having had the closest relationship with our father, Kieran had sought solace with his peers, who probably had a very different idea about what constituted appropriate behaviour. But even so, Kieran's patriarchal views had only really come to the fore after father's death, and I was starting to think I knew why.

Kieran had been left with a farm he'd never shown any interest in before and had no idea how to run. But he knew that I did. Instead of asking me for help, though, he'd resented me for the fact and cut me out of its management out of spite. And having declared himself the man of the house after father's death, intent on managing Niall himself, he could hardly come running to me for assistance once he realised he couldn't do it himself. And so, he'd continued to oppress me at every opportunity, most likely to make himself feel like he had control over *something* at least, justifying his behaviour with the widely-held belief that women were inferior to men and needed to be told what to do—a belief he himself had come to share over the years.

He'd given no thought to how his actions might be affecting me, blinded by his bruised pride and his bitterness, resenting me first for knowing how to manage the farm when he did not, and then for not doing the very work he'd forbidden me from doing, work he couldn't do himself. By now, it seemed to make very little difference to him what I felt or what I thought—he was intent on pushing me further and further away, until our interactions were limited to the sort we'd just experienced.

Thinking about the past two years, it pained me to remember how he'd treated me, when things could have been so very different if he'd only turned to me instead.

Coming back to the present after my lengthy contemplations, I realised the best way to forget about the morning's events was to occupy my mind elsewise. And so, I decided to visit Quin immediately after breakfast, instead of waiting until the afternoon, as I had intended. Fortunately, Kieran had already left for Ballygawley, where he would be spending most of the day, having meant to meet some acquaintances at the town's famed brewery.

He was unlikely to miss me.

When I arrived at Glaslearg, Quin himself met me at the door, evidently on his way out.

"Alannah," he said, breaking into a heart-stopping smile. "I am delighted to see you. I hadn't expected you until this afternoon. I was about to go visit some of the tenants to see for myself under what conditions they've been living." His green gaze met mine and my stomach gave a lurch. Suddenly, Kieran and his antics seemed entirely irrelevant. "But now that you're here, I can postpone my visit, if you would like to join me in the drawing room?" He started turning back toward the door.

"No, don't change your plans," I objected, and he stopped, looking expectantly at me. "I would be happy to join you…if you'll let me," I added, thinking that allowing me to translate for him didn't necessarily mean he wanted me actively involved in his business.

"Of course, Alannah, I would be most pleased to have your company. Besides, my Gaelic hasn't improved overnight, so your joining me would, in fact, be most fortuitous."

He winked and offered me his arm. We walked across the courtyard toward the stable, where he ordered the elderly groom to ready two horses for us—in English, I noted with some amusement.

"It turns out the servants can speak more English than they were letting on," Quin said, seeing me smile at the groom's unquestioning reaction to his English command. "I suppose they were pleading ignorance in the hopes I would soon grow tired of the dire state of communications on the estate and go running back to England, thus leaving them to their own devices once more." He paused, before slowly shaking his head. "Although why they would want to continue living in the state they're currently in is anybody's guess."

"Better the devil you know than the devil you don't," I suggested and looked up at him.

"Oh, and what sort of devil am I then?" he asked, grinning down at me.

"Well...that remains to be seen. Though I'd wager you're not the sort to sacrifice small children and seduce innocent young women."

"Am I not?" He gave me a direct green gaze that made my heart leap into my throat and start pounding furiously.

"Horses...ready, sir."

Grateful for the groom's interruption, I quickly mounted the waiting mare— one of Quin's four horses, my own enjoying a rest after our short ride here—and led her to the edge of the courtyard. Quin came up behind me and nudged his horse in the direction of a narrow trail that disappeared into the hills behind the stable.

"This way."

He led me along the path, which ambled away from the manor house and grounds, down into a small valley of luscious green countryside that bordered the small river. The grasses and delicate flowers of the hills gave way to reeds and lilies at the edge of the gently flowing water, which we traversed over a small wooden bridge. Orange-breasted robins flew around us while wrens whirred from bush to bush, breaking into surprisingly loud but sweetly melodious song.

41

I closed my eyes, enjoying the sunshine on my face and relishing in the beauty of a sky that was bright and blue, with not a cloud in sight.

"It's beautiful, isn't it?" Quin's voice was soft and filled with wonder.

I opened my eyes and found both horses had come to a stop on the other side of the stream, my mare nibbling contentedly on the succulent grass, nose to nose with Quin's brown gelding.

"It is. It's wonderful. It's...home."

He smiled at me and looked around him, shielding his eyes from the sun.

"It's rather unlike my own home," he said after a moment, turning back to me. "Do you miss London?"

"Yes...and no. I do miss the comforts and familiarity of my own house, of course. Not to mention the pleasure of being able to speak to everyone in English! But...right now...I wouldn't trade places with anyone," he said softly, holding my gaze.

I swallowed and looked down onto my hands. When I looked back up, he was still looking at me, but with a good-natured smile on his lips.

"Mind you, I would trade my best pair of boots for a good old-fashioned traditional English meal, one that doesn't involve potatoes!"

We laughed and continued on our way, emerging, after a short while, at the crest of the hill—which revealed a scenery not nearly as riveting as that by the river below us. From this vantage point, the entire estate was spread out before us, and I could clearly see what I'd already glimpsed the day before. Acres and acres of farmland were covered in scraggly vegetation that was a far cry from the orderly rows of crops to which these neatly demarcated fields had once been accustomed.

"Look at all that unused land," I exclaimed. Having lived on a farm for most of my life, I found such disarray offensive.

"It is astonishing, isn't it?" Quin said, a note of irritation in his voice. "Mr Brennan was hired to oversee the running of the estate, and this is what's become of it! Not only did he neglect the crops and livestock to the point we're making no money, but he also exploited scores of people who are already poor as dirt!"

Quin was visibly disgusted at his father's erstwhile steward, a sentiment I shared entirely.

I sighed. "Greed begets greed. There's good reason it's one of the seven deadly sins.—He will receive his judgment, in this life or the next."

Quin exhaled in a puff of annoyance. "I'm sure you're right, Alannah. But it's difficult to be entirely satisfied with the prospect of the Lord's eventual vengeance when the wickedness of the man is clear to see from where I stand." He gestured toward the ill-managed land. "Just look at what he's done to the place! Let acres of prime farmland be reclaimed by the wilderness...and why? Because he couldn't be bothered with the effort of farming it? Or to spare the expense of hiring hands to do the work?"

"Probably both. I imagine he thought he would make easier and better money by exploiting the tenants."

I could see Quin's jaw muscles tighten at this remark. He was quiet for a long moment.

"I shall see them done rightly by," he said at last and turned toward me. "I swear it."

WE RODE ALONG in silence, each absorbed in our own thoughts. I glanced furtively at Quin, riding beside me, back straight, looking ahead with a slight frown on his face. I supposed he was contemplating his options and marvelled at his evident sincerity in promising to improve the lives of the poor Irish families who were completely dependent on him—with a word he could protect and provide for them...or turn them out, destitute and homeless.

The fact he tended toward the former gave me a warm feeling I immediately tried to suppress.

"You barely know the man, Alannah Mór!" I hissed under my breath.

"I beg your pardon?" Quin turned his head in my direction, his brown hair lifting off his forehead in the breeze.

"Oh...um...it's nothing. I mean...I was just wondering," I finally pulled myself together, "how you came to be here as your father's agent. Could he not have sent someone else? Having as little personal interest in the place as you say, it seems peculiar he would have wanted his son to come in person to see to matters here."

"Well," Quin answered in a grim voice, "as we've recently discovered, good stewards are hard to find. And my father had had quite enough of entrusting his business to virtual strangers." He paused before going on. "As to why *I* am here and not one of his acquaintances...I must admit this circumstance is entirely of my own making."

He gave me a wry smile, his amusement hiding something else I couldn't read.

"I volunteered to come here in his stead when he threatened to travel to Glaslearg and see to matters himself." He made a grimace. "I couldn't possibly let innocent people be subjected to *that*!"

He grinned at me, and I laughed.

"And you evidently care a great deal about innocent people," I said with sincerity. To my surprise, though, Quin's smile vanished, and his face hardened.

"I am my father's son, whether I like it or not. And I am here to abide by his wishes. These being to achieve the maximum amount of profit with the minimum amount of effort, without any thought to who might suffer as a result. And filial responsibility demands I perform my duty as his agent to the best of my ability."

"That may be so," I countered, "but filial responsibility does not require you to have a conscience. If your father is only interested in making money, as you say, it would befit you, as his agent, to concentrate on increasing the estate's productivity, while leaving the tenants to their own devices, no matter how ghastly their circumstances might be, relishing in the fact the otherwise useless Mr Brennan increased the amount of rent to be collected.—And yet, you don't seem to be so inclined."

Quin looked at me for a moment before answering.

"It would be easier to take that approach," he finally said, "to ignore the plight of the tenants and think of them only as a source of income—far easier than thinking of them as people...with dreams and fears, emotions and needs. But I simply cannot sit idly by when there are people who are suffering as a direct consequence of my actions, or lack thereof."

He paused as he guided his horse around a crumbled stone wall. He stopped a short distance behind the fallen rocks, waiting for me to catch up.

"For better or worse, I am here now. I made the choice to be here. And I can't pretend not to see the downtrodden faces of the men who live here, who expect no better treatment than they've already received, but hope for it nonetheless.—If I can do some small thing to make the lives of these people a little more bearable, then I shall count my own life well spent."

I was deeply moved by his speech and increased my resolve to assist him in whatever way I could.

"Won't your father be angry at you, though?"

Quin shrugged. "I expect he might be, not being philanthropically inclined. But fortunately, I shall be far away and unable to hear his complaints. Besides," he added, "I have every intention of improving the condition of the tenants whilst also increasing Glaslearg's earnings. So there really won't be anything for him to complain about!—In any case, the estate won't be his forever, so he shall simply have to accept the decisions I make. About *my* property."

"I see...um..." I mumbled, rather shocked at this casual reference to his father's demise.

"Oh, I'm not talking about my inheritance," Quin objected hastily, evidently having divined my thoughts. "As much as my father makes me want to tear the hair off my head, I hope the old codger lives to be a hundred! No. There's an arrangement between us, well...between him and my mother really...that Glaslearg shall be passed onto me upon the occasion of my marriage." He glanced toward me at this, and my heart skipped a beat. "Luckily for him, this happy event is likely to be some years off."

He had clearly meant this statement to be said in jest, but I detected a note of anger in his words. Before I could say anything further, he had turned his horse back onto the path and was gesturing to me to follow.

After a short and silent ride, we arrived at the edge of a small field that seemed to lie somewhat apart from the others. It was laid out in orderly rows of potato vines, at the base of which stood a tiny ramshackle cottage that appeared to have no adornments of any kind, including windows or a chimney. The whitewash on the walls did nothing to improve its dilapidated appearance, serving merely to prevent the washing away of a structure made entirely of mud.

In silent agreement, Quin and I dismounted and approached the cabin on foot, leading the horses. Our approach was met with the furious barking of a mangy looking dog that came rushing toward us from the far side of the cabin, followed by a number of wild-eyed children, who stopped in the dooryard and looked at us suspiciously, the chickens they'd evidently been feeding pecking the ground at their feet in search of further nourishment.

At the racket, a woman dressed in drab homespun emerged from the cottage and eyed us warily. As we got closer, I could see she was younger than I'd thought, probably no more than a few years older than I. The trials of a hard life had etched themselves in her face, magnified by a hollowness in her cheeks that echoed the uncertainty of her family's existence.

"*Maidin mhaith, a bhean uasal,*" I said to her in greeting, smiling warmly.

She narrowed her eyes at me at the formality, and I quickly introduced myself and explained Quin was the newly arrived owner of the estate who'd come to inspect his tenants. The look of suspicion abated somewhat at this, although it didn't entirely disappear. Her husband must have told her of his meeting with Quin and his promises, I thought. Based on her expression, they had reservations that these promises would be met.

Looking around the small plot of land on which they depended for their very existence, I couldn't blame them.

I continued to smile at her and spoke to her encouragingly, finally coaxing her into introducing herself—"Mary Murphy," she murmured shyly—and her children, who she lined up in front of the cabin. There were four of them, three girls and one boy, ranging in age from about two to six, all dressed in rags.

Next to me, Quin started rootling in one of the large saddlebags on his horse, finally coming up with a small canvas sack. This contained numerous glossy brown pebbles I recognised as toffees, having tasted them once before when Mr Henderson had brought me some upon his return from a trip to England. Quin offered the beads to the eldest girl, who glanced at her mother before taking one and, having observed Quin's gesture that it was to be eaten, cautiously placing it on her outstretched tongue. Her eyes popped open, and she smiled in obvious delight, which encouraged her siblings and their mother to try one too.

I took a toffee myself, enjoying the sweet, creamy taste, and relishing in the joy the treat elicited in Mrs Murphy and her children. I eyed the family inconspicuously while we ate. They were all very thin and Mrs Murphy looked older than she probably was, but the children had ruddy cheeks and brightly gleaming eyes, as well as a natural curiosity that emerged once their initial wariness had worn off.

They were clearly very poor, but not starving.

Much of this, I knew, came down to the family's dependence on potatoes. Originally cultivated as a garden crop, the potato had first made its way onto Irish fields as a rotational crop—a purpose for which it was still being widely used—only to become the staple food for the large population of labourers that worked the grain fields of Ireland to meet the demands of the British market.

On average, an acre of land could yield about eight tons of potatoes, which was enough to feed a family of six for a year. This was why thousands upon thousands of people across Ireland, including tenants who rented tiny plots of farmland and labourers who were dependent on garden plots or conacre for their sustenance, had taken to farming potatoes almost exclusively, with the nutritious—though monotonous—harvest able to sustain its dependents year after year. But while few people were dying of hunger, most Irish were wretchedly poor, and being solely reliant on one harvest for their survival meant worry over crop loss and spoilage accompanied each mouthful, with the knowledge there was little or nothing else to fall back on.

And crops had failed before.

Most farmers had experienced occasional crop damage or loss caused by agricultural hazards such as heavy rains, frost or drought. Fortunately, the effects of these losses tended to be localised and neutralised by local relief efforts, which meant that, on the whole, the Irish people tended to have enough to eat—although not much else.

This became quite clear when I asked Mrs Murphy if we might have a look around. She nodded and showed us what there was to be seen in the yard—not much besides a small pile of turf—before leading us into the cabin. This was stuffy and gloomy, lit only by the wavering light of a single oil lamp hanging from the wall. Once my eyes had adjusted to the darkness, I could make out a rickety, three-legged stool and an oblong box that seemed to be used for storage and seating, as well as a small, ancient-looking loom. Besides these three objects, the cottage contained no furniture. The family slept on the hay that covered the floor, evidently sharing this space with their animals, as emerged when a sudden heave in the corner revealed a medium-sized black pig I hadn't noticed in the gloom.

"Cú Chulainn," the little boy piped up excitedly from the dooryard, pointing to the pig.

I laughed, and Quin gave me a questioning look.

"Cú Chulainn is the name of a famous Ulster hero. According to legend, he is the incarnation of the god Lugh come to Earth, who single-handedly defended his people against Queen Medb of Connacht, before going on to become a fierce warrior who fights from his chariot drawn by horses."

"Rather a difficult feat for a pig to replicate," Quin said, smiling at the little boy.

"He is also known for his monstrous battle frenzy, in which he knows neither friend nor foe."

"That sounds rather more like pig behaviour, at least when it comes to dinnertime."

We laughed together, and Mrs Murphy, who evidently hadn't understood our exchange, smiled shyly, looking proudly at the pig, which was sniffing at her feet, curly tail wiggling back and forth. She explained Cú Chulainn was being raised for sale, not as food for the family, and that she had high hopes he would grow big and fat on the potatoes he shared with the family and bring a decent income.

"Well, that explains how they pay the rent," Quin said after hearing my translation. "I didn't think it was possible to make enough money off the potatoes they're able to grow on this tiny plot of land. Not if they also want to eat and have clothes on their backs."

Catching the English word for potato, which she evidently knew, Mrs Murphy led us back outside to show us the location of the storage pit, which was situated a short distance from the cabin. It was now early June and Mrs Murphy told us that only a small pile of the lumpy brown vegetables remained of last year's crop, all that would sustain the family until September or October when the new harvest was in.

I looked at her thin frame and the children's knobbly legs and wondered how they managed to survive on the short rations of the summer months. Before I could ask, she explained they supplemented—as they did throughout the year— with whatever they could find; eggs from the chickens, fish from the stream or any small amount of milk and grain they could buy.

I blinked in the sunshine, marvelling at the nonchalance with which the woman before me was describing her precarious existence. Almost entirely dependent on a single crop, living in conditions that could at best be described as barely tolerable, Mrs Murphy nevertheless found the heart to exclaim in pride how young Robert had caught his first fish just a few months before and how Bridget had managed to clean and cook it all by herself.

I smiled at her, enjoying her company, and the joy she managed to find amidst the struggles she faced every day. We exchanged a few more pleasantries about her children and her husband, who had found temporary work on a nearby farm and would soon be leaving her to handle affairs here in his absence.

She seemed capable enough, but I promised to look in on her from time to time to see how she was faring.

After heartfelt farewells, Quin and I mounted our horses and rode off to continue our exploration of Glaslearg, the children running alongside, until their mother called them back to continue with their chores. In the relative silence that descended upon us with their departure I contemplated the Murphys' situation.

Having seen the men gathered in Quin's drawing room the day before, I'd known from the outset Glaslearg's tenants were poor—it could hardly be otherwise with just two acres of land at their disposal. I knew this wasn't the case for all Irish tenant farmers, many of whom tended to live fairly comfortably. The amount of land rented by tenants could vary considerably, though, with some laying claim to plots twenty or thirty acres in size, or more, making them quite wealthy in their own right. Such tenant farmers frequently sublet parts of the land they rented to undertenants—who inevitably paid a comparatively higher rent per acre than their overtenants and didn't usually have a lease, thus making them more vulnerable to evictions and rent increases. The small plots of land rented by the undertenants—much like the small plots rented by the tenants of Glaslearg—made it impossible to amass much in the way of riches, even working their fingers to the bone.

An overwhelming sense of helplessness came over me as I thought of Mrs Murphy and her children, living from day to day, never quite knowing what the next day would bring.

And yet...they had seemed reasonably content.

Yes, their situation was uncertain, but for the moment they had a small patch of ground to live on, food to eat and a cottage to sleep in. While this might not seem like a lot to some, there were others who had even less—landless labourers who relied on a few days' worth of meagre wages to see them through the year or hired a rood of conacre to see them fed; and those who had nothing, who were too old to work, slept under bridges and relied on handouts, facing the very real danger of starvation during the lean months, when the previous year's potato crop was eaten or spoiled and the new crop not yet ready for the harvest.

"At least they have a roof over their heads," Quin said suddenly, echoing my own thoughts, "even if it is only thatch." He was silent again for a moment before going on, "But damned if I'd want to live like that, in a tiny cabin without any windows, sharing my patch of hay with a pig! And to be so utterly reliant on one year's small crop...what if it should fail?—No. I shall not allow the Murphys to starve, nor shall I sit idly by whilst they live in conditions such as we have seen!" After another pause, he added, "One can only hope the other tenants are better off."

Unfortunately, this proved not to be the case, as every plot we visited showed variations of the same theme—whole families, and their animals and measly possessions, crammed into ramshackle cottages smaller than some rich people's boot rooms; cottages that were stashed away at the edges of the estates they occupied, far away from the manor houses, so the gleefulness of the noble lords and ladies wasn't besmirched by the unsightliness of the less fortunate who resided on their land.

When we bid the last tenant goodbye as heavy clouds started rolling across the sky, I mounted my mare with an equally heavy heart. Several hours spent face to face with the chasm of injustice that separated the rich from the poor had left me exhausted.

Returning to the manor house after a largely silent ride back, we left our horses in the care of the groom, before shaking the road dust off our clothes and going into the house, just as the clouds opened to release their watery burden in a steady downpour. Denis the butler met us at the door and Quin asked him to bring us some refreshment. Denis scuttled off as fast as his aged legs could carry him while Quin led me toward the drawing room, which had acquired the sparse furniture previously located in the reception room. I gratefully collapsed onto one of the wooden chairs, leaning my head back and closing my eyes.

"Are you all right, Alannah?" Quin asked.

"Yes, thank you." I opened my eyes to see Quin's anxious face looking down on me. "I am just a little tired. Seeing other people's misfortunes tends to take it out of me."

Quin sighed. "My sympathies exactly." He turned and looked contemplatively at the mantelpiece, picking up a candle stub and toying with it idly. "Two acres of land. Imagine being completely dependent on two acres of land. Yes, it's enough to grow potatoes to feed the family and provide fodder for the pig—at least in times of plenty—but there's hardly enough to spare, to sell and earn some money, to build a better house or save for a rainy day."

He stopped talking suddenly but continued to turn the candle stub over and over in his hand. "And what if the potato crop fails?" He looked up at me, green eyes intense.

"Disaster," I whispered. "I used to hear tales, tales my grandmother told me, stories she'd been told herself...about the *Bliadhain an áir.*—The year of the slaughter..." I paused for a moment before going on, "A terrible frost destroyed the entire potato crop, leaving tens of thousands of people without food, dying of hunger, succumbing to disease..."

"The famine of 1741," Quin said softly. Seeing my surprised look, he gave me a wry smile. "I too had an excellent tutor. One who didn't shy away from non-English history."

He grinned at me and went to pour some of the cordial Denis had brought. It was sweet, tangy and cold, and I drank it greedily, before slowing down to a more ladylike sipping. Quin eyed me with amusement but made no comment as he drained his own glass in a few healthy gulps.

Thus restored, I suddenly felt too restless to sit.

I got up from the chair and started pacing the room, wanting to use up some of my pent-up energy. What I needed to do was to find a way to help the people we'd just seen, to make their lives a little more bearable, a little easier. But what could I do, a lone woman with no resources? What could I possibly achieve on my own?

"You want to help them, don't you?" Quin's voice interrupted my pacing and I stopped in the middle of the room.

"Yes," I answered simply. "It's not because I offered to assist you...or not only because of that, at least. I feel...I feel like I'm obligated to do so, because of who I am...my position in the world." I looked up at Quin, wanting him to understand, but struggling to find the words to explain. "You see, if things had been different, if my great grandfather had been thrown off his land like so many others, it could have been me. It could have been my family living in a hovel, at the mercy of a foreigner who doesn't care one bit about the local people." I looked down, unable to hold Quin's gaze. "Instead, I'm living in luxury, while thousands of my countrymen are being treated little better than animals."

Quin took a step toward me, reached out his hand and gently lifted my chin.

51

"You don't need to feel guilty about that, Alannah," he said softly, his eyes meeting mine. "It wasn't a choice you made. You couldn't have done any differently than live the life you were born to.—Besides," he added with a smile, while he gently stroked my cheek with his thumb, "if you had been born into poverty, we probably never would have met."

He was standing very close to me. My breath was coming fast and shallow, and my heart was thumping steadily beneath my breastbone. He bent his head toward me and gently touched his lips to mine. I closed my eyes, feeling as if I were about to dissolve, melting into him like a stub of wax placed into the fire. When at last he released me and I opened my eyes, I felt like the world was spinning around me, with everything a blur except Quin's face.

"And I hope you know that I am not a tyrannical foreigner who doesn't care about the local people," he said quietly, his hands still cupping my face, which was only inches from his.

I nodded, unable to speak.

"I promise you, Alannah, I shall do everything in my power to assist your countrymen."

He let go of my face and took hold of my hands.

"And if you will do me the honour of aiding me in this endeavour...I shall be most delighted at your company."

QUIN SHUT THE door to his bedchamber and gratefully removed the tight cravat around his neck.

"Dreadful accoutrements," he said, flinging the piece of fabric against the wall. Now if Alannah should choose to remove it for him...that would make it worth the discomfort of wearing it.

He closed his eyes, savouring the memory of her touch.

He didn't know what had come over him that afternoon, but he'd simply had to touch her, to hell with social etiquette. He'd been half expecting her to strike him in shock at his audaciousness, but instead she had leaned into him, kissing him with a fervour that mirrored his own, quite unlike anything he'd ever felt with any woman he'd held in his arms before.

"And I've held a few," he muttered, with a slight frown at the memory of the last woman he'd held in his arms.

But not one of them had made him feel how he did when he was with Alannah.

52

From the moment he'd laid eyes on her she'd captivated him, pulling him into her orbit like the gravitational force of a planet. He could not resist the pull even if he wanted to, which he most certainly did not. He couldn't get enough of her, wanted to know everything about her.

When she'd shown up unexpectedly that morning, his heart had begun racing like a youth's—as it was doing again now at the thought of holding her in his arms again. And he was determined there would be a next time. Having tasted the sweet pleasure of her embrace once before, however fleetingly, he couldn't now imagine his life without it.

The thought stopped him in his tracks, astonished at the depths of his feelings toward her. He'd only seen Alannah four times and yet he felt like he'd known her his whole life, that she was already part of his life—an irreplaceable part.

"Then I shall just have to hold onto her!" he said to himself, resolute that nothing would stand in his way.

RETURNING HOME THAT afternoon, my mind was in a spin.

The day was a blur that revolved around one central moment, and I could scarcely remember what else I had done. I kept replaying the scene in my mind, the minutest detail etched into my memory, wanting to savour every instant of the connection Quin and I had shared. I had never experienced—or even imagined—the surge of passion that had held me in its grip while Quin had held me in his arms.

Arriving at the house, the sun emerged between the remaining wisps of rained-out clouds, Ireland's changeable weather reflecting the day's equally changeable mood.

Completely preoccupied with the memory of Quin's touch, I opened the door without remembering how I got there, dropped my hat and riding gloves where I stood, unable to recall where I customarily put them, and floated up the stairs.

"Where have you been?"

I jumped and let out a screech, whirling toward Kieran, who was sitting on the loveseat on the upstairs landing, lurking in the shadows.

"Out," I responded, heart pounding.

"Where?" Kieran growled, his voice thick with anger and distrust.

"Visiting a nearby farm," I answered vaguely, suddenly afraid he'd found out I'd been visiting Quin. Had Quin spoken to Kieran and told him I was helping him?

"Why? Have you been off cavorting with stable boys like the whore that you are? Well...have you?"

I stared at Kieran in disbelief, completely stunned both at what he'd said and the hatred with which he'd said it. Even at his worst, he had never insulted me so and with such fury in his eyes.

"I was invited to tea by the lady of the house," I lied, lifting my chin in defiance.

At least his outburst seemed to indicate Kieran didn't know anything about Quin.

Kieran narrowed his eyes at me, mere slits in the darkness. He got up slowly and came toward me, making me take an automatic step back, coming up hard against the balustrade. He loomed over me, his eyes burning into mine.

Clearly, he hadn't believed a word I'd said.

"Don't go anywhere without my consent," he commanded, enunciating each word, "especially not on your own."

He started turning away, but suddenly turned back and took a step closer, raising his fist and making me cower in front of him, my heart racing in fear.

"As I've told you before, it's time you learnt your place."

I could see the urge to hit me in his eyes and braced myself for the blow. Instead, he spun away from me abruptly, pounded down the stairs and rushed outside. When I heard the front door slam shut, I slid down the banister, shaking all over.

I put my head down and breathed deeply until I finally felt I could get up.

I made my way to my room on trembling legs and shut the door behind me. Still shaking, I undressed mechanically and unpinned my hair, sitting down at my dressing table to brush it. Hand held at the ready with the brush, I stared at my refection in the mirror. I looked frightened even to my own eyes, and seeing my fear reflected back at me made me put down the brush and place my head in my hands, tears welling in my eyes.

"I am such a fool," I whispered as a tear spilled over and rolled down my cheek.

There could never be anything between Quin and me, I should have known it from the first. With how Kieran had treated me over the past two years, it was clear my brother would never allow me to have anything to do with any man not of his own choosing, much less an Englishman.

He wouldn't even let me assist Quin on his estate, I thought, even to improve the lives of Irish people—Kieran wouldn't be able to see past the fact I was helping somebody English.

My brother had been less vocal about his dislike of the English while my father was still alive, although it had been obvious even then. In the two years since, his hatred had grown along with his expression thereof—and his mistreatment of me—but it had taken a substantial upturn over the last few months, with Kieran imbuing me and anyone who would listen with endless examples of English tyranny, both past and present, trying to rouse the listener into condemning the English alongside him.

I wasn't sure what had caused Kieran's demeanour—and his temper—to go from bad to worse, but the hairs on the back of my neck rose at the thought of what he must be getting involved in. I knew there were groups of Irish people who plotted against English rule, waiting for the right moment to launch a rebellion, in the hopes that this time it might be successful, when numerous similar attempts over several centuries had been in vain.

Such actions were considered traitorous by the English crown—rightfully so, I supposed—and punishable by death.

I swallowed and stared at my reflection. My lashes were stuck together in wet spikes and my cheeks were blotched with tears, when only an hour ago I'd been deliriously happy.

"Well, that's it then. It's best you forget all about Quinton Fletcher Philbert Williams and resign yourself to marrying a loyal Irishman. No doubt Kieran will pick a suitable match..." Old, rich and vile were characteristics I thought my brother would find appealing. Another tear rolled down my cheek, but I took a deep breath, sat up straight and willed myself to accept my fate.

"There are worse things in life," I said to my reflection, reminding myself of the abject poverty I'd been confronted with during the course of the day—and the knowledge there were many hundreds more who had even less.

Still shaking, I rose from my dresser and prepared to go down for supper, where I would sit meekly at the table with my brother, pretending all was right with the world.

7.

OVER THE NEXT few days, Quin busied himself with reading through the estate's ledgers—insofar as these were available—familiarising himself with the layout of the land, the positioning of the fields and their possible usage, and pondering the difficulty the tenants' situation presented. The latter caused him the most trouble, as he contemplated the best way to make good on his promise to right the wrongs Mr Brennan had done them. His initial impulse was to simply double the size of each tenant's land, thereby restoring them to the four-acre plots they should have received in the first place.

The difficulty with this approach was that it would mean sacrificing one-hundred acres of his own farmland, which he needed to increase the estate's revenue. With Glaslearg's dismal performance while Mr Brennan had been in charge, he needed every possible acre to maximise the estate's output and resultant profit; if he doubled the size of the tenant's plots, half of Glaslearg's land would be unavailable for him to farm.

Then again, Quin reflected, the unscrupulous Mr Brennan seemed to have neglected the estate's food production efforts almost entirely, focusing only on exploiting the tenants—and numerous labourers to whom he'd leased conacre at an exorbitant price, as Quin had discovered the day before—which meant even farming a good deal less than the previously available land should still result in a considerably greater income than was achieved the preceding few seasons.

"Mmph," Quin grumbled, wishing he had somebody to confer with.

Since his arrival at Glaslearg, he'd several times attempted to engage Rupert in conversation regarding the estate's business—having gotten into the habit of voicing his thoughts quite freely around his valet, having no other confidante to hand—but the poor boy's eyes tended to widen in apprehension while his hands twitched nervously when Quin asked him for his opinion. Although Rupert was by no means stupid and was usually talkative enough, he was still young, and his experience of the world was limited—he simply had no assistance to offer Quin as far as running a large estate was concerned, though he did his best to listen attentively, nonetheless.

Such a one-sided conversation would be of little help to him now, however, making Quin wish suddenly he could discuss the matter with Alannah, who was not only intelligent herself but had also been actively involved in the management of her family's estate for many years. After a moment's thought, though, Quin came to the conclusion that he likely knew what her response would be—she didn't strike him as the type to quibble over a few acres of lost farmland when there were people's lives to consider.

"Then I shan't quibble either," he declared, determining to find a plausible way to increase the size of the plot each tenant could farm.

Thinking of Alannah made him wonder where she was.

She'd said she would come back to Glaslearg the day after they'd visited the tenants, evidently eager to help them in any way she could. Having offered him her assistance as translator, she'd initially been reluctant to otherwise get involved in his affairs. He had, however, assured her he valued her input and indeed needed it, as he was thoroughly unschooled in Irish customs and traditions and thus likely to put his foot in his mouth at any given moment, which he wanted to avoid even if the residents could barely understand him. Laughing at his self-deprecating remark, she'd cautiously agreed to discuss his ideas. Though she'd seemed genuinely hesitant to interfere, Quin was sure he'd detected a spark of interest in her deep blue eyes at the opportunity to be directly involved in a matter that so clearly lay close to her heart.

It was therefore puzzling she hadn't shown up.

Her maidservant had sent word that her mistress had been otherwise detained, but that had been three days ago. What could be keeping her away still, especially considering what she'd told him about her brother's refusal to involve her in anything on his own farm?

Unless she was avoiding him?

Perhaps he'd overstepped his boundaries after all when he'd kissed her?

Making a sudden decision, he closed the ledger in front of him and marched toward the door to confront her.

ARRIVING AT THE O'Neills' house a short time later, he found himself unsure how to proceed. Having made the impulsive decision to confront Alannah, he now had no idea what to say to her. He had no claim on her whatsoever and had no right to ask her why she'd reneged on her promise, much less to demand the answers his wounded pride cried out for.

Clenching his jaw muscles and blowing out through his nose, he steeled himself and knocked.

He waited.

He knocked again.

And waited some more.

Finally, the door opened. To his surprise, Alannah herself stood before him.

"My apologies, the servants seem to have disappeared, I..."

Alannah's voice trailed off and her eyes widened as she recognised him. She quickly glanced behind her and pulled the door closed, leaving them standing in the dooryard.

"Quin," she said, the surprise evident in her voice. Quin also detected something else, perhaps a hint of fear. "What are you doing here?"

"I came to see if you were alright," Quin replied boldly, trying to look her in the eyes, which kept flitting to either side as if searching for something. At this she stopped.

"Oh...yes...I'm quite alright, thank you." She looked at him for a moment before averting her gaze once more. "I've just been...um...busy."

"Your brother has found you something to do then?"

"I beg your pardon?"

"Your brother, you said he hadn't allowed you to do anything on the farm. With you being busy now, I suppose that must have changed?"

"Yes...yes, that's it."

Alannah sounded as unsure of her answer as Quin felt. He didn't know what was going on, but he was sure she wasn't telling the truth. He decided to take the bull by the horns.

"Alannah, have I offended you in any way?"

"What? No, Quin...no." She searched his face, suddenly looking very sad, and very young. "You have been nothing but courteous and considerate of me." She lowered her eyes again. "I just..."

"It's alright, Alannah, you don't need to explain," Quin interjected, seeing her struggling for words. "If you have changed your mind about assisting me, I completely understand. You are under no obligation to do so."

"Quin, you don't understand." Alannah looked back up at him. "I want to help you...I feel that I *need* to help you. It's only that..." She broke off, shaking her head slowly.

Quin took a step toward her, wanting to take her hand, but before he could reach her, Alannah pulled herself up to her full height, shook back the black mane of her hair and took a deep breath.

"I am sorry Quin," she said. "I made you a promise I did not keep. I intend to make up for it. I would like to come visit you at your house as planned." She glanced around her again, seeming nervous of something. "I am not sure exactly when I shall be able to do so, but I shall send word. Would this be agreeable?"

"Yes, certainly, that would be more than agreeable. I look forward to hearing from you at your earliest convenience."

Quin bowed to her, and they said their goodbyes, before Alannah went back inside, closing the door on Quin, who was left wondering what she was keeping from him.

I ADJUSTED MY riding habit for the tenth time and fiddled with my hat for the twentieth time, trying to work up the courage to go downstairs.

Kieran had told me he was going on one of his ever more frequent excursions— this time to meet some business acquaintances in Dublin, he'd said—and that I shouldn't expect him back for a week or so. He'd left early in the morning, and I'd waited until midday before dispatching Finnian the hall boy with a note enquiring whether Mr Williams of Glaslearg might be willing to receive a visitor that afternoon. As soon as Quin's response had arrived, I'd asked John to ready my horse and raced upstairs to get dressed.

Now that I was ready, though, I was filled with doubt.

My encounter with Kieran on the stairwell a week earlier had disturbed me deeply. While we'd had our differences in the past and his views had often left me wondering how we could possibly be related, I'd never been afraid of him before, had never thought he was capable of doing me physical harm. After all, this was my brother, whom I'd grown up with, the person closest to me in all the world. Despite his poor treatment of me, I'd always remembered how close we'd once been and had held onto the hope that we might be that close again, to bridge the gap that had come between us.

But the look I'd seen in Kieran's eyes that day had shaken me to the core.

This was not merely irritation at my apparent stupidity or contempt at my resistance to bending to his rules, nor yet the dismissal that so frequently ended our conversations, with Kieran content in the knowledge I had no power to change anything despite my most vehement objections.

What I had seen in Kieran's face that day was hatred, utter loathing for me, a sister he'd once held dear, with no sign of the brother I had once loved.

"Oh, Kieran," I whispered, tears prickling at the corners of my eyes. "What's becoming of you?"

I braced myself on my dressing table, letting the fear and confusion I felt wash over me. When I thought I had myself under control again I straightened up and adjusted my hat once more. The thought of Kieran finding out where I was going and what I was doing filled me with dread.

But I needed to see Quin.

When I arrived at Glaslearg I made an effort to put my worry over Kieran behind me and focus on enjoying Quin's company. Quin himself did much to assist me in this effort, simply by his presence. The moment I laid eyes on him my heart leapt, and I felt myself break into an enormous smile—one, which I was happy to see, he returned.

"Alannah," he said, greeting me in the drawing room. "I am so pleased you've come."

"Quin, I'm sorry...I would have come sooner. It's only that..."

"Think nothing of it, Alannah. You are here now. So let us not waste time in obsessing about the past and focus on the present instead."

This so clearly echoed my own thoughts that I only smiled and nodded, waiting for him to tell me what he had planned for the afternoon. To my surprise, he suggested we take a ride.

"The countryside is beautiful, and we didn't really get a chance to enjoy it last time. The weather is fine for the moment, and I thought we could have a picnic by the river. I've discovered a beautiful spot."

He beamed at me in delight, and I couldn't help sharing his enthusiasm.

I declared myself more than happy to join him—and indeed I was—and so, offering me his arm, we set off to the stable. I experienced a moment's hesitation when I thought about how Kieran would react to seeing us walking arm in arm, on our way to spending the afternoon together, but I shoved the thought to the back of my mind, to be locked away with the rest of my worries for the remainder of my visit.

I glanced at Quin, who was regaling me with anecdotes of the listless food he'd been made to eat since his arrival in Ireland—"Boiled potatoes...again!" His close proximity made my heart pound, and I was infinitesimally aware of him, every twitch of the muscles in his arm, the brush of his thigh against my skirt, the arc of his neck as he bent down to catch something I'd said.

And yet, I was unsure how to act around him.

For me, the kiss we had shared had brought about a moment of defining clarity, crystallising in my mind the simplicity of what I wanted—to be by Quin's side. I still felt the same, but the possibility of a future for us seemed bleak, no matter how much I wanted it.

So what I am doing here, then? I berated myself, scolding myself mentally for having agreed to come.

And what about Quin?

I had thought at the time he must feel the same as I. But perhaps, for him, it had been just a kiss. Perhaps, I mused, he was in the habit of kissing impressionable young women charmed by his smile and impeccable manners. I frowned at the thought, although I had to admit that under the circumstances it might actually be better if the kiss had meant nothing to him, upsetting as it might be to me.

I should never have come here! I thought once more, wishing suddenly Quinton Williams had never shown up on my doorstep.

I was interrupted in my gloomy contemplations by the announcement of the groom that my horse was ready. I thanked him and led the mare—one of Quin's, the same one I had ridden on our previous excursion—to the mounting block. As I was about to climb up the solid construction, Quin suddenly appeared beside me and leapt onto the highest step. Without pausing for breath, he reached down, put his hands on my waist and lifted me onto the saddle in one smooth motion, seemingly without the least bit of effort.

"Oh." I found myself looking into his bright green eyes, which were mere inches from mine, twinkling with mischief.

"My lady," he said and inclined his head toward me. His hands were still on my waist, and he pulled me forwards gently. I braced my hands on his chest as I fell toward him, unable to stop the pull between us, my mouth finding his like a compass finding North.

It was a chaste kiss, no more than a peck, but the depth of feeling it awoke in me unsettled me in its intensity.

"This way," Quin said, having jumped grinning off the mounting block and rapidly gotten on his own horse.

He led me down the same path we'd taken a week earlier, down to the small river and over the bridge. But instead of continuing along the path, we turned east and followed the water some ways downstream, through a small valley between gentle peaks that rolled along under a warm summer sun. The scenery was as beautiful as Quin had promised and I felt intoxicated, as much by his presence as the delicate perfume of the wildflowers that dotted the lush hills.

We came to a stop at a bend in the stream, where a gentle, grassy slope covered in tiny blue flowers paid homage to the towering oak tree that rose on the banks on the far side of the water, long leafy branches nodding toward the surface. Quin produced a picnic blanket from his saddlebag and spread it out on the grass with a flourish. He gave me his hand and saw me comfortably seated before returning to the hobbled horses to collect the picnic basket he had strapped behind his saddle. This revealed itself to contain a small loaf of bread, a dish of butter and a bowl of wild strawberries, all nestled between two bottles of ale.

"I'm afraid it isn't much," Quin said apologetically. "Between the spontaneous nature of your visit and the state of the pantry at Glaslearg, there wasn't much choice in the way of picnic fare."

"It's perfect," I responded, feeling touched.

We ate tiny, sweet strawberries and thick pieces of bread off fine porcelain plates, slathering on butter with ornate silver knives, and washed it all down with ale drunk from delicate silver cups, laughing at the delicious simplicity of the meal, which outshone the pretentiousness of the tableware.

"I found the picnic set in the manor house," Quin explained between mouthfuls. "I can't say who it might have belonged to—perhaps one of Glaslearg's previous stewards—but I assumed no one was going to return to claim it. So when I heard of your intended visit, I thought it could be put to good use."

"This was a wonderful idea!" I said, savouring the feeling of the sun on my skin, the sound of the gurgling water of the stream and the pleasure of enjoying a meal in good company. "Although," I added with a smile and a sideways glance at Quin, "with what you've told me, I was half expecting a picnic basket filled with boiled potatoes."

Quin laughed, a hearty, infectious sound.

"It would have been, had I not managed—over the course of several gruelling hours last week—to explain to Denis the desirability of a more varied form of nourishment. The concept seems to have taken some time to take root in his mind, and I had almost resigned myself to my potato inundated fate, when Denis produced the remarkable new addition you see before you. Baked this very morning, with flour obtained from a nearby market, Glaslearg currently producing nothing much but potatoes."

"I'm sorry I wasn't there to help you."

"I beg your pardon?"

"You had wanted my help conversing with your servants. I could have assisted you with Denis, or your cook."

"Denis currently *is* my cook."

I stared at him, dumbfounded. "So you really do have only two servants?"

"I'm afraid so. It seems Mr Brennan rid the estate of all things he considered superfluous, in order to maximise his own gains by minimising expenditures.— Come to think of it, if he hadn't run off with the money, he and my father would have gotten on splendidly!"

He grinned, jumped up from the picnic blanket and offered me his hand. "Come along."

We wandered along the river, which was wider and shallower here than up at the house. We took off our shoes and stockings, and I hiked up my skirt, and we squelched through the soft mud along the water's edge, laughing and exclaiming over the beauty of the landscape, the chirping birds that flitted through the oak's branches and the insects that buzzed around us.

The sun continued to shine down on us, unusually constant in its affections, the sky unmarred by even a wisp of cloud.

"I never imagined myself hiking through the mud on an Irish farm with an Irish maiden by my side," Quin said, smiling at me as he pulled one long foot out of the muddy bank with a sucking sound. "Much less enjoying it!"

I laughed, realising that I too was enjoying myself, immensely so.

I felt invigorated, more alive than I had in years, away from Kieran's suffocating presence and in the company of a man who demanded nothing of me and yet made me want to give him everything I had to offer, without restraint.

"The Right Honourable The Lord Williams," Quin was saying as we wandered along the streambank, carefully articulating each word. "The Baron Williams of Wadlow, third of that name."

I nodded slowly, suitably impressed. "And what does that make you?" I asked after a moment, looking up at Quin.

He leaned toward me conspiratorially and raised his brows. "The son of a baron," he pronounced with a straight face, before breaking into a wide grin that made me laugh. "I'm afraid I have no honorifics of my own with which to adorn my person. While my father's title is an hereditary one that will eventually be passed down to me, my sole distinction currently lies in being my father's only heir—a role which, I might add, can be exceedingly trying at the best of times."

"Your father sounds like an interesting sort," I observed with some amusement.

"He is that." A slight frown appeared on Quin's forehead.

"But tell me more about yourself," I said quickly to distract him from his thoughts.

"Well," he began, smoothing out his brow, "let's see now.—I was eighteen when I bought my commission. My father was terribly pleased, of course, having fought under Wellington against the French himself." He gave me a wry smile. "A retired major of the British Army wants nothing more than to see his son follow in his footsteps!" I smiled back at him, although I sensed a tinge of resentment in his tone. "I was stationed with the 49th regiment," he continued, "and so I ended up in India, only to be dispatched to China in 1840, to battle the Chinese and their outlandish views on diplomatic relations and trade." He was silent for a moment, looking ahead. "I had wondered for years what it might be like in China and the other places I'd read about in my mother's books, and here I found myself in a position to find out."

"Was it how you expected it to be?"

"I can't really say. We were at war. There wasn't much opportunity to appraise the local customs, much less to converse with the locals themselves...even if they had been able to understand us. And had we not been at war, we still would have been greatly restricted in what we would have been able to see."

Quin paused, bending down for a drink of cool water from the stream. I followed suit, cupping my hands, and taking a few refreshing sips myself.

"You see, the Chinese weren't particularly trusting of the Europeans when we started visiting their shores for trade. So they set up a central trading post in Canton that dealt with all imports and exports—the only port foreigners were allowed to visit. In peaceful times, I imagine even this limited access to a world unknown would have been fascinating to behold. As it was, travelling between military encampments and battlegrounds along the coast, I saw only glimpses of what the rest of China must be like...tall, multi-tiered buildings, as alien to me as the dress of the Chinese, in their flowing robes with intricate tracery and pointy hats, like the tops of the towers that rose high above the surrounding countryside."

"And did you see much fighting yourself?"

"A good amount." Quin smiled at me, a smile that didn't reach his eyes. "The 49th was involved in several battles during the campaign. As a newly commissioned lieutenant I'd been rather disgruntled by the lack of action I was likely to find within Europe's reasonably peaceful borders.—Unbeknownst to me, I was soon to experience my fair share of combat on foreign shores." He compressed his lips for a moment and frowned. "Nonetheless, two years later the war was won, and I resigned my commission and came home," he ended his account abruptly.

I looked at him, wanting to ask why he had resigned his commission, but not daring to ask. There was obviously more to the story, something he didn't want to tell me.

"I wanted to become a farmer," he said, laughing at my surprised expression at having read my thoughts, his good humour returning. "What about you, have you lived at Niall all your life?"

"Most of it. My parents, my brother and I went to live there with my grandmother when I was two."

"And Niall is the family estate?"

"Yes," I agreed with a nod, a sense of pride blooming within me at the thought of my home. "It's actually called Talamh na Niall, although we call it Niall for short.—It simply means Land of Niall," I added, seeing Quin's confused look at the unfamiliar terminology. "It's named after Niall Noígíallach, an Irish king of old from whom the O'Neills are said to derive their name. It belonged to my many times great grandfather, Cathal O'Neill." I glanced at Quin out of the corner of my eye for a moment before going on. "He managed to cuckold the English into believing he'd become a loyal servant to the Crown, thereby preventing seizure of his land." I paused, waiting to see if Quin would find the action offensive, but he only smiled, waiting for me to continue. "Cathal O'Neill was a distant cousin of Hugh O'Neill, the Earl of Tyrone. But instead of following Hugh during the Flight of the Earls, Cathal decided to save his own skin—and his property—by swearing his allegiance to King James and converting to Protestantism. His performance was evidently believable, as he was not supplanted by British settlers during the Plantation of Ulster that began soon after the flight, and his land stayed in O'Neill hands for the next two hundred years—although rather substantially diminished in size."

"And what makes you think your many times great grandfather did not, in fact, become a loyal servant to the English crown?"

"I might have thought so, had the story of his deception not been passed down through the generations—usually with great pride, I might add." I laughed. "Beyond that, though..."

"Yes?"

"It's...well, it's a feeling...the feeling of belonging here, of being Irish—not British, or part of the United Kingdom—but Irish. The feeling...no, the knowledge...that this is our land, that this is our home...not just another acquisition of the British Empire." I looked across the stream at the green hills I called my home. "I doubt the sentiment would have persisted for two hundred years if my ancestors had supported the English in their hearts."

"The English aren't all bad, are they?" Quin asked, teasing.

"Some are worse than others," I responded with a smile, making Quin grin.

"And have you travelled much outside of Ulster?"

"Not much." I shook my head. "For the most part, my parents were content to live their lives on the farm...although I think my mother would have wanted things to be different.—My father was never meant to take over Niall, being the youngest of two sons. He went to study at Trinity College in Dublin, with the dream of making a name for himself as a lawyer. Before he could fulfil his dream, though, my uncle died unexpectedly, leaving the farm in my father's care, my uncle having had no wife or children of his own, nor any other living relatives besides my ageing grandmother, who was left behind on the farm after his death. My father had loved his brother dearly and knew he would have wanted the farm to be well taken care of and so, instead of hiring somebody to run it for him and bringing my grandmother to come live with us in Dublin, my father moved to Niall himself, bringing along his two young children and my mother, whom he'd met and married in Dublin."

I paused, as a warm breeze tickled my face, lifting wisps of hair off my forehead.

"I think my mother always felt cheated of the grand life she thought she would have lived in Dublin had they stayed. As for my father, he took over the farm without complaint. He did miss the law, though. Fortunately, he was able to take on the position of the region's justice of the peace, dealing with all manner of misdemeanours and criminal cases. I think the office gave him a sense of purpose, although it wasn't always easy for him to deal with local politics and the challenges faced by the Irish peasants, especially as many of them saw him as an enemy.—Rural magistrates tend to be part of the Protestant ascendancy, a group that isn't particularly popular with most Irish people, as they're thought of as English, rather than Irish."

I gave Quin a sideways glance, but he only inclined his head toward me as he listened intently.

"My father persevered, though, and immersed himself in his duties, passing judgement fairly and justly, no matter who appeared before his bench. I think the people came to respect him in the end, even though he was a Protestant. He knew the law and acted accordingly, while upholding local customs when it was in his power to do so."

"That explains why you know so much about Irish politics yourself," Quin said.

"Yes. I could hardly become a lawyer myself, but having my father relive his cases with me made me feel like I was in the courtroom with him, making a difference. And he indulged me...I think because he enjoyed my interest, which was in such contrast to Kieran's lack of interest in almost everything my father tried to teach him."

I breathed in deeply, looking at the beautiful countryside around us.

"If things had been different, I think father would have wanted me to take over the farm. As it was, my father was worried...worried Kieran would do a poor job of running the farm once the time came." I flipped a hand, dismissing my brother and his failings. "He invested some of his earnings, just in case. This meant he occasionally went to Dublin on business, especially in the last few years before he died. He took me with him on one such trip. I was seventeen and couldn't get enough of the sights. Even though I was born in Dublin, I hadn't been back since and couldn't remember seeing anything but farmland and the occasional village all my life. I was awed at the sheer size of the city. And the gas lighting of the streets and squares—it was like nothing I had ever seen before!—And the steam locomotive! What a marvel of engineering! I insisted to father we must go see it, even though we didn't get a chance to ride it."

Quin smiled as I retold my adventures.

"But to you Dublin must seem awfully small and primitive, in comparison to London."

"Well, London is rather a lot larger, of course.—As to it being less primitive though...the slums in London are unlikely to be any less ghastly than those in Dublin, and there are a lot more of them! If you ask me, a good measure of a society's primitiveness is the way in which it treats its poor...in which case, all of the British Empire is equally primitive."

He gave me a sideways glance, eyes glinting with humour.

"I trust you will not repeat such unpatriotic views as I have expressed in your company today."

I laughed and shook my head.

"No one will learn your secrets from me," I promised.

We carried on walking and talking for what seemed like hours, until a look at Quin's pocket watch signified it was time for me to go. My heart sank at the thought, knowing I had nothing to go home to and would be one day closer to Kieran's return.

When we arrived back at the manor house, Quin tried to persuade me to let him escort me home, but I insisted I would have no trouble on my own.

While I was reasonably sure Kieran wouldn't be home for a few more days, I didn't want any of our servants to see me in Quin's company, for fear they might tell Kieran—as to what they might tell Kieran of my absence, I tried not to think. Quin finally agreed to let me ride home on my own when I promised I would come back again the next day—in the morning, so I wouldn't have to ride home too late a second time.

I exchanged Quin's horse for my mare and waved him goodbye, turning reluctantly toward the prison that was my home.

QUIN STOOD IN front of the stable, holding Gambit's reins while watching Alannah ride off into the distance, wishing fervently she could have stayed. Talking to her this afternoon had been like shriving his soul. He couldn't remember a time when he'd ever felt so at ease with anyone, knowing he could tell her everything that lay on his heart, but without the need to say anything at all. Simply being in her presence was enough.

And yet, something had been different about her.

She had smiled at him, laughed with him, exchanging witty banter and making intelligent conversation...but there had been moments when she'd seemed unutterably sad, when her eyes had focused inwards, on some unseen memory she could not share with him.

He'd hoped the tenseness he had sensed in her when he'd gone to see her a few days before would have disappeared, but it hadn't. She had seemed just as edgy when she'd arrived, making him wonder whether it was his own presence making her uncomfortable. His ego hadn't enjoyed this line of thought one bit, prompting him into showing off for her with the ridiculous manoeuvre on the mounting block. He grinned at his own absurdity, which had nevertheless resulted in the exchange of another—although regrettably fleeting—kiss.

She hadn't cuffed him, at least, which would suggest Quin was, in fact, not the reason for her anxiety.

But it did leave him wondering what was.

She had voiced her displeasure at her brother's treatment of her, her inability to do anything she considered useful. Quin had thought this had changed when she'd declared herself too busy to attend him, but if so, why wasn't she happier? Instead, the opposite appeared to be true, which affirmed Quin's original supposition that she'd made up the excuse to avoid him. Not because she didn't want to see him, Quin thought, remembering how she'd looked at him when he'd pulled her close, but because somebody had told her not to.

The most likely person to have done so was her brother, Kieran.

Alannah had told him Kieran wasn't enamoured with Englishmen—to put it mildly—and that he had plans to arrange a marriage for his sister that would benefit him above all else. Evidently, he, Quin, didn't fit the requirements for an appropriate suitor for her, and so Kieran had forbidden Alannah from seeing him.

He narrowed his eyes at the thought. "We'll just see about that!" he said firmly as he handed his horse's reins to the groom, before crossing the courtyard and marching up the steps and into the house.

8.

OVER THE FOLLOWING four days, Alannah came to Glaslearg every morning and Quin invited her to assist him in cleaning up the mess Mr Brennan had left. Together, they went through the estate's meagre ledgers and interviewed Denis and Bryan, the elderly groom, attempting to piece together the estate's history and how this differed from what Quin and his father had been told by Mr Brennan and the stewards before him, in order to decide how best to go about restoring the estate's productivity.

While Alannah was initially shy and somewhat hesitant to offer her opinions, she soon relaxed when she saw Quin genuinely respected her advice. For his part, Quin found her presence and assistance invaluable, and found it more and more difficult to bid her goodbye every afternoon.

"I've decided to increase the size of each of the tenant's allotted land to four acres," he said on the last day, having finally decided on the matter the night before. "With only a minimal increase in rent," he added, with some smugness.

Alannah looked up at him from across the wooden table and broke into a wide smile. "Quin, that's...that's very generous of you."

"Perhaps not as generous as it might seem." He cocked his head. "My father had agreed to a rent of twenty-two shillings per acre, but Mr Brennan was charging thirty."

"Meaning the tenants are currently paying sixty shillings for their two-acre plots when they should have been paying eighty-eight for four."

"Precisely.—I shall propose to reduce the rent to eighteen shillings per acre, bringing the tenants' new total to seventy-two." He frowned. "I really can't reduce the rent any further if I wish to have a reasonable income from the leased land—there will be two-hundred acres of it, after all!" He shrugged his shoulders in some regret. "I shall, however, also endeavour to cancel the additional charges Mr Brennan had the tenants pay, and I shan't charge them a lease fee, which I hope will offset the slight increase in rent."

"That sounds like a generous proposal."

"I think so too."

"What made your father want to lease out four-acre plots to begin with?" Alannah asked after a moment. "He must have known there was little chance of the tenants being self-sustainable with so little land."

Quin compressed his lips. "I rather think that was the point. He thought it would be useful to have a large number of tenants at his disposal—to work as labourers on the estate, knowing they would have to supplement their income." He gave a humourless laugh, as this was precisely what he was intending to do with the tenants himself.

"I also think, though," he continued, "that part of his reasoning was based on his general distrust of people. He thought it better to rent out numerous small plots of land rather than four or five large ones, because he was convinced he was more likely to collect his rent if there were more people paying it.—An entirely illogical conviction, I dare say!" He gave Alannah a wry look. "I told him the exact opposite was true...that farmers with more land were more likely to be able to pay their rent, and that a greater number of those with less land were likely to fall into arrears, therefore making the greater number of tenants a hazard rather than a benefit." Quin sighed. "My father doesn't tend to take anybody's advice when he's convinced himself of something.—Fortunately, I'm not nearly so intractable myself, nor quite so cynical."

"I can see that," Alannah responded with a laugh.

"*Un*fortunately," Quin said, "I can't do too much about the size of the plots the tenants are renting, beyond increasing them to the four acres that should have been available to them in the first place. I can hardly evict half the tenants to increase the size of the other crofts!—Besides, the remaining tenants wouldn't be able to pay the additional rent."

"I think you've come up with a good solution."

Alannah held his eyes for a moment, and Quin's heart gave a pleasant thump.

"It will require some work," he said. "I shall have to map out the new plots and assign one to each family, and then the tenants will have to move to their new homes—all before the winter sets in. I also plan on assisting each and every one of the families in building proper houses, not made of mud, and with windows and chimneys—one of each at the very least!"

Quin paused and absently ran a hand through his hair. "Of course, they won't want to move from their current plots until this year's potato harvest has been collected in the autumn. But once the harvest is in, I want them all moved into their new homes so they can focus on preparing their larger plots for next season's planting—and assist me with mine."

"Um, Quin...how exactly do you propose to build fifty cabins within the space of a few months?"

Quin smiled crookedly at her and shook his head. "I rather doubt we'll be able to manage all of them this season, as much as I would wish it to be otherwise. It will have to be a long-term project, dependent as much on when the work can physically be done as on the availability of the building materials. I haven't quite worked out all the details, but one way or another, I shall see all my tenants suitably housed!"

"Perhaps you should start with the largest families and move those to currently unoccupied fields, where new cabins would have to be built anyway," Alannah suggested.

"That's an excellent idea. Half of the families will have to move to land that was previously being used for crop production, which presently doesn't contain any huts...not even single-roomed ones made of mud."

"And what will you do with the remaining farmland?"

Quin pursed his lips in thought. "I shall still have a good bit of land available, far more than was evidently utilised in the last two years or more. Based on your suggestion, I have narrowed down my options to growing oats, wheat, potatoes and barley. But I am wondering whether I should start with all four on a few fields each or whether I should focus on just one or two and possibly introduce some livestock."

"I thought the estate already had livestock?"

"It had, yes. But no longer—aside from a few chickens. Just one more thing our Mr Brennan managed to run into the ground."

Quin felt resigned, rather than angry at this further evidence of Mr Brennan's uselessness, but he also experienced a sense of determination. Determination to make a success of a farm that was currently in shambles.

He did enjoy a challenge, after all.

"No doubt he dragged the last cow with him when he left, after eating its fellows over the duration of his stay," he said, making Alannah smile. "What are you smiling about?" he asked teasingly.

"Oh, nothing," she replied and blushed.

He lifted an eyebrow and looked at her expectantly.

"I was just wondering whether you were enjoying the prospect of becoming a farmer."

He broke into a grin. "Well, I can't say it ever crossed my mind before I came here. Although I knew Glaslearg would one day be mine, I had always thought I would play a more distant role in its running. Much like my father...only better, of course!" He laughed at his own self-righteousness. "I am a soldier by trade...but I do know one end of a spade from the other!"

Alannah laughed with him, and Quin's heart lifted at the sight. While she genuinely seemed to enjoy his company and was eager to offer him her help, she still carried with her a sense of sadness and nervousness...even fear.

He frowned inwardly at the thought, wanting to do something to appease her anxiety, but not wanting to intrude on her privacy.

"Perhaps a fresh perspective is just what Glaslearg needs," Alannah said. "Just like my brother's farm," she added under her breath, and suddenly, her air of cheerfulness was gone.

Quin decided that enough was enough.

"Alannah," he said, looking at her with urgency. "What's bothering you? How can I help you?"

She averted her gaze. "I don't know what you mean."

Quin could hear the anxiety in her voice and could see the blood pounding in the delicate vessels of her neck.

He gently reached across the desk and took one of her hands in both of his.

"Is it Kieran? Does he not want you to see me?"

Her head snapped up and she looked at him, startled. "How...?"

"I guessed as much when you didn't come back after we visited the tenants. I gathered he had told you to stay away."

"Kieran doesn't know I've been seeing you."

Now it was Quin's turn to be startled. "But then..."

"He doesn't want me to see *anyone*. He doesn't want me to do anything at all without his permission.—But I'm reasonably sure this would extend particularly to you."

Alannah couldn't hide the sarcasm in her voice and her eyes were filled with anger. They looked at each other for a long moment. Finally, she sighed.

"I had promised to help you, and I hope that I have done so," she said softly, with a visible effort at appearing calm. "Kieran has been away on business, but he will be back any day now. So...I cannot return...at least for a while...if ever."

She compressed her lips briefly before hardening her face, withdrawing her hand from his and rising from her chair. Quin quickly followed suit.

"I thank you for your hospitality, Quin, and for giving me the opportunity to contribute to the wellbeing of your tenants. I...I greatly appreciate it...truly."

She swallowed visibly and looked at him for a moment before turning to go. Quin bounded around the desk and jumped in front of her, blocking her way to the door.

"Alannah, please, don't go! Perhaps I can come with you to speak to your brother, to introduce myself, to assure him I have nothing but good intentions."

Alannah shook her head. "It won't do any good. He is set in his ways. He has other plans for me, plans that don't include you."

She tried to push past him, but he pulled her toward him. She started to respond, but quickly pulled away.

"Quin, please.—There is no future for us, as much as I would want it to be otherwise. Please don't make it even more difficult." She looked up at him and her eyes were shining with tears.

Every fibre in his body screamed at him to take her in his arms, to hell with the consequences. But he could see the pleading in her eyes, could sense her fear at the thought of defying her brother.

So he forced himself to step aside.

"My lady," he managed to say. "I am honoured at having had the pleasure of your company."

He bowed. Rising, their eyes locked, and they stared at each other for a long moment before Alannah turned on her heel and left, closing the door behind her with a dull thump.

I RODE HOME with an aching heart, wanting nothing more than to turn my horse around and fling myself into Quin's arms. But the look on Kieran's face on the staircase haunted me and I was afraid, and in my fear, I was ashamed.

I should defy him, I thought, tell him he couldn't order me around, that I would choose my own path.

And if I should do so, I thought angrily, Kieran would cast me out, leaving me even more destitute than the tenants on Quin's estate, with nobody to turn to for help. For despite Quin's evident liking for me, I found it doubtful he would defy his own family and traditions to take in a disgraced and penniless Irishwoman whom he barely knew.

Much less marry me, I thought, tears welling in my eyes.

"Stop it!" I said aloud. "You knew from the start there was no future with Quin, especially not with a brother like Kieran."

I angrily wiped my tears away, straightened my back and continued toward home, resolutely trying not to think about Quin, or the joy I'd felt in his company over the past few days.

When I arrived at the farm, I instantly knew I was in trouble.

Kieran's grey gelding was standing in front of the stable, waiting for John the groom to remove his saddle and rub him down. Kieran was nowhere in sight, although he must have just arrived. Hands shaking, I left my mare in the gelding's company and hurried into the house.

Maybe I could sneak past Kieran and pretend I'd been home all along, I thought, without any real hope of being able to do any such thing.

I let myself in through the servants' door and used the back staircase to go up to my room. Heart pounding, I quickly crept up one step after another, listening out for approaching footsteps. I managed to avoid notice until I turned the very last corner onto the corridor leading to my quarters.

With a sinking heart, I saw that Kieran was standing in front of my door, looking thoroughly irritated.

There was no point in going back downstairs—there was nowhere to hide and no point in doing so, as I couldn't pretend I'd been anywhere else but out. I was dressed for riding, and he'd probably noticed my horse wasn't in its stall when he arrived.

"Kieran," I said boldly, stepping into the corridor.

He turned toward me, narrowing his eyes at me and lifting his chin.

"Where have you been?" he demanded.

"I took Milly out for a ride," I answered, doing my best to sound nonchalant. "She needed some exercise, and I needed some air."

Kieran took a few steps toward me, looking me up and down in disdain. "And you wore your finest riding habit for that?"

I could feel heat rising in my cheeks but willed myself to remain calm.

"You told me I wasn't allowed to see anyone without your permission," I said slowly through clenched teeth, suppressing the urge to scream at him. "With you being absent and unable to give such permission, the prospects of social engagements requiring fine attire were limited. I therefore took the opportunity to dress smartly for taking my horse for an outing.—Is that also forbidden, dear brother?"

"I told you that you were not allowed *out* without my permission," Kieran said, ignoring my question. "You have defied my orders." His blue eyes, so like my own, were filled with disgust. "But, fortunately," he added, his demeanour visibly brightening, "your insolence will not be my problem for much longer."

A cold shiver ran down my spine at his words. "What do you mean?"

"I have found a husband for you, dear sister. Negotiations for the marital contract should be completed within the month."

"Who...?" I managed to croak.

"Oh, I can't reveal too much until everything is official. But rest assured it will be a suitable match."

I doubted this in the extreme. "I'm not marrying anybody!"

Without warning, Kieran lunged toward me and grabbed me by the upper arms, his fingers digging painfully into my flesh. His eyes were burning, boring into me.

"Oh, yes, you are!" he hissed, drops of spittle flying. "You are going to do exactly as you're told, or you'll live to regret it! Do you think I give a damn about what you want? You are nothing but a pawn in a much bigger game.—One with no use if you don't play your role!"

He was glaring at me, bearing me down with the weight of the hatred in his eyes. I had to look away.

"Do you understand me?"

"Yes," I managed to whisper.

"Look at me!" He grabbed me by the chin and forced my head up to face him. "Look at me!"

I did, and the loathing I saw in my brother's face hurt me more than any physical pain he could have inflicted on me.

"Father was far too lenient with you.—Things are different now. You are going to play the role that's been set out for you, or you aren't going to play at all.—

It's really very simple, if you think about it. Easy enough for a scholar like you to understand."

He squeezed my jaw painfully, before releasing me, turning on his heel and storming away.

I went into my room, closed the door and lay down on my bed.

I was too stunned to cry, too afraid to move.

I didn't know how long I lay there, but eventually my body calmed enough for my mind to start replaying what had happened, to try to make sense of it.

Kieran had been almost berserk when I'd said I wouldn't marry the husband he had chosen for me. Who was this man? And what significance would our marriage have? I doubted very much it was a simple matter of farmland. Kieran had bigger plans, plans that required capital to succeed. So somebody rich, undoubtedly, but probably also somebody who hated the English, who could sway others to join the cause of rebellion.

But who was Kieran dealing with?

The more I thought about it, the more it seemed to me Kieran hadn't come up with this plan himself. His mysterious trip to Dublin—along with a slew of similar absences over the past few months—and subsequent announcement of my imminent betrothal seemed like a strange coincidence.

He must have gone to Dublin to meet the rebels he'd gotten entangled with— I'd never known him to have any business acquaintances. Our overseer, Mr Smith, handled the running of the farm and had done so successfully for the past twelve years. My father—and through him, I—had been actively involved, always working closely with Mr Smith, but after his initial failed attempts at being in charge of Niall, Kieran had generally left the overseer to his own devices, doing the barest minimum himself.

Idleness truly is a sin, I mused.

If Kieran had been busy seeing to the farm, finding newer and better ways of doing things, and trying to increase productivity, he would never have had the time to plot and plan as he was evidently doing.

Plotting and planning he was, though, and by all accounts I was a key player in his scheme. Just how I fit into it, I had no idea. Why would the support of a rich rebel depend on my marrying him?

Unless it was only a pretence, or an added benefit for someone looking for a young bride?

My head was spinning with all these suppositions.

I rolled onto my back and stared at the ceiling. I suddenly thought of Quin and my heart sank. I couldn't see him anymore. The past five days had been wonderful, but they were all I would ever have of him. I was not free to choose my own path. Kieran had made that abundantly clear—he would decide my future for me.

And by his own words, I was worth nothing to him if I didn't follow his orders.

I shivered. He hadn't used the words, but I'd known what he'd meant, nonetheless. If I didn't agree to the proposed marriage, he would have me killed—or do it himself.

The pain I felt in my heart at the knowledge that my own brother would even think such a thing was almost unbearable. I curled myself into a ball and started rocking back and forth, as the tears I'd so far managed to hold at bay overwhelmed me. I cried in great gasping sobs, my soul overflowing with the anguish it couldn't escape, until I at last lay still and finally drifted off to an exhausted sleep.

9.

THE FOLLOWING MORNING, I dressed and went down to the dining room, where I was greeted by Kieran, who acted as if nothing out of the ordinary had happened.

"Sleep well?" he asked cheerfully.

I stared at him tiredly. I knew my eyes were puffy from crying and lack of sleep, and I let my features answer the question for me.

I didn't want to talk to him in any case.

"A bit wet out this morning." He waved an arm toward the window, through which I could see nothing but a sheet of water in the gloom.

A perfect reflection of how I feel, I thought.

I turned away from Kieran and stood in front of the sideboard to contemplate the selection of breakfast foods Mrs O'Sullivan had prepared that morning. I had no appetite but took a few plump red apples from the laden bowl in the centre.

"I'm going to the stable," I said. "If that is permitted, of course," I added, without any attempt at hiding the bitterness in my voice.

"Of course, Alannah. Why shouldn't you go to the stable? You are free to peruse the grounds as you please."

I looked at him for a long moment before heading toward the door, trying to see the brother I used to love in the heartless man sitting before me.

Stepping outside was like stepping into a waterfall. I hurried along the path to the stable as fast as I could but was soaked within moments. Drenched and out of breath, I stood inside for a minute, waiting for my eyes to adjust to the darkness.

It was a small stable, with only four stalls, but it was peaceful inside, with the feeling of the horses around me, the sounds of their gentle movements mingling with the wisps of hay floating in the air. I breathed in deeply, feeling some of the weight lift off my shoulders in the stable's warm embrace.

I walked slowly between the stalls, stroking a soft nose here and scratching a pointy ear there, distributing apples as I went, wishing I could leap onto one of the sturdy backs and race away into a distant land, one without controlling relatives and societal restrictions. A land where Quin and I could squelch through muddy streambanks to our hearts' content without fear of discovery.

I stopped in front of Milly's stall and stroked her head. She blew out softly through velvety nostrils, large shiny eyes looking intelligently at me. She nuzzled my shoulder affectionately and we leaned into each other, the horse offering me comfort in the only way she could.

"Well, isn't that a lovely sight to see."

I spun around at the sound of the unfamiliar voice, and Milly shied away at my sudden movement.

"Who are you?" I demanded, heart hammering, Milly prancing around nervously behind me.

"And what sort of question is that to ask your brother's honoured guest?" the man said and took a step toward me.

I took a step back, eyeing him with distaste.

He was probably a few inches shorter than I, with oily brown hair that hung in a messy tail down to his shoulders. Beady black eyes roamed over me impertinently, with such wanton appraisal I felt dirty just being in his presence.

He rubbed his pointy, rat-like nose before suggestively running his fingers over his lips. "Your brother's description doesn't do you justice at all, my dear," he said, assessing my rain-bedraggled countenance, his gaze lingering on my breasts. "You are much prettier than Kieran would have us believe." He licked his lips, eyes travelling slowly down my body. "And I do like the lasses wet."

My heart started pounding furiously, and I pressed myself back against the stall door, hands braced against the rough wood.

He made no move toward me, though.

"But we haven't even exchanged pleasantries," he said suddenly, breaking into what almost—but not quite—looked like a genuine smile. A smile that didn't touch his eyes. "My name is Martin Doyle."

He bowed and stuck out his hand. When I made no move to give him my hand, he dropped his and shrugged, unperturbed.

"Who are you?" I repeated my earlier question, although I was starting to suspect, not precisely *who* he was, but what sort of character he was.

"Has Kieran not mentioned me at all, then?" He sounded offended. "Tsk, tsk...I shall have to have a word with him.—I, madam, am a distinguished member of the Ulster band of ribboned brothers who seek to find justice for the unjustly oppressed."

A Ribbonman—so that's what Kieran had gotten involved in.

I'd heard of them. Ribbonmen, so named because of the green ribbon tucked into the front pocket of their shirts, were locals who banded together to defend the rights of the poor Irish people, frequently with violence. Targeting mostly landowners or their middlemen, but also others who employed Irish labourers, the Ribbonmen acted against anything they saw as unjust—the eviction of tenants, the hiring of cheaper labourers from other counties and similar real or perceived crimes—showing up in the dead of night with pitchforks, torches and pikes to attack the homes of the offenders.

"I can see you're suitably impressed," Doyle said and winked at me.

"What are you doing here?"

"I was just having a nice lie-down on a pleasant pile of hay when I was awoken by the sweet sound of your skirt rustling between your legs." He gave me a lewd look and I glared at him. "But if you're meaning what am I doing here, on this farm... Your brother, good friend he is, invited me to stay, me having to leave Dublin in something of a hurry after our visit...what with a few uniformed men being on my tail." He sniggered, and my heart gave a sudden thump at the implications of what he'd said. "And to think your brother had only just arrived..." He shrugged dismissively before unselfconsciously scratching his backside.

"Why aren't you staying up at the house?"

"Kieran did offer me a room with a very nice bed, but before I could make myself comfortable, my presence was required elsewhere...a young lady of the night of my acquaintance desiring my company on a particular bale of hay."

He grinned at me, showing surprisingly white teeth. This nevertheless did nothing to improve my opinion of him, particularly as the grin was accompanied by a hand rubbing the front of his breeches and an unmistakably vivid motion of his hips.

"And where is this...lady now?" I asked, averting my gaze, looking unobtrusively around the stable for protruding naked limbs.

"Oh, off to find more profitable entertainment elsewhere, I'm sure.—I dare say, though...now that you're here, Mary would pale in comparison."

His eyes travelled insolently over me once more and I wanted nothing so much as to get away from him as fast as possible.

"Thank you, Mr Doyle," I said, hoping politeness would distract him long enough for me to make my escape. "I welcome you at Talamh na Niall. I do hope you will enjoy your visit with us."

I inclined my head toward him in a gesture I hoped portrayed respect—as opposed to the repugnance I actually felt for him. I picked up my skirts and strode purposefully toward him. He had a sneer on his face but moved out of the way to let me pass, and I hurried out into the downpour.

This time, the rain felt refreshing, cleansing me of the filth I felt clinging to me as a result of Doyle's presence.

I didn't wait to see whether he would follow me but went back into the house and ran up the stairs. I closed the door and leaned heavily against it.

Yet again, I thought with a sinking heart, I was a prisoner in my own home.

QUIN WAS PACING around the study, picking up random objects and putting them back down. He had planned on mapping out the proposed changes to the estate this morning but had found himself unable to concentrate for even the briefest period of time.

His mind was entirely preoccupied with only one topic: Alannah.

If he was being honest with himself, she hadn't left his mind once since she'd left his house, but until now, he had at least been able to complete his daily tasks despite his reeling thoughts. But today, he could do absolutely nothing but replay the scene that had played out in this very study three days before and obsess about the longing he felt for the woman who'd told him there was no future for them.

"But why shouldn't there be?" he demanded, thumping his fist onto the desk in frustration.

Because her brother would never permit it, his mind supplied the answer. Because he would force her to marry somebody else, whether she liked it or not, or throw her out and leave her in disgrace.

He couldn't stand the thought of Alannah being subjected to ridicule and snide remarks. He knew how quickly rumours could go around—had good reason to know it—and if Alannah's brother was as callous as he suspected, it wasn't unlikely he would make every effort to besmirch her character if she didn't abide by his rules. Let him make up a story about her having loose morals and a line of lovers waiting in the wings, and no man would ever wed her. She would be ruined, and completely destitute if he cast her out.

The thought constricted his heart in pain. He wanted to march out to the stable, get on his horse, ride over to Alannah's home and rescue her from her fate.

But he could see no simple way of doing so.

"And when have you ever done things the simple way?"

"Pardon, Master?"

"Oh...Denis...it's nothing. Thank you." Quin waved away the butler, who had stuck his grey head through the open door expectantly.

"I really ought to stop talking to myself," Quin said to himself.

He frowned. He simply couldn't resign himself to the thought of never seeing Alannah again. Despite their brief acquaintance, he felt more for her than for anyone he'd ever met.

And suddenly, it all seemed very clear to Quin. He couldn't let her go and so he simply wouldn't. He put down the letter opener he hadn't realised he'd been holding and walked out the door.

I WAS RUMMAGING around in the vegetable garden, randomly picking out weeds—or what I thought were weeds, in any case. I didn't really know what I was doing but I'd had to get out of the house. The garden, tucked away remotely behind a low wall, out of sight of the house, struck me as a place Martin Doyle wasn't likely to venture to on his own. I'd also never seen him eat a vegetable, so I thought I would be safe enough in this small sanctuary.

I gave up my attempts at horticulture and sat down on the small bench beside the gate. I leaned back and lifted my face to the sun, which had finally come out in full force after days of nearly incessant rain. I basked in the sun's welcome warmth, breathing deeply, enjoying the smell of the freshly turned earth and the spicy scent of the herbs that grew against the wall.

"Psst...Alannah...psst..."

I sat up in a rush of fabric, turning my head toward the sound I knew I couldn't have heard.

"Alannah," the voice came again.

I narrowed my eyes against the sun and saw Quin's face peeking out of the bushes lining the garden's western wall. Before I'd made a conscious decision to move, I was standing in front of him, and he was pulling me into a tight embrace.

"You shouldn't have come," I whispered into his shirtfront while I clung to him.

"Hush..." he said, stroking my back. "Everything will be alright."

I leaned my cheek against his broad chest, breathing in his musky scent, and closed my eyes, wanting to pretend everything was right with the world, that we could stay locked in this embrace forever.

After what seemed like a long time, but wasn't nearly long enough, I lifted my head and looked into his eyes, which shone bright green in the sinking sun.

"You shouldn't have come," I repeated.

He stroked my face and bent down toward me, until our noses were almost touching.

"Alannah...you asked me once before to stay away from you. And I tried.—I tried for three days, until I found myself lurking around your house for two more days like a common criminal, waiting for the opportunity to speak with you." He smiled and ran his thumb softly over my lips. "I simply cannot stay away from you."

He lowered his head and kissed me. I responded hungrily and without restraint, wanting to lose myself in his arms. He lifted me off my feet and wrapped his arms around me, while I ran my hands through his hair and cradled his head.

When at last he put me down, out of breath and dishevelled, I hung onto him, not yet willing to let him go.

"Quin," I finally said, looking up at him. "I wish things could be different...that I was free to choose. But...my brother..."

"Your brother will not be a problem for us."

"What do you mean?" I asked, puzzled, stepping back a bit to get a better look at him.

"I shall talk to him, introduce myself...make my intentions clear." He gave me a green gaze that made it clear to me exactly what those intentions were. "I hope thus to be able to persuade him of my upright character." He winked at me. "But..." he went on, his face hardening, "if he should still have objections...then I shall send him to the Devil and take you anyway!"

He had said this with some violence, and I gaped at him. "But..."

"Alannah, I can take care of you. You won't need him. And it won't matter what he says about us if we're together."

"I..."

"I know it's frightening to think about. But he won't be able to hurt you if you're with me.—And to hell with anyone's opinion!"

"It's not that...it's...I...Kieran has found a husband for me. He told me so on the day I last saw you."

I swallowed and looked down. Quin was silent for a moment.

"Who is he?" he finally asked.

"I don't know. He wouldn't tell me...not until all the arrangements have been made..."

"I see."

I glanced at him. His expression was blank, giving nothing away. After a moment, he set his jaw and looked down at me, determination stamped on his features.

"There's still time," he said. "We shall have to act fast, before any papers have been signed, but...there's still time."

"Wha...?"

"Alannah...I know we barely know each other, but...I cannot imagine my life without you." He held me by the shoulders, his eyes searching mine, wanting me to believe the sincerity of his words.

I did.

"This is not the way I would have wanted things to transpire, but I see no other way out of this predicament. Alannah..." He suddenly dropped down onto one knee in the dirt in front of me, startling me. "Will you do me the honour of being my wife?"

I felt tears prickling at the corners of my eyes as I looked down at the earnest expression on his face, the longing he showed plainly and the fear he tried to hide—the fear of being rejected...and the fear of what it would mean to be accepted.

"Quin...I...I" I took a deep breath to get my feelings under control. "I want nothing more than to accept your proposal..." His eyes lit up. "But...Kieran would be furious. He would never agree..."

"Kieran doesn't need to agree," he said violently, jumping to his feet. "If we have to travel to England to be married because he'll stand in our way here, then so be it. And if he threatens to cast you out or abuse you in any way, then you will simply come and live with me immediately. I can protect you. And I have my own resources. We have no need to be dependent on his. As for any rumours he should choose to spread about us—we shall deal with those in due course."

I so dearly wanted to believe him, but I feared it was not that simple.

"But what about your father?" I had another try. "Shouldn't he have a say?"

Quin narrowed his eyes and scowled. "My father sent a one-line note telling me my mother had died while I was off at war.—He can hardly expect me to be any more considerate of him."

I gaped at Quin with my mouth open, having no idea how to respond.

"Besides," he went on, flipping his wrist in dismissal. "My father complains about everything. Marrying you without his consent would simply give him one more reason to do so, which he would in any case, no matter what sort of wife I should choose." He had said this with a sense of irritation and something else I didn't understand. "Under the circumstances, though, I suspect he would be relieved I had finally gotten married at all...old and decrepit as I am."

He grinned, and I couldn't help smiling in return.

"Alannah," he said softly, sobering up and taking my hands in his. His hands were large, warm and capable, engulfing mine in their grasp. "I know you're frightened. So am I. But this is the only chance we have.—Will you take it?"

His eyes implored me to join him on the path he had laid out before us. Doubt and fear swirled around me, colliding in my mind at the memory of the expression on Kieran's face when I'd told him I would not marry the suitor he had proposed, the hatred in his eyes and the violence he had threatened.

But before me stood a man who drew me to him by his very presence, who had made me feel more in the past few weeks than I had in my whole life. A man who was gentle but strong, supportive but decisive, who had given me a purpose when I'd been drifting on a foreign sea; someone who wanted me for who I was and not for the person I'd been pretending to be.

"Yes," I whispered. "Yes, I'll marry you."

10.

MY HEART WAS pounding, and my legs were shaking. My eyes were huge blue orbs in the large hall mirror and fear was stamped clearly on my features. I breathed deeply a few times, until my hands stopped trembling and my reflection took on a more normal hue. Slowly, I turned toward the staircase and started descending the steps to the interview with my brother.

Alone.

QUIN HAD WANTED to go with me to tell Kieran of our plan, but I'd insisted I go alone.

"I know my brother," I said. "I know how to handle him." I had known—once. "If you come with me, he'll feel like he's been ambushed. It will make things even worse."

I thought it most likely that this was true, although in reality I had no exact idea what to expect of Kieran, changed as he was. I did know he would not take kindly to an Englishman telling him what to do—especially this particular Englishman, his soon-to-be unwanted brother-in-law—and this was my main motivation for going alone.

Not that I had any particular intention of telling him outright I was going to be marrying an Englishman. He hadn't bothered telling me the identity of the man he had selected for me, so why should I be any more forthcoming with him?

Besides, I thought, he's going to be furious anyway, so why make it any worse?

"I don't like this, Alannah," Quin interrupted my thoughts. "You shouldn't have to carry this burden on your own." He frowned at me. "I was the one who suggested the plan in the first place!"

I laughed.

"What?" he asked, startled, but breaking into a smile nonetheless, dimple showing.

"I wouldn't necessarily describe your actions as 'suggestive'.—Persuasive, yes, in the extreme; demanding, even, but I certainly didn't get the feeling that saying 'no' was an option you would have considered acceptable."

He looked slightly abashed at this.

"I haven't made you do anything you haven't wanted to do, have I?" His eyes met mine, questioning—drawing me to him in physical denial of his words.

"No," I breathed into his chest, "you haven't.—But that doesn't mean it's going to be easy living with the consequences."

"I know. I'm sorry."

"It's not your fault. It's my brother's narrowmindedness that's to blame—and his foul temper."

My heart started racing at the thought of how Kieran's temper would react to what I had to tell him. He'd been frightfully angry just a few days ago when I had objected to his plans. What would he do now, when I told him these plans would not come to fruition?

I buried my face in Quin's shirt to hide my fear. I didn't want him to know how Kieran had threatened me, didn't want him to have to worry about my safety. For if he did, he would never let me speak to Kieran on my own, and Quin's coming with me might make things even worse, with the hostility he wouldn't be able to hide. And despite how I felt about my brother now, he was still my brother and I had once loved him. I could not abide the thought of him and Quin fighting over me—with swords and pistols to hand, and tempers and fists flying, things could rapidly get dangerously out of control.

No, I would simply have to face Kieran on my own—no matter the risk.

"It will be alright," I said quietly into Quin's shirt, trying to convince myself as much as him.

"IT WILL BE alright," I whispered to myself again now, as I walked down the hallway to the study, where Kieran was wont to spend his afternoons, pretending to be doing some work, in reality probably staring out the window and twiddling his thumbs.

I stopped in front of the door and took a deep breath before knocking. There was no answer. I knocked again and waited. Silence.

"Kieran?" I called and slowly opened the door. The study was empty. The breath I'd been holding went out of me in relief.

A few more minutes of respite, I thought cowardly.

I searched the house, but found no trace of Kieran anywhere, and the servants I came across said they hadn't seen him all afternoon. I ventured down to the stable and the outbuildings, but these too held no sign of my brother. Not sure whether I should be relieved or disappointed, I went back to the study, thinking he might have returned while I was out.

My heart jumped into my throat when I saw that the door to the study was ajar. I was sure I had closed it. Heart pounding, I knocked briskly and entered, seeing no point in delaying matters further.

"Kieran, I..." I stopped talking abruptly as I realised it was not my brother sitting at the desk, but Martin Doyle, lounging with his feet on the tabletop, looking cleaner than when I'd last seen him, but no less vile, nonetheless.

He smiled a slimy smile at sight of me and swung his feet down.

"Well, if it isn't the beautiful Miss O'Neill." He eyed me lasciviously. "I'm afraid Kieran isn't here. I sent him off to run an errand for me.—He should be back this evening."

"Thank you," I stammered and turned to go.

"Not so fast." Doyle sprang up from his chair and stepped in front of me, blocking my way out. He grabbed me by the arm and spun me back into the centre of the room.

"Why not stay for a bit of conversation?" he asked in a pleasant voice, while his eyes remained cold.

"I have nothing to say to you." I tried to pull my arm out of his grasp but for all he was shorter than I, he was incredibly strong. My efforts had absolutely no effect.

"Oh, but that you do, lass, that you do."

He let go of my arm, took two steps to the door, and closed and locked it with an ominous click. My heart started pounding furiously and I inched away from him.

"There's a story I want to be telling you," Doyle began in a conversational tone, advancing toward me while his eyes roamed over me, "about a most pleasant scene I happened upon this very afternoon.—I was out on a stroll, when I saw a beautiful young lass locked in a warm embrace with a tall handsome man." He stared at me as the blood drained from my face. "Why, imagine my surprise when I realised the beautiful young lass was none other than our own Kieran's dear sister...letting herself be fondled by an Englishman."

He spat the last word with revulsion and lunged toward me. I tried to scream, but he clapped a hand over my mouth, restraining me with his other arm. I tried to get away, until I felt a cold sharp pain on the side of my neck, just under my jaw. He pressed his forearm hard over my windpipe and brought the knife up, so I could see it out of the corner of my eye.

I stopped struggling.

"That's better," he said, pulling me against himself with his arm across my throat, making spots appear before my eyes. "Now, can we continue our most enjoyable conversation?"

I nodded. He let go of me and I collapsed onto all fours on the floor, wheezing and retching.

"You see, Miss O'Neill, your brother and I have worked very hard to arrange your marriage, to a man who can do much to further our cause—once his baser urges have been satisfied with you in his bed." He came to stand in front of me. When he spoke again, his voice was filled with anger. "And the man you were frolicking with this afternoon is not the man you're supposed to be marrying!"

He crouched down in front of me and lifted my head with one hand, holding me painfully by the chin, while he held the knife in his other hand, in line with my eye.

"Are you beginning to see the problem?" he hissed.

I made no response, my body frozen in fear as my eyes kept traveling to the knife I could see in my peripheral vision. I tried to turn my head away from it, but Doyle tightening his grip on my chin, making me cry out in pain. Suddenly, he grabbed me by my hair and pulled my head back, further and further until I thought my neck would break under the strain. My vision started to blur, and I made an incoherent sound, trying to breathe.

"Do you see the problem?" he asked in an awful voice as he laid the knife against my outstretched neck.

His face was right in front of me, and his eyes were burning into mine. I tried to nod, but was unable to move, answering instead with a pitiful mewl that sounded terrified even to my own ears.

He dropped my head and stood up, leaving me gagging and gasping on the floor. Finally, I could breathe again and opened my eyes, only to be confronted with the sight of his boots—recently polished I noticed. Suddenly, like lightning striking, he pulled back one foot and kicked me, the soft flesh of my midsection meeting hard leather in a sickening thud.

He kicked me again, and again, and again.

I lay on the floor, rolled into a ball, unable to move, unwilling to think, trying only to breathe.

He kneeled down in front of me again.

"I think we can agree you will not be seeing this Englishman again...is that not so?"

I nodded.

"If it were up to me," he said, stroking my hair and trying to infuse his voice with honey but failing utterly, "you could marry whoever you want." I didn't believe a word. "But, alas, your intended insisted on having you as his wife, and his wishes must be met. It's a sacrifice we're willing to make—for the greater good. Wouldn't you agree?"

I said nothing, only looking up at him with hatred in my eyes. Evidently, he took this to be agreement.

"That's what I thought," he said coldly and got up.

He started walking toward the door, but suddenly stopped and turned back toward me.

"Oh, before I forget," he said in a voice one would use at Sunday afternoon tea, "if you ever see your Englishman again"—he drew back his right hand, curling the fingers into a fist—"the bastard will not live to see another day."

The blow landed on my cheek. The last thing I saw was Doyle's face, suffused with red hatred, eyes blazing with madness, lips moving as he said something I couldn't understand.

Then everything went dark.

11.

I STOOD IN front of my dressing table mirror, trying to locate myself in the reflection staring back at me.

The front of my body was covered in large blue and purple bruises that spread from my lower ribs down to my hips, and I had an ugly bruise on my left cheek. Not too bad, I thought abstractedly, it might have been worse. I twisted to the side and flinched. It hurt. It hurt a lot. But there seemed to be no internal damage. I wasn't bleeding, and I could breathe without difficulty, although not without discomfort. There also seemed to be no broken bones in my face, and my teeth were all intact. I rubbed the back of my head, gently fingering the large bump where my head had hit the floor when Doyle's fist had hit my face.

That had probably been an accident, I mused; he hadn't meant to knock me unconscious. The rest of the damage he'd done had been calculated, almost precise in its application—enough to bruise, but not enough to maim...and easy enough to hide. Nobody would see the bruising on my body, and the contusion on my cheek could easily be explained away with an excuse of clumsiness.

Only the expression in my eyes would give away the truth.

I noticed my hands were shaking and quickly locked them behind my back. This brought my abused body full into view, though, and I turned away from the mirror, looking for my shift. I slipped it over my head and crept back into bed, trying to suppress the crippling fear that had been bubbling up to the surface of my consciousness since the moment Margaret had found me.

Doyle had disappeared, and the little maid had rushed to my side, exclaiming in horror at sight of me. I'd sat up groggily, stammering that I must have tripped on the rug and fallen. I doubted Margaret had believed me, but she hadn't said anything, only offered me her arm—which proved to be surprisingly strong—and helped me to my bed. I'd lain there fully clothed for a long time, staring at the ceiling, seeing and feeling nothing, until I had finally dragged myself off the bed, with the sudden and urgent desire to wash away the filth I felt was clinging to me, before assessing the damage Doyle had done.

"You can only blame yourself," I whispered to myself now.

I had known from the start Quin's plan would never work. Had known it the moment the words had crossed his lips, as the sudden joy soaring within me stirred the memory of hatred in Kieran's eyes at the thought I might defy him.

Except it hadn't only been Kieran I'd needed to be afraid of.

Evidently, my marrying my unknown suitor was more than just an added bonus for him—whatever assistance Kieran and Doyle hoped to get from the man seemed to be dependent on our nuptials. That made me wonder again exactly what my brother and his repugnant acquaintance were up to. With Kieran's leanings and Doyle's character, I could guess, and it wasn't something that would brook interference from a lone recalcitrant woman.

Kieran and Doyle, and no doubt several others who were in league with them, believed my proposed husband's influence—political, monetary or both—would sway their attempts at rebellion in their favour. A rebellion they hoped would free Ireland of English rule...a goal they would consider of infinitely greater importance than indulging any sensibilities I might have.

I was just a pawn in their game—as Kieran had already told me.

I rolled onto my side, wincing in pain. I stared out the window, where the setting sun had lit the cloudy sky in red and orange flames. I watched the light fade until darkness descended. I let the black night surround me, hiding the wounds on my body and the deeper ones in my soul.

WHEN I OPENED my eyes the following morning, after a restless and uncomfortable night, Kieran was standing by my bed, looking down at me with an expression of shock on his face. As soon as he saw me looking at him, he adjusted his features into a scowl, which nevertheless couldn't hide his uneasiness.

"You only have yourself to blame," he growled, echoing the thought I'd had the night before.

I pulled up the blanket to cover the deep bruises that could be seen clearly through the thin fabric of my shift.

"Go away," I told him and turned my face away.

"Alannah," he said in a rush of breath, "I..."

I looked at him expectantly, waiting for an apology I knew would never come. He dropped his gaze.

"If you would just do as you're told, then this would never have happened!"

"Yes, Kieran," I responded tiredly, wanting only to be left alone.

To my surprise, Kieran suddenly bent over my bed and looked intently at me.

"Please, Alannah, just do what he wants.—What *we* want." He straightened up and turned toward the door. "You don't know what he's capable of."

I wasn't sure if I'd meant to hear his last remark, quietly as he'd said it, but before I could say anything else, he was gone.

I lay there, trying to decide what to think and what to feel.

By all appearances, my brother seemed to be having second thoughts about the kinds of pastimes he'd gotten himself involved in. Perhaps, in his mind, there was a difference between threatening me and acting on those threats and being confronted with the aftereffects of the latter had shaken him.

What was clear to me was that Doyle was the one in charge. Kieran had said *do what he wants*, before correcting himself and had warned me, perhaps intentionally, of the danger Doyle posed.

You don't know what he's capable of.

I had some idea, I thought, looking down at my battered body and gently stroking my swollen cheek.

What I didn't know was what Kieran was likely to do.

Yes, seeing his sister beaten had evidently shaken him, but I doubted it would extend as far as him breaking away from Doyle's influence. If I knew one thing about my brother, I knew his life's aim was to see Ireland rid herself of the English; he'd said as much for as long as I could remember, contemplating a free Ireland even as a boy. Maybe it was only that seeing me fall prey to the results of his rebellious thoughts had awoken in him a sense of brotherly protectiveness he had forgotten—something he could no doubt suppress again, I thought with a sinking heart.

Kieran knew rebellions weren't likely to be won with words alone, that violence would be involved. I thought he must be capable of violence himself; he had demonstrated as much to me when he'd threatened me in the past. Although he hadn't actually struck me, I'd seen the urge to do so in his eyes, the knowledge he could and would do what he felt necessary. And what was necessary was evidently decided by Doyle, or others like him.

I sighed, looking up at the ceiling. After a few minutes, I slowly edged to the side of the bed and swung down my legs. Sitting up made my head pound terribly and I sat still for a moment, waiting for it to ease. It didn't much, but I slowly stood up and walked gingerly past my dresser, avoiding looking at myself in the mirror, to a small table that stood in the corner of the room. I opened the drawer, removed a sheet of yellowed paper, and picked up the quill and inkhorn.

It was time to write to Quin.

QUIN WAS PACING restlessly in the drawing room, wanting urgently to ride to Niall without delay.

Something's gone wrong, he thought to himself; I never should have let her confront her brother alone.

From what she'd told Quin about him, Kieran sounded like a disillusioned, insecure man who wanted to feel better about himself by reminding his sister at every opportunity that he was the one in control. She'd never said anything about him being physically violent toward her but...

Quin swallowed heavily. He knew he would never forgive himself if Alannah came to harm because of him.

A knock on the door interrupted his thoughts.

"Yes, Denis?"

"Master Williams. Letter...for you," the butler said in his broken English, handing Quin the advertised paperwork.

Quin's heart jumped into his throat. "Thank you, Denis."

It was from Alannah. He knew it before he'd torn away the seal to reveal her elegant hand.

Dear Quin, he read.

I apologise for my tardiness in getting this note to you. I have been much occupied with my thoughts and have only now found the opportunity to write to you.

I have considered the situation we find ourselves in and am sorry to say I cannot accept your proposal, despite my earlier, hasty acquiescence. My life is meant to follow a different path and I must accept this.

I deeply regret any pain I might have caused you.

Please do not try to contact me. It will be easier that way.

Sincerely

Alannah Mór O'Neill

Quin stared at the piece of paper, unable to make sense of the words written upon it. Alannah had gone home defiantly to tell her brother she would be marrying him, Quin, no matter what Kieran's thoughts on the matter might be. Instead, it now seemed she'd resigned herself to the fate Kieran had decided for her, without even telling him about her betrothal to Quin—which she'd also reneged upon.

"I don't believe it!" Quin angrily tore up the page. "Not one bit of it!"

He looked at his newly acquired clock on the mantelpiece: seven p.m.—rather late for a formal visit, but he had no intention of being formal about it in any case. He threw the shredded paper onto the ashes of the hearth and went to get his coat.

I WAS STANDING at the open window, watching the sun go down amidst shredded clouds. I was dreadfully tired and ached all over, but I was afraid to sleep. Not because I thought I might have nightmares, quite the opposite. I knew I would dream of Quin—and the happy life we might have lived if things had been different. I didn't want to face the prospect of waking up in the morning only to realise none of it was real.

He must have read the letter by now.

I had sent Margaret to Glaslearg hours ago. I hoped he would accept my decision and move on with someone else, a nice English girl at home, perhaps. It hurt me to think of him with someone else. And I despaired at not being able to help the tenants on Glaslearg as I had promised. But I would break every vow I'd ever given to see him safe. I could not risk Quin's life by giving into my longing for him. For I had no doubt Doyle had meant what he'd said. He would kill Quin without hesitation if he thought he stood in the way of his plans.

It was a warm night. As the last of the sun's rays faded away, I drew the curtains, leaving the window open, and reluctantly got into bed. I tried to stay awake, but my eyelids drooped and within moments, I was asleep.

QUIN AND I were having a picnic on the streambank, the oak's branches throwing long shadows over us as we lounged on the blanket. He picked up a strawberry and gently placed it in my mouth. He smiled and bent down to kiss me, his mouth coming away sticky with the sweet juice. I ran my finger along his lower lip and brought it to my mouth.

"Alannah," he whispered and stroked my cheek.

"ALANNAH."

"What?" I sat up, gasping at the pain.

A dark figure loomed up beside the bed and my heart leapt into my throat, cutting off the shriek that had risen in me at the sight.

"Alannah. It's me. Quin."

"Quin?"

A flurry of emotions flowed over me as I said his name. Relief that it was not Doyle who'd shown up at my bedside; anger that Quin had ignored my plea to stay away; fear about what consequences his actions might have…but outweighing all of these was the feeling of pure joy at the sight of him. I wanted nothing more than to fall against his broad chest, for his strong arms to surround me, to make me feel safe again.

But for *him* to be safe, I had to send him away.

"Quin. You shouldn't have come. I'm sorry if I've upset you, but I'm afraid I've changed my mind. I cannot marry you.—I shall do as my brother commands."

He stood stock-still for a long moment, looking down at me. Then he turned away. My heart sank. He was leaving. It's what I'd hoped for—but it wasn't what I wanted.

I watched him go, but when he got to the door, he didn't open it as I'd been expecting, instead removing the oil lamp hanging from the hook beside it. After a series of rattles and clicks a spark came to life, and within moments the lamp was burning brightly. He came back toward me, holding the lamp before him.

My heart started pounding and I shrank back against the pillows, trying vainly to hide. I knew Quin would recognise the truth the instant he saw me in the light.

He stopped next to the bed. I turned my head away.

"Look at me, Alannah," he said gently.

My eyes were filling with tears, and I swallowed the lump in my throat. I looked up.

Quin's expression was unreadable. His face was blank, hiding all emotions. He put down the lamp, knelt down next to me and reached out a hand to gently stroke my bruised cheek. He dropped the mask, and I could see shock and anger flit across his features, his jaw muscles clenched tightly as he took stock of the damage. He reached out to me and pulled me roughly toward him.

I cried out in pain.

He let go of me and jumped back. "What is it? What else has he done to you?"

Without looking at him I pushed down the blanket and lifted my shift up to my breasts.

He was quiet for a long moment, and I risked a peek at his face. It was hard-edged, laced with fury.

"I'm going to kill him for this."

It was spoken softly, but with an intonation that left no doubt as to the truthfulness of his words. He looked up from my battered body, and when his eyes met mine my face crumbled. He held me in his arms, gently, that he wouldn't hurt me, stroking my back and rocking me softly. I clung to him, seeking comfort in his arms.

When at last I'd cried my last tear and lay exhausted and dazed against his chest, he gently laid me down on the bed. I refused to let him go, though, so he lay down next to me, pulling me close. He stroked my hair, and he stroked my back, and I suddenly became aware of the fact that I was wearing nothing but a thin cotton shift, this currently rucked up around my waist, my modestly preserved only by the summer blanket, which had crept dangerously low.

I stiffened slightly in Quin's arms and his hand abruptly stopped moving.

"What is it?" he whispered.

"Uh...um...nothing." I blushed and looked down.

He followed the direction of my gaze and realisation swept over him. He was silent for a long moment, as he made an obvious effort to compose himself.

"You needn't worry," he said finally, sounding a little breathless, "*I'm* still fully clothed, so your virtue is safe from me."

I laughed nervously and our eyes met.

I reached for him, pulling his head toward me until our lips touched and, suddenly, I desperately wanted him to remove the last scraps of fabric that lay between us. Heart pounding, I took his hand and deliberately placed it on the naked skin of my hip. He froze. I pressed closer to him, and his hand slowly caressed my side, before sliding down over my buttocks, making me shiver.

Abruptly, he stopped moving and gently extricated himself from my embrace, rolling slightly away from me.

"Not now. Not like this," he said softly, breathing heavily.

"Please."

"No, Alannah. You're hurt, you're scared.—You don't really want this."

"Yes, I do!"

He chuckled and rolled back toward me. He stroked my cheek and kissed me softly. "I promise you, when the time is right…"

"But how can it ever be right?" I interrupted him irritably. "We can never be together."

"I promised I would take care of you, and I shall. Tomorrow, you will pack your things and come live at Glaslearg with me. Then Kieran won't be able to hurt you anymore."

"It wasn't Kieran."

"What?"

"It wasn't Kieran who did this to me."

Quin was visibly startled by the revelation. "Then who…?"

"A man named Doyle. Martin Doyle. An acquaintance of Kieran—of sorts." I shivered at the recollection.

"Martin Doyle? I seem to have heard that name before…" Quin wrinkled his forehead, evidently trying to remember what, if anything, he knew about Martin Doyle.

I shuddered at the thought of Quin having anything to do with the man.

"You needn't be afraid," he said, seeing my reaction. "I can protect you from both of them." He took my hands in his, determination etched on his face. "No one will hurt you while there's breath left in my body."

"But that's what I'm afraid of," I whispered.

He stroked my head, trying to soothe me. "I'm a trained soldier, Alannah. I can take care of myself…and you."

"Doyle…he said…he said if I ever saw you again…he would kill you."

The words were barely a whisper, but Quin had understood. He was quiet for a moment.

"Alannah, I know that you're afraid…afraid for me. And your concern for me moves me deeply. But the only thing that scares *me* is the thought of living without you. I'm willing to take any risk that comes with being by your side."

"He said he doesn't work alone." I searched his face, trying to make him understand the danger he was placing himself in. "Before I blacked out…after he did…this"—I waved vaguely at my cheek—"he said something, something I couldn't understand. I saw his lips move but couldn't make sense of what he was saying. But it came back to me last night. He said, *I don't work alone.*"

I left the statement hanging in the air, not needing to explain what it meant. If Doyle didn't kill Quin himself, somebody else would do it for him—and we wouldn't know from where the danger would come.

Quin gathered me into his arms without saying a word.

"I shall think of something," he said softly, holding me tight. "He will be none the wiser in the morning, and I shall think of something." He kissed me lightly on the forehead.

"How did you get in here?" I asked, the question having suddenly occurred to me when I'd contemplated how Quin was to leave without being seen.

"I climbed up the lattice against the wall and in through your window—which you'd thoughtfully left open for me." He smiled and despite myself, I smiled back. "I had been watching the house for hours. I didn't know where I might find you. When I saw your silhouette at the window I knew where to go. So I waited until it was dark and invited myself in."

He pulled me close again, his lips brushing the top of my head. "I just couldn't ignore what my heart was telling me...that you hadn't meant what you'd said in your letter."

"I didn't. I..."

"Hush. It's alright. We're together now and everything will be alright."

12.

I CONFINED MYSELF to my room for two days.

I didn't want to see anyone, to have to pretend nothing had happened. I particularly didn't want to have to run into Martin Doyle, who I assumed was still staying at the farm. Kieran didn't come to visit me again and I saw no one but Margaret, who brought me food and cleaned the commode. I was grateful for the solitude, needing to come to terms with what had happened...and what might happen in the future.

Quin had stayed with me through the night, despite my protests that he was placing himself in danger. He'd closed the window and placed a chair in front of the lockless door, ensuring himself no one could enter unannounced, doing something to allay my fears. But I'd continued to jump at every creak, expecting Doyle to burst in on us and take Quin unawares.

"Martin Doyle..." Quin repeated to himself some time during night. "Where have I heard that name before?"

"Not in polite company, I would guess."

"No, I wouldn't think so either," Quin said distractedly, tapping a finger on his chin to aid thought. "But I can't remember...hmm...wait a moment...I seem to think. Yes, I recall now where I heard the name! It was in connection with a brawl at an inn in Dublin several months ago. An acquaintance of my father mentioned the happenstance upon hearing of my imminent departure to Ireland, having himself returned from Dublin not long before. I'd mentioned to him I would be travelling by ship to Dublin, from whence I would continue on to Glaslearg."

He frowned.

"Now that I recall the occasion, I can remember the details of the tale. Evidently, several men who'd had rather too much to drink started harassing one of the other patrons, an elderly Englishman. By all accounts, the man ignored the insults, focusing on his meal instead, but took offense when the group started taking turns trying to push him off his chair. When he got up to defend himself, one of the Irishmen threw a punch, knocking the Englishman flat. The innkeeper and some of the other customers tried to assist the Englishman, but in the ensuing brawl one of the Irishmen dragged the man outside, whereupon he laid into him with fists and feet, leaving him lying gravely injured in the street before fleeing the scene."

Quin looked at me and the hair on the back of my neck rose at the certain knowledge of what he would say next.

"The Irishman was reportedly one Martin Doyle, who is by all accounts well known to the Irish Constabulary, having been linked to several instances of unrest and violence across Ireland dating back at least a decade, most of an Anglophobic nature."

Although shocking in itself, this revelation didn't surprise me. A character like Doyle's was unlikely ever to have been wholesome.

"And he's also wanted for murder," Quin said, looking pointedly at me.

I swallowed.

"You mean…"

"The Englishman died. Doyle beat him to death.—And it wasn't the first time he's killed."

"I CAN'T HIDE in here forever!"

I was talking to my reflection—something I seemed to be doing a lot of late. The bruise on my face was still prominent, but had faded to a lighter blue, tinged with green and yellow; much like the ones on my belly, although these were still much more apparent.

It had been three days since my encounter with Doyle and I was starting to feel restless.

I needed to get out of my room, where I had been stewing in Quin's revelations about Doyle and what it all meant. Quin had said he would think of a way to rid us of the threat he posed. I hoped with all my heart he could, but I was unable to see how—it wasn't just Doyle we had to fear, it was his unknown acquaintances who might do his bidding, violent or otherwise. And then there was Kieran…he had threatened me himself, had promised me retribution if I didn't do as I was told.

But then there was the moment the morning after Doyle had beaten me, when he'd shown only shock at sight of me and, perhaps, regret.

I didn't know what promises Kieran had made Doyle, what arrangement there was between them, or how Kieran fit into Doyle's plans—which I surmised went beyond the burning and looting of the Ribbonmen he'd associated himself with when he'd introduced himself to me. But the fact Doyle was here, in our house, suggested it was far too late for Kieran to make a quiet exit from whatever shady organisation they were involved in—should he even want to do so.

I needed to stop thinking, I decided.

Wanting to escape my thoughts, and the confines of my apartment—but avoid seeing anyone—I waited until it was dark before cautiously opening the door. The house was quiet, and I heard nothing but the creaking of the floorboards as I made my way downstairs to the library, where I thought I might find some distraction in a favourite book.

As I was walking down the corridor toward the library, I heard a sudden noise coming from the study. The door was slightly open, and I could see shadows flickering in the wavering light that spilled through the gap.

"It's not enough!"

I recognised the voice of Martin Doyle and froze in my tracks.

"Burning down a few houses and scaring a few landlords isn't enough! It's not going to get us any closer to getting rid of the English than printing pamphlets.—We need to strike against them...with force!"

"We don't have any force!" I could hear my brother respond in protest.

"We will! Our ranks are growing even as we speak."

"Our ranks?" Kieran's scepticism was clear in his voice. "A score of men dredged up at the poorhouses of Dublin?—They're unlikely to grow into an army in our absence, nor will they be any more capable of battling the English when we return!"

"You're not going soft on me now, are you, Kieran?" Doyle's question was filled with a quiet menace. "Just a few days ago you were proclaiming your willingness to die for Irish freedom."

Both men were quiet for a moment, and I stood stock-still, barely daring to breathe. They would be furious if they found out I'd been eavesdropping.

"Is this because of your whore of a sister?" Doyle asked suddenly in a nasty tone and my heart jumped into my throat. "You're not upset that I taught the little bitch a lesson, are you?"

Little? I thought. I'm taller than you, you bastard.

"Well...no," Kieran responded, without much conviction. "It's just that I hadn't thought..."

"If you're going to be squeamish about it, lad, then you'd best go crawling back to your cradle right now and leave the real work to men! There's always a price to be paid for freedom. And if we have to pay with the virtue of some of our womenfolk, then so be it! Your sister has a role to play, and she'll play it..."

Doyle left the unspoken threat hanging in the air. He, evidently, had no qualms about going to any lengths to get what he wanted.

"We don't need soft-bellied, lily-livered farm boys to join the fore. We need men who are willing to stand up and do whatever is necessary—*whatever* is necessary! Do you hear me?" His voice was rising, although he wasn't quite yelling. "Did Wolfe Tone balk at fighting his own countrymen if they were against him or worry about the fate of peasants coming up against English canon? No!" There was a loud thump, as someone—Doyle, I presumed—brought his fist down on the desk. "He fought!"

"And he failed," Kieran said in a small voice. "The whole rebellion of 1798 failed, and you well know it!" His own voice was rising now. "And with the Act of Union that followed his failed attempt, Ireland is even worse off than before! Not only are we still under English rule, they've gotten rid of our own parliament, making us even more subjected to their whims.—And Tone had the backing of the French!"

"Who didn't make it to the battle in big enough numbers to count! At least we won't have to worry about bad weather preventing the landing of our supporters on Irish shores if our supporters are already here!"

"Tone had local supporters, tens of thousands of them. And he still failed!"

"They weren't organised, and they didn't have enough weapons! Pikes and pitchforks against firearms and heavy artillery? It's hardly surprising they failed! But things will be different this time. With Andrews' money, we'll arm the rebels!—And then we'll strike the English bastards right in the heart. This time we *will* take Dublin and rally the surrounding counties to revolt. There won't be enough resistance to stop us!"

"And what if it's a trap? Can you trust the man?"

There was a sudden scraping sound, as of a chair being pushed violently back.

"Can I trust *you*?" Doyle hissed. "You say you're for Ireland, for freedom...that you'll gladly give Andrews your sister in return for his money. And now, at the first hurdle, you're acting like a sick puppy whining at the loss of the teat!—A man like me trusts no one but himself, especially not some Anglo-Irish whoreson who earned his riches off the British Army! But to win this war, we must take what's available. We need money to buy arms, and if your sister's sweet arse is going to loosen Andrew's pockets to give it to us, then so be it!"

There was a brief pause before Kieran responded. "I've done everything you asked," he said softly, sounding defensive. I was sure I could also detect a note of fright in his voice. "Haven't I?" The question sounded almost pleading to my ears and I wondered what else had passed between the two men.

"So far," Doyle sneered. "You'd better have your sister meekly accepting the proposal when I get back...or you'll live to regret it! Do you know what I do to people who get in my way?—Why don't you ask Thomas if you're not quite sure."

Doyle sniggered cruelly, a sound that made the hair on the back of my neck stand on end.

"Are you going to slit my throat like you did his?" Kieran asked in a low voice.

My heart gave a painful thump both at what he'd said and the obvious fear I could hear in his speech. Clearly, it was no idle question. Suddenly, I saw Kieran's violent outbursts toward me in an entirely different light.

"He got what he deserved!" Doyle snapped.

"For disagreeing with you?"

"For betraying me!" Doyle yelled, accompanied by a loud thump as his fist hit the desk once more.

My heart was hammering in my ears, drowning out the silence that had abruptly descended following Doyle's outburst. I carefully edged back toward the staircase, my breath coming short and shallow. I quickly climbed the steps to the first floor and hurried back to my room, hoping they hadn't heard me. I closed the door and leaned against it, waiting, but nobody came, and my heart finally began to slow.

I sat down on my bed and breathed in deeply several times, trying to suppress the fear bubbling up inside me.

Doyle was a murderer.

I'd already known that, but now... I swallowed heavily as I remembered the cold brutality of his voice as he threatened Kieran—something he seemed in the habit of doing to get his way. How many people had he killed already, I wondered? For I had no doubt Doyle had meant what he'd said.

106

I took another deep breath, letting it out slowly as I forced my mind away from Doyle, thinking about what else I'd overheard.

Andrews, I mused, so that was the name of the man I was supposed to marry.

From what I'd heard, I surmised they must mean Herbert Andrews, the landowner and businessman. I had met him once, when I was seventeen, when father had taken me with him to Dublin, where he'd had dealings with the man. Fascinated with all there was to see in the city, I hadn't paid much attention to what my father had said about him, but from what I could remember, Andrews' family had arrived in Ireland from England many years earlier and had taken possession of a large plot of land still largely covered in native forest. Instead of cutting down the trees to plant crops, as was being done across Ireland, Andrews' family had decided on timber farming as a means to make money. This decision had paid off handsomely during the Napoleonic wars, as the British Navy had required enormous amounts of timber during the campaign.

Being an enterprising sort, Herbert Andrews—who had taken over the family business during the course of the wars—hadn't been satisfied with this, though, and had become involved in numerous other ventures, which meant he hadn't suffered markedly from the drastic economic downturn that followed the end of the war. While peace was likely a desirable prospect for most people, it did have financially detrimental effects on those who relied on the exigencies of war as a source of income.

Not Andrews, though, who'd barely paused in his financial advance and amassed a substantial fortune while others had struggled to survive.

A fortune that was now to assist Doyle and his rebels if they had their way.

I shuddered at the thought that I was the key to this arrangement, that my marrying the man would be required for Doyle to receive the money. Herbert Andrews must be more than old enough to be my father. But beyond this, there was something in the way he'd looked at me when I'd met him in Dublin I'd found most disconcerting. It wasn't anything in particular—he had been nothing but outwardly courteous—but he had held my hand just a little too long, had scrutinised my appearance just a little too closely.

Evidently, he remembered me and now insisted I was to be part of the arrangement with Doyle.

And what sort of arrangement was it exactly?

On the surface, it seemed like the perfect solution for Doyle. Get the support of a rich man capable of providing the money necessary to arm the rebelling masses, thereby increasing the chances of the rebellion's success—for how many uprisings had failed when unarmed rebels, no matter how fierce, had come up against fully trained and equipped soldiers?

Placing guns and swords in the rebels' hands would surely increase the chances of success.

But how many guns could one person's money possibly buy? Doyle seemed to think Andrews would be willing to provide vast quantities of arms, but I wasn't so sure. Being a shrewd businessman, he was unlikely to overinvest, and with thousands of rebels to arm—not to mention feed—even a large portion of Andrews' fortune was unlikely to make enough of a difference.

And why would Andrews want the rebels to succeed in the first place? What would he gain from Irish independence?

Nothing, I thought, for he relied heavily on Ireland's trade with England for his earnings. And if the Irish rebels should defeat the English, the vanquished would be unlikely to promote trade with their conquerors for some years to come. And if the rebellion should fail and Andrews be found to have supported it, he would be arrested for treason and lose everything, including possibly his life.

No, I could see no reason for Andrews to fulfil his end of the bargain, which made me think it was all a ruse—apparently to get to me.

I doubted he'd been planning anything of the sort for the past five years, but being as successful as he was, he was probably also an opportunist. And when Kieran's name had come up in connection with a potential rebellion that required funds, he probably thought it was an excellent opportunity to bag himself a wife—one he'd seen before, and evidently fancied. Why he didn't simply ask Kieran for my hand, I didn't know—after all, he had plenty of money and could easily have made him an offer, which Kieran would have accepted, no doubt. Nor could I understand what a man of his social standing would possibly have been doing in circles where rebellions were discussed.

I shook my head. There were more questions than answers, and I wasn't any closer to figuring out how to get rid of Martin Doyle and the danger he posed. I hoped Quin was having better luck. The thought of Quin filled me with longing. What I wouldn't give to have him here, to find comfort in his presence and his embrace.

I checked the window. I'd promised Quin I would leave it open for him at night, so he could sneak in again when he deemed it safe. I'd argued against his coming, afraid he would be seen. But he had insisted, wanting to have a way to visit me. I opened the curtain and looked out into the night, letting the cool breeze caress my face, before turning toward my bed, in hope—and fear—that Quin would come tonight.

QUIN LAY AWAKE, unable to sleep. Every fibre of his being screamed out for him to do something, no matter that it was three o'clock in the morning. He had felt restless since he'd seen Alannah two nights ago; restless and powerless, two feelings he didn't enjoy one single bit.

He jumped up, deciding he'd stayed away long enough.

He got dressed quickly, in dark, drab clothing that would fade into the night. He quietly opened the door to his quarters and tiptoed past Rupert's small adjoining closet. He could hear regular snoring coming from the other side of the door. His valet was unlikely to notice his leaving; nor would Denis or Bryan hear him up in their rooms in the attic.

He decided to go on foot, as he had the last time, so as not to risk notice with his horse. The farmhouses were only about one mile apart, Quin could easily reach his destination on foot. He loped along the dark road as a light drizzle fell from the sky, keeping low, eyes and ears alert to anything suspicious.

A short distance from Niall's manor he slowed and crept behind the clump of low shrubs that grew in front of the house. The rain had stopped; it was quiet, and the house was dark, with no signs of disturbance or unrest. He dashed across the open space between the bushes and the house and pressed himself against the wall. He waited, but there was no sign of alarm and so he eased his way along the wall until he reached the corner of the house. He risked a glance but saw nothing untoward and continued along the wall until he reached the lattice he'd climbed up two nights before.

He looked up at Alannah's window and saw she'd left it open as she'd promised.

His heart started pounding and he scrambled onto the flimsy-looking framework, which groaned frightfully under his weight, as it had the last time. Hoping it would hold a second time, he climbed cautiously upwards, expecting at any moment to be shot in the backside as he made his ascent. No volley of gunshots ensued, though, and he reached the windowsill without incident. He scrambled through the window, ending crouched on the floor.

He stood up and walked slowly across the room to Alannah's bed, not wanting to frighten her.

"Alannah," he whispered when he reached the bed.

There was no reply.

He knelt down and patted the humped shape he could see by the dim light coming from the banked fire.

"Alannah," he repeated, but discovered the lack of a response was not due to Alannah being asleep, but rather due to her absence. The shape he'd thought was her was in fact just a pile of bedclothes. He looked around, startled. He could hear no sounds coming from the commode behind the screen and he couldn't see her anywhere else in the room.

She wasn't there.

Quin's mind started racing, supplying him with images of Alannah being dragged away by Doyle, while Kieran held quill and inkhorn at the ready for the marriage contract awaiting her signature.

He snorted in anger and marched toward the door, intending to wrench it open and tear down the house in search of her. Before he could get a hold of the handle, though, the door opened, and Alannah came in. He stood there gaping, with his hand extended, as she yelped in alarm and dropped the book she'd been carrying with a loud thump, her lamp swaying dangerously.

They both froze and stared at each other, but the house remained quiet.

Quin quickly closed the door and, before Alannah could say a thing, had dispossessed her of the lamp and lifted her off the floor in a tight embrace.

"Quin," she whispered and hugged him fiercely.

He held her for a few moments longer before reluctantly setting her down.

"I went to fetch a book," she explained softly as she picked it up. "From father's library.—I couldn't sleep."

"Neither could I. I needed to see you."

He reached out a hand and gently stroked her cheek. The bruise had faded, but it was still all too prominent for his liking, even in the dim light. He clenched his jaws as a sudden wave of fury overcame him.

"How are you feeling?" he asked, making an effort to suppress his anger.

"Well," she replied, and he looked at her sceptically. "As well as might be expected," she amended, and he narrowed his eyes at her. She returned the favour. "If you want to know whether I'm in pain...then the answer is yes, yes, I am.—But it isn't anything I can't handle."

She looked at him defiantly for a moment before lowering her eyes. "As for the other...I'm trying not to think."

He took a step toward her, but she turned and walked to a small table that stood in the corner of the room, where she placed the book.

"I went to Ballygawley," Quin said to her back. "I spoke to the constable of the Irish Constabulary Police Force who's stationed there with his men. The name of Martin Doyle was only vaguely familiar to him, but he said he would be happy to arrest him nonetheless when I listed his crimes."

Quin snorted and walked to the window.

The farm lay quietly below him on a night that was dark with the lingering clouds hiding the light of the waxing moon. He turned back toward Alannah, who was now facing him, a slight frown between her brows.

"I was reluctant to have the constable come here directly. I was afraid Doyle would be scared off.—I shall not place you in danger by risking his escape." His tone brooked no argument. "I thought it better to bring him in myself and deliver him to the police."

Alannah's eyes flew open, but before she could say anything, Quin pressed his point. "If a dozen men show up here, he'll get wind of it and disappear before anyone gets close to him. I can sit in wait, watch the farm and its grounds, take him unawares without him even knowing anyone's hunting him."

"But..."

"I'm a trained soldier, Alannah," he said and stepped in front of her. "You needn't be afraid for me."

She glared at him. "If you think your saying so is going to make the slightest difference to how I feel, you are very much mistaken. Of course I'm afraid for you. I have reason to know what sort of animal you'll be lying in wait for.—But that's not what I meant in any case," she muttered, waving away his objection. "Doyle isn't here," she went on more gently, "or at least I don't think so.—I overheard him talking to Kieran earlier. It sounded as if he were going somewhere for a few days. He left Kieran with instructions...to keep me in line until his return."

She couldn't hide the scorn in her voice and Quin frowned.

"At least we don't have to worry about him catching you sneaking in here," she said with an attempt at a smile.

"No, I suppose not," Quin agreed, not smiling, but holding her gaze.

Suddenly, she reached for him. "Quin."

He pulled her to him roughly, his mouth finding hers.

She came to him willingly, pulling him closer as his heart pounded in his chest. He relished in the feel of her, the touch of her skin, the scent of her hair, wishing only to lose himself in this moment for the rest of his life. But too soon she broke away from his kiss, breathing heavily, but in control of herself.

"It will be alright," she whispered into his chest as she gently ran her hands up and down his back.

He laughed, making her pause in her caress and look up at him quizzically.

"Have I not been trying to convince you of the same thing since virtually the moment we met?"

"I suppose you have," she agreed. "But what do we do now?"

"We wait."

13.

A FEW DAYS later I came down to breakfast and ran into Kieran, who was on his way out of the dining room as I came in.

I'd been avoiding him since my encounter with Doyle, waiting until I thought he'd finished eating before having my own meals and staying confined to my room for most of the day. Since his visit at my bedside the morning after the attack, he'd made no effort to see me, to ask me how I was feeling.

His lack of interest hurt me, but I tried to smile at him as he passed by me.

His eyes widened when he saw me—in surprise and a hint of guilt, or even regret, I thought—but he quickly looked down, murmuring an excuse as he hurried away. I looked after him for a moment, my heart heavy, before perusing the selection of breakfast foods. I ate sparingly. I hadn't had much of an appetite since Doyle had beaten me and food had become nothing more than a form of sustenance for me.

I looked out of the window.

It was a beautiful morning, bright and sunny with the promise of warmth. It made me think of the day Quin and I had gone on our picnic. It seemed like a lifetime ago, but only two weeks had passed. I missed Quin terribly. I hadn't seen him since his last night-time visitation. We'd agreed another visit would be too risky, as we didn't know where Doyle was or when he might return.

As to what we would do when he did return...

I shook off the thought. I had regained my strength and the bruise on my face had almost faded. Those on my abdomen were still quite prominent but didn't hurt anymore.

I can't keep hiding in my room, I thought, irritated, feeling like a coward for letting Doyle intimidate me so. Making a sudden decision I dared not question, I got up. Surely, there was nothing stopping me from taking Milly for a turn around the grounds.

I quickly climbed the stairs to my room and donned a riding habit, went out to the stable and saddled Milly myself, before I could change my mind. Leaving the house made me feel vulnerable and exposed, and I chided myself for my weakness. I breathed out heavily and lifted my chin defiantly, determined to conquer my fears.

I rode around the farm aimlessly, slowly feeling my anxiety start to fade away. The sun shone warmly on my face and a sense of freedom started to awaken in me as I left the house and its memories behind. I led Milly along the fields of wheat and oat, grain heads heavy with their bounty, almost ready for the harvest. We passed the small herd of sheep grazing on their pasture, awaiting the shearer with their shaggy coats.

The sights, sounds and smells of the farm invigorated me.

Talamh na Niall had shrunk considerably since Cathal O'Neill had secured the land for his offspring, as his neighbours encroached on his territory and political upheaval resulted in the redistribution of farmland. But the original simple farmhouse and a moderate acreage remained, a small farm that faithfully sustained its inhabitants, year after year.

A farm that was thriving under Mr Smith's management. I was happy to see the results of his efforts to go beyond what had been expected of him when father was alive. But it saddened me to think my brother had been unable to rise to the challenge of running the farm himself.

I rode along the edge of the pasture, coming to a stop at the foot of a small grassy hill. I hobbled Milly and let her nibble the succulent grass while I lay down on the spongy carpet, looking at the vast sky above me, feeling very small. Everything else faded into insignificance as I beheld the immensity of creation, my very existence receding to the background of the constancy of the heavens. I watched fine wisps of cloud float by and felt my worries float away alongside them. An unexpected feeling of contentment descended upon me, something I hadn't experienced in years—except in the presence of Quin these past few weeks.

Quin.

He was like no one I'd ever met before, made me feel like I was the centre of his universe, that everything I thought and did truly mattered to him. Even though we'd only known each other for a few short weeks, it felt like I had known him for years, for my whole life.

I thought about the past two years, how Kieran had tried to control me, to bully me into submission. And I had let him. I could have tried to defy him, told him where I stood. I could have left.

But I hadn't—because I'd been afraid of the consequences.

I had grown up privileged, with a father who had catered to my unladylike whims. The thought of facing a hostile world on my own and with barely any resources at my disposal had filled me with dread. And so, I'd succumbed to Kieran's threats and tried to accept my fate.

But that was before Quin had come into my life. A future without him was something my mind simply couldn't accept. And if I wanted a future with Quin, I could no longer hide behind my fears.

I sat up, feeling like a weight had been lifted off my shoulders. I breathed in deeply, filling my lungs with the sweet scent of the luscious grass, the pungent aroma of the sheep that looked curiously at me from behind the fence, and the heady smell of my sun-warmed skin.

Amidst all of my troubles, I had found an oasis of peace.

I ambled slowly back toward the farmhouse, wrapped in a cocoon of serenity, as a layer of clouds spread across the sky. I came around the bend that led to the outbuildings and walked Milly toward the stable, which stood at the very end of the path.

"Well, if it isn't the lovely Miss O'Neill."

I pulled Milly to a stop, tugging on the reins more forcefully than I'd meant to as my brain registered the voice I had heard. She rolled her eyes and stamped her hooves, but I managed to control her before she could throw me off. My eyes scanned the buildings and I saw a dark shape detach itself from the shadows behind the granary.

"And what's happened to your cheek, then?" Martin Doyle said in mock concern. "Had an accident no doubt?"

I glowered at him and made to move past him, but he grabbed Milly's reins with one hand and my left leg with the other. He jerked forcefully on my calf, unbalancing me, and I quickly had to pull my right leg from the pommel and jump off the horse to stop myself from falling. I landed in a heap at his feet, cursing the invention of the side saddle, determining to ride astride from now on. I stood up and wiped my dirty hands on my riding habit, trying to glare at Doyle in anger while my heart raced in fear, the tranquillity of a moment before forgotten.

"Tsk, tsk." He looked me up and down. "You should be more careful. I hear you've been confined to your bed these past few days...an indisposition of sorts, I believe." His eyes gleamed as he seemed to be recalling the details of our last encounter. "Getting up before you're quite recovered can cause a relapse, I'm told."

His eyes hardened and he took a step toward me.

I took an automatic step back, but his hand shot out and he grabbed me by the arm. He pulled me forward until he had me in a tight embrace. I could smell his stale sweat and his sour breath and tried to push away from him. He pulled me closer, holding me with one arm, while the hand of his other arm fastened on my breast, making me squirm.

"You shouldn't fight so much, sweetheart," he said in a conversational tone, hot breath caressing my cheek. "Much better for everyone if you just play along."

He removed his hand from my breast, replacing it lower down. He pushed my hips toward him, and I thought I could feel a hard bulge pressing against me through the layers of fabric. I felt panic starting to rise within me but squashed it down. Surely, I thought fervently, he wouldn't accost me in broad daylight in the middle of a farm with farmhands likely to show up at any moment.

"I'm afraid I have to disappoint you, sweetheart," he said apologetically while his hand caressed me all too familiarly. "Your intended insisted I bring you to him unspoilt." He licked his lips, looking down at my breasts while continuing to fondle me elsewhere. "If that wasn't so, I would've had you on your back on the nearest haystack long since."

He made a lewd motion with his hips and pressed me into him.

"But don't worry." He suddenly released his grip on me. "There'll be plenty of time for that once the contract's been signed.—While I'd like to be the first one to have a taste of your quim, I don't mind a bit of a wait. When your man's had his fun, we'll get our chance."

He winked at me with dead eyes, and I stared at him in shock as my heart carried on pounding.

"Now," he continued, as if we were discussing a point of business interest, "I've got a meeting planned in four days' time to finalise the arrangement. Being the good girl you are, you'll be coming with me to meet your husband...won't you?" He hissed the question into my face, his eyes boring into mine.

"Yes," I whispered, looking away.

"Good. I see your obedience is improving. I told Kieran you just needed a bit of motivation." He smiled at me with unblinking eyes and patted me on the cheek.

"Just make sure you remember it. We really can't be disappointing the groom by showing up with a battered wife...or no wife at all." His cold eyes glared at me for a long moment before he turned on his heel.

"Good day, Miss O'Neill."

He waved as he walked away unhurriedly while I stood trembling in the middle of the path, staring after him as the first raindrops began to fall.

THE CANDLELIGHT FLICKERED, and Quin put up a hand to shield it from the breeze coming through the window.

He had no idea what time it was, but he knew it was late. The servants had long since gone to bed. He himself had gone to bed—repeatedly—but had been unable to sleep. Sitting around waiting was not something he'd ever been good at, and his capacity to do so hadn't improved in the present circumstances, waiting for Martin Doyle to return.

He scowled, wishing the man would show himself forthwith so he, Quin, could send him, Doyle, to his maker.

A sound outside the door made Quin turn toward it with a frown.

He thought he could hear soft footsteps in the passageway outside the sitting room. The sound stopped suddenly, and Quin froze. There was no knock at the door, but Quin saw the handle turn slowly, as somebody evidently tried to gain entry without making a noise. He blew out the candle and silently crept to the door, before turning the handle and yanking it open in one smooth move. Without pausing for breath, he grabbed his unannounced visitor, pulled him into the room and locked his arm around his neck.

"Quin," came a strangled voice.

"Alannah?"

Quin quickly released his stranglehold and spun her around. Heart racing, he pulled her toward him and embraced her, but froze as his hands encountered her hips.

"What in God's name are you wearing?" he said in astonishment, forgetting to ask what she was doing there in the first place, as he ran his palms over the smooth expanse of fabric.

"Breeches," she explained, her eyes shining in the semi-darkness. "They're Finnian's...my hall boy." Quin stared at her, dumbfounded. "I found the shirt and breeches airing out by the servants' entrance, so I thought... I couldn't very well walk here in a voluminous skirt, now could I?"

"You walked here?" he hissed. "On your own? In the middle of the night?" His voice was rising as anger welled up inside him.

"Yes, I did," she said, scowling. "Contrary to what the English believe, the Irish countryside isn't riddled with murderers lurking behind every bush."

"That may be so. But we do know of at least one...one who has a particular interest in *you*.—How could you be so reckless?" He was barely able to stop himself from shouting at her, as he struggled to contain his rage.

"Doyle isn't going to kill me...at least not while he thinks he can get his money from Andrews through me."

"Is that supposed to make me feel better?" Quin growled. "Look at what he's done to you already! Do you think he would simply accompany you back home if he came across you on your own?"

"No," she admitted, looking down.

Quin breathed deeply a few times, trying to suppress his fury. She was unharmed, she was here, she was safe.

Not for any lack of trying on her part, he fumed.

"I'm sorry I frightened you, Quin," she said suddenly and took his hand. "But...I had to come."

He looked down at her and squeezed her hand, his anger slowly melting away. "It's alright. You're safe. But please, Alannah...don't ever do something like this again."

"Um..."

"What?" His earlier apprehensions returned in full force. "What have you done?"

"Well...the reason I needed to talk to you is that I...I've devised a plan...to capture Doyle.—Using myself as bait."

"You what?" he roared.

"Quin, please," she said softly. "Stop yelling at me. I'm not doing any of this to upset you.—Besides, you'll wake everyone in the house."

Quin blew out slowly through his nose and made a stab at civility. "Alright," he said as calmly as he could manage through clenched teeth. "Let me light a candle and then you can tell me about this plan of yours. And if my hair doesn't stand on end, we may—and I say *may*—discuss it."

He plastered a smile on his face and led her to the small table he'd been sitting at, still fuming, but sufficiently calmed to enjoy the dim view of her backside in the ridiculously tight and entirely inappropriate—yet strangely enticing—breeches.

He snorted.

"You are a veritable cacophony of sounds tonight," Alannah said with a sideways glance at him as he lit the candle.

Despite himself, Quin chuckled. "Don't test me, woman," he muttered. "If you continue with your present demeanour, you'll have me howling at the moon and yapping at your heels."

She laughed and sat on one of the two chairs, while he lowered himself onto the other.

"Now"—he took a deep breath—"tell me about your plan."

She began talking hesitantly, cautiously examining his expression as she told him how she'd come upon Martin Doyle that morning, evidently returned from whatever shady errand he had been on. Quin's jaw tightened at the thought of the vile man anywhere near Alannah, but he said nothing.

"He wasn't exactly courteous, but not...violent, either," she said, looking up at him through dark lashes. "Although he was more than happy to threaten me."

She shuddered in remembrance and Quin made a growling sound, scowling angrily. She ignored him and continued with her tale, recounting how Doyle had seemed sure their previous encounter had convinced Alannah her only choice was to go along with his plans—to marry this Andrews she'd told Quin about.

"And so, I agreed," she concluded, and Quin's breath exploded in a puff of anger as he understood at once what she intended to do.

"No!"

"Quin, it's the perfect plan. He thinks I'll be leaving with him in a few days' time to go to Andrews. He thinks he's cowed me sufficiently that I wouldn't dare to defy him. He won't suspect a thing."

"No, Alannah, it's too dangerous!"

"But I won't *be* in any danger. The police will arrest him the moment he shows up to meet me."

"Something could go wrong. It could become violent.—No, Alannah, I won't have you involved in any such thing."

"But..."

"No, Alannah! I forbid it!"

"You *forbid* it?" she hissed, face suffused with anger, blue eyes sparking fury. "You have no right to forbid me from doing anything!"

He glared back at her, outraged at the thought of her willingly putting herself in danger—a danger she didn't see.

"I am not stupid, Quin. I know what sort of man Martin Doyle is...I know it better than you do!—And that's exactly why I'm doing this. Martin Doyle needs to pay for his crimes, and I am going to see to it, with or without your help! I am not going to sit by helplessly any longer!"

They stared at each other, each waiting for the other to back down.

"I know I have no claim on you," Quin conceded finally in a tight voice, "but I can ask." His expression softened. "Please, Alannah, don't do this, don't put yourself in danger. We'll think of another way."

"It's too late, Quin. If I back out now, he'll know something's wrong." She reached for Quin's hand and clasped it tightly. "I know you're trying to protect me, to keep me safe...but your best chance of doing that is to see Martin Doyle arrested for his crimes."

Quin looked at her earnest face, and countless thoughts and emotions tumbled through his mind.

"Alannah...if anything should happen to you..."

"Hush," she said and stroked his cheek, giving him a tired smile. "Everything will be alright."

QUIN INSISTED THAT he walk me home after we'd concluded our impromptu meeting and I meekly agreed. I knew he was furious with me for sneaking off in the middle of the night. He would never let me walk back on my own and, in truth, I wasn't keen to repeat the experience.

When I'd made up my mind to go see Quin myself instead of sending a discreet note with one of the servants the following day, the unexpected peace I'd found on my morning ride had still been fresh in my mind, despite my encounter with Doyle. And so, I had started out bravely enough, convinced I was taking my first steps toward bettering my life and that of others, and obtaining my freedom, proud that I would be making a useful contribution to society by arranging the arrest of a violent criminal. I had felt bold in my plan, like nothing could go wrong with my noble quest, powerful even, as I donned the breeches and shirt ordinarily confined to men.

My valiant disposition had declined rapidly on the way to Glaslearg, though, as I crept slowly along the road, feeling increasingly vulnerable in the dark, my heart beating rapidly in my chest. I had started at every sound, expecting Doyle to come upon me at any moment, imagining that I saw him at every turn.

It was a trip I had no desire to repeat and, in hindsight, couldn't believe I'd even contemplated in the first place.

Quin's solid presence next to me on the way back now was a welcome addition, as was the small lamp guiding us along the way.

"You said Doyle threatened you," Quin said as we walked along in our small pool of light, his mind evidently still on our earlier discussion. "What exactly did he say to you?"

"Oh...um..." I stammered, not quite sure how to tell him about the hidden threats in Doyle's lecherous comments.

Quin paused in his stride and looked down at me with narrowed eyes, clearly expecting an answer.

"Um...well...he made it clear that he wanted to...um..."

I must have looked uncomfortable enough in my attempted explanation that Quin understood what I was trying to say. His nostrils flared in an expression of anger that was becoming all too familiar to me and he breathed out like a steam engine, the cords in his neck standing out in anger.

"If that man lays another hand on you, I will kill him with my bare hands." His eyes were burning with fury even in the dim light. "Did he say anything else?"

"Isn't that enough?" I asked, surprised at the question.

"It's more than enough," he grumbled. "I simply wanted to ascertain the complete schedule of events the man has prepared for us."

"Oh, well...he did also imply that...that he would kill me if I didn't do as he says." I glanced sideways at Quin, who looked like he was just about ready to explode.

"And yet you had no qualms about sneaking out of the house in the middle of the night to see a man he expressly forbade you from seeing? And when you knew Doyle was back at the farm and might easily have seen you leave?—Is this not precisely the kind of action he warned you about?"

He was glaring at me, obviously enraged.

I looked down, as the fear and doubt I had tried to suppress since Doyle's unexpected appearance suddenly overwhelmed me. My hands started shaking and I felt tears prickling at the corners of my eyes.

"I'm sorry, Alannah," Quin said, pulling me to him roughly and stroking the back of my head. "I didn't mean to upset you. I'm angry. No...I'm furious! It makes it difficult to be rational." He shrugged apologetically. "I know you're afraid. And to come to me in spite of that...I know why you did it, I understand.—I just can't stand the thought of you being in danger. And me not being there to protect you."

I wrapped my arms around him and leaned my head against his chest. We were quiet for a moment, and I could hear his heart thumping steadily under my ear.

"That's why we have to catch him, have him locked up," I said after a while. "So we don't have to be afraid anymore."

"I know." He stroked my cheek. "But I don't like the thought of you having anything to do with it!"

He hugged me tightly to him and kissed me on the forehead, before releasing me. We walked on for several minutes in silence.

"How did you know where to find me?" Quin asked suddenly. "In the house, I mean," he added with a smile.

"I saw the light of your candle under the door," I answered, smiling back at him. "I assumed none of your servants would be sleeping in a room that size. And since you're the only other person who lives there, I thought it likely I'd found my mark."

"And what would you have done if I hadn't had a candle lit? It was well past midnight after all. I might have been asleep." He gave me a sideways glance and lifted his eyebrows questioningly.

"Well...I thought it likely that you *wouldn't* be asleep," I said quietly. "I wasn't..." I looked at him as he walked along the path, strong and sure, and felt a tugging at my heart. "If I hadn't seen the light, I would have opened every door and looked into every room until I found you."

"And risked waking the servants?" he asked with a grin.

"I highly doubt either Denis or Bryan would have noticed if I'd entered the house with an entire battalion. As for waking poor little Rupert..." I waved a hand in dismissal. "I didn't think he would cause me much trouble."

He laughed at my assessment of his staff. "But how did you get into the house in the first place?"

"One of the small windows on the ground floor was ajar. So...I let myself in."

I looked up at him out of the corner of my eye, waiting to see his reaction, but he only chuckled to himself.

"I shall have to berate the servants for leaving the house open for such dangerous trespassers."

I laughed myself. "Fortunately, I *was* able to get in that way. It was rather a tight squeeze. I should never have managed in a dress."

We were in sight of the house by now. Quin stopped walking and put down the lamp, shielding it behind a small bush that grew along the path. He turned toward me and took a few steps closer, until he was standing right in front of me. He looked down at me with a dubious expression on his face.

"I am by no means saying I in any way approve of your choice of attire," he said and gently pulled me toward him. "However"—his hands skimmed my hips, moving slowly along the contours of my body, lightly cupping my buttocks—"there are advantages," he breathed into my ear.

I leaned into him, weak-kneed, but he only kissed me gently on the forehead before turning toward the house, motioning to me to stay. I stood there waiting for my heart to stop racing while he quickly checked the surroundings. When he'd assured himself it was safe, he took me by the hand and led me cautiously to the servants' door I had left unlocked at the back of the house. He preceded me up the stairs, carefully scrutinising each corner before allowing me to proceed. When we at last reached my door, he checked the room thoroughly while I waited at the threshold, before closing the door and pointing me toward my bed.

"What about you?" I whispered, stifling a yawn as the exertions of the night caught up with me. The thought of collapsing into my bed was suddenly very appealing.

"I'll use my usual escape route," Quin murmured with a smile in his voice, nodding toward the window. "Will you be alright?"

"Yes. I'll send word..."

"Hmph..." A frown appeared between his brows. "I'll make the arrangements."

He gave me a brief kiss on the cheek and, without another word, crossed the room in three strides and disappeared out the window. I leaned my head out after him and watched him make his descent, holding my breath as the lattice creaked ominously.

When he reached the ground, he looked up. Seeing me standing there, he waved, before loping off into the dying night.

I turned toward my bed as the darkness started fading, hoping my exhausted mind would find some rest.

14.

I WAS SHIVERING. Not because I was cold, but because I was awaiting the arrival of Martin Doyle to escort me to my intended bridegroom.

I moved closer to Milly, leaning against her strong neck. She turned her head toward me and whickered softly into my ear. Kieran fidgeted nervously next to me. I looked in his direction and saw the moonlight glinting off the pistol he was carrying.

My heart had leapt into my throat when I'd seen him pull out the weapon when he'd fetched me from my room an hour or so earlier.

"What is the meaning of this?" I hissed, my heart racing.

"It's nothing, Alannah." He looked down, avoiding my eye. "Just a precaution."

"Against what?"

"To make sure you don't change your mind," he said, trying to sound menacing but failing, his voice tinged with fright instead.

I glowered at him, ignoring my shaking hands.

"Please, Alannah, just do as he says," Kieran burst out suddenly, pleadingly, and grabbed me by the arm. "Then nobody will get hurt."

He had pulled me through the door and led me out of the house and to the stable, where the horses had been waiting for us. We'd ridden a short distance along the road before veering onto a small dirt track, until we'd reached an abandoned farmhouse, where we were to meet Doyle.

I hadn't seen the man since the day he'd pulled me off my horse.

All communication from him had come to me through Kieran. Evidently, Doyle hadn't felt himself safe at the farm and had avoided being seen there. The thought made me slightly nervous. If Doyle suspected something, he would come prepared, making it all the more difficult to capture him.

And all the more dangerous.

My palms started sweating as I thought of Quin out there in the dark, waiting for Doyle, who was likely to be heavily armed.

But Quin will be armed too, I said to myself, and so will the men from the police.

For we had gone along with our original plan, to ambush Doyle as he tried to lead me to Andrews. Quin had intended to alert the police constable at Ballygawley of Doyle's presence, waiting only to hear from me when and where the meeting was to take place. We'd agreed I would send a note with Margaret when she went to the town market on Friday morning, to be passed inconspicuously to Quin. They had met before, the first day he'd come to Niall, and would be able to recognise each other.

The difficulty had been obtaining the information.

I'd only had a day or so to get it for it to be passed on at the Friday market, and I hadn't been able to ask Doyle anything directly without raising suspicions. In the end, I hadn't been able to ask him anything at all, having to rely exclusively on what Kieran could tell me, which wasn't very much. Doyle didn't seem to be particularly trusting of his erstwhile accomplice, which made me wonder what else had passed between the two of them since I'd overheard them in the study. The only thing Kieran could tell me was that the rendezvous was to take place on Friday night, not Saturday morning as I'd thought, making it clear Doyle was trying to avoid notice by leaving in the dead of night. I had been informed that I should pack nothing but the clothes on my back and that I should be ready to depart one hour after sunset.

With no further details forthcoming, I'd written a brief note to Quin, hoping he would be able to find me.

Looking around now at the empty countryside, which was clearly visible by the combined light of the full moon and the lamp Kieran had hung beside the delipidated door of the farmhouse, I felt panic rise within me that our plan would fail, that Quin would arrive too late to catch Doyle as he sped me away. For far worse than being forced to marry Andrews would be the fate that awaited me if Doyle knew he was being pursued while he had me in his grasp. He would know Quin would fly to Andrews' side to await Doyle as he attempted to deliver me. And I knew, without a shadow of a doubt, that under those circumstances Doyle would choose to save his own skin rather than risk arrest by carrying out his plan.

And to save himself, Doyle would run, dragging me with him.

The thought of being at Doyle's mercy made me gasp for breath in fear. He had made it abundantly clear what he wanted to do to me. If he were on the run, and I with him, he would take what he wanted—and there would be no form of restraint. There would be no reason to spare me, as he would have no further use for me. He would keep me alive for his own pleasure, to take out his anger and use me as he wanted, discarding me when he was done.

I leaned against Milly, trying to breathe slowly as dark spots started appearing in front of my eyes. My hands were shaking, and my heart was racing. I clung to the saddle, and slowly my breathing started to return to normal and my heart began to slow.

I saw Kieran glance at me, his face suffused with an undoubtable look of fear, but when he saw me looking at him, he quickly turned away.

"He's coming," he murmured a moment later.

I lifted my head and saw a rider coming down the hill that rose steeply behind the farmhouse. He was moving slowly, the horse carefully picking its way through the jumble of stones that lay scattered on the ground. Suddenly, another rider appeared at the top of the hill. I gasped. Quin, I thought, but realised immediately it couldn't be him. The man was too short and looked awkward on his perch, nothing like Quin's effortless grace. As I watched, two more figures materialised, and I felt bile rise in my throat.

Doyle had brought reinforcements.

"Ah, the lucky bride," Doyle said when he reached Kieran and me, jumping off his horse. "So good of you to come."

His eyes flashed in the moonlight, the brightness doing nothing to hide the wickedness of the soul behind them. He took a step closer to me and gripped me firmly by my upper arms.

"You'll not be trying anything foolish, now, will you?" He narrowed his eyes, his face mere inches from mine. I could see the dark stubble of his beard, which matched the dishevelment of his hair.

I shook my head mutely and looked down, not daring to meet his eyes.

"Good," he said and patted me familiarly on my rump. "You really should feel flattered, you know," he added, his hand lingering on my hip. "Being carried off in the middle of the night must mean you're worth something."

He sniggered nastily at the suggestion that I was being abducted for my dowry. Herbert Andrews hardly needed to resort to the sorts of tactics some poor labourers and smallholders used to acquire a better-off bride, forcing her into a marriage she didn't want by compromising her to the point she had no other choice.

Doyle pinched my cheek with a sneer and turned away, moving off to confer with the three men he'd brought with him, who were standing in a huddle talking in hushed voices amongst themselves. Kieran stood apart from the rest, alone.

After a moment, the three men disappeared into the ruins of the outbuildings that stood a short distance from the house. I looked after them, wondering what they were doing.

"They've hidden supplies," Kieran's voice came from behind me.

I turned around and looked at him, but his eyes flitted away, avoiding my gaze. Before I could say anything, there was a loud shout from the outbuildings, succeeded by a series of yells, several loud bangs, and the sounds of a scuffle. This was followed in short order by the emergence of a roiling mass of limbs as the fight spilled out of the ruins and onto the hillside. A figure dashed out from behind a crumbling wall, pursued by a man in a dark green, army-style uniform.

"Stop, in the name of the Queen!" the uniformed man yelled dramatically after the escapee, who paid no attention to these instructions, redoubling his efforts instead, the policeman hot on his heels.

My heart had leapt into my throat at the start of the ruckus and continued to beat rapidly as I turned away from the outbuildings, anxiously observing the policeman's progress. Suddenly, out of the corner of my eye, I saw someone running in my direction, toward the horses that stood clustered together next to the derelict farmhouse.

It was Doyle, I realised with a small shock, obviously trying to escape.

I couldn't let that happen.

I ran at the horses and started shouting and waving my arms, spooking them so they scattered in fright. Doyle emitted a torrent of filthy language and turned burning eyes on me, lifting his pistol and pointing it at me. He fired, and I threw myself onto the ground, the bullet whizzing over my head as it missed its mark by the barest of margins.

Doyle roared in anger, and I scrambled to my feet and ran away from him in dread. I ran without conscious thought, past the house, scrabbling up the hill as I lost my footing, hampered by my voluminous skirts. A hand grabbed my foot and tried to pull me down as I struggled to keep going, scraping my palms painfully on the ground.

"You fucking bitch," Doyle hissed behind me. "You've ruined everything!"

I kicked at him frantically, but he got hold of my ankle and pulled me down under him.

"I'm going to kill you!" His spittle flew into my face as he tried to close one hand around my throat with murder in his eyes.

I twisted and turned, trying to push his hands away from me and get out from under him, but he was far stronger than I. In desperation, I jammed my knee up into his side as hard as my skirts allowed and clawed at his face with my nails. As he leaned his upper body away from my outstretched fingers, I pushed at his chest with all my might, causing him to lose his balance on the steep slope. He fell heavily onto his side, and I rolled onto my hands and knees and scrambled away from him as fast as I could, trying to get to my feet.

He was after me before I'd gotten very far, and his hand started closing around my foot once more.

Fuelled by panic, I yanked my foot up before he could tighten his grip, pulling my knee up as far as I could, and viciously brought my foot back down with as much force as I could muster. I heard a crunching sound as the solid heel of my shoe made contact with a delicate body part. Doyle screamed, and I could see him lifting his hands to his face as I finally managed to get up and started running back down the hill toward the farmhouse, where I should have headed all along.

"You filthy whore," Doyle screeched after me through the blood pouring down his face.

I slid down the hill, tumbling the last few feet, up and running as soon as I hit the ground. Suddenly, a dark figure loomed in front of me, and I shrieked as I ran headlong into it.

"What?" Quin said in surprise as he caught me in his arms, and my knees almost buckled in relief.

He looked back up the hill and, seeing who was in pursuit of me, put me behind him and drew his sword.

"Martin Doyle, I presume," he said, in tones as hard as steel.

"Well, if it isn't the English bastard," Doyle spat, voice thick with the congested blood that blocked his ruined nose.

"Give yourself up, Doyle. There's nowhere to run."

Evidently Doyle didn't agree with this assessment, for he glanced around the abandoned farmyard and made a sudden dash toward one of the tumbled-down walls. Quin was off and running after him the next instant. Instead of vaulting the wall as I expected, Doyle bent down when he reached it and, quick as lightning, stood up again, holding a sword in his hand, making Quin come to a sudden stop a short distance away.

"You're not the only one who knows how to use one of these," Doyle snarled, holding the sword out in front of him.

The two men started circling each other, swords outstretched, while I watched in terror. Quin made a sudden lunge toward Doyle, who took a quick step back, barely avoiding being run through.

"But I am better trained," Quin quipped, continuing his advance.

I hoped sincerely he was right.

Quin was undoubtedly the more elegant swordsman, but Doyle was fighting for his life and was parrying Quin's every stroke—and more.

The moonlight flashed off Doyle's sword as the blade came within an inch of Quin's chest, and my heart hammered in my own chest in fear. I flattened myself against the farmhouse, my foot brushing something as I stepped back. I risked a quick look down and saw a large pistol lying in the dirt, evidently dropped by one of the men. I quickly stooped and picked it up. I'd never held a pistol before and had no idea what kind it was, nor what I might do with it now—I couldn't shoot while Doyle was in such close proximity to Quin for risk of hitting Quin himself—but I felt better for holding it.

I stood transfixed, both hands wrapped around the pistol's grip, while Quin and Doyle continued their murderous dance. Quin's face bore a mask of concentration, the absolute focus needed to stay alive, with no room for any thought outside the sphere of the sword in front of him. Suddenly, his face changed as Doyle swung his blade in a vicious arc across Quin's body. As Quin stepped back to avoid the blow, he tripped on one of the broken stones from the wall. He fell back with a look of dismay and Doyle advanced on his incapacitated prey.

"Quin!" I shrieked in terror, as Doyle lifted his sword.

Quin had somehow managed to keep hold of his own sword during his fall and brought it up in the nick of time as Doyle came upon him with a deathly stab. Quin parried the swipe, but Doyle advanced on him again, knocking the sword out of Quin's hand.

I was shaking in terror, but suddenly, belatedly, remembered the pistol in my hands. I lifted it and pointed it at Doyle, who was advancing on Quin once more. I didn't know whether the pistol was loaded, much less whether it was cocked and primed, but I pressed the trigger and prayed.

It fired with a mighty roar and a cloud of smoke, and I felt my shoulders snap back as the pistol recoiled.

Doyle looked at me in surprise and staggered backwards, holding his right arm as his sword fell to the ground. Quin jumped up and got Doyle in a stranglehold, while two men from the police force ran toward him, belatedly coming to his aid.

I dropped the pistol and slid down the wall of the farmhouse as my body started shaking in reaction. I lowered my head as dizziness overcame me, and I started to sway. Suddenly, Quin was there. He wrapped me in his arms, stroking my back, stroking my hair, murmuring words I didn't understand as I lay against him, numb with shock. Finally, the buzzing in my head subsided and the fragments in my mind realigned themselves into a world I recognised.

I looked up at Quin, touching his back, touching his arms, stroking his face, wanting to assure myself he was there in front of me.

"It's alright," he said, stroking my cheek, "it's over now.—It's alright."

"I wonder if we'll ever find anything else to say to each other," I mumbled as a hysterical need to laugh suddenly threatened to overcome me.

Quin grinned and shook his head. "I'll never stop saying it. No matter what we're up against, everything will be alright as long as we're together.—No matter what sort of filth we have to deal with," he added, looking in the direction of Martin Doyle, who was being led away in handcuffs. He kissed me on the forehead and stroked the top of my head, but stopped suddenly, bringing his hand down in front of him.

The lamplight showed a dark smear on his fingertips.

"Doyle shot at me," I said, staring at my blood on his fingers.

Quin looked at me in shock and clenched his jaws, all colour draining from his face. He carefully probed my scalp.

"The bullet must have grazed your head," he said in a low voice filled with fury. "Does it hurt?"

"It stings a little," I admitted as the scrape started to make itself felt. Thinking about how close the bullet had come to lodging in my head made bile rise in my throat as the world started spinning around me. I breathed deeply a few times until my hands stopped trembling and I felt I could stand up.

Quin pulled me gently to my feet, wincing slightly as he got up.

I looked at him in concern and saw that the left side of his shirt was torn, a large stretch of dark-stained fabric gaping open ominously. I held onto his arm as he tried to turn away and gently pulled up the ruined shirt, modesty forgotten.

I gasped.

A foot-long gash marred his smooth flesh, running at an angle from his ribs to below his waist, oozing blood that trickled into the waistband of his trousers.

"Quin," I said, shocked.

"It's nothing." He gently removed my hands. "I've experienced worse. And would have done so again tonight if you hadn't fired that gun with such impeccable timing and aim." He smiled at me tiredly. "Where did you learn to shoot like that?"

"I've never used a gun before in my life," I answered mechanically, staring at the torn shirt and the damage it hid. "I wasn't aiming at his sword arm...I wasn't aiming at all...except at Doyle of course," I said, making no sense at all as sheer exhaustion descended on me like a smothering blanket, wrapping me in a sheath of detachment as I continued to stare at Quin's shirt.

I swayed and would have fallen, but Quin caught me in his arms and picked me up. He carried me to the horses that the policemen had gathered and helped me onto Milly's back. He climbed up behind me and turned the horse's head in the direction of the road, ignoring the glances from the other men.

"I'm taking the lady home," he declared in a tone that brooked no argument, wrapping one arm firmly around my waist.

I closed my eyes and leaned back against his chest, letting the world recede into the haziness of the fog around me. I drifted along without conscious thought, taking no notice of my surroundings, until I could at last lay my head and fall gratefully into oblivion.

"SIR...SIR..."

"Mmmm." Quin turned away from the intruding voice, grunting in pain as he rolled onto the heavy dressing on his left side.

"Sir...I'm sorry to wake you, sir, I truly am, but...there's a constable here to see you."

Quin grumbled and slowly opened one eye, looking over his shoulder at the anxious face of his valet as he tried to ignore the throbbing in his side.

"It's alright, Rupert," he croaked, before yawning hugely. "I must have had at least five hours of sleep over the past week, so I really oughtn't to be tired, now, ought I?"

"Yes...I mean, no...sir?" Rupert said uncertainly, not being the keenest observer of sarcasm. "I shall have your clothes laid out for you in a moment, sir," he added anxiously, eager to please his master.

"Thank you, Rupert," Quin responded sincerely as Rupert scuttled off toward the wardrobe with a worried glance behind him.

Quin rubbed his eyes vigorously and sat up, wincing slightly and swaying with tiredness for a moment before getting up. He splashed some cold water from the ewer onto his face, until he felt as invigorated as he was likely to get any time in the near future.

Thoughts of the future made him think of Alannah, and his heart contracted painfully.

He had taken her home and seen her safely handed over to her maid and the other servants, with strict instructions to tuck her into bed without delay. Margaret had looked at him with big eyes as he gave a brief account of the night's events to the staff, who had tumbled into the foyer at his abrupt arrival, nightcapped and dressed for bed. They'd exchanged looks of horror amongst themselves at his tale and gaped at him and Alannah, who stood motionless beside him, slumped and dishevelled, staring into the distance as he held her upright around the waist.

She'd barely said a word after they'd left the abandoned farmhouse, stunned and exhausted by everything that had happened—not just the night before, he thought, but the last few weeks.

"Since I came into her life," he muttered to himself with some irritation.

He knew he wasn't entirely to blame but couldn't help feeling Alannah's life would have been less complicated if he hadn't shown up. Then again, if he *hadn't* shown up, she probably would have been forced into the marriage Kieran and Doyle had arranged for her, and who knew what would have happened to her then—or if she'd tried to refuse the proposal, as he was almost certain she would have done even without his presence.

"At least I can protect her."

He was relieved beyond expression that he and the three policemen had been able to track her and Kieran from Niall to the abandoned farmhouse. They might easily have lost the two riders, on foot as they were. But Kieran had led Alannah at a slow pace and Quin and the others had been able to follow undetected at a safe distance, hiding in the abandoned outbuildings when it became clear they'd reached the meeting point. If they hadn't...

Quin's jaw tightened thinking about how Doyle had shot at her without the slightest hesitation, intending to kill, and how close he had come.

Trying to quell his thoughts, he rather painfully got himself dressed with Rupert's assistance—recoiling in horror at the sight of his bloodshot eyes in the mirror—before sending his valet in search of some coffee. Quin was normally thoroughly English in his tastes, considering anything but tea to be an offense to the very concept of a hot beverage, but under the circumstances, he felt something stronger was merited.

As Rupert hurried out of the room, Quin ran his hands energetically over his face once more, before making his way downstairs to meet the constable. It was Constable Ryan, who'd led the charge the night before.

Quin was pleased to see the man didn't look any better than he felt himself.

"Good morning, Mr Williams," Ryan addressed him with some irony.

Quin inclined his head and returned the greeting in exactly the same tone of voice.

"The prisoners have been taken to Omagh gaol," Ryan announced without further preliminaries. "There's an assize scheduled in a week or so. Might be that the judge will address them then."

"Thank you," Quin said to the constable as Rupert came through the door with a tray bearing a steaming pot and two cups.

"Are the other men familiar to you?" he asked, accepting a cup with some hesitation.

Quin had only had coffee once before, several years earlier, and hadn't particularly enjoyed the experience. He sniffed delicately. Finding the coffee's aroma to be tolerable, he took a cautious sip. He made a face and reached for the sugar and cream, plying his cup liberally with both, before gulping down the contents without pausing for breath. Ryan eyed him with amusement as he came up for air, mouth burning from the scalding liquid.

"Yes," Ryan said before draining his own cup in a similar fashion. "They've been causing some trouble in these parts for several months. Stealing livestock, setting sheds on fire and the like."

"Did they have a particular motive for their actions?" Quin blinked tiredly as he waited for the coffee to take effect.

Ryan shook his head. "We don't think so. Their activities seem to have been based on convenience rather than any political or religious reasons—or even agrarian unrest. They've stolen and vandalised across the county, without any apparent preference of victim."

"But you can't be sure of that."

"No," Ryan replied tersely. "But we shall most assuredly ask them."

"I apologise for what must seem to you to be a noisome interest in your captives, constable," Quin said. "I only wished to assure myself these men are casual acquaintances of Martin Doyle, not his henchmen."

Ryan sobered up at this and rubbed a hand across his face, opening his eyes wide as he looked at Quin. "I understand, Mr Williams. But I'm afraid I can't give you that assurance. We have no reason to believe the three men are anything more than common criminals.—But that isn't to say they definitely aren't, nor that they aren't in the permanent employ of Martin Doyle."

Quin tapped his fingers together thoughtfully.

"Thank you, Constable Ryan," he said after a moment. "Then we shall hope they are indeed simply common criminals and will not be a danger to us upon their release...which I hope will not be occurring any time soon?"

Quin raised his eyebrows expectantly, but Ryan only shrugged.

"I can't say, Mr Williams. The punishment for such crimes isn't always clear-cut. It often depends on the judge..."

"Hmph," Quin grumbled, unsatisfied with this answer, but deciding to address the likely reason for the constable's visit instead of arguing with him. "I assume you've come for my statement?"

"Yes, sir, if you would be so kind to oblige me."

STATEMENT GIVEN, AND two further cups of coffee consumed—without any obvious improvement to his muddled state of mind—Quin staggered up to his room to freshen up. Dousing himself with ice-cold water was likely to be the only action that would have any invigorating effects on this particular day, but Quin settled on splashing his face with water from the ewer in a repeat of the morning's proceedings.

"Will you be having a rest, sir?" Rupert asked behind him as he handed him a towel.

"No, Rupert," Quin said as he emerged from the soft sheet. "I shall be visiting Miss O'Neill."

"But sir"—Rupert's eyes went wide—"you look like the Devil himself with your red eyes and wild hair...will you not frighten her? Um...meaning no disrespect, sir!" He looked down suddenly, face aghast, a furious blush creeping up his young cheeks.

Quin chuckled at his mortified valet. "If you would be kind enough to make me a little more presentable, I'm sure Miss O'Neill would be most appreciative."

"Oh, yes, sir," Rupert declared eagerly and set to work with brush and comb.

Quin had very little hope Rupert's efforts would make any noticeable difference to his dishevelled appearance, but he let his valet do as he liked, trying to use the opportunity to gather his thoughts before setting off to Niall.

Besides the troublesome nature of the night's events and the ensuing arrests, he was sure the three men who'd appeared with Doyle were preying on Alannah's mind. Doyle had said he didn't work alone and here, it seemed, was the evidence thereof, he having rustled up three thugs to take Alannah to Andrews against her will. Yes, they had been arrested and their presence the previous night didn't necessarily mean they would do Doyle's bidding blindly, but it did show he had criminal connections—connections that possibly included others he might call upon now to enact his vengeance.

Quin was sure these connections worried Alannah.

He didn't want to dismiss her concerns outright—there might be reason for concern, after all—but he didn't want her to dwell on them either.

"That's better, sir," Rupert interrupted his thoughts.

Quin looked at himself in the mirror and had to admit it was an improvement.

Rupert had brushed out his hair, flattening stray wisps into submission so the brown mass lay meekly against his skull with a few flattering waves. The stubble on his cheeks and chin had been removed—when did that happen? he wondered—and he was wearing a becoming green necktie, which brought out the colour of his eyes, making them look slightly less bloodshot.

"Thank you, Rupert." He smiled at the beaming face in the reflection.

Rupert gave him a quick bow—pausing momentarily to frown worriedly at Quin's midsection—and bustled off, tidying up the tools of his trade. Quin got up, breathed heavily a few times in an attempt to clear the fuzziness in his brain and, finding this to be only marginally effective, set off toward the stable.

When he arrived at Niall, he was met by Finnian the hall boy, a tall and gangling youth of about sixteen, who seemed to have aspirations of becoming a butler, interrupting his usual tedious chores to open the door for Quin. The boy bowed in a low and sweeping manner normally reserved for more formal meetings between members of the gentry, a gesture that looked rather comical conducted by such a gawky frame, despite its attempted elegance. Upon its completion, Finnian straightened up with evident pride at having managed such a complex manoeuvre and looked expectantly at Quin.

"Can I help you, sir?" he asked while trying inconspicuously to tuck the front of his shirt into his waistband, apparently feeling he wasn't suitably dressed for the occasion.

"Yes, thank you," Quin said, as his overwrought mind provided him with a distracting image of Alannah in the form-fitting breeches now adorning the servant before him. "I wish to call on Miss O'Neill."

As he followed Finnian down the hall toward the parlour, Quin mused that the breeches had been rather a lot more form-fitting on Alannah than they were on their current wearer, the latter being substantially less curvaceous than the former. His fingertips tingled in remembrance of the smooth curves he'd caressed, so tantalisingly close to the surface, separated from him by a single thin sheet of fabric that could so easily be removed. This train of thought rapidly led to a vivid recollection of the touch of her naked skin when she'd pressed herself to him on the first night he'd snuck into her room.

"For God's sake, Quinton, can you think of nothing else?" he chided himself under his breath as he quickly sat down on one of the chairs Finnian pointed out to him, hoping Alannah would give him a moment's respite before making her appearance.

As it was, Alannah entered the room approximately thirty seconds later, having evidently heard him arrive.

"Quin," she said from the doorway as he got up from his seat, marginally restored.

"Alannah." He took several quick steps toward her as she came into the room.

She stopped just short of him and seemed to reach for him, but dropped her hand, glancing sideways at the maid, who was lurking by the door.

"I'm glad you came." She gave him an attempted smile that didn't quite reach her tired-looking eyes.

Quin started to lift a hand toward her but lowered it when she averted her gaze. "Are you alright?" he asked instead.

"Yes...yes...I'm quite alright." She gently ran a hand over the top of her head, barely looking at him before turning toward the window.

Quin frowned at her back, unconvinced.

"But how are you?" she asked suddenly, spinning around and coming to stand in front of him. She reached a hand toward his side, stopping just short of touching him, and looked up at him with worried eyes.

"I'm quite alright," he replied, echoing her words with some irony. "My groom Bryan very ably saw me patched up. He's generally more accustomed to dealing with horses, but he proved to be a most gifted physician even for a non-equine patient. Between his attentions and those of Denis and Rupert, I shall be back to my old self within the next day."

This wasn't entirely true.

The lower end of the gash had been deep enough to require several stitches, which had been administered by his terrified valet under the watchful eye of Bryan, whose gnarled hands hadn't been up to the task in the middle of the night. Rupert's experience being restricted to darning his shirts, the operation had taken considerably longer—and been considerably more painful—than Quin had thought was strictly necessary. He would hardly be surprised if the haphazard doctoring he'd been subjected to left him fevered and at death's door within a day.

But he smiled at Alannah now, hoping to crack the armour she seemed to have put on overnight. She didn't return his smile, though, only staring at the sight of his injury, her eyes becoming unfocused as her thoughts turned inwards.

"Good," she said finally, sounding dazed.

She dragged her gaze away from his midsection and looked up at him, eyes glazed with exhaustion—and more.

"Doyle...?" She let the question hang in the air.

"He's behind bars, in Omagh gaol," Quin assured her firmly and she breathed a sigh of relief.

"Good." She nodded to herself. "I thought this morning I must have dreamt the whole thing. I feel...not quite myself."

Quin took a step toward her, but she turned away from him, feigning an interest in the bookshelf.

"The men will likely appear in front of a judge within a week," he said with a heavy heart, wishing she would let him comfort her. "There's an assize scheduled...rather fortuitously I suppose. With the likely seriousness of the charges, Kieran and Doyle could hardly be tried by a local magistrate."

"Kieran?" Alannah turned back toward him, all colour draining from her face as she breathed her brother's name. She looked at Quin with huge eyes filled with shock.

"I thought you knew," Quin said softly, coming to stand in front of her. "He was arrested last night, along with Doyle and his accomplices."

"Of course...I knew...I mean, I must have known. I just didn't think..." She shook her head, looking down. "What a fool I am."

Quin gently placed a hand on her shoulder. "You are not a fool, Alannah, far from it. He is your brother. It's understandable that it's difficult for you to imagine him being placed under arrest, no matter what he might have done."

"Still, I..."

"You've had a lot to deal with. You shouldn't be so hard on yourself."

She looked so defeated, so vulnerable, Quin wanted nothing so much as to take her in his arms. But she stayed aloof and so he kept his distance, carefully removing his hand from her shoulder.

"The most important thing is that Doyle and his associates are no longer a threat to us," he said with conviction, wanting to impress on her the vital outcome of the night's work.

"Yes, you're right," she said, sounding uncertain.

"Alannah, you needn't be afraid of him anymore," he insisted, looking urgently into her eyes. "He can no longer hurt you. With his history, no judge will dismiss the charges. His fate is sealed."

"I'm sure you're right."

She continued to look doubtful, and Quin thought she must be thinking about Doyle's promise of vengeance. He was about to say something to counter her fears when she spoke again. "I want to see Kieran."

He was silent for a moment as she looked at him expectantly, almost daring him to deny her request.

"Of course. I wouldn't have expected anything less."

15.

I WAS WRINGING my hands nervously as I looked around the confines of the small room, waiting.

We had come to Omagh that morning, hoping to be allowed to see Kieran and provide what support we could. Constable Ryan, who'd arranged Doyle's capture with Quin and had come to Omagh to testify against him, had been sympathetic to our request, although guardedly so, seeming to find it peculiar that I would want to see such an errant brother. Considering how Kieran had treated me in the past, I harboured my own doubts about my presence here. But while I couldn't forget the actions that had led Kieran to his fate, I also couldn't forget he was my brother—and my only living relative. I felt it was my duty to stand by him in his time of need, but part of me also wanted to be there for him.

Part of me still loved him, even after everything.

Kieran and the other men were being held in the town gaol while they awaited trial, and Constable Ryan had promised to set up a brief meeting in one of the rooms of the keep, he having had dealings with Omagh's sheriff before. Turning up in Omagh had given me a strange feeling, evoking memories of my father and the work he'd done in his capacity as justice of the peace. I wished he could be with me now, although in some ways I was relieved he wasn't, that he hadn't had to watch his son's fall into disgrace with the shameful company he kept.

I shuddered as I thought of Doyle's close proximity while we waited for Constable Ryan and Kieran in the small office we'd been shown to.

Quin looked at me curiously but didn't say anything, returning to his perusal of a large volume of some legal description someone had left on the small desk. Quin had insisted on coming with me to see Kieran, not wanting me to face him alone. I looked at his strong back, wanting suddenly to wrap my arms around him and seek the comfort I knew he would provide, but that I was reluctant to take.

The feeling of detachment that had settled on me on the night of the arrests still clung to me, making me feel like I was somehow watching myself from outside myself. I spoke when spoken to and performed everyday tasks without difficulty, but at times I felt like something in me had been irreparably altered that night, like I was no longer the person I had once been. The numbness I felt was interrupted by brief stabs of normalcy that disappeared as quickly as they'd come, replaced momentarily with panic as my warped mind envisaged Quin's slashed skin, convinced the wound had been inflicted on him because I had chosen defiance instead of obedience.

When the world wasn't spinning around me at a safe distance I was plagued with anxiousness—anxiousness about losing myself in the fog and the role I'd played in getting myself into it. Beset with guilt and fear, I reproached myself for putting Quin in danger and worried about what the future might hold, for me, for Quin, for Kieran; until I was safely cocooned in oblivion once more.

If I let Quin come too close, I knew the shell around me would shatter, leaving me exposed—and afraid.

A knock at the door brought me back to the present.

Constable Ryan stuck his head through the door and seeing us, opened it wide to let in his prisoner.

"Kieran," I gasped.

When I'd last seen him at the abandoned farmhouse, his curly hair had bobbed above a face masked with fear and uncertainty. His features showed the same emotions now, enhanced with a sense of defeat, but his pale skin was marred by dark blue bruising on his left cheek and a black eye, which matched the marks on his throat.

Left by someone's hands, I realised in shock.

Constable Ryan cleared his throat, seemingly embarrassed. "It seems Mr Doyle and Mr O'Neill aren't quite as companionable as we'd thought."

"Doyle did this to you?" I asked Kieran, coming to stand in front of him.

He nodded once, before averting his gaze. I looked helplessly up at Quin, who came to stand next to me, eyeing Kieran with interest.

"Punishment for not keeping Alannah under control, perhaps?" he suggested with some scorn.

Kieran glared at him, and Quin nodded to himself in confirmation.

"The two of them have been separated," Ryan said into the awkward silence. "Mr Doyle is being kept apart from the other prisoners. After his violent outburst..." Ryan's voice faded away as he looked at the marks on Kieran's neck, which suggested Doyle's hands had come very close to accomplishing their goal.

"Thank you, Constable Ryan," Quin said politely as I continued to stare at Kieran.

I finally tore my eyes away from his bruises and realised I had no idea what to say to him. I couldn't pretend nothing had happened, nor could I promise him everything would be alright—it was far too late for either of those two options. I struggled to find a third, until I finally realised there was one thing I could say, the only thing I could say.

"I'm here for you, Kieran, no matter what."

He looked at me and his face changed, like the surface of a smooth lake disturbed by a pebble, as a flurry of emotions flitted across his features, ending in an expression of mingled pain and longing—and regret. His mouth compressed in a tight line, and he blinked several times before looking at me again.

I took his hand and squeezed it tight.

"I mean it," I said, blinking away tears.

He gripped my hand hard and swallowed audibly. Our eyes locked for an instant, but he quickly turned away and walked to the door, where his captor awaited him.

THINKING ABOUT THE scene the following afternoon, I experienced the absurd hope that we could convince the courts to let Kieran go, that it had all been a mistake, that he'd had nothing to do with Doyle and his rebellious plans. I glanced at Quin, who was pacing up and down the courthouse corridor while we waited to see the magistrate, and my mind was flooded with vivid memories of the night Kieran had been arrested and everything that had happened before.

My heart sank. Kieran had hardly been an innocent bystander, not least of all in the harm done me.

Quin suddenly stopped his pacing. Looking up I could see the door to the office where we were to meet the magistrate was opening, revealing a sparsely built, neat-looking young man. Instead of inviting us in as I'd expected, he looked at Quin, who'd come to a stop in front of the door.

"Mr Williams?" he asked in a nasal tone.

"I am," Quin answered in his deeper voice.

"I'm afraid the magistrate is otherwise engaged." He flitted an apologetic glance toward me. "I am the clerk," he added by way of explanation for his own presence in the courthouse.

Quin narrowed his eyes at the clerk.

We'd arranged to see the magistrate upon our arrival the day before, to see if there was anything to be done for Kieran. Like most rural justices of the peace, including my father, Omagh's magistrate was a landowner who was tasked with the upkeep of local laws and the maintenance of order, presiding over petty sessions twice a month and quarter sessions four times a year. The assize scheduled for the following day—where serious crimes, including capital crimes, were trialled—would be presided over by the circuit judge, who'd arrived in Omagh to great fanfare and excitement that morning. Being unable to speak directly to the judge, we'd hoped the magistrate might be of some assistance, and Constable Ryan had told us he'd managed to arrange a meeting for us through the clerk. Evidently, though, no such meeting would now be taking place. Perhaps the man truly was too busy to see us, or perhaps he simply didn't want to.

"Um...can I help you with something myself?" the clerk asked, looking uncomfortably up at Quin.

"I rather think not." Quin's civil tone was strongly spiced with irritation. "We had hoped to discuss with the magistrate the case of one Kieran O'Neill, currently residing in the gaol."

"Oh...yes...ah...I'm familiar with the case." The clerk gave me another sideways glance. "The bills of indictment were handed in about an hour ago. A charge of treason I believe..."

My stomach dropped, and I gasped.

I hadn't really thought about the grounds on which Kieran had been arrested, but I hadn't quite expected this, despite what I knew about his political leanings.

"But...surely..." I stuttered, as I suddenly realised why the magistrate hadn't kept his meeting with us. He hadn't wanted to see us because there was no point. The local landlords who made up the grand jury had ruled there was enough evidence against Kieran to support a charge of treason and that he would be brought before the court the following day to face said charge.

I stared at the clerk in disbelief.

"I'm sorry, ma'am," he said, looking uncomfortable. "I'm afraid I can't say more than that. The judge will hear your brother's case tomorrow, and that of his accomplice." He looked at me apologetically, awkwardly shrugging his shoulders. "Court opens at nine a.m."

With that, he gave us a brief bow, spun on his heel and was gone.

Quin and I gawped after him in astonishment, before looking at each other.

"I suppose we shall be here tomorrow at nine," Quin said shortly and offered me his arm.

WHEN WE GOT to the courthouse the following day, it was already packed. It wasn't every day people could escape the monotony of their existence to see two men trialled for treason, and the crowds had flocked in to take advantage of the occasion.

With no place to sit, Quin and I stood in the back against the wall. With all the people pressed together the courtroom was stifling, even early as it was, and sweat started trickling down between my breasts. We waited for what seemed like ages until at last the clerk made his appearance and announced the arrival of the judge, a squat middle-aged man with greying sideburns and moustache, and a severe expression. This was followed by the swearing in of the petty jury, those members of the public who would be deciding my brother's fate. I eyed them nervously as a measure of silence descended on the courtroom, along with an unmistakable air of anticipation—or bloodlust perhaps, I thought, looking at some of the expressions around me.

Having kept his audience waiting, the judge now proceeded swiftly, spending the barest amount of time on each delinquent brought to his bench, handing out justice rapidly and precisely with the backing of the jury, as thieves, rioters and assailants received their dues.

The prisoners were judged in groups, with the jury discussing the verdicts once each case had been heard. My mind started drifting as the session proceeded, but I gave a start when the clerk admitted the next set of prisoners into the courtroom.

I recognised the three men who'd been with Doyle on the night of his arrest and held my breath as their charges were read. There was no mention of Doyle, though, nor Kieran or anything to do with either of them. Still, the three men seemed to be well-known criminals, accused of numerous counts of thievery and destruction of property, and the judge wasted no time in sentencing each of them to transportation to Van Diemen's Land for twenty years once the jury had found them guilty of their crimes.

I goggled at the speed at which these men's lives had been irrefutably altered and swallowed a lump in my throat, dreading the fate that awaited Kieran, who was being accused of a far more serious crime.

I shifted uncomfortably on my feet and took a deep breath, letting it out quickly as the rankness of my fellow spectators crept up my nose. Standing pressed against the hot, sweaty bodies was extremely unpleasant, not least of all because the continuously shuffling feet tended to tread painfully on my toes.

It did afford us an advantage of viewpoint, however.

And so it was that when Kieran and Doyle were at last brought into the courtroom mid-afternoon, my brother's eyes immediately found mine. He looked tired and dirty, and terribly nervous—an expression that, combined with his big blue eyes and light-brown locks, made him look even younger than his twenty-four years, even marred as he was by the bruising on his face and neck.

My heart contracted painfully at the sight of what had become of the sweet, curly haired boy I had known and loved.

I tried to smile encouragingly at him, but my heart started pounding in fear of what might be in store for him, a reaction intensified by the murderous look aimed at me by his co-accused. Doyle was staring at me with an expression of sheer hatred, his face suffused with a loathing that was all the more obvious as his eyes glared at me above his grotesquely discoloured and swollen nose.

My hands started trembling and my breath came short, and I had to look away. I tried to retreat into the safety of the surrounding fog, but it was spreading out away from me, becoming thin, unable to smother my doubts and fears as it had before, leaving me to face them alone.

I felt a tug on my arm as Quin pulled me closer to him, and I suddenly felt overwhelmingly grateful for his strong and solid presence next to me.

The audience, who'd been looking as wilted as I felt, began livening up as the clerk started reading out the charges against one Martin Patrick Doyle, who was being accused of plotting a traitorous rebellion against the Crown, with the intention of overthrowing the English regime in Ireland, as well as the murder of the English gentleman Augustus Pummell and an Irishman named Aiden Moran. Hearing the latter, I suddenly remembered the conversation I'd overheard

145

between Doyle and Kieran and wondered how many other people Doyle might have murdered in his lifetime. There was the man named Thomas the two of them had referred to—who hadn't been mentioned by the clerk—and who knew how many others? Doyle seemed to have few scruples about removing anyone he thought would stand in his way. I shuddered briefly before turning my attention back to the front of the courtroom, where the rest of the charges were being read, these including numerous counts of rioting and inciting unrest—events that seemed almost mild in comparison to the other crimes Doyle was being accused of. The defendant himself was staring unblinkingly in my direction throughout the clerk's recitation, a leer appearing on his face as loud murmurs broke out in the crowd.

I held my breath as I waited for the next set of charges to be read.

My heart started hammering loudly in my ears as the clerk began speaking—as he'd already informed me the previous day, Kieran was being accused of colluding with Martin Doyle to treasonously oust the English government. I gulped for air and had barely caught my breath when the prosecutor called the first witness in the case against Doyle.

One Kieran Timothy O'Neill.

"What?" I said out loud, too shocked to remember to keep quiet. A few irritated faces turned in my direction, amidst grumbled complaints at my outburst.

Quin laid a warning hand on my arm and whispered in my ear, "It looks like Kieran is testifying against Doyle. Perhaps he's made a deal."

This seemed to be precisely what Kieran had done and my heart started pounding in my chest at the thought that he might be able to save himself. Then I looked over at Doyle's face, which was flooded with fury, his eyes radiating hatred as he stared at my brother with the same look of abhorrence he'd been bestowing upon me.

I swallowed and looked away.

"What evidence have you to bring against the accused?" the prosecutor was asking Kieran, who was shuffling nervously from one foot to the other and wringing his hands.

Kieran looked uncertainly at Doyle, who glared back at him. After a moment's hesitation, Kieran squared his shoulders and, giving me a brief glance, started talking, hesitantly at first, but with more conviction as he proceeded with his account of events.

His testimony descended on a blanket of whispers, as the English speakers amongst the crowd translated for those who understood only Gaelic.

Kieran told the court he and Doyle had met at an inn in Belfast where disgruntled Irishmen made a habit of voicing their dissatisfaction with the state of affairs in Ireland. This particular inn had become something of a refuge for those who felt unjustly treated by the English who ruled them and dreamt of an Ireland no longer under English control.

"A condition the majority wanted to achieve with violence, not quiet politicking," Kieran added with a sideways glance at Doyle, who was now staring straight ahead, jaw clenched tight with rage. I noticed his upper arm was wrapped in a filthy looking bandage, although he seemed to be feeling no lasting effects from the bullet wound I'd inflicted on him.

"At first," Kieran went on, looking away from Doyle, "some of the lads were content to resort to scare tactics to frighten those they felt were particularly unjust in the treatment of the Irish, but after a while"—he glanced at Doyle again—"it became unsatisfactory. Some...felt that violently, and permanently, removing the English from Ireland was the only answer."

"Who felt this?" asked the judge in a stern voice, double chin wobbling.

"Martin Doyle and a few others."

"You fucking bastard," Doyle shouted and tried to leap at Kieran in the witness box but was prevented from doing so by the quick reactions of the sheriff, who was standing next to him. "You were shouting for English blood as much as the rest of us, you cowardly swine."

The courtroom erupted into an excited racket, with some onlookers, I was sure, agreeing with Doyle's anti-English sentiments, aiming leering glances in Kieran's direction. The sheriff held Doyle's arms behind his back to keep him under control while the bailiff tried to silence the crowd. When proceedings finally got under way again, Kieran was visibly sweating under the strain.

"What plans, exactly, did Mr Doyle describe for his proposed enterprise?" the judge asked once the onlookers had quietened down.

"He wanted to join others who felt a repeal of the Act of Union was not enough, that Ireland shouldn't only be able to govern itself under English rule, but that it should be liberated entirely and become a free state.—Doyle spoke of war and rebellion, intending to decimate English law enforcement so Ireland could rule itself once more. He hoped he could persuade others that a rebellion would be successful by commissioning a large number of weapons to arm the rebels he had begun recruiting."

"And how did he mean to procure such arms?"

"He made an arrangement with a rich landowner," Kieran said vaguely, darting a brief glance in my direction.

"What exactly was this arrangement and who was the landowner?" the judge asked in a harsh tone, moustache quivering.

"He proposed to arrange a marriage for Herbert Andrews in exchange for ten-thousand pounds."

There was a collective gasp from the audience; ten-thousand pounds was more money than they would ever see in their lifetime.

"And who was Mr Andrews to marry?"

Kieran looked around the room, evidently uncomfortable.

"Mr O'Neill?"

"My sister," Kieran responded in a small voice, looking down onto the wooden railing in front of him.

The spectators erupted again, this time in outrage.

"Silence! Silence, I say!" the judge shouted above the racket until he had the crowd under control once more. "How was it that a marriage was proposed between Mr Andrews and your sister, when you seem by your own account to have been present during the negotiations?"

"I didn't suggest it!" Kieran objected, looking directly at me, imploring me to believe him. "Andrews had met her years before and when he found out who I was and who she was…evidently he wanted her, so he and Doyle decided on the plan…"

"And why did you not object to this plan?"

"Because I wanted the money," Kieran admitted in a defeated tone, shoulders slumping. "I'd hoped I could somehow take the money for myself."

I stared at Kieran, my throat constricting.

Quin gently squeezed my hand, which I hadn't realised he was holding under cover of the folds of my skirt. The judge and the prosecutor looked disgusted at Kieran's admission, but neither questioned Kieran further, the judge dismissing him instead. The next witness, Constable Ryan who'd arrested Doyle, testified that the Irish Constabulary had identified him as the same Martin Doyle also wanted for murder in Dublin and several riots in connection with anti-English sentiments, with Kieran's involvement in Doyle's affairs limited to his presence at the old farmhouse where Doyle was arrested. The constable's testimony was quick and uneventful, and the judge dismissed him without further questions, the prosecutor clearly satisfied with the evidence brought against the accused.

"If there are no more witnesses..." the judge started saying but was interrupted by a loud bang as the door behind the witness box flew open.

Amid surprised exclamations and affronted cries, an attractive, middle-aged gentleman made his unhurried way into the witness box, depositing his top hat on the bench beside it and leaning his walking stick against the balustrade.

My legs might have given way when I recognised the man, had Quin not gotten a firm hold on my arm to keep me upright. For here in the courtroom stood none other than Herbert Andrews, my erstwhile—and now presumably scorned—betrothed, looking a little older than when I'd met him five years before, but unmistakable, nonetheless. His short hair and pointy moustache were now almost completely grey, but he had the same tall frame he carried with the same arrogant set to his shoulders, and the same calculating eyes, which were roaming the courtroom, eventually coming to rest on me, a small smile on his lips.

I shuddered, and Quin gave me a curious look.

"And who are you?" asked the judge, professional courtesy forgotten in his annoyance at the interruption.

"I, sir, am Herbert Charles Robert Andrews," he answered slowly, with a distinct air of superiority.

Quin squeezed my elbow encouragingly, understanding my uneasiness at seeing the man. I managed a slight smile in reassurance.

"Oh." The judge stroked his voluptuous chin. "Not, perchance, the same Herbert Andrews accused of plotting to fund a traitorous rebellion?"

"The very same, sir," Andrews said coolly to the stunned faces in the courtroom.

"And have you come to counter these claims?"

"Indeed, I have.—The accusations against me are false."

This statement was met with loud murmurs, and every eye in the room turned toward Kieran and Doyle in speculation. I felt the blood drain from my face and clutched Quin's hand for support.

"Do explain yourself, pray tell," the judge ordered in a loud voice to be heard above the racket.

Andrews looked haughtily at the onlookers until the noise had subsided to his satisfaction before he began speaking.

"The accusations against me are false," he repeated. "I never planned to support a rebellion against the Crown, financially or otherwise."

"You lying whoreson!" Doyle shouted angrily. "You're just trying to save your own skin!"

"And how do you respond to this, sir?" the judge asked, putting out a hand in a quelling gesture toward the accused. Doyle continued to fume but said nothing further.

"I am indeed trying to save my own skin," Andrews replied with an arrogant look at Doyle. "But not," he added, raising his voice above the murmurs that had broken out again, "because I am guilty of the crime of which I'm being accused.—On the contrary, I am in the employ of the British government to root out such treasonous behaviour to which I have been witness."

"You mean you're a spy?" The judge couldn't hide the surprise in his voice, which matched my own astonishment at Andrews' declaration.

"That is correct. Or I should say, I *was* a spy"—he narrowed his eyes in annoyance—"for I can clearly be one no longer, being as publicly ousted as I have been today."

"Just one moment," the judge said with a puzzled expression on his face. "If you were worried about being found out, then why did you involve yourself personally in the affair in the first place, instead of staying in the background where your identity as a spy would not have been discovered?"

I had been wondering the same thing.

Andrews sighed. "Regrettably, that was an oversight. I had hoped I could lure Mr Doyle and his co-conspirators into a trap that would lead to their arrest without implicating myself...beyond our acquaintance as businessmen. He and Mr O'Neill had come to see me with the intention of investing some money, seeking my assistance in maximising their capital output in the minimal amount of time. Mr Doyle had introduced himself under a false name. I, however, knew who he was and thought I could use his fortuitous appearance to my advantage. He was already wanted for murder, but I thought I could provide clear-cut evidence of his treasonous activities and root out others like him in the process."

He paused, fingering his moustache.

"Making him believe I shared his sensibilities, I inveigled him into telling me he needed money to arm and support the rebels he was rallying to his cause. I had already learnt from my associates that Mr Doyle had indeed started gathering some men, and so it came as no surprise when he revealed to me he intended to deploy these men, as soon as he was able, to strike against the army troops and police forces situated in Dublin, as well as numerous other British strongholds in the surrounding counties."

He lifted his chin self-importantly as he looked at the judge. "And should you doubt my word," he said, sounding offended at the very possibility any such thing might occur, "I have in my possession a list of names, written in Mr Doyle's own hand"—Andrews paused for dramatic effect as he slowly placed a hand into the inside pocket of his jacket and withdrew a yellowed sheet of paper—"of high-ranking officials within the army and the police force whom his rebels were to target, with plans for their assassination to ensure a lack of government resistance."

Amidst the murmured voices of the onlookers, the judge's eyes bulged as he perused the list of names the clerk had handed him, while the prosecutor looked like he was about to leap into the air in delight.

I risked a quick glance at Martin Doyle.

His face was suffused with rage as he stared at Andrews, hissing something uncomplimentary under his breath. I thought I could make out the words *lying whoreson* once more but was recalled back to Herbert Andrews as he continued speaking, ignoring Doyle and everyone else in the courtroom as he went on with his tale.

"As you can imagine," he began with a long-suffering air, "I was of course exceedingly eager to see Mr Doyle and his confederates arrested before such a cowardly venture could begin." He pursed his lips in disgust. "However, in my haste to see the would-be rebels arrested, I made the mistake of offering to contribute to the funds Mr Doyle needed myself, hoping this would win his trust and allow me access to the deeper echelons of such conspiracies to which he was privy. Not wanting to appear too eager to part with my money, though, I said I required something of value in return. When I found out Mr O'Neill's family connections, I feigned an interest in his sister...and so...when the prospect of the betrothal came up...I agreed." Andrews spread his hands in a gesture that suggested he could not possibly have done any differently. "Alas, the plan never came to fruition. We had meant to meet the following day to discuss the arrangement, but Mr Doyle disappeared, only to show up again here under the circumstances we have seen."

Andrews folded his hands in front of him, evidently done with his testimony.

The audience, and the jury, gaped at him as if mesmerised. They had hung on his every eloquently spoken word and clearly believed each one, even though the onlookers probably wouldn't ordinarily feel much sympathy for a self-proclaimed British spy.

I wasn't so sure about Andrews' testimony myself. Something didn't seem quite right about his tale.

The judge, though, seemed to share the general opinion that he was telling the truth. "Thank you, Mr Andrews," he said, his chin wobbling as he nodded toward the witness while refolding the sheet of yellowed paper, "your service to the Crown is greatly appreciated by all, and your testimony today has been of immense service in the case against Mr Doyle." He frowned and tapped his index finger on the list of names. "As to the involvement of Mr O'Neill…"

My heart jumped into my throat, and I looked at Kieran, who stared back at me without seeing me, face pale and awash with fear.

"Mr O'Neill made no treasonous declarations in my presence," Andrews interrupted the judge, making Kieran's head snap around to look at him. "The transaction I described was conducted solely between Mr Doyle and myself, with no more than a few pleasantries exchanged with Mr O'Neill, who seemed only interested in securing a most excellent marital match for his sister.—I am not convinced he shares Mr Doyle's traitorous intentions and indeed, I heard no mention of his name from any of my associates."

Kieran gaped at Andrews in utter confusion while Doyle snorted loudly through his nose. He didn't say anything, though, instead looking at Kieran with unconcealed hatred on his face, before lifting his head and turning toward Quin and me, staring at us with such loathing in his eyes that the hair on the back of my neck stood up and I broke out in a cold sweat.

I tore my eyes away and, shaking, looked toward the judge.

"I see," the judge muttered before dismissing Andrews from the stand. Sitting up straight as Andrews left—throwing a backward glance in my direction—the

152

judge turned toward the accused. "Mr Doyle," he said, "you may present your case and call your witnesses, should you have any."

He looked expectantly at Doyle, who continued to stare at me without blinking.

"I'm innocent of all charges," he declared, before spitting a thick globule of mucous onto the courtroom's pristine floor and glaring at the judge, who narrowed his eyes and puffed up in indignation at Doyle's unrefined behaviour.

When it became evident Doyle would say no more and would call no witnesses to defend him, the judge summed up the case against him in clipped tones, before turning toward Kieran, who swore to his own innocence in a wavering voice that I thought might condemn him as easily as save him. Having already been declared innocent by the chief witness against Doyle and having no one else to turn to, Kieran professed himself unable to produce any further witnesses in his defence. He darted a quick glance in my direction, before lowering his gaze as the judge instructed the members of the jury to deliberate and consider the verdicts.

I sagged against the wall as hushed conversations broke out around the courtroom. Quin gave me a worried look but didn't say anything. Nothing happened for a few minutes but, just as I was wondering how long we would have to wait, the clerk announced that the jury had reached its verdict.

"That was quick," Quin said under his breath, echoing my own thoughts.

When everyone had settled down once more, the judge leaned over to the jury box. A brief exchange of words ensued before he gave a nod and turned back toward the courtroom.

"Based on the evidence presented here today," he said, "the jury finds Mr Martin Patrick Doyle guilty of all charges."

The crowd erupted, and the judge turned toward Doyle, looking sternly at him down his nose.

"Mr Doyle, do you wish to address the court before your sentencing?"

"Go to hell," Doyle spat at him through clenched teeth.

The judge's eyes narrowed in anger, and when he spoke again, his voice was harsh. "Martin Patrick Doyle, the court hereby does order you to be taken from hence to the place from whence you came, and thence to the place of execution, and that you be hanged by the neck until you are dead, and that your body be afterwards buried within the precincts of the prison in which you shall be confined after your conviction. And may the Lord have mercy upon your soul."

The judge's words fell gravely upon the onlookers, who continued to mutter noisily amongst themselves, while Doyle himself stared straight ahead of him—at me. His dead eyes locked with mine and he lifted his right hand, slowly, drawing it across his throat in an unmistakable gesture of menace.

I tore my eyes away, heart pounding.

"In the case of Mr Kieran Timothy O'Neill..." the judge was shouting above the racket. I held my breath and squeezed Quin's hand. "...the charge of treason against him is dismissed. However"—the judge gave Kieran a severe look—"I sentence you to one month in prison and a fine of twenty shillings...for keeping poor company."

"I RATHER DOUBT the fellow can be trusted."

Quin held a forkful of stew lifted halfway to his mouth but seemed completely unaware of it, so engrossed in his thoughts was he. We were having supper in a quiet corner in the taproom of the inn, having arrived bedraggled and exhausted from the courtroom an hour earlier.

"No, I wouldn't think so," I agreed. "I thought as much when I met him the first time and a second encounter hasn't improved my opinion.—You should eat that, it's getting cold."

Quin looked down at the fork, evidently wondering where it had come from, before finally tucking it into his mouth. I laughed, and he grinned back at me.

"I just don't find his story believable," he said after he'd swallowed. "It simply doesn't make sense for him to offer his own money as bait if he was indeed working as a British spy. He must have known it was a sure way for his cover to be blown, for he could never have expected Doyle to keep quiet about his own involvement after his arrest. And the only way Andrews could then have saved his reputation would have been to do exactly what he did...to come forward and make his name known publicly, including his supposed secret activities."

"Unless he really was interested in financing a rebellion and only made up the story about him being a spy when it looked like he might be charged himself..."

"Hm...that's the other thing that's troubling me. Why would Doyle have gone to see Andrews in the first place? Yes, he's a rich man who knows how to make a profit, but surely Doyle couldn't have expected a speedy turnaround of whatever measly amount of money he would have been able to amass. And Doyle doesn't strike me as the type of character who would be willing to wait around for a few years for his investment to pay off."

"If he'd heard rumours about Andrews being of a like mind, though…"

"He would have gone there hoping to persuade a fellow rebel to put his substantial fortune where it might be of best use."

Quin ate the last mouthful of stew and washed it down with a swig of wine. He made a grimace at the quality. Not much better than vinegar, he'd assured me with a moue of distaste. I was drinking cider myself and found it to be quite refreshing.

"That would also explain why he would risk such a visit, being wanted for murder," he continued. "Even with an assumed name, it would have been dangerous to see Andrews himself. He might have recognised him, from a picture in the Dublin papers perhaps. It wouldn't have made sense for Doyle to risk being recognised if it was only a matter of an investment."

"Whereas if it was about rallying supporters for a rebellion, he would have wanted to go himself, especially if he'd hoped Andrews' contribution would buy him greater influence with the other rebels."

"And a murder charge would hardly seem like an impediment to someone who was plotting to commit treason, so Doyle must have felt himself reasonably safe of betrayal by Andrews, thinking him equally inclined."

"That would also explain why Doyle revealed his plans so quickly. If he hadn't known of…or at least strongly suspected…Andrews' own leanings before, Doyle surely wouldn't have been so open about his at their very first meeting. And giving him that list of names…"

"Hm." Quin frowned. "I'm not sure Doyle would necessarily have *given* the list to Andrews.—Besides, I was watching Doyle while Andrews was testifying against him, and I'd swear he was as surprised to hear about the list as everyone else."

I nodded, having observed Doyle's reaction myself. "So Andrews fabricated the evidence."

"Why not?" Quin shrugged. "It's unlikely anyone would try to verify its authenticity. And if Andrews wanted to see Doyle condemned, either because he truly is a spy for the British or to prevent being arrested himself, he would have known such a piece of hard evidence would make a conviction all the more likely."

Quin paused briefly before going on. "What I can't work out, though, is how *you* fit into all of this." He looked at me across the table and gently took my hand. "Why would Andrews go as far as agreeing to marry you? If he was indeed a spy and trying to set a trap, promising Doyle the money would surely have been enough. And if he was actually a rebel, then why would he not simply contribute his funds to the cause instead of insisting on a proposal that might not materialise and would do him no good should he be arrested for treason."

"I think..." I looked down and slowly extricated my hand from Quin's grasp. "I think he just...wanted me." I lifted one shoulder uncomfortably and looked back up again, my hands in my lap.

"That's what your brother said too. But it still makes no sense at all, whether Andrews is a spy or a rebel.—As to why a man of his position would choose to plot an uprising against the Crown..."

He paused, and I could almost see his mind working as he mulled over everything we'd learned over the course of the day.

"And if he really is a spy, why did he only come forward now? Why didn't he immediately inform the Dublin Metropolitan Police of Doyle's intentions and possible whereabouts when he didn't show up for their scheduled meeting? Even if he couldn't catch any of his co-conspirators, Andrews' testimony might have been enough to convict Doyle himself—as indeed we witnessed today—and yet he chose to keep quiet until Doyle was arrested, coincidentally at that."

Quin rubbed his chin in contemplation. "And Doyle told you he'd arranged to meet with Andrews to hand you over, so they must have been in contact since their first meeting. Yet Andrews made no mention of any such thing." Quin shook his head. "I really can't make head or tail of any of this."

"Neither can I," I said, my own head spinning with suppositions. "But speaking of convictions, I was rather surprised at the speed at which Doyle's was handed out today."

"So was I."

"It almost seemed like the verdict against Doyle had been decided on before the case had appeared before the court. That's not unheard of, of course, but it was incredibly fast...particularly for a charge of treason based largely on circumstantial evidence..."

"Perhaps the jury simply found it easier to convict him of all charges without much ado, knowing he would be hanged anyway." Quin waved a hand. "Or perhaps," he continued, narrowing his eyes as a thought obviously occurred to him, "somebody wanted our Mr Doyle to be tidied away as speedily as possible.—Somebody with some influence, perhaps, who knows the Irish legal system isn't quite up to the standards of the English equivalent?" Quin gave me an apologetic look.

"Possibly," I said slowly. "You do have a point.—Even my father lamented the state of the Irish legal system. Although it's meant to be the same as the English system, that often isn't the case, especially in rural villages, where the magistrates tend to be English landowners, who rule the Irish people ineffectively or not at all, and who themselves feel threatened by the increasing presence and power of the police." I frowned. "My father often said local enforcers of law and order are at odds with the people they're trying to govern, who distance themselves ever further from a government they believe to be perpetuating English and Protestant rule. This means juries are often biased too, frequently sympathising with the accused, who in their minds is being charged of defying *English* laws." I gave Quin a wry smile. "My father often said it was easier to get away with murder in Ireland than any other nation in the world, as the charge was not infrequently dismissed as an accidental death.—He worried, though, that this would make people believe they *could* get away with it, knowing there was a good chance the charge would be dropped...not a good premise in a society with such political and religious animosity."

"In this case, though, the jury found *against* the accused, at least in the case of Doyle."

"They could hardly have done otherwise, with the man's history! Even an Irishman can't expect any sympathy from his fellows under such circumstances. And it didn't take long to convince the jury of that.—No doubt the sentence will also be carried out speedily to ensure the matter is settled promptly." I shuddered.

"I can't say that would give me sleepless nights," Quin said in a cold voice that rather shocked me. "You haven't forgotten what he did to you, have you?" he asked, seeing my reaction. "And what more he might have done?"

"No. I haven't forgotten." I paused and looked up at Quin. "I also haven't forgotten that he said he doesn't work alone. Even if Doyle is hanged tomorrow, somebody else might come after you."

Quin shook his head. "I doubt that in the extreme. On the night he came to take you to Andrews, he brought along reinforcements, presumably men who would follow his commands and believed in his ideals, for him to trust them with such an important venture. Yet, by all accounts, the three men with him that night were nothing more than common criminals, who Doyle probably encountered by chance...and the three of them are being transported.—And I highly doubt your brother is going to be a danger to us when he's released!"

"What about the rebels?" I asked softly.

"Scattered to the four winds," Quin said firmly. "Whatever plans Doyle might have had, you said yourself you overheard him and Kieran allude to only a handful of men, none of whom are likely to have any particular allegiance to Doyle himself. Otherwise, where were they on the night of the arrests?—Such wretched souls as he likely managed to gather have probably never travelled past the outskirts of Dublin in all their lives, and they're unlikely to have followed him here!"

Quin's voice was rising in anger, and he gave me a long look. "Uprisings attract those who have nothing to lose...or nothing better to do. Such men are unlikely to unerringly follow a leader who cannot lead and whose promises of arms and supplies have come to nothing...much less one who has managed to see himself arrested and condemned to death!" He snorted irritably. "They're more likely to turn on him than to stand by his side.—And if Doyle did have a loyal army at his back, we would have heard of it!"

He scowled and breathed in heavily, before exhaling slowly and reaching a hand toward me. I pulled mine away. He looked across at me with sad eyes, his hand lying open in front of him, waiting for me to take it.

"We can't live in fear for the rest of our lives," he said quietly.

"I know, but..."

"Alannah, I know what I want. And I shall not forgo the having of it for fear of an unknown future, even for fear of my own life."

"But..."

"Even if we sacrificed our own happiness for the off chance somebody of Doyle's acquaintance might make an attempt on my life, there is no guarantee such an attempt might not still occur. It's gone far beyond the point of me being an inconvenient hurdle in his plans. I have now seen him condemned to death for treason.—I would imagine he would not look kindly upon this act."

I had to laugh despite myself. "No, I wouldn't suppose so. But Quin...I'm afraid."

"I know you are." He reached for me again and I reluctantly placed my hand in his. He squeezed it tightly, while his eyes looked deep into mine, revealing the depths of his feelings. "Alannah, I know we've only known each other for a short time, but my feelings for you are not going to change. I want you. All of you, and everything that comes with that, no matter the risk."

"I..."

"I had asked you if you would marry me. My offer still stands...if you'll take it."

He had said this in a business-like tone, but his eyes couldn't hide the emotions he felt, the longing, the fear.

My heart was hammering in my ears. I took a deep breath and slowly pulled my hand out of his grasp. "I'm sorry Quin...I can't promise you anything. I'm not saying no. But...I need some time. With everything that's happened in a few short weeks my whole life has been turned upside down. I need time to think about what it all means...for me...for us."

Quin leaned toward me and looked at me for a long moment. "I'll wait."

THE FOLLOWING MORNING, we again found ourselves at the courthouse.

We'd gone to pay Kieran's fine and try to reduce his sentence. While I personally thought Kieran had been exceedingly lucky to get away with such a light sentence—given all I knew about his rebellious proclivities—Quin had promised he would put in a good word to see if Kieran might be spared time in prison, for my sake.

I waited outside, wandering up and down in front of the columned portico of Omagh's courthouse, trying to decide how I should feel.

I was relieved, of course, that Kieran hadn't been convicted of treason, despite the fact I wasn't entirely sure he was innocent of the charge. For as long as I could remember he'd voiced the opinion that Ireland needed to be freed of English rule, an opinion that had grown in intensity in recent times. What exactly he'd done in pursuit of this belief, I didn't know. Not much, it seemed. Perhaps his conviction had been based on words, not actions, much like his plans to take over Niall after father's death.

This, perhaps, might be forgiven.

But then there were the threats he'd issued against me, the hatred I'd seen burning in his eyes, the belief I'd held in those moments that he would kill me himself if I got in his way. I wasn't sure if I could ever forgive him for that.

Or for bringing Martin Doyle into our lives.

And yet, he was my brother, a brother I loved and for whom I had come here even after everything he had done—despite the fact I didn't agree with his opinions much of the time and didn't support his actions most of the time. More than anything, I wanted us to find a way back to each other, but I was afraid the rift between us was too deep to cross.

Deep in thought I hadn't noticed that someone had come up behind me and so I was startled to hear a loud thump, as of somebody forcefully shutting a book. I turned toward the noise and my eyes grew wide with surprise as I recognised the man who stood in front of me, a large leather-bound volume in hand.

"I see you remember me," Herbert Andrews said in a pleasant tone of voice.

"Um…"

"I knew I'd left an impression on you."

He smiled while he fingered his greying moustache, dark eyes roaming over me impertinently, making me feel as uncomfortable as I had the first time I'd met him, despite his attractive appearance.

I noticed a large burly-looking man lurking behind him, scanning the surroundings while keeping a close eye on Andrews. A guard, I thought.

"You know, you really ought to have gone along with my plan," Andrews said suddenly in an irritated voice. "We would have made an excellent match. And you would have been able to buy much prettier things to wear than that."

He eyed my serviceable dark blue gown with a look of disapproval on his face, as if I had offended him in some way by wearing it. The dress was made of sturdy cotton, rather than delicate cashmere with lace trim, and its simple design, with loose sleeves and a high waistline, was no doubt several years out of fashion. Being rather unaffected by such trends in any case and living in rural Ireland where they didn't much matter, I didn't care. Besides, I knew the blue fabric suited me as it brought out the colour of my eyes.

I stood up straighter and glared at him.

Andrews smirked. "On second thought, I dare say you could wear a flour sack and look enticing.—Or nothing at all." He laughed as if he'd said something uproariously funny, having to take off his hat to stop it from falling off his head.

"I must tell your brother about our chance encounter here in the middle of nowhere," he wheezed. "Oh, but I forgot. Your brother is currently being detained. Something about questionable intentions, I surmise?" The smile he'd kept on his lips suddenly disappeared and the blood froze in my veins. "But it's only questionable if there's no evidence, isn't it?"

He tapped his index finger on the side of his nose and gave me a knowing look, his eyes boring into mine. Then, suddenly, the smile returned to his lips, and he bowed to me.

"It has been exceedingly gratifying to re-establish our acquaintance, Miss O'Neill. I wish you a pleasant day and bid you farewell. Until we shall meet again."

He walked off without another word, followed by his burly servant, leaving me standing baffled in the middle of the courtyard.

QUIN WAS MAKING his way out of the courthouse, deciding how best to tell Alannah he'd failed.

He had tried his utmost to convince the local magistrate to speak to the judge about reducing Kieran's sentence, even casually dropping the names of not only his father but every other high-ranking official in the British Army he'd had personal dealings with, but to no avail. The man had stayed as stern as his expression, telling him the judge had made his ruling and that was that. He'd even refused the guarded hint that Quin might pay a little extra on top of the fine for Kieran's immediate release.

He got what he deserved, Quin was given to understand.

Not that Quin didn't agree with this assessment, in fact he rather felt the bastard should have been locked up for the foreseeable future for the trouble he'd caused Alannah.

But he was Alannah's brother and Quin had promised her he'd try his best to get him released. And he would do anything to spare her further pain.

It was clear to him that the events of the past weeks had severely distressed her, although she was trying to put up a brave front. Quin had hoped she would let him comfort her as he had before, but ever since the night Doyle and Kieran had been arrested, he'd felt she was pushing him away. He knew Kieran's betrayal had hurt her deeply and that Doyle's assault had left her badly shaken, but he was worried her fears for the future were consuming her now.

She'd said she needed time and he would give it to her.

With Doyle arrested, there was no longer the need for haste. But if she spent too much time thinking about what had happened and what it might mean for the two of them, Quin thought she might try to cut him out of her life, for fear she would put him in danger if she stayed with him. He himself was certain any danger their union might bring was no greater than the danger they'd already placed themselves in by setting up Doyle for capture. Unlike Alannah, though, Quin did not believe anyone other than Doyle himself was likely to harm them, and with the man now condemned he saw no reason for them to forgo their own happiness.

"And why should I give up on her if I'm already doomed in any case?" Quin grumbled as he entered the courtyard.

He caught sight of Alannah standing a few feet away, looking into the distance with a slight frown on her face.

"Are you alright?" he asked when he reached her.

"Pardon?" She startled, having evidently not noticed Quin's arrival. "Oh...It's nothing...I think..."

"What do you mean?"

"I've just had an encounter with Herbert Andrews. And it was...strange."

Quin's eyes sprang open in surprise at the name, but he didn't say anything. Alannah looked up at him and pursed her lips.

"He didn't say very much, but I could have sworn he threatened me."

"Threatened you?" Quin asked, voice raised in outrage. "How?" He curled his hands into fists, turning this way and that, ready to defend her bodily if he must.

A few curious glances turned their way from the people milling around the courthouse.

"Nothing like that," Alannah assured him with a small smile. "He just made some comments...that he would testify to overturn Kieran's verdict if he were so inclined."

"You mean..."

"Have him convicted of treason."

"Oh," Quin said, temporarily at a loss for words.

162

"He didn't say anything of the sort outright, of course, but I understood the hint."

"But what does he want?" Quin asked, recovering his voice.

"I don't know. I don't know how he fits into any of this. —I don't believe he's a British spy, but it also seems exceedingly unlikely he's plotting *against* the British." She looked at Quin, her confused expression mirroring his own.

"I think you're right," he said after a long pause. "But if he's neither a spy nor a rebel, what would he have to gain from your brother being condemned as a traitor? And if he did want to see Kieran so condemned, why did he not see to it himself yesterday when he had the chance, instead of making himself largely responsible for Kieran being found innocent by speaking out in his favour?"

Alannah shook her head, no more able to answer Quin's questions than Quin himself.

"Did he say anything else to you? Hint at something you're supposed to do in return for his silence?"

"No, nothing. Although I would imagine..." She broke off, blue eyes troubled. "I would suppose it has something to do with our proposed marriage...presumably he's unhappy the deal fell through. Perhaps he thinks he can blackmail me into marrying him anyway..."

Quin frowned. "But if he wanted to blackmail you into marrying him, then surely he would have just come out and said exactly that a few moments ago. What would he gain from waiting? It's unlikely we'll see him again once we leave here."

"Yes, I suppose you're right," Alannah said, sounding suddenly very tired. "Perhaps I've just become paranoid. Perhaps he didn't threaten me at all."

Quin could see confusion and uncertainty flitting across Alannah's features, and he wanted suddenly, urgently, to take Herbert Andrews by the collar and ram his fist into his aging face. And then repeat the same process with Martin Doyle, and Kieran bloody O'Neill just for good measure.

He reached out a hand to Alannah but stayed himself from touching her.

"You're not paranoid. That man is up to something. And I have the unfortunate feeling we're going to find out what that is, at whatever point in time he chooses to enlighten us."

Looking at her standing there, Quin wanted desperately to take Alannah by the hand and run away with her. To the coast, across the sea and to his house in

England, where he could keep her safe. Where the men who'd threatened her were reduced to names hidden in the depths of their memories.

"Come," he said and offered her his arm. "Let us leave the courthouse and the unpleasant characters who lurk about here."

"What about Kieran?"

Quin cringed, having forgotten all about Alannah's brother in light of her revelations about Andrews.

"I'm sorry," he said, turning toward her, "I did everything I could, but the magistrate refused to speak to the judge about reducing his sentence.—And he wouldn't grant a visitation either."

He held his breath, waiting for her reaction. But she only breathed a deep sigh and gave him a tired smile.

"Thank you, Quin." She gently squeezed his arm. "Thank you for trying. Now please, take me home."

16.

I WAS WORKING in father's study—or Kieran's study, I corrected myself, although it would always feel like father's study to me. With Kieran locked away, I'd started tackling some of the farm's managerial tasks again. Mr Smith, the overseer who'd come to take over the farm's management, had expressed himself happy at my assistance, and I had been happy to believe him.

I frowned down at the records lying before me.

I'd been calculating the farm's disposable income in preparation for the harvest. As we did every year, we would hire labourers to assist the farm's usual staff to bring in the crops. Being a small farm, Niall had no cottiers, who exchanged their labour for the use of small patches of farmland, nor did we rent out conacre, my father having been averse to the practice. Instead, we paid labourers a wage of two shillings per day of reaping. The farm had done well the season before and we would be able to cover the labourers' costs for the upcoming harvest; however, I was trying to decide whether we also had sufficient funds to buy a new cow. Niall's two cows had both died unexpectedly within days of each other a few weeks before, having stopped eating one day, only to be struck with a high fever and collapse a few days later. None of the other animals on the farm seemed to have been affected, but the loss of the cows was noticeable, as we no longer produced our own dairy.

Having to meet our dairy needs at the market was slowly cutting into our available capital, which was a limited resource at the best of times. While Niall was prospering and its inhabitants lived comfortably enough, our wealth lay in the farm itself, not in shillings and pence. Almost everything we needed was produced onsite and so we seldom relied on money, but when we did, it was sometimes hard to come by.

I tapped my fingers on the desk in thought, looking at the numbers in front of me.

Rather wait until after the harvest, I decided, once the surplus produce had been sold.

Content with my decision, I put the ledger back onto the shelf and looked around for something else to do. Having been deprived of the opportunity to be involved in the farm's management for the past two years, I was enjoying doing the work.

Beyond that, though, it kept my mind occupied.

I'd managed with reasonable success to suppress the memories of the courthouse and everything that had happened leading up to Kieran and Doyle's arrest. In some moments, Kieran's behaviour and Doyle's appearance in my life felt like nothing but a dream. An unpleasant dream, but a dream, nonetheless. Submerged in numbers and calculations, and the innumerable practicalities that came with running a farm, I could almost convince myself that nothing was amiss, that father was still alive, and that Kieran was simply visiting an acquaintance on another farm.

Except when I thought of Quin.

Quin filled my dreams, sleeping and waking, sneaking up on me in unguarded moments, his green eyes twinkling above a radiant smile. I wanted to reach out to him, caress his cheek and lay my head upon his chest to hear his heart beating under my ear; let him take me in his arms and carry me with him to a world where we could be together and live without fear.

But I was afraid that world didn't exist.

We lived in a world where my brother had betrayed me, his friend had beaten me, and Quin's life had been threatened because of his association with me. I could barely think of Quin without remembering the hatred in Doyle's eyes when he'd confronted me about my meeting with Quin in the garden, the coldblooded way in which he'd told me he would kill Quin if I saw him again, and the brutal way in which he'd demonstrated his seriousness with his fists and his feet.

I'd managed, for a time, to forget the encounter.

When Quin had snuck into my room to see me despite my half-hearted attempts to keep him away, had seen my bruises and vowed to find a way for us to be together, I had believed him—because I'd wanted to. And I'd thought I could achieve the future he foresaw for us by luring Doyle into a trap, thinking Doyle's capture would make us free to live our dream.

But the dream had faded on the night of the arrests, when I was faced with the wound inflicted on Quin because of me, and it had vanished almost entirely at the courthouse when the last vestiges of the numbing fog that had surrounded me since that night had been ripped away. Seeing the hatred in Doyle's eyes had brought back all the fears I'd tried to suppress, the memory of his menacing words.

I don't work alone.

I could not ignore Doyle's threat and see Quin come to harm. My actions had already seen him injured, more gravely than he'd let on, I knew. He'd tried to downplay the seriousness of the wound inflicted by Doyle's sword, but I'd seen the pain that flitted across his face when he moved, the thick bandage he'd worn under his shirt for many days afterwards and the way he favoured his right side even now. My choices had led to Quin being harmed and my defiance had seen me beaten and almost killed, and my brother arrested.

I would not also be responsible for Quin's death.

Quin thought it unlikely there was anything to fear. And in truth, when I thought about it rationally, so did I—after all, Doyle's dealings with Andrews were surely over, whether I now had anything to do with Quin or not. But I was afraid to take that chance, irrational though it doubtless was.

And so, I'd forced myself to keep my distance, had tried to stay away from him, cowardly hoping he would tire of my antics and move on.

But Quin had been persistent, insisting on visiting me three times a week after our return, to ensure himself of my welfare in Kieran's absence, he said. For once, our meetings were properly chaperoned, with Margaret, Mrs O'Sullivan or even Quin's valet Rupert lurking in the corner of the room when we met, thus ensuring our encounters were chaste. I'd suggested the presence of a chaperone, as a ruse to continue our acquaintance in the acceptable social form, in reality to stop myself from losing my resolve.

I knew Quin's touch would undo me, that my determination to stay away from him would crumble if I let him come too close—and while I actually wanted nothing more, I was simply afraid to take that step.

A knock at the door interrupted my thoughts.

"Come in," I called, trying to make my voice sound welcoming.

There was a moment's silence. I was about to repeat myself when the door creaked open, hesitantly, as if the caller were uncertain about entering. I looked up expectantly.

When my visitor finally stood in the room it took me a moment to recognise him. He was filthy, unshaven and with dirty, scraggly hair.

But his blue eyes were the same, the same as mine.

"Kieran," I exclaimed and jumped up from my chair. "Kieran!"

Without conscious thought, I ran around the desk and flung myself at him. He smelled dreadful, but I pulled him to me, tears welling in my eyes and over-spilling. He raised his arms hesitantly and slowly wrapped them around me, awkwardly patting my back. As I held onto him, the strength of his embrace increased, until we were clinging to each other, both of us weeping.

"I didn't expect to see you for at least another week," I said when I finally pulled away from him, wiping the tears off my cheeks. Kieran glanced uncomfortably at me before looking down.

"I was released early," he explained through his unfamiliar beard, his eyes darting away from mine as he awkwardly shrugged his shoulders. "For good behaviour...apparently." He snorted. "I think it was actually because there wasn't enough space to put all the criminals.—So, they let one of us go."

"You're not a criminal."

"Am I not?" Kieran's expression hardened as he took a step back. He was quiet for a moment, and I thought he would say no more, but suddenly he burst out, "I am guilty of everything I was accused of and more. If things had been different, I'd be rotting in jail still...or dead."

I looked at him uncertainly, unsure what to say, feeling suddenly hesitant. With everything that had happened between us, we'd become virtual strangers.

But whatever else he might be, Kieran was still my brother.

"Well, I'm glad you're home." Another tear escaped at the words.

"Why would you be? I've brought you nothing but trouble.—You're better off without me."

"Kieran," I said softly as his shoulders slumped, "I..."

"I know what you're going to say," he interrupted me. "You're going to make excuses for me, justify my behaviour like you used to do...when we were younger."

I swallowed. I knew it was the truth.

"You were always looking out for me, trying to stop me from getting myself into trouble. And how have I repaid you?"

He lifted his eyes to look at me. They were filled with sadness and regret, and I wanted to weep for him and the bond we had lost, the bond we might have had.

I blinked away the tears that were threatening to overflow yet again.

"I have insulted you, mocked you, gone out of my way to be cruel to you at every turn, to take away any joy you might find.—And at the last, I saw you beaten and threatened with your life." His lips quivered as his own eyes filled with tears. "What sort of brother have I become?" he whispered. "What sort of man have I become?"

I had no idea how to answer this and just stared at him helplessly. I groped for something to say but found only lies and half-truths, words that would mean nothing to either of us and would do nothing to bridge the distance between us.

With a look of defeat, Kieran turned away from me and walked to the window, where he stood silently, staring out at the farm that was his birthright. Neither of us spoke for several minutes, and the silence between us grew, until I thought I could bear it no longer.

"Kieran..." I said, coming up behind him.

"I was jealous," he started suddenly, so softly I could barely hear him. I stopped and looked at his back, seeing the hunched shoulders of a broken man. "I was jealous," he repeated quietly, turning to face me, his disheartened eyes meeting mine briefly before flitting away, "jealous of the attention father showered on you."

"But..."

"I know it was my own fault, that things would have been different if I'd shown an interest in the things he tried to teach me, the things Mr Henderson tried to teach me." His eyes took on a faraway look, seeing something beyond the contents of the room. "He used to spend hours with you, poring over the farm's ledgers or some ancient manuscript or discussing legal matters.—I wanted that time too."

He gave me a long look that gave me an inkling of the dejection he must have felt, a dejection that—in truth—I had seen, but had done nothing about, thinking it to be misplaced self-pity.

"But mother..." I said hesitantly as he lowered his eyes once more.

"Mother doted on me, yes. But all she ever did was complain about everything. How miserable her life was, how much better things would have been if father hadn't inherited the farm, how much he'd changed since we moved here..." He sighed and shook his head. "Just like her, I started believing everybody else was to blame for my problems. And then mother died.—And I was left with a bad attitude and a father who thought I was useless."

"Father didn't think you were useless," I countered automatically.

"Yes, he did. I know he thought so. I know he worried about me taking over the farm one day. I heard him say so to mother and Mr Smith on more than one occasion. And I know he invested his money to plan for my failure." A tear escaped the corner of his eye as he lifted his face, his features distorted with pain and remorse. "I might not have had much interest in mathematics and philosophy, but I can hear and see just fine, even things that people try to hide."

"Oh, Kieran," I cried and pulled him toward me in despair.

"I'm sorry," he sobbed, shaking in my arms. "I'm sorry," he repeated over and over as I held him, stroking his back, my heart breaking for him as he fell apart.

"Hush," I whispered. "Hush. You're home now. Everything will be alright."

I SAT AT the dining table, a single candle fluttering in the breeze that blew in through the open window. Supper was long over, and the servants had retired, leaving me to my thoughts as the last of the daylight vanished.

I had held Kieran until his hiccupping sobs had finally subsided, before leading him to his room, where Margaret had placed two basins of warm water for shaving and washing. I'd left him to his ablutions and gone to speak with Mrs O'Sullivan about setting an extra place for supper. I didn't customarily eat much for my evening meal, but the industrious Mrs O'Sullivan had a table full of food prepared in the time it took me to change my gown.

Kieran had come downstairs and lurked at the door, waiting uncertainly, until I called him in and invited him to his accustomed seat. He ate ravenously, polishing off more food than I would have thought possible after three weeks of hunger. I watched him covertly as I picked at my own food without appetite. Cleanly shaven, washed and in fresh clothes, he looked like the brother I knew. His light brown hair bobbed around his ears, still damp from his wash. The curls lent him an air of innocence that was abruptly broken when he lifted his head and looked directly at me.

His face had hardened in his absence, his eyes turned colder—with regret, I thought, but perhaps something else.

"Pass the salt, please," he asked politely, but without smiling.

I obliged.

"Mmm, this is delicious," he said around a mouthful of food. "I haven't eaten anything but potatoes in weeks."

The statement gave me a start, as it reminded me of Quin's light-hearted complaints about his bland diet when he'd first arrived in Ireland. I pushed the thought away.

"And practically nothing for the past two days." Kieran helped himself to some more sliced beef. "It took me two days to walk back home," he explained in response to my startled expression. "I kept turning back...I didn't know if I should come..."

"Oh..."

"They kept me for three weeks before deciding they needed my patch of ground for someone else." He looked up at me with tired eyes, eyes that had seen the misery of the men in his company, a misery he had shared. "Three weeks can seem like a very long time when you spend your days behind bars, thinking you might go mad if you're not released soon."

He paused, mopping up the last of his gravy with a thick slice of bread.

"I had a lot of time to think.—About what I'd done in the past, how I'd treated people...about what kind of man I want to be." He sighed, put down his napkin and leaned back in his chair. "I want to change, Alannah," he said, his eyes imploring me to believe him. "To make up for lost time...to be your brother again."

I took a deep breath and made an effort to smile at him. "It will be alright. Get some rest and we'll talk in the morning."

Kieran had gone to bed and the servants had cleared the table, while I'd sat unmoving in my chair.

And I was sitting there still, in the dark, as the events of the day swirled through my head.

I wanted to believe Kieran had changed. I *did* believe he had changed. But how much? I could imagine being imprisoned might make one face one's own shortcomings, as regrets surfaced and the desire for freedom burned. I had felt Kieran's grief over the harm he'd done me, had believed he'd meant his apology. But was it likely he would now support my decisions wholeheartedly? Let me take over the running of the farm and marry whom I pleased?

My brother was weak.

I had known it for years, although I'd always tried to deny it and make excuses for him. I had seen it in the way he constantly took the easy way out, in the way he treated others, and in the way he always blamed others for his own

171

shortcomings, taking responsibility for nothing. Today was the first time I'd ever heard him apologise for any one of those things. I had believed him. And yet I had doubts, doubts over how far-reaching his promise to change would turn out to be, and how long it would last.

It was one thing regretting one's actions and resolving to change when confined to a prison cell, it was another to live the change in the outside world. And I couldn't imagine Kieran submitting meekly to my commands as I took over the farm that was rightfully his, no matter how much he might regret his treatment of me in the past.

And there was more to his past than his mistreatment of me.

He hadn't mentioned Doyle and his involvement in rebellious activities, but I doubted very much that his leanings in this regard would have changed. He had complained about the rule of the English over Ireland for most of his life, he was unlikely to change his tune now. Was he likely to act on these feelings of injustice again? Or would he be content to complain about the English around the dinner table, while accepting his fate?

I didn't know. I had so many questions and so few answers.

I closed my eyes for a moment in the darkness, seeing the candle's flame dancing behind my eyelids. There was one thing that had become crystal clear to me as I'd comforted Kieran in his regret—time lost could never be regained.

I needed to speak to Quin.

QUIN WAS MUCKING out the stable, cursing under his breath.

He'd done any amount of physical labour in his youth and during his time with the army, but he'd hoped living in a manor house would have provided him with the benefit of fitting staff to do such work for him. As it was, he ended up doing much of the farm work himself, as the two servants who were available to him were so old and decrepit it would take either one of them most of the day to clean out the four stalls currently in use.

As for his valet...

Rupert was a sweet boy who performed his duties with enthusiasm and efficiency, always seeing to it that Quin was suitably groomed and dressed. But he'd never been outside of London in his life and had never set foot on a farm before. He didn't have the slightest clue about agriculture or animal husbandry and was as likely to stab himself in the foot with the pitchfork as he was to move any hay with it. And so, Quin had assigned Rupert to taking care of the household, with the instructions to make the manor resemble the grand house it was pretending to be, while he, Quin, tackled all manner of physical labour.

It wasn't so much that Quin objected to getting into the grubby side of farm life, it's that he had other work to do.

He'd promised himself he would see the tenants suitably housed and taken care of, and the estate steered back in the right direction, but he hadn't taken a single concrete step toward achieving any such thing. His plans had been dramatically interrupted by the advent of one Martin Patrick Doyle, the bloody bastard, and since Quin's return from the trial he seemed to be spending most of his time tackling one menial task after another.

What he had at last managed to do was to hire one additional member of staff, in the form of a new overseer, a Mr Dunne introduced to him by Constable Ryan after Quin had described the state of Glaslearg to the constable during one of their rare casual conversations. Mr Dunne was only set to arrive at the estate at the beginning of September, though, which was still some ways off.

Besides this iota of progress, he'd gotten as far as laying out the land he intended to allocate to each tenant family, but he was no closer to building them suitable homes. He'd also decided on using the remaining land to plant potatoes, oats and wheat—on a few fields each to begin with, to be planted in rotation over future seasons—with a small section retained for the possible grazing of some livestock.

As to the procurement of building materials for the tenants' houses, seeds for the new season's planting and the animals themselves, and the hiring of additional servants and labourers to do the work...

Quin snorted irritably through his nose and uttered a rude word.

At that exact moment, a shadow crossed the dooryard, making him look up. Alannah was standing outside the stable, holding her horse by the reins, a look of uncertainty in her eyes.

Quin dropped the pitchfork and took three quick steps toward her, wiping his hands on his breeches as he went.

"Alannah."

"Quin, I..." She took a deep breath and lifted her chin in determination before going on. "I apologise that I've come unannounced, I can see you're busy." Quin waved away her apology. "I was hoping we might speak...in private."

173

Her eyes met his and the blood started pounding in his head.

"Of course."

He quickly led Alannah's mare to one of the empty stalls, yanked off the saddle, tossed in a few wisps of hay and put the gate on the latch. The horse would have to do without grooming.

He strode purposefully back to Alannah and stopped in front of her.

"Would you care to join me in the drawing room?" he asked, trying not to sound too eager.

She gave him a nervous smile. "I would."

They walked in an awkward silence down the path from the outbuildings to the courtyard of the manor house.

"One moment, please," Quin said when they reached the small fountain in the centre.

He quickly cleaned the muck off his hands and washed his face, taking the time to compose himself. His heart was racing as he contemplated what Alannah's presence here meant. For the past three weeks, she'd kept her distance, agreeing to see him only in the presence of a chaperone. She'd held herself aloof, had been quiet, restricting conversation to the barest minimum. He was fairly sure she'd agreed to meet with him only because he'd insisted on it and had been expecting a note from her telling him his attention was no longer welcome.

So what did it mean that she was here now?

Ablutions complete, Quin straightened up and ran his damp hands through his hair, rivulets of water running down his neck and into his shirt.

"Here."

Quin turned toward Alannah, who was holding out a large white handkerchief. Their eyes met, and the world froze. As if in a trance, Quin slowly lifted his hand toward the piece of fabric, grazing Alannah's fingers as his hand closed around it. He dabbed his face and neck, his eyes locked with hers.

"Thank you," he said, handing the handkerchief back to her as time resumed.

Alannah shook herself and Quin swallowed heavily, before leading her into the house. Neither Denis nor Bryan was in sight, and Quin hoped Rupert would make himself scarce. He had no desire for a chaperone on this particular day. He opened the door to the drawing room and let Alannah precede him inside.

"It looks like somebody lives here now," Alannah said as she looked around the room.

174

Rupert had not only acquired a few additional items of furniture but had also added some vases with flowers he'd collected around the grounds, as well as several decorative odds and ends he'd unearthed in the rubbish that currently filled the attic. Quin had to admit the addition of a few personal touches made him feel a bit more at home.

"My valet," he explained. "He has no agrarian inclinations whatsoever, but he does know how to make things look good."

"I noticed." Alannah glanced at him and blushed.

Quin quickly turned to close the door before coming to stand in front of her. "Would you like to sit?"

"No, thank you," she said, surprising him. "Quin, I..."

He braced himself for the rejection he feared was coming.

She paused for a long moment before speaking. "Kieran's back."

"What?" This wasn't at all what he'd expected to hear. "How? It hasn't been a month yet."

"He was released early...too many inmates." Alannah waved away her brother's return and took a step closer to Quin. He could see her pulse beating rapidly in her neck. "Quin...I've been trying to push you away...to forget you and move on without you. But"—she swallowed and licked her lips—"I don't want to live my life with regrets." The words were barely a whisper.

She looked up at him, and he could read her eyes like an open book—the fear and the doubts that harboured there, overshadowed only by the longing she couldn't hide, not even from herself.

"I know it's foolish, Quin, but...I am afraid...afraid of what might happen to you because of me." Her voice was shaky with emotion and a single tear rolled down her cheek. Quin's heart clenched like a fist at the sight. "But I am even more afraid of living my life wondering what might have been..."

Quin reached out a hand and wiped away the tear, caressing her cheek. She closed her eyes and leaned into his hand, filling him with tenderness. He moved closer to her and took her face in both of his hands, tilting her chin up to him.

"It will be alright. Everything will be alright."

He kissed her then, gently, slowly, while his hands softly caressed her waist. She brought her arms tentatively around his middle, resting her hands lightly on the muscles of his back, making him shiver through the thin shirt. He gently pulled her closer with a hand on her lower back and she pressed herself into him, moaning softly against his mouth, making him feel dizzy as the blood rushed from his head.

Making a terrible effort he gently pushed her away from him and stood panting in front of her. She still had her eyes closed and he made a quick adjustment to the front of his breeches.

"Quin." She opened her eyes and reached a hand toward him.

He took a quick step back. "Alannah, please," he said in a strangled voice, "if you touch me now, I shall have you naked on the hearth rug within the next minute...which will be all the more impressive considering there is no hearth rug in this room." He stopped talking abruptly as he suddenly realised what he'd said.

Alannah only laughed nervously, though, while a soft blush crept into her cheeks. "Alright, I promise not to touch you."

He cursed himself for idiocy.

"At least not this instant." She laughed again, seeing the look of horror that must have sprung up on his face. "But...perhaps...when the time is right..."

"Take all the time you need. I shall wait for you...my whole life if I must."

"I don't want to wait anymore," she said quietly and took a step toward him. "I have spent my entire life waiting for the world to change, wasted the past two years letting Kieran push me into a corner instead of standing up for myself.— Why?" Her voice was rising, her blue eyes intent. "Because I was afraid. Afraid of what others might think, afraid of what others might do, of what Kieran might do if I didn't act like the submissive woman he wanted me to be, that society wanted me to be. But that's not who I am. And I'm tired of pretending otherwise.—I know what I want, and it isn't limited to sitting at home looking pretty, discussing poetry and having babies...although I want that too," she added with a sideways glance at Quin.

She was quiet for a moment.

"I am afraid still. Afraid for you...afraid of what might happen. And of what's happened already...what's happened to you because of me." She extended her hand and gently touched the site of his injury.

"You are not responsible for any of this!" Quin objected, his heart aching at the thought that she blamed herself. He took her hand in his and gripped it tightly. "You cannot blame yourself! Nothing you did justifies what happened to you…what happened to us. Kieran's cowardice and Doyle's wickedness are to blame. Nothing else."

He searched her face, wanting her to believe him. "Alannah," he said, gently stroking her cheek, "you are not to blame. Please believe me."

He could see doubt flitting across her features, as her desperate desire to believe him fought with the fear that still held her captive.

"You don't need to be afraid anymore."

"I don't *want* to be afraid anymore, Quin," she said quietly, slowly shaking her head. "I have been afraid of so many things. Of being judged for being different, of being forgotten if I comply, of being forced into a life I didn't want…of being cast out.—But all of those fears pale in comparison to the fear I felt when I saw you facing the end of a sword because of me." Quin was about to speak when she continued, "I am still afraid. I want to believe we're not in any danger and that none of this is my fault, but every time I try, I see Doyle's eyes, filled with hatred as he beat me…and threatened to kill you."

Quin swallowed a lump in his throat and pulled her toward him, his heart aching for her and the burden she felt she had to carry alone. She leaned into him for a moment before pulling away and looking up at him, big blue eyes still filled with doubt.

"Quin," she said softly, looking so vulnerable Quin wanted to pick her up and cradle her in his arms, to keep her safe, always. "I came here today…because I don't want to let my fears control me anymore.—I don't want to wake up ten years from now with regret."

"Alannah, I have wanted you since the moment I laid eyes on you. Nothing is ever going to change that. I am yours…if you'll have me."

He stood stock-still, waiting. She looked at him for a moment, pulse beating steadily in her throat.

"I'll have you," she whispered and came into his arms. He pulled her to him roughly as his emotions threatened to overwhelm him. He lifted her off the ground, cradling her head next to his.

"I know you're afraid," he murmured into her dark hair, breathing in the scent of her, "but we have each other now. We'll face our fears together."

"THE DARK GREY morning coat and the fawn trousers, sir?—With the double-breasted burgundy waistcoat?" Rupert's young face shone with excitement at his master's suggested wardrobe. "A bit formal for daywear, but it'll let him know your intentions!"

Quin smiled at his valet's eagerness. He hadn't told Rupert the whole story, but his young romantic heart knew enough to understand that today's meeting with Kieran was important.

"Thank you, Rupert. I think you've made an excellent choice."

Rupert beamed at Quin and started laying out the clothes on the big tester bed that had recently made its appearance in his bedroom.

Quin had no idea where Rupert had acquired the thing—whether he'd dug it out of the rubble in the attic, bought it at the market (that seemed unlikely), or made it himself (that seemed even more unlikely)—but he had to admit getting into the monstrosity every night made him feel rather regal. And the thought of sharing the bed with Alannah...

He quickly smothered the thought.

It would do his chances of getting dressed no good.

He had decided there was no point in delaying an interview with Kieran once Alannah had made her decision—he having made his weeks ago. She had agreed, but he could see the thought of Quin and Kieran in the same room together made her nervous.

She had told him about Kieran's supposed change of heart, how he'd apologised for how he'd treated her in the past, that he'd said he wanted to make amends. Quin had declared himself pleasantly surprised at this turn of events—and he was surprised indeed—but he could see Alannah harboured doubts.

Doubts that he shared.

"I'm not convinced people ever really change," he'd said cautiously when she voiced her concerns. "Of course, you grow as you get older, but to change a fundamental set of your beliefs? To change who you are in the depths of your soul?"

She sighed. "You're probably right. No doubt he'll revert to his normal behaviour once he's gotten over the shock of spending time in gaol."

"I'm sorry." Quin took hold of her hand. "I didn't mean to upset you. I hope he *has* changed, I really do! But...I think we shouldn't depend on it."

"Yes...you're right, we shouldn't depend on it. I want to believe him. To believe I have a chance...of having my brother back." She paused. "But even if he hasn't changed...Quin, it won't make a difference. I'm not going back to the way things were...to a life where I had no choices and no voice. A life that didn't include you." She turned her blue gaze toward him, eyes shiny with emotion, her voice barely a whisper. "I love you, Quin. I've tried to deny it, but I've been lying to myself."

He took her face in his hands, gently stroking her cheeks, his heart ready to burst with joy. He bent his head toward her, his lips just touching hers.

"I love you too."

SITTING IN KIERAN'S parlour awaiting his arrival, Quin thought to himself that Kieran really ought not to have any objections to Quin's proposal. He had money to his name, had been a lieutenant in the British Army and was of noble blood— of the lower rank, true, but noble nonetheless, with the coat of arms to prove it.

He was certainly capable of taking care of Alannah, financially and otherwise.

He wasn't sure, though, whether these qualities would be marred by his basic Englishness in Kieran's eyes. He'd said he'd changed, but Quin doubted his emotional rehabilitation would have extended to his political leanings. Quin couldn't quite imagine Kieran accepting an English brother-in-law with open arms.

"Hmph." He suddenly wondered whether he should have brought his sword.

"Mr Williams."

Quin jumped up from his seat and turned toward the door where Kieran had appeared. He looked much improved from the last time Quin had seen him, although rather thin. With his light brown, curly hair floating like a halo around his head, he had an angelic look about him—quite in contrast to the picture of Alannah's brother Quin had just been contemplating.

"Mr O'Neill." Quin offered Kieran his hand.

They shook hands civilly while Kieran surveyed Quin with eyes that were uncannily like Alannah's. Quin returned the frank appraisal but found it difficult to read the man. Outwardly, he seemed nothing but welcoming, but Quin's scepticism refused to accept Kieran's hospitality at face value.

"Mr Williams."

Quin let go of Kieran's grasp and reached Alannah in two strides. He bowed, took the hand she offered and brought it to his lips, holding her gaze. "My lady."

She curtsied, a smile on her lips. "Sir."

Quin couldn't help smiling, too, in response to the formality.

Remembering where he was, he looked back at Kieran to see his reaction. He didn't seem visibly perturbed, but Quin continued to be cynical, expecting at any moment Kieran to declare that this was all a hoax, and that Quin would be forcibly removed. No such threat came, though, and they all sat down while Margaret bustled about pouring cups of tea and offering sweet and savoury treats.

Quin didn't have much of an appetite but selected a few small savouries so as not to offend his host. Not that refusing his food would be the most offensive thing I could do today, he thought as he took a bite.

A few moments of silence followed as the servants melted away, broken only by the loud ticking of the longcase clock in the corner, and the soft chime of plates being placed on the table.

Quin glanced at Alannah, who looked back at him encouragingly, but with a slightly nervous expression. Evidently, he wasn't the only one who continued to harbour doubts. She showed no signs of wanting to leave Quin to confront Kieran alone, though, and so he shrugged and decided to grasp the nettle.

"Mr O'Neill," he said, "I have come to ask for your sister's hand in marriage."

He raised his chin ever so slightly, daring Kieran to deny his request. But Kieran only looked at him for a moment before turning toward Alannah.

"Is this what you want?"

Alannah's eyes popped open in surprise at being asked for her opinion. Evidently that hasn't happened in a while, Quin thought with some irritation.

"Yes," Alannah responded, looking first at Kieran then at Quin. "With all my heart." She held Quin's gaze and the blood thumped through his veins.

"Good," Kieran said after a moment's hesitation, "then it shall be so. You'll be married as soon as the banns have been called."

He gave Alannah and Quin a brief smile, nodded to himself, and turned his attention back to his plate without giving them a further glance. Alannah looked at Quin, wearing an expression that must mirror his own—one of complete astonishment. Kieran had said he'd changed, but Quin had not expected the meek compliance he'd just witnessed.

Nor did he believe it.

Perhaps it was just his natural scepticism for all things that seemed too good to be true, but he found it exceedingly unlikely Kieran's behaviour was a true

180

reflection of his feelings, he who had been highly vocal about his hatred of the English only a few weeks before. Whether or not he'd meant to improve his relations with his sister, it was doubtful in the extreme Kieran would happily abide by her choice of an English husband without even the slightest objection. At the very least Quin would have expected a thorough interrogation of his intentions, perhaps even an exhaustive examination of his background.

But this? No, Quin thought, there's something suspicious going on here.

He frowned, and Alannah scowled at him. He quickly readjusted his features into something he hoped resembled a smile and busied himself with his teacup.

An awkward half an hour followed, with conversation limited to trivialities and requests to pass the sugar. When at last Kieran declared he had matters to discuss with the farm's overseer—which caused Alannah's eyebrows to rise to her hairline—Quin breathed a sigh of relief. He rose from his seat and bid Alannah farewell, experiencing a thrill at the thought she would soon be his wife.

Turning toward Kieran, though, he made no move to offer him his hand.

"Mr O'Neill, before I depart so you can go about your business, might I have a private word with you?"

Alannah gave him a startled look and he unobtrusively shook his head. She continued to stare at him for a moment, a blue gaze he interpreted as instructions not to do anything stupid. He narrowed his eyes at her to indicate he'd understood the hint. She raised her eyebrows, expressing her doubtfulness at his ability not to do anything stupid under the circumstances.

"Hmph," he grumbled as Alannah left the room.

He turned back to Kieran.

"Mr O'Neill, I wish to be frank with you," he began without preamble. While pleasantries and diplomacy were highly prized social niceties, some situations called for brutal honesty, Quin felt. "I am not convinced of your benevolent disposition regarding your sister's betrothal to me," he said as tactfully as he could.

Kieran gaped at him uncomprehendingly.

Quin sighed. "I think you're lying about your intentions." Kieran's eyes grew wide, and Quin narrowed his. "Considering your very recent near traitorous actions, I find it highly doubtful you would be happy to welcome an Englishman into your family."

Kieran stared at him for a moment.

"I'm not happy about it," he finally responded in clipped tones. "I'm not happy about it at all.—The English have brought nothing but misery and despair to Ireland. And now I'm supposed to sit by quietly while my sister marries one of them?" Kieran's voice was rising, and Quin was about to respond but Kieran continued. "We would all be better off if every last one of you shipped off back to England! Unfortunately, though," he said as Quin opened his mouth to speak, "I made my sister a promise. And whether you believe it or not, I intend to keep it." He suddenly sagged visibly and lowered his head. "She's the only person in the world I can count on."

"And you repay her for that by trying to sell her off to some rich, old bastard?'

Kieran lifted his head, eyes blazing. "That wasn't my idea!"

"But you were happy enough to go along with it hoping to make a profit."

"I didn't want the money for myself. I wanted it for the rebellion...to free Ireland."

"But on the stand, you said..."

"I lied! I lied to save my own skin.—Is that what you wanted to hear?" Kieran started pacing irritably around the room. "Doyle and Andrews thought up the plan. I didn't think anything of it. She needed a husband anyway, so I thought, why not a rich and old one who was likely to be dead in a few years, leaving her a rich widow while providing us with the money we needed...to arm and feed the rebels we were trying to gather to rid Ireland of the English. That was the point of the arrangement all along."

Kieran stopped in front of Quin with an angry expression on his face. "Are you going to have me arrested for that now?"

"No," Quin spat at him. "While I would like nothing better than to see you back behind bars, Alannah has suffered enough because of you."

Kieran stared at him with loathing in his eyes. "It was the perfect plan," he said, ignoring Quin's comment. "She should have gone along with it and married Andrews! She would have if it wasn't for you!"

"And Andrews would have turned you over to the police the instant the ink was dry on the contract.—Besides, if that's what you think of your sister you don't know her at all!"

"Oh, yes? And you do?"

"Yes, I do," Quin hissed. "I was the one she confided in about your ill-treatment of her, her sadness that her own brother could care so little about what she might think or feel, how you had oppressed and threatened her for the past two years." Quin's voice was rising as he was struggling to control his own anger. "And I was the one who comforted her when your friend Doyle beat her black and blue!—Or have you forgotten about that?"

"No," Kieran said quietly, suddenly looking ashamed. "I haven't forgotten. I..." He stopped talking abruptly, a look of disbelief blooming on his face. "You *comforted* her?" He gaped at Quin with raised brows and wide eyes. "When? How?"

"I visited her," Quin said shortly, scowling at Kieran. "In her bedchamber," he added, thoroughly provoked.

"You...you...in her..." Kieran stammered, a red hue creeping up his neck.

Quin lifted his chin defiantly while Kieran continued to sputter in outrage. "You didn't seem to care overly much yourself," he snapped.

He stared at Kieran, who stared back until at last he dropped his gaze. Quin could see Kieran's jaw muscles working as he evidently made an effort to control himself. When he lifted his head, Quin was surprised to see a look of sadness in his eyes, which were so like his sister's.

"I never meant for it to happen," Kieran said quietly, shrugging his shoulders uncomfortably. "I thought we could keep her in line with a few threats.—I didn't think she would resist so much." He looked vaguely surprised Alannah would object to being forced to marry a man to advance her brother's traitorous ambitions. Suddenly, he frowned. "But then you came along..."

Quin exhaled explosively. "Do not blame me for your own shortcomings! Your execrable treatment of Alannah started long before I even set foot in Ireland!"

Kieran was silent for a moment. "I know," he said abruptly, surprising Quin, who breathed out like a steam engine once more. "I...I have no excuse. I treated her badly, I know that now. Seeing her beaten and afraid...and she still came to me when I was arrested, tried to help me, even though it was all my fault..." He looked down and Quin could see he was struggling to contain his emotions. "I know you don't believe me, but I *have* changed.—At least when it comes to Alannah!"

He lifted his head defiantly, making it clear some of his other opinions hadn't changed one bit.

Quin took a moment to respond, until he felt he could speak without shouting. "Alright, Mr O'Neill, let us try to come to an agreement." Kieran looked at him sceptically but didn't object. "I shall do my utmost to believe your mistreatment of Alannah has come to an end…if you do your utmost to eliminate your prejudice against me and judge me for the man that I am, not the *Englishman* you see."

Quin lifted his eyebrows expectantly.

"Agreed," Kieran said after a long moment and stuck out his hand.

Quin shook it and turned to go. Just before he reached the door he turned back and gave Kieran a piercing look.

"Just one last thing, Mr O'Neill. If I ever hear of another indiscretion against Alannah by your hand, no matter how trivial, you will personally find out just what sort of vengeance this particular Englishman is capable of."

He stared at Kieran for good measure before walking through the open door.

"Good day, Mr O'Neill," he said without turning back.

17.

THE FOLLOWING DAY, I found myself sitting in the parlour again, awaiting Quin's arrival once more. With Kieran's unexpectedly swift agreement to our betrothal, there were a few legalities and practicalities to discuss, including my dowry and the question of where we would live once we were married.

The latter was giving me some pause.

If we stayed in Ireland, I would of course go live with Quin at Glaslearg, leaving Kieran—or rather, Mr Smith—to run Niall. But I thought there might be a chance Quin would want to take me back to England instead, a prospect that gave me distinctly mixed feelings.

Quin had stated with absolute conviction we had nothing to fear from Doyle, but he might have some doubts, doubts he was trying to hide from me. And if so, the possibility of Doyle's vengeance—however slight it may be—and the question of Andrews' intentions might make Quin feel the only possible course of action would be to take me right out of Ireland to see me safe. Besides, I was reasonably sure he'd never meant to settle down at Glaslearg, only intending to see it steered back on the right course before returning to his home in London.

"Mistress, your gentleman caller has arrived," Margaret's voice intruded on my thoughts.

"Thank you, Margaret," I said to the maid as she bobbed her capped head.

I smiled to myself. The way Margaret had enunciated *gentleman* was one of many signs she was rather taken by Quinton Fletcher Philbert Williams—a sentiment I shared entirely. His thoroughly English name aside, Quin truly was a gentleman, courteous to a fault and considerate of everyone, including the servants. And his physical appearance didn't disappoint either, usually having a rather alarming visceral effect on me instead.

I took a deep breath and rose to meet the object of my reflections. Seeing him walk through the door made a smile break out on my face.

"Mr Williams," I said and extended my hand.

"Miss O'Neill," came his deep voice in response.

He kissed my hand, green eyes twinkling with mischief, as we both tried to ignore the presence of Margaret, who was waiting for Kieran to come down to join us.

"Are you well this morning, Miss O'Neill?"

"Yes, very well, thank you, Mr Williams. I am to be married to a wonderful man, so I couldn't be happier."

"I am delighted to hear so. And, may I say, what a lucky man your betrothed may consider himself to be."

I laughed, and Quin responded in kind, the worries of the last few weeks evaporating with the sound.

"He is lucky, indeed, Mr Williams," I agreed, "lucky the negotiations with my brother went so smoothly...after the betrothal had been settled." I raised one eyebrow at Quin, and he cleared his throat.

"Why, Miss O'Neill, have you been eavesdropping perhaps?"

"I would hardly call it eavesdropping when your voices were raised high enough to be heard through most of the house even without the open door."

This wasn't entirely true. They hadn't been yelling—not quite—but I could hardly admit I'd purposefully waited in the hallway to overhear their conversation, although I was reasonably sure Quin suspected as much.

"You reminded me of two cockerels fighting in the yard," I said, and Quin coughed, turning pink around the ears, making me laugh. "I wanted to thank you," I continued softly.

"Thank me?" Quin was visibly startled.

"For promising to give Kieran the benefit of the doubt. I know you have reservations...and I know you made the promise for me. I hope...I hope his intentions are true. That he can find it in himself...to be the brother he once was to me."

"I hope so too," Quin said, eyes tender, "for your sake. I only want to see you happy...and safe."

My heart gave a painful thump at his words, but I had resolved to suppress my fears about the future.

"At least Martin Doyle won't be able to harm us anymore," I said, shuddering slightly. Doyle's hanging had been scheduled to take place a few days earlier.

"I wouldn't be so sure about that."

Quin and I turned as one toward the door, where Kieran was entering with a frown on his face. My heart started pounding at the sight.

"What do you mean?" Quin asked in a tone that demanded answers.

"He's not dead."

"But…" I sputtered, "I thought…the verdict…"

"The sentence hasn't been carried out."

"Why not?" Quin's voice sounded like thunder.

"He's awaiting a royal pardon."

"He's what?" I asked in astonishment.

"On what grounds?" Quin demanded.

Kieran shrugged uncomfortably. "All I know is his sentence was postponed the day before it was to be carried out, which was the day I left."

Quin and I looked at each other, utterly shocked. Quin took a step closer to me.

"He was found guilty of treason and murder," he said in a hard voice. "There's no chance he could possibly be pardoned!"

"Perhaps…" I started and stopped abruptly. "Perhaps…he's trying to buy time," I whispered, trying to suppress the panic starting to rise within me.

"Time to escape," Kieran said softly, clearly having thought of this before. "That would seem likely to me. Of course, he would try to escape…in which case…"

It occurred to me belatedly that my brother was also in danger from Martin Doyle, probably more so than Quin or me. It was in large part Kieran's testimony, after all, that had seen Doyle convicted, testimony Doyle would no doubt see as a personal betrayal, Kieran having previously been his ally. And he had tried to strangle Kieran in the gaol before the trial had even started, before he knew Kieran would be testifying against him on the stand.

I looked helplessly up at Quin.

"Just wait one moment," he objected. "I forbid either one of you from continuing the line of thought upon which you have embarked! You are assuming Doyle is not only going to attempt to escape, but that he is going to succeed, followed in short order by a visitation from the man to act out his vengeance upon one of us.—You are forgetting he currently *is* in gaol, behind bars. And likely to stay there for the foreseeable future, until the welcome execution of his sentence, which no judge worth his salt is going to overturn, much less the Queen herself!"

Quin narrowed his eyes, daring Kieran or me to object to his assessment of the facts.

"Now," he continued, "I shall make some enquiries as to the state of Doyle's legal affairs, which I'm sure will proceed swiftly up the scaffold. There is absolutely no chance he could possibly be pardoned!—In the meantime," he said in a gentler tone, "let us also remember he is only one man. A vile and callous man, but just one man, nonetheless. Even if he *should* escape, he is unlikely to take us unawares or appear on our doorstep with a mob."

Quin's face was determined, sure of himself, and his strength gave me strength.

"We cannot live in fear," he said softly, looking at me, echoing the same sentiment I had expressed a few days earlier.

"You're right," I agreed quietly. "It would just be easier…"

"…if Doyle were dead," Kieran finished the statement for me.

Silence descended on us as each of us was preoccupied with our own thoughts.

"How did you hear of Doyle's appeal?" Quin asked after a time.

"Oh," Kieran said, coming out of his reverie. "At the gaol. He must have told someone, or one of the inmates overheard something…before long that was all anybody talked about. The other prisoners would speculate whether he would be pardoned or whether their own convictions might be overturned, wondering jokingly whether the Queen might pay the debt that had seen most of them land in gaol." Kieran snorted. "It was hard not to notice. At first, we thought it was all just for show, that there was no appeal…but then, when Doyle's hanging was postponed…"

"Did you have any contact with him yourself?" Quin asked.

"Little. He was in a different cell, and we were only rarely let out. I avoided him when we were…"

I looked at Kieran, trying to imagine what it must have been like for him being imprisoned, succeeding only too well.

At this moment, Margaret arrived with the tea tray. While she proceeded to lay out cups, saucers and tea pot, I made an effort to obliterate Martin Doyle from my mind.

"Are you alright?" Quin whispered into my ear.

I hadn't heard him come up behind me. I turned, meeting a worried green look, and wanted nothing so much as to feel his strong arms wrapped around me.

"Yes," I said barely audibly.

Quin narrowed his eyes at me but didn't say anything. He lowered his head down to mine until our foreheads were touching and gave my hand a gentle squeeze.

188

Kieran's throat clearing behind us made me take a quick step back and release my grip on Quin's hand, but Quin held on for a moment longer before turning unhurriedly toward his future brother-in-law, his expression daring Kieran to make a comment about our behaviour. He didn't. Instead, he invited Quin and me to sit at the table to discuss the details of the marital contract.

My dowry was to include all my personal belongings currently in my quarters, my parents' fine porcelain dinner set and a few pieces that were of greater sentimental than monetary value, as well as a portion of the farm's earnings from the upcoming harvest and a small number of livestock.

"What about your inheritance?" Quin asked.

"My mother's jewellery," I answered with a pang. Thinking about it always brought back painful memories of my parents' deaths. I hadn't looked at the small box in months. "There are a few pieces of some value, but on the whole, it isn't worth very much. Most of my parents' money went into the farm. And Kieran inherited that, of course."

As I was talking, a strange expression started blooming on Quin's face as he looked at Kieran across from him.

"What is it?" I asked.

Quin was staring intently at Kieran, who was squirming in his chair.

"Kieran?" I tried to look him in the eye but was unable to do so because he was studiously examining the tabletop. I got a sinking feeling when I saw a red hue creeping up his neck.

"What did you do, Kieran?" I demanded.

"Um...I..."

"What did you do?" I repeated, almost yelling.

"I'm sorry Alannah."

I stared at my brother, suddenly wanting to strike him. He must have read the inclination on my face, for he put up his hands in a defensive gesture.

"Please, Alannah, I really am sorry! It was before...before...all of this..."

He spread out his hands, encompassing the events of the past few weeks. I blew out my breath with an unladylike sound and glared at him.

"What did you do?" I asked for the third time, enunciating each word in a menacing tone.

"I... Father had put some money aside for you. But...well...I...I spent it," he said and lowered his head.

"You spent it? You spent my inheritance? Without even telling me I had one? How could you do such a thing?" I was fuming, sputtering with rage.

"How much was it?" Quin asked, laying a restraining hand on my arm.

"Three-hundred pounds," Kieran responded quietly.

"What?" The word barely came out as a whisper.

I was utterly astonished, could barely breathe in my shock.

How had father managed to put aside three-hundred pounds for me? While we lived comfortably enough at Niall, it was a small farm, and once all the expenditures had been subtracted, there was very little income left to save. Even the money father had invested hadn't amounted to much. And we'd spent most of that the year before to buy seeds for our newly tilled fields.

Three-hundred pounds.

If I'd had access to that amount of money while Kieran was trying to control me, I probably would have left, gone to rent a room somewhere, try to make it on my own—to find a family that would hire me as a governess, perhaps. It would have been a hard life, far from the one I'd been born to, but I would have been free, or as free as I could be as a woman. The irony of the times was that as a single woman, anything I owned or money I earned legally belonged to me, whereas if I married, everything would automatically belong to my husband.

My husband.

I looked up at Quin and he gently took my hand as I struggled to control my emotions. I never would have met Quin if I'd left. I closed my eyes and breathed deeply a few times. When I looked back up, I held Kieran's gaze.

"On what did you spend my money?" I asked him in a controlled voice.

"On the cause," he answered quietly.

"You mean the rebellion? You couldn't possibly have thought it would make much of a difference!"

While three-hundred pounds was a potential treasure trove for one lone woman, I didn't think it would go all that far when plotting an uprising against the Crown.

"Not for arms or supplies..." Kieran broke off, looking down and fidgeting with a loose thread on his sleeve.

Quin eyed him askance. "You used it to buy your influence.—Didn't you?"

Kieran clenched his jaws and made a fist with his right hand. "Yes," he hissed.

I gaped at him, dumbfounded. I didn't understand this at all. "But...why?"

"I would imagine it's much like in the British Army," Quin said. "If you wish to be more than a common soldier and have some rank, you have to purchase your commission." There was a sense of resentment in the way he spoke the last three words and I looked at him quizzically. He shrugged and gave me a weak smile.

On the other side of the table, Kieran wasn't smiling at all. Instead, he was fuming, nostrils flaring. I took this behaviour to indicate Quin's assessment had been correct.

"But surely rebels wouldn't be so particular?" I insisted.

"I wouldn't think so either," Quin said. "Was it Martin Doyle who demanded the money?" he asked Kieran suddenly.

Kieran glared at him angrily. "Yes," he admitted through clenched teeth.

"So he had you pay him to keep his company, is that right?"

Kieran's nostrils flared again, and he braced his hands on the tabletop. I held my breath, expecting him to jump up angrily. But instead, he blew out his breath slowly, with an effort that made the muscles in his neck tremble, before removing his hands from the table and folding them across his chest.

"He promised I would be his right-hand man," he said in a strained voice, "that I would lead the rebels alongside him and his accomplices. The money was meant as a show of faith...proof I was serious about joining the rebel ranks. He said it would be used to help him and his fellows infiltrate the Dublin Metropolitan Police...to make sure we didn't end up with another failed uprising like in 1798."

The rebellion of the United Irishmen. The rebels had meant to capture Dublin at the outset but failed because their plans had been thwarted by informants who rallied government forces against them before they'd even assembled.

"And I'd hazard a guess Doyle had no accomplices?" Quin asked with a hint of irony.

"No...at least none that stuck around. There was one when I met him, a man named Thomas, but Doyle..." Kieran compressed his lips briefly and shook his head. I shuddered, remembering what I'd overheard, that Doyle had killed the man because he'd felt he'd betrayed him. "Most of the people we met found Doyle's ideas...too extreme." Kieran paused, giving me a quick glance. "Not that I knew any of this to begin with," he burst out suddenly.

He got up abruptly and started pacing around the room. "I was angry, angry at the world. Father had died, and I was in charge of a farm I knew nothing about...that I didn't know how to run." He shrugged his shoulders uncomfortably before going on. "I felt like a failure. Deep down I knew...I knew it was my own fault...because I'd never shown an interest in the farm before." His voice was filled with sadness and remorse, his eyes hooded with memories as he looked into the distance, seeming to have forgotten Quin and I were there. "I knew...that I should swallow my pride, that I should ask for help...but instead..." He looked up suddenly, his eyes meeting mine, and my throat constricted at all he had kept from me. "I looked for somebody to blame.—You," he said, his face hardening, "for the affection father showered on you instead of me...and then the English." He looked at Quin. "I convinced myself my life would be better if Ireland were free...which wasn't all that difficult, since I'd already felt that way for most of my life."

He stopped pacing and sat back down at the table, slumping in his chair as he exhaled forcefully.

"I started spending more and more time with people who felt the same. They're not that hard to find," he added as an aside to Quin. "That's how I met Doyle. The others...they wanted to bide their time, but Doyle spoke of action. He wanted to make things happen...fast. And I wanted something to believe in, to take my mind off other things..."

He ran a hand tiredly across his face.

"We spent some time with the Ribbonmen, but that was just a bit of fun for Doyle...and he had no time for their secret rituals. He wanted to start a war, to get rid of every last Englishman and Scotsman in Ireland, and he didn't want to wait. He started gathering some men in Dublin, desperate souls who followed him because they had nothing to lose, but most of the others...they said we needed to take our time, plan everything carefully to prevent a repeat of the failed uprising of the United Irishmen, and that we should concentrate on the British military forces, the police and law enforcement. If we had control of those, Ireland would be free.—But Doyle didn't want to waste time scheming and planning, he simply wanted to arm as many Irishmen as possible and he wanted them to murder and pillage, as revenge for the same courtesies done to the Irish over countless years."

"But..." I interrupted him as a thought occurred to me. "What about the list?"

"The list?" Kieran gave me a quizzical look. "Oh"—his features suddenly cleared—"you mean the list of names Andrews produced at the trial?" I nodded. Kieran frowned and shook his head. "I never saw Doyle make a list...in fact, it seems rather out of character." He shrugged. "Maybe Andrews wrote it himself.—It's not as if anyone would question him about where he got it. A nice piece of evidence against Doyle, though." Kieran gave a brief snort. "Making lists and detailed plans isn't really how I would describe Doyle.—Violence as it pleases him is more his approach."

My stomach gave a lurch at Kieran's words, but I tried to ignore it.

"That was all he ever talked about," Kieran went on, "violently removing as many of the English as possible. He insulted and ridiculed anyone who spoke up against him, or worse. When people started turning away from him, he got desperate...he tried to buy his influence with Andrews' money...just like I tried to buy mine with yours."

Kieran sat back in his chair and looked at me, with eyes that seemed to have aged ten years in the past month.

"I told him to wait. Wait and see if Andrews could be trusted before going through with the plan." He emitted a humourless laugh at the irony. "I said he should ask for some of the money before handing you over, but he wouldn't listen, didn't want to wait. He yelled at me, accused me of going against him, told me he wasn't stupid, that he knew what he was doing." Kieran compressed his lips at the memory. "That's how he treated people who tried to reason with him..."

"But..." I started as something suddenly occurred to me, "if Doyle is as unpopular as you say, even in suspect circles...is it likely he has any supporters who would do his dirty work for him?" I swallowed and looked at Quin.

"You mean, is someone other than Doyle himself likely to be a danger to us?" Quin asked with a frown.

I nodded.

"I don't know," Kieran said, and my heart sank. "He didn't seem to have any earnest supporters for his rebellion, at least none with any influence, but...there are those who take pleasure in violence...and Doyle is a violent man, make no mistake! He killed one of his only allies because he thought he was turning against him...and his wasn't the only body Doyle left in his wake..." Kieran shook his head slowly. "The other men who followed him, the ones we were gathering in Dublin, they were desperate, men without food, without work, without families...men who could find no help even at the workhouses. But I doubt any of them felt any particular loyalty toward Doyle, when he couldn't offer them anything but words himself..."

Kieran paused briefly. I glanced at Quin, who was nodding earnestly; clearly, Kieran's portrayal coincided with what Quin himself had deduced about Doyle's band of rebels—broken men whose only hope lay in overturning a government that was letting them starve, but who owed their allegiance to no one, having been abandoned by everyone in the past.

"Then again," Kieran said, making Quin scowl, "Doyle spoke to a lot of people, anyone who would listen—and a good number who wouldn't. He often had rough-looking characters in his company, like the ones he rounded up for the night he..." Kieran's voice tapered off as he looked at me for a moment. "Although none of them seemed to be...allies, exactly, and I don't know if any of them would act on his orders while he's imprisoned. But...I can't say for certain he *doesn't* have associates who would..."

He cut off with a forlorn expression on his face. Quin looked at him angrily from across the table.

"Nobody is going to harm you, Alannah," he growled, staring at Kieran with narrowed eyes, before turning toward me. "Doyle is not going to send anybody after us, and he is not going to come after us himself! And even if he did, I wouldn't let him or any of his thugs anywhere near you! Do you hear me?"

Quin's nostrils were flaring as he tried to suppress his growing rage, the words hissing through his teeth as he tried not to yell. I nodded meekly without saying a word, Quin's eyes locked with mine, urging me to believe him.

"I'm sorry Alannah," Kieran said suddenly, barely audibly, "for getting you into this...and the money."

I looked at Kieran, who sat hunched and dejected in his chair, and my eyes filled with tears. I blinked them away and took a deep breath.

"The money isn't important," I said in a shaky voice. "You are. Both of you." I looked from Kieran to Quin and reached out a hand to each of them as my eyes overflowed. "We can't change the past. But we can work together to make the most of our future."

"WHAT I WANT to know is, who would apply for a royal pardon on Martin Doyle's behalf?" Quin asked, frowning into his whiskey glass.

After the shock of finding out Doyle hadn't yet been hanged and that Kieran had squandered an inheritance I hadn't known existed, we had decided a restorative was in order.

"He can't possibly have been recommended by the courts, not with the crimes he committed," Quin went on, "and there certainly is nothing in his history or his character to suggest he might be deserving of a pardon."

As Quin was talking, I became aware of someone lurking at the door.

It was Finnian the hall boy, evidently deployed by Mrs O'Sullivan to collect the empty tea things. I waved him in politely as Quin gave him a curious look. Finnian seemed rather shocked to see his employers drinking hard liquor in the middle of the morning. Tableware collected, he scuttled off with a wide-eyed glance behind him that almost caused him to trip over his own feet.

I laughed at his antics but sobered up quickly when I was recalled to the topic of conversation.

"From what we've heard, Doyle has no particular allies," Quin was saying, "least of all any who could possibly obtain a royal pardon for him."

"Perhaps it was a desperate family member," I ventured, "and the courts took pity on him and agreed to hear the plea."

Quin looked sceptical. "I doubt even Doyle's own family would describe him as a wholesome man deserving of a second chance." He was quiet for a moment. "Perhaps it's somebody who was paying Doyle to perform personal favours of an unsavoury nature. It must be somebody with some influence, in any case, someone whom the courts would take seriously...seriously enough to hear the appeal at least.—Knowing, of course, that no pardon will be granted even so," he added with narrowed eyes, lest Kieran or I start envisaging Doyle's release. "I wouldn't think somebody like Martin Doyle would have any relatives with such social standing."

"No," Kieran said slowly, "but I don't think the man is just another ordinary criminal, either."

Quin and I turned toward him with curiosity.

Kieran shrugged awkwardly. "He didn't reveal too much about himself, but...there's something in the way he talks and acts...I don't know what it is exactly, but I think he's maybe...a bit higher born than your average felon."

"That would explain why you two got along so well," Quin quipped acerbically.

Kieran narrowed his eyes at Quin and scowled. I put a hand on Kieran's arm and gave Quin a stern look. "Please," I said.

"Hmph," Quin grumbled as Kieran exhaled forcefully out of his nose.

"What you're saying, Kieran, is that you think Doyle may come from a better family and perhaps be better educated than one would assume based on his criminal history?" I looked at Kieran expectantly and he nodded.

"Perhaps I can find out a bit more about him when I travel to Dublin next week," Quin said.

"Oh?" I hadn't heard anything about an impending trip before.

"I do apologise, Alannah," Quin said, looking slightly abashed. "I had forgotten to inform you of my plans. With all the excitement of the last few days…"

His eyes locked with mine as we both recalled the reason for his distraction. I smiled at him, and his face lit up.

"I had intended to travel to Dublin to make the necessary arrangements for my tenants, and for the estate. I really can't delay any longer if I wish to begin the process of seeing them suitably housed and prepare for next season's planting."

I nodded in understanding but felt a moment's qualm at the thought of his absence, when we had only just found each other again.

"You could come with me," he suggested, raising his eyebrows at me.

"I would love to!" I agreed enthusiastically, delighted at the thought, but glanced at Kieran as I suddenly remembered he might have a say in my whereabouts.

"By all means." Kieran waved his hand—without smiling, I noted. "Now if you will excuse me." He got up abruptly, draining the last of his whiskey. "I have some things to attend to."

He bowed briefly to Quin and was gone before either of us had said another word. I looked at Quin quizzically.

"He isn't overly fond of me.—And he hates the fact the promise he made you means he can no longer stop you from seeing me," Quin said, an expression of smugness settling on his features, "or from marrying me."

He leaned across the low table toward me. I followed suit and we ended up nose to nose over the whiskey decanter. His green eyes sparkled as a slow smile spread across his lips. He reached for my left hand and gently ran his thumb over my ring finger.

196

"Soon," he said, and his expression changed to one that made my heart start pounding in my chest.

He leaned in closer and kissed me, slowly, while gently caressing the nape of my neck. When we finally broke apart, I felt breathless. Quin grinned at me, and I grinned back, trying to ignore the distracting scenes my mind was imagining for me. I felt a blush creep into my cheeks and Quin chuckled.

"Soon," he said again in an entirely different tone of voice, his eyes smouldering, and kissed the back of my hand, his soft lips lingering on my sensitive skin.

Completely flustered, I took a restorative gulp of whiskey, which I didn't usually drink. The amber liquid burned up the back of my throat and into my nose, and I gasped for air. Quin looked at me with amusement, his eyes crinkled into triangles as he tried not to laugh.

"Um..." I croaked after a moment, trying to regain my dignity, "speaking of marriage..."

"Yes? You're not having second thoughts, are you?" He raised an eyebrow at me, and I shook my head.

"No! Not at all! I just wondered...whether you had decided where we would live...after the wedding."

A frown appeared between Quin's brows as his smile disappeared, and I was sorry I had brought up the topic.

"I haven't," he admitted with a sigh.

He took both of my hands in his and looked at me intently.

"If I thought for even a moment staying here would place you in danger, I would ship you off to England in a heartbeat. But I believe you are safe. Safe from Doyle and any associates he might have. He *will* hang, Alannah, I'm sure of it." His eyes displayed the conviction he felt. "But Doyle isn't the only consideration..." He shook his head. "I don't know what Andrews' intentions might be.—I doubt he means you any harm, but he could be a nuisance at the very least. But should that deter us from staying here? Should we forego the opportunity to build a life for ourselves here, just because there is a small chance somebody might come along to ruin it?"

He shrugged. "In some ways, it would be easier to live in England. We would be well off, could be part of society, entertaining the lords and ladies of the upper classes. There would be no farm work to worry about, no tenants to take care of, no labour disputes to deal with. You wouldn't need to worry about a thing!—But would you be happy?"

His eyes searched mine and he gently stroked my cheek.

"More than anything, I want you to be happy," he said softly. "I came to Glaslearg to set the estate on the right course. When I saw the state of the tenants, I vowed to see them taken care of. And I meant it. But if I have to rely on a steward to do it for me, then so be it. Alannah"—he pulled me closer to him—"*you* are what matters to me most now, your safety and your happiness. Everything else is trivial. And so, I shall let you choose. And follow as you command."

I gaped at him, not sure whether I had heard him correctly.

I hadn't been able to do a thing of value over the past two years, had felt utterly at the mercy of somebody else's choices, and here he was letting me decide where we would live. And not just where we would live. For the choice I made would also determine the kind of life we would live, whether we would be draped in finery and mingle with aristocrats or be covered in the sweat of our labours as we oversaw the running of a farm—and nurtured the people on it.

I looked out the window at the green hills that had greeted me every morning of my life, and back to the man in front of me, who sat patiently awaiting my decision, knowing he would abide by my wishes without complaint. My heart thumped heavily with the magnitude of the choice in front me, even as it burst with joy at the knowledge Quin would be by my side no matter what choice I made.

I closed my eyes briefly and said a quick prayer. When I opened them, Quin was looking at me expectantly, his eyes radiating the trust he had in me to decide on our future. I took a deep breath and gripped his hands tightly.

"We'll stay."

18.

QUIN WANDERED DOWN Capel Street toward the river Liffey, taking in the sights and sounds of the city, enjoying his brief return to metropolitan living. While life on a farm in rural Ireland had thus far proved not to be the slightest bit boring, he had at times felt rather isolated, as if he'd been cut off from the rest of the world. Then again, he'd never felt as connected to anyone as he did to Alannah and was looking forward to spending time in isolation with her.

He grinned at the thought, making an elderly gentleman give him a suspicious look. Quin lifted his hat and bowed to him, and the man's expression took on a note of surprise as he hobbled off. Quin laughed, looking after the man's receding form, the morning's success bolstering his mood.

They had arrived in Dublin the evening before, and Quin had wasted no time getting to work. After a quick visit to the bank that morning, Quin had set off to enquire about buying seeds and building materials, thinking it likely he would have to spend several hours wandering the city to find what he needed. But he had been in luck. One thing to be said about city living was that it came with a degree of convenience. While Dublin wasn't nearly as large as London, it nevertheless provided an abundance of services, if one knew where to look.

He hadn't known exactly where to look, but had headed toward the Corn Exchange, thinking this a good place to start his expedition. This had proved to be the correct course of action as, within moments of his arrival, he'd stumbled across a farmer dealing in precisely what he was looking to buy. The farmer's eyes had bulged when Quin had told him the quantity of seed he wanted to buy, but he'd been more than happy to accept Quin's coin in return. It wasn't nearly enough to plant all the available land on Glaslearg, but it was enough to begin with.

With luck, come next year's harvest season, the crop would yield enough bounty to feed the estate's inhabitants and allow for some sale, as well as provide the seeds necessary for the following season's planting. After that, Quin hoped it would become a self-sustaining enterprise that would pay off handsomely over the next few years, as the produce joined much of Ireland's harvest on its way to the profitable markets of England.

An acquaintance of Quin's father had once called Ireland the granary of Britain—and with good reason. Quin had heard it estimated that the food exported from Ireland each year was sufficient to feed approximately two million Britons. Although grain was the largest export commodity, Ireland also dealt in the trade of other foodstuffs, as well as livestock, textiles and several other diverse products.

With matters on the estate as they were, Quin had decided to focus most of his efforts on the export of crops, as he hoped he could make a reasonable profit within a season's planting by using land that had stood vacant for the past two years or more. Although dairy farming or the trade in livestock was likely to be more profitable in the long run, it would take longer to bear fruit and required a greater capital outlay to begin with, as animals first needed to be purchased and then raised for eventual use.

Quin had a decent bit of money at his immediate disposal, but buying seeds was already expensive enough, especially considering he would also need a good amount of capital to ensure the tenants were suitably housed.

With the latter task in mind, Quin had left Rupert in charge of arranging the transport of the seeds to the inn. His valet had puffed up at the importance of the job bestowed upon him, making Quin smile. He'd taken Rupert along on the trip to run such errands for him, and Rupert was taking the addition to his usual job description very seriously.

"I shan't disappoint you, sir," he'd said breathlessly, cheeks flushed with excitement as Quin bade him farewell.

Quin had tried hard not to laugh at Rupert's serious expression, instead enquiring if he was sure he knew how to get back to the inn from the Corn Exchange. Rupert had nodded vigorously, promising he would see the seeds safely at the inn before his own return, and Quin had turned his attention to the remaining tasks on his agenda.

He'd been tempted to enquire at the Brick and Tile factory about purchasing bricks for the tenants' houses, being of the opinion that a proper house ought to be built with bricks. He knew, though, this wasn't a feasible option for the large number of cabins he intended to see built, as it would be far too expensive, even if he were to turn to the smaller brickworks closer to the estate. Alannah had confirmed his reluctantly reached conclusion that a far easier, much more common and exceedingly less expensive option would be to use rubble stone from the surrounding countryside or a local quarry for the building, instead of bricks. She'd smiled in amusement that Quin had even thought of using anything else, commenting that he'd been thinking like a gentleman, not a farmer. Feeling rather sheepish at her bruising—yet accurate—assessment, he had however also been exceedingly relieved he wouldn't be obliged to transport several tons of bricks halfway across the island.

Dublin was situated some ninety miles from Glaslearg, and it had taken them almost three days to get there with their large wagon. Quin had nevertheless wanted to travel to Dublin rather than Belfast, which was closer by almost forty miles, in part because Dublin was about three times larger and he thought it more likely he'd be able to obtain all the necessary supplies there, not to mention that he needed to withdraw some of the money he'd deposited with the Bank of Ireland in Dublin upon his arrival two months before.

But the main reason for his decision was the presence in Dublin of several troops of the British Army, which happened to include some acquaintances from his time at officers' training. It was these acquaintances that had spurred him on to travelling to Glaslearg via Dublin in the first place, rather than taking the shorter route from Belfast, and it was these same acquaintances who'd made him want to travel to Dublin again this time around—a choice he was grateful for now as he hoped they would be of assistance in finding out more about Martin Doyle.

Thoughts of Doyle had occupied his mind since the day he'd learned the man hadn't yet dangled from the end of a rope.

Quin had assured Alannah he no longer posed a danger to them—and he still believed this to be true—but he would sleep better once the man was dead. Callous though the thought was, he knew it to be the truth. At times, the memory of the bruises Doyle had inflicted on Alannah were so vivid in his mind he wanted to march up to Omagh gaol and carry out the sentence himself, with his bare hands. This not being a socially acceptable option, though, he wanted to find out as much as possible about the man, including the ludicrous attempt by someone of his acquaintance to obtain a royal pardon for his crimes, just in case such information might be necessary in the future. He was quite sure the application would be summarily dismissed, but he was of the opinion that it never hurt to be prepared.

Thus preoccupied with his thoughts, he'd made his way from the Corn Exchange down to Grafton Street and then up to Capel Street, searching the shops for any that might stock the remaining supplies he needed. Amidst the booksellers, hosiers, goldsmiths and vintners beckoning passing customers, he'd come across a small smithy, worked by a burly young man dressed in shirtsleeves and drenched in sweat in the steamy confines of his forge. Quin had watched in fascination as the man swung a meaty arm, bringing it down forcefully on a red-hot piece of metal he held on top of a bruised and battered-looking anvil. Through repeated administration of the same treatment, the smith had forced the metal to bend to his will, finally emerging with a serviceable-looking ploughshare, which he'd immersed in the slack tub with a steamy hiss. Looking up, he'd seen Quin watching him and invited him in to inspect his wares.

Half an hour later, Quin had emerged from the shop, having commissioned the blacksmith to produce two sacks of nails, ten ploughshares and an assortment of hammers, spades, scythes and similar equipment for a fair price indeed. Feeling almost like he was taking advantage of the man, Quin had promised to pay a good bit extra if he could have the wares ready within the next two days. The smith's eyes had bulged slightly at this deadline, but he'd declared himself willing and able to meet his customer's demands. Quin had bowed formally and gone on his way, searching the bustling streets for the last few odds and ends he still required.

Thinking the day a roaring triumph, Quin now cheerfully made his way back across Essex Bridge toward the inn, where he'd arranged to meet Alannah and Margaret for afternoon tea. A glance at his pocket watch indicated he still had ample time to return and so he stopped for a moment halfway across the bridge, leaning against the railing. He looked down at the dark water of the Liffey as it swirled beneath him, hurtling inexorably on in its rush toward Dublin harbour, where it spilled into the Irish Sea. His eyes followed the course of the water to the opposite shore before travelling back upstream, until he was looking across to the other side of the bridge, where the tall buildings of Parliament Street rose on either side of the wide thoroughfare—a product of The Wide Streets Commission of 1757.

Officially known as the Commissioners for making Wide and Convenient Ways, Streets and Passages, the commission had been established by parliament with the aim of reshaping medieval Dublin to make it more spacious and elegant. One of the commissioners' first acts had been to widen the heavily trafficked bridge Quin currently stood on, followed by the demolition or widening of old streets and the building of new ones.

"There's some merit to the practice," Quin said to himself as he looked across at the white columns of the Royal Exchange, which was clearly visible in the open space provided by the generous width of the street leading up to it.

Quin enjoyed the vista for a moment longer as a few rays of sunshine broke through the clouds that had been his sporadic companions over the course of the day. He smiled at the sight. Ireland's weather never quite seemed able to make up its mind, vacillating continuously between sunshine and rain, with periods of dry cloud cover filling in the gaps. An entire day spent in any one climatic condition was a very rare event indeed.

Quin laughed at the thought before continuing on his way.

He ambled slowly through the city toward the inn, a spring in his step at the day's success and the prospect of his impending wedding. He had a moment's pause as he considered there might be some in London who would object to his intended nuptials but recovered his good humour when he reminded himself these individuals were not, in fact, around to voice any such objections, even if he would have paid any attention to them in the first place. He was determined to have Alannah as his wife, and he wasn't about to let anyone or anything get in his way. The thought that it was only a matter of days until he could call her his own made his heart soar with joy and he hurried on, filled with a sudden and urgent desire to be in her presence.

When he got to the inn, the taproom was empty, except for a few drunkards lounging at one of the rear tables, looking blearily at him with bloodshot eyes, a whiff of beer fumes wafting in his direction. He nodded toward them, getting a few grunts in return, before heading up the staircase that led up to his room. He paused at his door, looking toward Alannah and Margaret's apartment, which adjoined his own, imagining sharing a room with Alannah on future trips—without her maid.

While a lady might be accustomed to traveling with her maid, Margaret was actually a housemaid, rather than a lady's maid, although she did provide such services for her mistress. Alannah had brought Margaret along to Dublin because she'd been concerned it would be unseemly for her to travel with him unaccompanied, they not being married yet—or so she'd led him to believe. He rather doubted Alannah believed any such thing or that she was the slightest bit affected by any gossip her behaviour might provoke—the thought hadn't bothered her before, after all. Instead, he was quite sure she'd insisted on Margaret's presence to avoid being alone with him, for fear the delights of their wedding night might be prematurely explored. He grinned at the thought, his vanity thoroughly delighted at the effect he seemed to be having on her. Of course, she was having exactly the same effect on him and in some ways, he was glad she'd insisted on her chaperone. It had taken all of his restraint to keep his hands off her thus far. It would be almost impossible to do so now, were they to find themselves alone together in a private room with a convenient horizontal surface…

"Are you quite alright, sir?"

"What?" Quin spun back toward his door, where Rupert had appeared, his head protruding into the corridor like a turtle emerging from its shell.

"I heard your footsteps approaching, sir, and expected you to come right in. But, well, you were just standing there, staring…with a strange look in your eyes, like you were about to devour a prime slice of the roast beef…"

"Ah, yes, I'm quite alright, thank you, Rupert," Quin stammered and cleared his throat. "I am rather hungry, though, as you surmised…" Not for roast beef, but still. "Perhaps you would be kind enough to assist me with my wardrobe, so I might freshen up before I join Miss O'Neill for a bite?" Or a gentle nibble on her earlobe if he had his way. He looked expectantly at his valet, trying to suppress such diverting thoughts.

"Yes, sir. Of course, sir," Rupert said eagerly, opening the door wide to let Quin into the room. "I've already laid your clothes out for you, sir. We'll have you ready in no time."

"I take it you had no difficulty with the seeds then?"

"Oh no, sir. I told you I wouldn't disappoint you, and I haven't now, have I?" There was a note of nervousness in Rupert's tone, and he looked anxiously up at Quin.

"No, Rupert, you've done exceedingly well." Quin smiled, glad to have found something to distract his overly lewd mind. "I can't thank you enough for your assistance in this endeavour, which will be of the utmost benefit to the tenants of Glaslearg, and to me forbye."

Quin inclined his head toward Rupert in a gesture that made his valet puff up with pride, his cheeks flushed and eyes bright with delight at his master's approval. Quin managed not to laugh, only giving Rupert a wide smile.

The young man had been with him for about eight months now, and Quin had gotten rather fond of him.

With Rupert's assistance, Quin was suitably dressed and combed within a few minutes, and he made his way back downstairs to the taproom. A few more patrons had arrived in his absence, but Alannah not being among them, Quin found a table in a quiet corner and sat down. He didn't have to wait long until Alannah appeared, walking into the inn from the street with Margaret, the two of them laughing and deeply engrossed in what appeared to be an utterly enthralling conversation.

Quin stood up, catching Alannah's eye. A blush broke out on her cheeks at the sight of him, but she made her way toward him as Margaret continued on upstairs, carrying several neatly wrapped parcels.

"Mr Williams," Alannah said when she reached him, her blue eyes sparkling with amusement at the formality demanded by public discourse.

"Miss O'Neill." Quin kissed the hand she offered and broke into a huge grin.

They sat down, and Quin ordered some refreshment. Although they were technically meeting for tea, the inn in which they found themselves wasn't known for its gentle tea-time infusions, being better versed in the sale of something far more fundamental, namely, beer. When the barmaid brought their drinks, Alannah sipped demurely at her small ale while Quin eyed his Guinness extra stout with approval. Inky black in colour with a thick layer of light foam, the aroma of deep roasted malt that rose from the glass made his mouth water. With a sense of reverence, he lifted the vessel to his mouth and tilted it gently, making the creamy foam float over his lips, accompanying the smooth flavour of the beer as it flowed into his mouth, leaving a rich smoky flavour on his tongue.

"Good, is it?"

He opened his eyes to see Alannah looking at him in amusement.

"Quite," he said, feeling a little sheepish.

"I would have thought you would have tasted Guinness beer in London." She raised a sleek black eyebrow enquiringly.

"I have, but some time ago.—A London gentleman is expected to drink fine wine, port and sherry, with perhaps a bit of brandy thrown in for variety, but certainly not a working-class drink such as stout!" He shook his head in mock outrage at the thought, making Alannah laugh. "I drank a fair bit of beer with the army, but I haven't had anything quite like this for years."

He took another healthy swallow, savouring the subtle sweetness that mingled harmoniously with the bitter tang of the hops.

"When I arrived in Dublin a few months ago, I sampled only the wine."

"Was it only a few months ago?" Alannah looked stunned at the thought.

"Barely two, actually," he said softly.

Their eyes met, and he could see his own thoughts reflected in her eyes, as she contemplated everything that had happened since then.

"Um...were you successful in your endeavours today?"

"Yes, very," Quin said, glad of the change of topic. "I was fortunate enough to find a farmer selling seeds for winter wheat and winter oats that are to be sown in the autumn. I thought it best to purchase these instead of the traditional variety, as the seeds won't have to be stored very long before their use, so there will be less chance of spoilage. I've also ordered a number of farm supplies, as well as materials for the building of the tenants' houses.—All in all, I would venture to say the trip has been highly successful thus far." He leaned back with an air of satisfaction, his arms loosely draped across his midsection. "And I expect it to only get better. I shall visit a glass factory tomorrow to enquire about windows. Every house should have at least one window!" he declared, making the corners of Alannah's mouth turn up in amusement.

"And have you decided how to go about building all those cottages?"

He wrinkled his brow in thought. "Well, as much as I would like to be able to build all of them before the end of the season, that likely won't be feasible...not least of all because I won't be able to procure the necessary materials for so many in such a short time. However," he added, brightening up, "I shall endeavour to have a good number built by the winter and I've thought of a way to do so.—I would imagine the tenants themselves would be fairly eager to have the building completed as soon as possible. Many of the men will be working outside of Glaslearg, though, trying to earn some money before their potato crop is ready for the harvest. So I have the choice of hiring external labourers to do the building for me or I could pay the tenants to return to Glaslearg, thereby ensuring they don't lose any earnings they might have made elsewhere."

Alannah looked at him for a moment before breaking into a broad smile. "You mean, you're going to pay the tenants to build their own cottages?"

"I suppose I am," Quin admitted. "Although I shall also require them to prepare the farm's fields for the autumn planting and assist in the harvesting of what little produce is currently growing on Glaslearg.—It's rather an archaic custom to have one's tenants working one's own fields, but with the small plots they're renting, they have to supplement their earnings anyway." He shook his head with regret. "I shall not force any of them to assist me or threaten them with eviction if they don't, nor shall I allow them to neglect their own crops. But, I hope, by providing them with a monetary incentive, they can be persuaded to assist me if we come up with a reasonable strategy." He shrugged. "If they don't, I shall have to hire labourers to do the work."

"Regarding the cottages," he continued, "I shall propose that the tenants work together in groups of five families, with the men of each group joining forces to build one cottage after the other until all five families are suitably housed. I hope this will speed up the process, as the tenants assist one another, but I hope also that the completed cottages will be able to house those families through the winter whose homes are not yet complete, should their existing huts be uninhabitable."

"That sounds like a good idea. And there's some time yet before the potato crops need to be harvested, so you should have several cottages standing before the cold sets in."

"Indeed." He smiled at the excitement she seemed to be feeling about his plan.

She smiled back at him, and their eyes met. He held her gaze for a long moment, his smile gradually being replaced with a look that no doubt portrayed the more visceral emotion he was beginning to feel. She blushed and looked down.

"Are you not missing the person of your maid, Miss O'Neill?"

"Um…" Alannah cleared her throat and lifted her eyes, looking at him boldly. His grin widened. "Yes, I am, as a matter of fact," she said, feigning dismay as the colour slowly faded from her cheeks. "I wonder what's keeping Margaret. She had meant only to take our purchases to our room and come right back down. Perhaps I should go check on her."

"Well if it isn't Lieutenant Quinton Fletcher."

Quin and Alannah turned as one toward the booming voice that had come from the doorway, where a large barrel-chested man in the red uniform of the British Army was making his beaming way through the growing throng of dinner-time customers, most of whom looked utterly bewildered by the deafening apparition.

"Archie, you old bastard." Quin got up from his chair and extended his hand toward the dark-haired man, who ignored the proffered appendage and pulled Quin into an embrace instead, thumping him on the back in apparent delight.

"Ham and Ollie said you'd arrived in Ireland, but I didn't think I'd see you for a while yet, being stuck on some farm in the middle of nowhere as you are."

Archie looked away from Quin and glanced at the table where Alannah still sat. His head snapped back toward her an instant later and his eyes went round as he took in her appearance, a look of approval appearing on his blunt features.

"And who's this beauty, then?" he asked Quin with a nudge in the ribs. "The lovely Miss Sarah, I presume?"

"Ah...no," Quin responded in a slightly strained voice, avoiding Alannah's questioning gaze. He quickly recovered, though, straightening up to his full height and lifting his chin. "Lieutenant Archibald Bellinger, might I present Miss Alannah O'Neill...my betrothed."

He bowed toward the lieutenant, who looked momentarily startled. After a brief pause, Archie smiled and bowed in Alannah's direction.

"I am delighted to make your acquaintance, Miss O'Neill."

"Won't you join us?" Quin offered, risking a quick glance at Alannah, who was smiling pleasantly enough but looked as if she was deep in thought. "It's quite fortunate you happened upon me here," he said as Archie took a chair from a neighbouring table and sat down. "I had meant to come past the barracks in the morning to arrange an opportunity to speak with you and the others, but now you've saved me the trip."

His friend waved over the barmaid and instructed her to bring him beer in the largest vessel she could find. Apparently, Quin wasn't the only nobleman who enjoyed the odd foray into less genteel beverages.

"The lads will be happy to see you. And to have me join in the celebrations to boot," Archie said, winking at Alannah.

"Archie was in England when I came to Dublin the last time," Quin explained. "By all accounts, he made a quick exit the moment he heard I was coming."

Archie laughed. "I would have, if you'd given us any warning." He turned toward Alannah, who was smiling at the exchange. "As it happened, news of Quin's plans arrived about two days before he did, by which time I was already on my way.—Our ships must have passed each other on the sea."

The two men continued their banter until the barmaid arrived, bearing what looked more like a vase than a beer mug, the sight of which made Archie break into a huge grin.

"There are times," he informed Quin and Alannah, lifting the pitcher in both meaty hands, "when sipping demurely at a glass of wine is entirely satisfactory. And there are times"—he lifted the mug to his mouth—"when something a bit more substantial is necessary."

The glass rim met his lips and the beer flowed down his throat, received in great gulps that seemed to find no end, until finally, Archie lifted his head in an explosion of breath and set the mug on the table with a loud thump—the level of the contents substantially reduced.

"Ah, that's better," he said with a look of contentment, leaning back in his chair.

Alannah laughed, and Quin joined in, laughing as much at Archie's antics as the joy he felt in seeing Alannah happy. He caught her eye, and she gave him a warm smile.

"You must tell me about this farm of yours," Archie said, making Quin tear his eyes away from Alannah to look at his friend. "And why in God's name you chose to come here in the first place. Um...meaning no offense, ma'am." He threw Alannah an apologetic look as he seemed to realise someone named O'Neill was likely to be Irish.

"No offense taken," Alannah responded in her soft Irish lilt, making Archie's ears turn pink. "But if you will excuse me, gentlemen, I believe I shall retire. It has been a long day, after a long trip to get here."

She rose from her chair and both Quin and Archie got up from theirs to see her off.

"Mr Williams, Lieutenant Bellinger, I wish you a pleasant evening."

"Miss O'Neill," Quin and Archie said in unison, bowing as Alannah made her way across the busy taproom and up the stairs to her room. When she reached the landing at the top she looked back down at their table and smiled at Quin, before disappearing down the corridor.

"You've got it bad."

Archie's mocking voice broke in on Quin's dreamy thoughts as he continued to stare at the spot where Alannah had disappeared.

Quin laughed and sat down, waving to the barmaid as she made her rounds. It was early evening by now and he was getting hungry. "You're right."

"She *is* one fine looking woman." Archie nodded his head in approval. "But an Irishwoman? And one you barely know?"

Quin looked at Archie and narrowed his eyes.

Archie was a tall man, about as tall as Quin himself, but much wider in proportions, with burly shoulders and fists as large as hams. His imposing physical presence wasn't the most disconcerting thing about him, though— instead, it was his brutal honesty. Archie said and asked what everybody else wanted to but was too polite to voice. Having grown up in circles where polite— and often meaningless—conversation was the order of the day, with harsh gossip conducted behind closed doors, Quin had found Archie's candid approach refreshing and had liked the man immediately.

That didn't mean it wasn't uncomfortable in his presence at times, though.

"Yes." He let the depth of his feelings for Alannah permeate the single word. "I love her."

Archie raised his eyebrows and Quin braced himself for an onslaught of further disconcerting questions, but Archie surprised him by asking one he hadn't expected.

"How do you know?"

"I just know," Quin said, a smile appearing on his lips as he remembered his mother giving him the same unsatisfactory answer when he'd asked her the same question as a boy.

Archie scowled at him, and Quin laughed.

"It's true. From the moment I saw her I felt drawn to her. And the more time I spent with her, the more I realised I wanted her in my life, no matter what obstacles might lie ahead."

"Obstacles such as those you left behind in London?"

Quin shrugged. "What my father might think doesn't bother me much, seeing as nothing I do is ever good enough for him anyway. As for the other..."

He waved his hand in dismissal as the barmaid arrived with their food.

The delectable smell of beef stew and freshly baked bread made Quin's mouth water, and he tucked into his generous portion with enthusiasm, savouring the rich flavour of the tender meat nestled between cubes of potato, carrot and turnip. The two men ate in silence for a few minutes, concentrating on their plates. Quin used a thick slice of bread to mop up the rest of his sauce, before sitting back with a sigh of contentment echoed by Archie across from him.

"Speaking of obstacles," Quin said, leaning forward on the table and looking at his friend with a serious expression. "There is something you could help me with."

"Of course." Archie straightened up and looked at him expectantly.

In as few words as possible, Quin explained his desire to find out as much as possible about Martin Doyle, describing the man's character and how he'd come into their lives, assaulting Alannah and threatening him, and outlining the events surrounding Doyle's capture. Archie's eyes grew wide as Quin explained how Doyle had come within a hair's breadth of shooting Alannah during the night of his arrest and how the events of that night had almost destroyed the possibility of a joint future for them.

"So you see, as long as he lives, Doyle is a threat…if not directly to Alannah or me, then certainly to our happiness. She's afraid of him…understandably so. Afraid he might harm me or herself…or perhaps her brother. That fear very nearly made her turn away from me and I won't have it come between us again!"

Archie looked at Quin for a long moment as he visibly sought to process everything he'd just heard.

"Martin Doyle," he said finally, scratching his chin thoughtfully. "Come to think of it, I've read about him…his arrest and his sordid history. It was in The Freeman's Journal a few weeks ago, only a brief article, with much said about him being convicted of treason and murder, but no mention of the details of his arrest…and certainly no mention of your name!"

"That's one good thing at least."

"You think if somebody knew about your involvement, they'd take revenge on you for Doyle?"

"No!" Quin objected firmly. "I believe no such thing! From everything I've heard about the man and the impression he left upon me during our brief and unsolicited acquaintance, I'm convinced Doyle prefers to work alone. He fancies

211

himself as a leader of men, as someone who could rouse rebels to the quest of liberating Ireland…and yet, he has achieved nothing of the kind, with the few men who responded to his call having dispersed as speedily as they arrived. He trusts no one, alienates those who might follow him by trying to force them to accept his irrational views, and insulting and threatening them if they don't, or worse. He picks up scoundrels to do his dirty work for him when he thinks it's necessary, but when something's important to him, he sees to it himself.—I highly doubt he has any loyal supporters who might lie in wait for me or Alannah to exact revenge on his behalf." Quin shook his head slowly back and forth. "If he wanted me killed for the role I played in his arrest—and I would imagine he does—he would want to do it himself. I'm sure of it. Still," he added with a frown, "I don't want to be widely known as the Englishman who sent an Irishman to the gallows, no matter what he might have done. The English are unpopular enough as it is."

"But you think he might escape?"

"I find it highly probable that he's trying to. He can't possibly think he has a chance of being pardoned, not after being found guilty of treason as well as murder, no matter who might be appealing on his behalf! But now he has more time. Time he's unlikely to spend peaceably awaiting his execution."

Archie grunted in amusement. "And you'd prefer the execution to be carried out sooner rather than later." It wasn't a question.

"Yes," Quin agreed coldly, daring Archie to object.

He didn't.

"I understand," he said instead, leaning his chin on his steepled hands. "I would feel the same. Scum who threatened me and mine…even a short life would be too long." He lifted his head and looked Quin in the eye. "I'll see what I can find out. I have some acquaintances at the Dublin Metropolitan Police who might know a few things. Ham and Ollie will help, of course." He grinned. "It'll give them something to do…keep them out of trouble."

Quin grinned back at him, bolstered by the knowledge he had friends he could count on, even when he was far from home.

"It does explain a lot," Archie continued before Quin had a chance to respond. "About you and Miss O'Neill," he elaborated when he saw Quin's curious look. "When I saw you together, I thought you must have known each other for years. Hence my comment about…" He shrugged his shoulders apologetically and Quin shook his head in dismissal. "I suppose going through something like that would bring people closer together."

"Or tear them apart," Quin said cynically, "as it very nearly did." He exhaled strongly through his nose as the fury he'd felt at the time resurfaced. "I won't let that happen again. I promised her I would keep her safe. And I shall! It will be all the easier if Martin Doyle is locked up—or better yet, dead—but if he isn't, I need to keep one step ahead of him to make sure he doesn't harm us before he meets his well-deserved fate."

"I'll find out what I can, Quin," Archie promised. "I doubt you have anything to worry about. He's unlikely to be pardoned and it's not as easy to break out of gaol as it once was. But I'll look into his background and enquire about his appeal. With any luck, it's already been overturned, and he'll be meeting the hangman's noose any day now."

"I hope so," Quin grumbled, wishing for the umpteenth time he could personally deliver Doyle's sentence, preferably upon the instant.

"Chin up, Quinton," Archie said, sounding irritatingly cheerful. "The man will be dead before you know it. Then you and the lovely Miss O'Neill can run naked through the green hills of this depressing nation without a care in the world."

He broke into a wide grin and Quin could feel a smile forming on his own lips in response.

"It's not as bad as you make it sound."

"Wait until you've been here for longer than two months.—Then again," Archie added, his eyes taking on a glazed look, "I don't have a beautiful black-haired maiden to keep me company at night."

Quin laughed as Archie got up and collected his hat.

"It's been a pleasure, Quinton Fletcher, as always." Archie bowed formally to Quin, who had risen from his seat. "We shall see each other tomorrow or the day after. I'll speak to Ham and Ollie and send word."

"Thanks, Archie."

"I haven't done anything yet." Archie winked, before making his way out of the inn through the boiling mass of dinner guests, who were enjoying the excellent food—and copious quantities of drink—on offer at the establishment.

Quin watched his departure before fighting his own way through the crowd and up to his room. This he found to be empty, Rupert evidently having gone in search of his own supper, leaving Quin to enjoy the relative quiet behind the closed door, the noise of the taproom reduced to a low buzz in the background. It was too early for bed, but Quin was happy to recline on the lounge chair to think about the day's events.

He was content with the progress he'd made, both for the upkeep of the estate and the welfare of its inhabitants, but beyond this, he was relieved he would soon have some answers about Martin Doyle. Answers he hoped he wouldn't need, but that he wanted, nonetheless. Although the logical part of his mind was telling him the man was as good as dead, he had a nagging feeling things were not quite settled between them, despite Doyle's sentence. And until the sentence had been carried out, Quin wanted to be prepared.

He would not let Alannah come to harm again.

I COULDN'T SLEEP.

I had enjoyed strolling through Dublin with Margaret during the day, perusing the shop windows and marvelling at the sheer quantity and diversity of goods for sale—and the number of people that bustled along the busy streets. With great excitement, I had purchased a few small items for my upcoming nuptials, thrilled at the thought that I would soon be Quin's wife, giggling with Margaret in delight.

But when I'd gone to bed and closed my eyes, my mind had not let me sleep.

I knew Quin wanted to ask his friends from the army for assistance in obtaining information about Martin Doyle. So he could be prepared, he'd said. Prepared for what, I didn't know. Beyond learning his fate was sealed, I never wanted to hear the name of Martin Doyle again for as long as I lived. The whole situation was making me feel uneasy.

The man has been condemned to death, I thought angrily, surely he is no longer a danger to us.

And yet, someone who knew him was appealing his verdict, presumably hoping Doyle could escape his sentence—or perhaps give him time to escape his cell.

When I thought about it in broad daylight, the idea of the verdict being overturned—or Doyle orchestrating an escape—seemed ludicrous, but in the dark hours of the night, when I lay alone in my bed, the fear I'd felt in Doyle's presence sometimes came creeping back, snaking its long, suffocating tendrils around my heart so it started pounding in panic at the thought of having to face him again. And in those moments, at the back of my mind, I could hear his threatening voice telling me he didn't work alone. Quin was sure it had been just an empty threat, but I still had my doubts, as much as I tried to suppress them. Especially now we knew someone had applied for a royal pardon on Doyle's behalf.

Who was this person and what were his motives for trying to help the man? And would this unknown acquaintance be a danger to us himself?

I needed to get up, I decided.

I threw back the covers and tiptoed across the room, past Margaret's sleeping form to the chair where I'd left my robe. I slipped the light fabric over my shift and carefully opened the door, stepping out into the darkness of the corridor. While the staircase landing was visible from the taproom—from which the occasional sound of clinking glasses could be heard, signifying the presence of a few remaining patrons—the rest of the passage was hidden from view. There was a small window at the end of the corridor, and I opened this to admit a blast of cool night air, sighing in relief. I leaned against the wall, letting the cool breeze wash over my face, feeling my lingering worries disappear—these being replaced with startling speed with diverting thoughts of my future husband.

I closed my eyes, imagining Quin's strong arms around me, almost giddy at the thought that we would be married in a few days' time. This line of thought led me straight to the contemplation of our wedding night, to the point I was so distracted I didn't hear the door opening further down the corridor. The footsteps that followed stopped abruptly as the visitor saw me standing at the end of the passage.

"Alannah?"

"Quin?" I felt blood rush into my cheeks as I encountered the object of my recent entertaining thoughts.

"I didn't mean to disturb you." He made as if to turn away.

"No, don't go," I said. "I couldn't sleep."

"Neither could I." His teeth flashed in the moonlight as he smiled.

He came slowly toward me, his eyes holding mine. I swallowed, my heart pounding. He stopped in front of me, and I could see he was still wearing the trousers and shirt he'd worn in the afternoon. Evidently, he hadn't even gone to bed.

"Are you alright?" I asked, looking up at him.

"Never better," he assured me as his eyes took on a calculating look.

Quite suddenly, he bent down and kissed me, pressing me against the wall so the lengths of our bodies met. I gasped but returned the kiss ardently as his hands roamed over me, caressing me through the thin layers of fabric that separated us, making me weak at the knees. With one hand, he gently stroked the side of my breast, then skimmed down to my hip and thigh, and lifted my leg to pull me closer, making it obvious he wanted more. His other hand caressed the nape of my neck, holding me locked in his embrace with far more than the power of his two hands. He moved his mouth away from mine and kissed along the side of my neck, making me tremble and my breath come short. When he finally pulled away from me, he was panting and had a slightly wild look in his eyes.

"This," I whispered, breathing heavily myself, "is precisely why I can't be left alone with you.—Argh." I clapped my hands over my mouth as I realised I had spoken aloud.

Quin chuckled. "You have a point, Miss O'Neill. I can't seem to keep my hands off you."

"I don't want you to." I reached tentatively toward him, gently stroking his chest, making him shiver.

"Unfortunately—or perhaps fortunately, for your virtue at least," he said, taking hold of my hands, "there is no convenient, unoccupied room in the near vicinity...and I'm not about to consummate our future wedding vows on the bare floorboards of this corridor, for all bystanders to see." He gently kissed the palms of my hands and stroked my cheek. "As much as I might be tempted," he added with a wry grin.

"Ah...how was the rest of your evening?" I asked, by way of distraction.

"Good. It was wonderful to see Archie again. It's been a few years since we've been in the same room together, although we've kept in touch by post."

"I gathered. He seemed to think...that I was...somebody else?" I looked at him expectantly, holding my breath.

"Oh," he said, shrugging his shoulders. "Just an acquaintance of the family. People assume things." He flipped a hand dismissively.

I must have looked doubtful at this explanation because he took my head in his hands and lowered his forehead to mine.

"There's nobody else, Alannah. Only you."

216

His soft lips met mine and I could feel the sincerity of his words reflected in his touch. There was something else I wanted to know, though.

"Um...Quin..." I started tentatively. He looked at me encouragingly and I cleared my throat. "I wanted to ask...ah...whether you've ever...um..." My voice trailed off and my cheeks started blazing.

He narrowed his eyes at me and looked at me askance before his features cleared when he understood what I wanted.

"Alannah," he said gently, "if you're asking me whether I've ever been with a woman before...then I'm afraid the answer is yes." He touched my cheek lightly. "I don't want to lie to you. But I can't deny my past."

He lowered his hand and stood in front of me, waiting for my response. I was silent for a moment, just looking at him.

"It doesn't matter," I finally said, reaching for his hand. "We all have a past...it makes us who we are. And I want you the way that you are."

He looked at me tenderly, with eyes so filled with love my heart overflowed with joy at the sight.

"I have a past, Alannah," he whispered into the top of my head as he pulled me close. "But my future is with you, always."

THE FOLLOWING EVENING, Quin dressed in the finest attire he had brought to Dublin, Rupert bustling about him like an agitated flee to make his master presentable. Archie had sent word that afternoon, asking Quin to meet him, Ham and Ollie at the Kildare Street Club, of which the three of them were members. As Quin made his way to the gentlemen's club, a spattering of rain started to fall, which nevertheless did nothing to dampen his mood. He was looking forward to spending the evening with his friends, reminiscing about the past, and simply enjoying one another's company, something that was some years overdue. He felt a brief qualm thinking about how unfortunate it was that the name of Martin Doyle would likely come up in conversation but promised himself to keep discussions of that disagreeable topic to the barest minimum before returning to more pleasant matters.

The man was locked up after all, and presumably still condemned to death, so the entire subject matter was likely to be of no consequence whatsoever, except to satisfy his own morbid curiosity.

Quin reached the club several minutes early. Being a non-member, he wanted to wait for the others to arrive before making his way in and so, to bide his time, he continued on down Kildare Street toward St Stephen's Green, which lay at the opposite end. He stopped at the edge of the park, enjoying the sight of the luscious green trees that dotted the pristine lawn and the ducks that floated on the pond, diving into the water without the slightest acknowledgment of the raindrops that stippled the surface. Humans, evidently, were far more sensitive to rain than ducks, with people rushing along the streets to disappear speedily into dooryards, with only one or two stragglers to be found on the green. Quin wasn't much bothered by the rain himself, wearing a coat and a hat. Besides, he was English, and it rained enough in England and the rest of the United Kingdom that the event was hardly worth mentioning, particularly a light rain such as was falling now. With a laugh at Man's peculiarities, Quin turned away from the park and made his way back toward the club. As he reached the building, a small group of men turned a corner onto Kildare Street a short distance away and started walking in his direction. He identified the three men immediately and broke into a huge grin, walking forward to meet them.

"Archie," he greeted the bear-like man with a handshake and a thump on the back. Archie grinned at him and returned the thump with a massive hand, while the other two men crowded around him. "Ollie, Ham. It's so good to see you!"

Ollie and Ham were wearing identical smiles of delight at the sight of their friend, but that was where the resemblance between the two of them ended. Oliver Penhale was fairly short and rather thin, with a homely face that wasn't likely ever to be called handsome. His stature belied his strength, though, which was possessed of a wiriness and resilience borne out of years of resisting being tormented by his bigger contemporaries and honed during his time with the army. His plain features masked the workings of a shrewd mind that could be relied upon to dissimilate all manner of problems to their most basic components. Hamilton Wolstenholme would be called handsome by most, an effect enhanced by the confident set of his shoulders and the almost arrogant way in which he carried his well-proportioned frame. The only blight to his features—which included wavy brown hair, a ruddy complexion and big blue, almost girlish eyes—was the presence of a rather large nose. Hamilton being Hamilton, though, he wore his aristocratic proboscis with pride, countering all

218

jests at his expense with his quick wit and a seemingly inexhaustible supply of retorts to every imaginable insult.

"Didn't I tell you?" Archie was saying, elbowing Ollie in the side while Quin greeted Ham.

"Tell him what?" Quin asked, feeling his spirits soar in the other men's company.

"That you look like a stallion that's come upon a mare in heat...wild-eyed and chomping at the bit."

Quin grinned. "*Stallion* being the operative word." He raised his eyebrows for emphasis, making Archie, Ham and Ollie roar with laughter.

"I doubt you've got quite the same equipment at your disposal," Archie said, wiping his eyes, which were tearing with amusement, "but I'd probably feel much the same if I had a mare as beautiful as yours to hand. How have you managed to keep your hands off her?—Or haven't you?" He eyed Quin askance, with a speculative look in his eyes.

"Trust you to ask a question like that, Archibald Bellinger! To answer it, I have not touched her...or not nearly enough at least," he added, which made the others break out in gales of laughter once more.

"So when's the wedding?" Ollie asked.

"In two weeks or so, as soon as we've made the arrangements."

"The sooner the better, ey?" Ham suggested, digging Quin familiarly in the ribs.

"Ah, what I wouldn't give to have a beautiful young lass in my bed at night," Archie said with a dreamy expression on his face. "Instead, I have to sleep in musty old barracks I share with these two." He made a face. "But come, we can't stand out here in the rain all night."

The rain had in fact abated to the point it was hardly noticeable, but Quin happily followed his friends into the club, which embraced them in a cocoon of warm wooden fittings and elegant leather furnishings, overlaid by the delectable aroma of roasting meat, fine spirits and a hint of cigar smoke, an ambience that made Quin feel right at home. Archie, Ham and Ollie were greeted courteously as members of the club and Quin was welcomed as an esteemed guest, whose presence nevertheless restricted the men's movement around the club to the single room available to non-members. None of them cared overly much, though, as they wouldn't need anyone's company other than their own.

"How did you come to be members of the club, Archie?" Quin asked as they made themselves comfortable around the table they'd been shown to. "You're hardly Anglo-Irish, even though you're Englishmen living in Ireland."

Ham snorted at Quin's attempted jest, while Ollie rolled his eyes. Archie gave him a broad grin before answering.

"A very astute observation, Quin. I see you haven't lost your touch. Living here for fifty years is unlikely to make any of us feel any more Irish than we do now." Ham and Ollie nodded in agreement. "As to how we came to become members of this respected establishment, that's a story better told by the one to whom we owe the honour." He nodded toward Ham, who leaned forward conspiratorially, as if he were about to impart some tantalising secret.

"Family connections," he enunciated carefully, rubbing a forefinger along his sizeable nose.

"Having had the misfortunate of being stranded in Ireland," Archie said with a mocking shake of the head toward Ham, "we'd thought to find some entertainment outside the usual army haunts."

"We asked around," Ham took up the story, "and discovered the Duke of Wellington had been a member of the Kildare Street Club while he lived in Dublin."

Quin raised his eyebrows in interest.

"So, of course, we had to come here, to find out what sort of place would attract a man like that!" Archie said.

"Hamilton thought his own military successes would be bolstered by breathing the same air that Field Marshal Arthur Wellesley once did," Ollie remarked dryly, making Ham narrow his eyes at him before they both broke into wide grins.

"It was worth a try!" Ham insisted with a laugh.

"Much good it's done us," Ollie grumbled, making the others laugh even more.

"But how did you get in?" Quin asked once the ruckus had subsided.

"Well, we couldn't just walk in uninvited, of course," Ham continued the tale. He leaned toward Quin and lowered his voice. "Fortunately, an…acquaintance of mine was able to procure a list of names of active members from her sister, who happens to work here as a maid."

"What a fortunate coincidence," Quin muttered.

Archie chuckled. "Isn't it just?"

"It gets even better," Ham went on, unperturbed. "As it happened, there was a Mr Wolstenholme on the list. This not being the most common of names, I thought perhaps we might use this auspicious happenstance to our advantage."

Ham paused briefly as their drinks arrived, waiting until they'd all sampled their sherry before going on.

"Now, I of course set out to observe this Mr Wolstenholme inconspicuously, and lo and behold...I found there to be something of a family resemblance." Quin glanced at Archie, who was tapping a finger against his nose. "I remembered my father mentioning a distant cousin of his had moved to Dublin some years earlier—God knows why." Ham shook his head at the thought that anyone might want to come to Ireland voluntarily. "So naturally, I assumed the Mr Wolstenholme of Kildare Street Club and myself to be related."

"Oh, naturally," Quin echoed. "And he believed you?"

"You know how he is." Ollie nodded toward Ham. "He could sell beer to a barmaid."

Quin laughed. Ham could in fact convince most people of just about anything. He always sounded like he knew what he was talking about—even on the rare occasions when he didn't—and loved being the centre of attention, regaling his listeners with his sharp mind and an endless supply of entertaining tales. Convincing a complete stranger he was a distant cousin was probably easy for him.

Ham shrugged, not the least bit apologetic. "We very well might actually *be* cousins, and I never specifically said we definitely were, only that there was a distinct possibility. Besides," he added with a dismissive gesture of the hand, "Peter Wolstenholme enjoys my company, relative or not, and was happy to present me to the committee, regardless."

"Where after, you got Archie and Ollie on board," Quin said. "How long did all of this take you?"

"Nine months or so," Archie responded.

"You *are* persistent."

"Or just bored!" Ollie grumbled. "What I wouldn't give for a bit of action. A nice rebellion to put down, perhaps. Something more than the local brawls and agrarian unrest we have to deal with." He sighed, his homely face suffused with regret at the tedium an army officer is faced with during times of relative peace.

221

"Speaking of rebellions," Archie said, looking at Quin, "I've found out a few things about your man Martin Doyle."

Quin sat up straight at mention of the name, fully alert, all traces of amusement forgotten. "Yes?" He leaned toward Archie and raised his eyebrows.

"It's an unfortunate tale." Archie rubbed his chin, getting straight to the point. "His parents were tenant farmers, but reasonably well off, renting a sizeable plot of land. They seemed to be doing quite well, until they fell behind on their rent one year after two consecutive poor harvests and were evicted."

"How do you know all this?" Quin asked.

"From one of the constables at the Dublin Police. I met him a few years back and we became friendly." Archie grinned wryly. "After a few drinks, he becomes even friendlier and his tongue becomes looser.—In any case," he continued, sobering up, "he told me the Doyles tried to convince their landlord to let them stay, that they could come up with the rent if he gave them some more time. But the man refused. He came to the farm the following day with three of his sons and two policemen to forcibly evict them. One of the policemen was a friend of constable Walsh before he died." Archie paused. "The official report says the Doyles resisted, and a fight ensued, during which both of them were accidentally killed. But"—he lowered his voice—"Walsh says his friend told him they were killed in cold blood. He says the Doyles pleaded with the landlord not to evict them. When he ignored them, the woman started crying and wailing, throwing herself on her knees in front of him. One of the landlord's sons took objection to this behaviour and shot her...right between the eyes. The husband was shot moments later by the landlord himself when he tried to attack the son who'd killed his wife."

Archie gave Quin a long look. "And young Martin Doyle saw the whole thing."

Quin's eyes flew open. "You mean..."

"He was there. His parents were murdered in front of him."

"How old was he?"

"Probably about twelve. The landlord threw him out to fend for himself after his parents were killed, with nothing but the clothes on his back...and presumably paid a handsome bribe to the police to keep the matter quiet."

Both men were silent for a while.

"And the landlord was English, I presume?" Quin asked finally.

"Yes, a Mr Baker. Arrived from England not long before the incident...to personally take over the management of his estate..."

Quin snorted.

"Mr Baker and one of his sons were found dead on a field several years later," Archie went on quietly. "The son had been shot between the eyes.—The murderer was never found."

"Martin Doyle," Quin said softly.

At that moment, he could almost understand the man's hatred of the English, which went far beyond a feeling of discontent about the English reign over Irish people. He wanted revenge for the life that had been ripped away from him. In one day, he had lost his family, his home and his future—all at the hands of an Englishman after his coin.

Quin shook his head. What was the world coming to, he thought gloomily?

"What about the royal pardon?" he asked.

Archie lifted one shoulder in a shrug. "Walsh didn't know anything about it. He'd heard the man hadn't yet been executed but he didn't know why. He certainly hadn't heard anything about Doyle being pardoned and found the very suggestion ludicrous."

Quin frowned. "Nobody in Omagh could tell me anything about it either. I went there the day after I learned the sentence hadn't yet been carried out, but the magistrate wouldn't give me any details. All he would admit was that the hanging had been postponed. He wouldn't say why and appeared to know nothing about who might have made an appeal on Doyle's behalf, nor on what grounds."

"It sounds like the person responsible doesn't want his name to be known," Ollie remarked.

"But why?" Ham asked, "if he wants the man to be pardoned, then surely he must be some sort of acquaintance."

"Perhaps it isn't an open relationship," Archie suggested.

Quin nodded. "I thought it was perhaps someone of prominent social standing who was using Doyle to undertake illegal activities for him and was hoping to find a way to continue the arrangement."

"In which case, he wouldn't want to be publicly linked with the man," Ollie agreed.

Ham gave him a sceptical look. "But why wouldn't this person simply find another criminal to do his bidding, instead of risking being identified as the man trying to get a convicted traitor and murderer to go free?"

"I have no idea," Quin and Archie said at the same time.

"Hm..." Ollie wrinkled his brow, making them all look at him expectantly. "I've only just thought...what makes you so sure anyone at all is seeking a royal pardon for Doyle?"

Quin was taken aback for a moment but answered readily enough, "Kieran, Alannah's brother. He was imprisoned with Doyle for a time and heard about the appeal before he was released." He stroked his chin in contemplation. "Now that you mention it, though, Kieran himself said Doyle was the one spreading the story about the appeal...there was no official announcement—and why would there be? He only believed it to be true when the execution was postponed."

"It might have been postponed for another reason," Ollie suggested.

"You're right, I hadn't thought of that." Now that Quin had thought of it, it made sense. Whatever the reason for the postponement, it likely had nothing to do with anyone wanting to set Doyle free, no matter what the man himself might have hoped for. "Nothing but a coincidence," he muttered, frowning into his empty glass.

Archie patted Quin on the shoulder. "I'm sure you have nothing to worry about, Quin. The hanging was rescheduled, that's all. And even if there is anyone wanting to see Doyle go free, he isn't likely to have any interest in you or Miss O'Neill. And the appeal, if there is one, won't come to anything in any case."

"Certainly not," Ham said while Ollie nodded.

Quin grumbled. It was what he'd been telling himself for days and it was good to hear his friends shared his opinion. Still...

"You'd prefer the man to be safely dead," Ollie observed in his analytical tone.

"Yes." Quin clenched his fists.

They were silent for a moment.

Finally, Quin took a deep breath and relaxed his hands. "Enough of such morbid conversation," he said, forcing himself to smile, remembering his resolve to keep the discussion of Martin Doyle to the barest minimum. "Let us turn our minds to more pleasant matters. Let us order some wine and something to eat, and then you can tell me what mischief you've been up to since you've been here."

PACKING THEIR BELONGINGS into the wagon three days later, Quin reflected how fortunate it was that he had friends he could rely on even when he hadn't seen them in years. He'd met other people whom he'd initially felt close to, only for the relationship to deteriorate when put to the test, by distance or some unforeseen circumstance. With Archie, Ham and Ollie, though, their bond was as strong as it had been when they'd first met, even though they'd only seen one another a handful of times over the past six years. And they'd gone out of their way to see him when he'd unexpectedly arrived in Dublin—not once but twice—and had gone to great lengths to assist him in the matter of Martin Doyle.

Beyond Archie's conversation with Constable Walsh, each of them had sought out every other acquaintance he could think of who might provide some answers to the question of the royal pardon and the postponement of the sentence—all within the four days that had passed between Quin's fortuitous meeting with Archie at the inn and his departure back to Glaslearg. Unfortunately, their enquiries hadn't resulted in any useful information, with nobody willing or able to disclose anything about why Doyle hadn't yet been executed, but Quin was exceedingly grateful for their efforts.

For one thing, their assistance had put his mind at ease, alerting him to the likely fact the royal pardon Doyle was waiting for was nothing but a desperate tale he'd spun himself. Quin had been sorry to bid Archie, Ham and Ollie farewell after only a few days, but he left with the certain knowledge he could count on them in any situation. A man was lucky to have such friends.

"Ready?" he asked Alannah, who had appeared on the other side of the wagon.

"Yes." She gave him a broad smile that warmed his heart.

Their eyes met, and her smile widened as she read the thoughts that must be plain to see on his face.

"Soon," he said in a hungry voice, making her blush.

Quin laughed. He could hardly contain his excitement at the thought of marrying her. Actually, he thought with a grin, he couldn't wait to share a bed with her. He wanted to be lawfully wedded, alright, but his mind was so preoccupied with the carnal aspects of matrimony he could barely think of anything else. Being around her every day for the past week, including in the close confines of the wagon, had been almost painful in its effect on him. He thought of their meeting in the hallway a few days earlier and was sorely tempted to repeat the experience right there in the stable yard.

Alannah cocked her head. "Shall we?"

"Please." He offered her his hand to climb into the wagon.

When she put her hand in his he lifted it to his mouth for a gentle kiss, holding her eyes over their entwined fingers. He could see his desire mirrored in her blue gaze and gripped her fingers tightly in a gentle promise. She breathed in deeply through slightly parted lips, squeezing his hand in reciprocity.

Mesmerised, he finally managed to tear his eyes away from her and helped her onto the wagon. Then he assisted the waiting Margaret, ignoring the knowing smile on her face. Once the seemingly oblivious Rupert had scrambled up behind him and Quin himself had taken his seat, he turned the horses toward home.

19.

IT WAS MIDDAY when we arrived at Niall, tired from the long ride back, but glad to be home, particularly so as our return meant we would soon be married. My heart jumped in excitement whenever Quin caught my eye, as he dimpled a smile at me or gave me a look that made the blood start racing through my body. As we turned toward the farmhouse, though, we were greeted by a scene that had a very different effect on me.

"What?" I said, looking at the piles of furniture and household items that littered the dooryard.

I glanced at Quin in confusion. He frowned, his face bearing a distinctly suspicious expression that made me feel even more uneasy.

"Come." He pulled the horses to a halt and gave me his arm to climb off the wagon.

"Ride on to Glaslearg," he told Rupert as he helped Margaret down. "I'll meet you there."

As we made our way toward the jumble of objects scattered in the yard, John the groom and Finnian the hall boy emerged from the house carrying a large trunk. Straightening up from setting it on the ground they caught sight of me. Both faces took on identical expressions of dismay, but before I could say a thing, they'd scuttled back into the house, with no more than a brief "Miss O'Neill" in acknowledgment of my appearance. A sinking feeling descended on me, and my heart started thumping in my chest.

Having reached the dooryard, I could identify most of the things that lay there—here was the casement clock from the parlour, there was the sideboard from the dining room and the table and chairs to match, all interspersed with countless other items I was accustomed to seeing in their familiar positions inside the house. I wandered through the chaos with a growing sense of anxiety, which was abated only by the discovery that none of my personal effects appeared to have made their way out of my room.

I looked at Quin helplessly, at a loss for words. Before he could say anything, the silence was interrupted by the sound of voices coming from the side of the house. It was Kieran and the overseer, deep in conversation, which ended abruptly when they came around the corner and saw Quin and me standing in the middle of the clutter.

"Miss O'Neill." Mr Smith doffed his hat without meeting my eyes, before turning around with speed and disappearing the way he'd come.

"Alannah." Kieran gave me a look that made it clear he wanted to follow the servants' example and make himself scarce. His eyes kept flitting away from mine and fine beads of sweat started dotting his upper lip and temples, his face looking unnaturally pale.

"What is the meaning of this?" I managed to ask, voice low and menacing.

"Ah…" Kieran shuffled uncomfortably from side to side, still avoiding looking at me, which banished any remaining hope I'd had he would tell me he was refurbishing the house.

"What have you done?" I hissed, barely able to get the words past my lips.

"I…I…um…"

My nostrils flared as I fumed in anger, remembering a similar conversation that had passed between us not long before, and I clenched my hands into fists. Quin gently touched my arm, and I slowly relaxed my hands.

"What have you done, Kieran?" Quin repeated my question in a controlled voice, but one that allowed no possibility of evasion.

"I…ah…" Kieran looked at me briefly and swallowed, before dropping his eyes once more. "I've sold the farm." The words were barely a whisper, but they might have been shouted from the rooftop for the effect they had.

I stared at him, utterly dumbfounded. The blood roared in my ears, and I exhaled heavily while I tried to find my voice.

"You what?" I finally croaked.

"I sold the farm," he repeated quietly while studiously examining the tops of his boots.

I blinked a few times in disbelief. "How could you?" I asked in a breathy voice, still stunned, but starting to emerge from my stupor.

When Kieran didn't answer or even deign to look at me, I exploded. "How could you?" I yelled, advancing on him with barely contained fury. "After everything father did for this place? He gave up the life he dreamed of to see the farm taken care of…a farm that's been in O'Neill hands for generations against all odds…and you *sold* it?"

228

I was screeching by now but didn't care. I was so furious I could have scratched his eyes out had he lifted them to look at me. When he finally did look at me, I was prevented from leaping at his throat by Quin's restraining arm around my waist.

I was in no mood to be manhandled, though, and turned irritably toward him. "Let go of me!"

Quin gently extracted his arm, eyes wide with astonishment, but hovered by my side, evidently expecting me at any moment to hurl myself at my brother in a violent frenzy. I wasn't entirely sure I wouldn't do exactly that if I was in his presence for an instant longer and so I spun on my heel and stomped off angrily, coming to a stop in front of the occasional table that had stood in the entrance hall. I breathed deeply for several minutes, trying to get my emotions under control, until I thought I could face Kieran without the burning desire to do him physical harm.

I turned back toward him, clenching my jaws in the effort not to yell.

"Could you be kind enough, Kieran," I started slowly, in as civil a tone as I could muster, "to explain the circumstances of the sale...of *my home.*"

He fiddled with the sleeves of his shirt for a moment before lifting his head in my direction, while shifting his feet back and forth. He worked his teeth over his bottom lip and shrugged his shoulders uncomfortably.

"It's not your home," he finally responded in a small voice.

"I beg your pardon?" I wasn't sure I had heard him right.

"The farm is *mine* by right. Father left it to *me* when he died."

"And I'm sure he's turning over in his grave at the thanks he's getting!"

Kieran narrowed his eyes at me. "I can do with the farm as I like. You're going to live with *him* anyway." He nodded his head in Quin's direction, with a distinct look of dislike.

I growled deep in my throat, nostrils flaring in anger, but bit back the retort that had sprung to my mind. I was beyond furious at what Kieran had done, but at the back of my mind, I knew he was right. Niall *was* his property—or had been—and he could do with it whatever he wanted. He didn't need to ask my permission.

"I know the farm is yours, Kieran," I said with great effort, "you've reminded me of that often enough!" I took another deep breath. "But you could have told

229

me.—I shouldn't have to find out like *this*." I waved an arm over the heaps of belongings strewn over the yard.

"I didn't plan it that way. It just..." He shrugged irritably. "You know I'm not a farmer!" He spat the words at me, as if they could justify his actions. "I didn't want it!"

"And how were you planning to live, Kieran?" Quin asked in a calm tone. He had come to stand next to me and now cautiously took my hand and gave it a gentle squeeze.

Kieran scowled at us for a moment before dropping his eyes. "I..."

"You mean to say you haven't given it any thought?" Quin's voice conveyed only a sense of curiosity, rather than the complete disbelief I was feeling myself.

"I haven't got it all worked out yet."

"And what were you planning on doing with all our things?" I demanded, not quite shouting.

"Um...well...I...I thought I'd take them to that abandoned farmhouse until I'd come up with another plan."

I shook my head. "After everything we've been through, how could you do this?" I looked at him for a long moment, suddenly feeling unutterably sad.

I turned away from him and walked back toward the road, wanting to get away. Quin caught up with me and took me by the hand, leading me along the path toward Glaslearg, as the door to my old life closed behind me once and for all.

QUIN CLOSED THE door to his bedroom and sank gratefully down on his bed. He was tired. It wasn't a state he was overly familiar with, usually feeling himself inexhaustibly energetic throughout the day until the moment he lay his head on his pillow at night.

The events of the afternoon had taken it out of him, though.

Alannah had been so angry she'd barely spoken a word on their way to Glaslearg. He'd tried to engage her in conversation, remind her of their upcoming wedding, but she'd only made passing remarks that quickly faded into insignificance, leaving them stranded in silence. When they'd reached the manor house, he'd seen her settled on the settee in the drawing room before going in search of Rupert, instructing him to ride back to Niall to arrange for Alannah's things to be brought to Glaslearg, where a room would be set up for her. He'd contemplated for a moment suggesting she move in with him straight away, but he knew that would upset her. She wanted to wait until their wedding night—and avoid the scandal such a move might arouse—and he would respect her wishes.

Quin had seen to the unloading of the wagon, making sure the seeds he'd purchased were stored cool and dry in the barn so they wouldn't spoil before the planting, and packed everything else away. Then he'd finally washed the road dust off his face and hands and gone back to join Alannah in the drawing room, only to find she'd fallen asleep. His heart had filled with tenderness at the sight, and he'd gently laid her on her side, put her feet up on the settee and left her with a soft kiss on her forehead.

He'd walked quietly out of the room and shrugged back into his coat, determining to use the opportunity to have a private word with his soon-to-be brother-in-law.

Thinking about the conversation now left him with a distinct feeling of distaste.

Kieran had neither been rude toward him nor overly civil, hovering instead somewhere in the vicinity of indifference, his demeanour as emotionless as if he'd simply made a poor choice of produce at the market. Quin hadn't had the impression Kieran didn't care, though, but rather that he was trying to hide some strong emotion he didn't want Quin to see. As to what that emotion might be, Quin wasn't entirely sure, and the possibilities kept running through his mind. He thought it likely Kieran would feel annoyance, and even anger, at his sister's reaction to his decision to sell the farm, which he obviously thought justified. He might be angry she had questioned his actions at all, much less as vehemently as she had, possibly feeling himself superior to her and beyond reproach, being the legal owner of the farm. It was also possible, though—and Quin thought this to be more likely—that Kieran felt a sense of failure, and perhaps shame, at his inability to hold onto the farm that had been part of his family's heritage for so many years.

Quin shook his head and got up with a groan. He had to get out of his dirty clothes before he could sleep. Rupert would skin him alive if he soiled the fresh sheets. He undressed quickly, throwing his clothes into a corner, and washed himself briefly with water from the ewer.

That would have to do, he thought, drying his face.

Scrubbing the cloth over his cheeks, another thought occurred to him, one that had been nagging at the back of his mind since his first glimpse of the mayhem

231

in Kieran's dooryard. The clearing out of the house had seemed chaotic, as if it had been done in haste, like the prelude to a speedy exodus. Kieran had told him the new owner wanted the farm vacated as soon as possible, but Quin thought it unlikely the man wouldn't have permitted Kieran a few more days to make the necessary arrangements. And Kieran hadn't made any arrangements at all, to the point he didn't even know where he would sleep or store his possessions, much less how he would earn money to support himself once he no longer had the farm's income at his disposal.

The question was, why?

Was it simply that Kieran was impulsive and hadn't thought it all through or was it something else, something more sinister perhaps? As much as Quin had told himself he would give Alannah's brother a chance to prove himself worthy of his respect, he couldn't help feeling he was up to something, that he hadn't quite closed the chapter of his life that had seen him thrown in gaol.

Quin grumbled as he pulled the heavy quilt off the bed and slid under the crisp white sheet. Soon he would be sharing this bed with Alannah. The thought sent a pleasant jolt through his body, and he tried to focus on it to relax his mind, but his thoughts kept straying to his earlier conversation with Kieran.

The man hadn't said very much, mostly giving Quin one-word answers to his questions, elaborating on nothing. He hadn't revealed the name of the man who'd bought the farm or said very much about him, except that he would be arriving with his own set of servants to attend to the farmhouse and see to the running of the farm. How much he'd paid Kieran for the farm, Quin didn't know. He only knew Kieran's abrupt choice to sell Niall had not only deeply upset his sister, it had also seen the entire farm's staff reduced to the masses of the unemployed in what seemed like the blink of an eye.

The instant this thought had occurred to him, Quin had known he would have no choice but to see to the servants' welfare himself—Alannah would want them taken care of. He'd at first felt irritated at having to clean up Kieran's mess, but upon further reflection, had realised it might not be a bad thing for him to take over Niall's workforce. His own estate was vastly understaffed—he'd lamented this fact repeatedly over the past weeks—and these were people Alannah knew and trusted. They'd been with the O'Neills long enough that he could rest assured they would know what needed to be done and act accordingly without the need for constant supervision, which would allow him to turn his attention to other, much-neglected matters on his estate.

With this resolve and having obtained all the information Kieran was likely to impart, Quin had bid him farewell and ridden back to Glaslearg, where he'd found Rupert overseeing the establishment of Alannah's quarters, her possessions disappearing up the stairs in the arms of Finnian and John. Alannah herself had watched the proceedings from the doorway to the drawing room, a slight frown between her dark brows, but seeming otherwise to have recovered from her shock. She'd expressed herself supportive of—and grateful for—his proposal to hire Niall's servants to work at Glaslearg, as well as his suggestion that the remaining items littering Niall's dooryard be kept at Glaslearg until Kieran decided what to do with them. Silence had descended upon them at the mention of Kieran's name, and Quin had found himself promising Alannah that, of course, her brother was welcome to stay with them as well until he was otherwise settled.

"You really are a fool," Quin said to himself now.

He could barely tolerate the man and here he found himself living under the same roof with him—and by his own invitation!

"Well, what was I supposed to do? Turn him out to starve?"

He flung the sheet back irritably and jumped out of bed, suddenly feeling too restless to lie down.

It had taken several hours to transport everything from Niall to Glaslearg, traveling back and forth with the two wagons and pair of small carts at their disposal. The manpower had also been limited, this being restricted to Quin himself and Kieran—who'd looked like he would rather eat a handful of nails than live with Quin but hadn't put his objections into words—and Niall's servants. Quin's own servants, Denis and Bryan, were far too old to be expected to lend much assistance and Rupert wasn't strong enough to lift the heavier items. Alannah had declared herself willing to assist with the lighter pieces, but of course Quin hadn't allowed her to do any such thing, encouraging her instead to arrange her new apartments to her liking, which she'd agreed to with minimal protest.

That had left Niall's staff, which included Margaret the maid, Mrs O'Sullivan the cook, Finnian the hall boy, John the groom and the overseer Mr Smith, who hadn't returned from the errand he'd disappeared on earlier in the day. The diminutive Margaret had scuttled off to assist her mistress with less physically taxing labours, while Mrs O'Sullivan had taken firm hold of a cart handle with one meaty hand and proceeded to walk tirelessly up and down the road between the two farmhouses all afternoon. John and Finnian had continued the job they'd been doing all day, moving the furniture they'd already carried out of one farmhouse into another, barely stopping in their progress to hear their new instructions. By the time Mr Smith had returned, the last few pieces were making their way to their new home while the sun's long rays disappeared beneath the horizon as the short summer night began.

Kieran had vanished without a word, presumably to find a bed somewhere, leaving Quin to contemplate the mess that had been relocated from Kieran's dooryard into his house. The manor was littered with tables, chairs, cupboards, chests and an assortment of other items, all strewn haphazardly across every available surface on the ground floor, filling up the rooms to bursting and spilling out into the entrance hall.

Thinking about the clutter that would require his attention in the morning—a time he'd hoped to spend in pleasant contemplation of his imminent nuptials— filled Quin with an intense feeling of annoyance.

Why should he have to deal with any of this? He wanted to marry Alannah, not act as her brother's nursemaid!

He paced irritably up and down the room, torn between wanting to locate Kieran and give him a piece of his mind regarding appropriate and responsible adult behaviour, and finding Alannah and releasing his frustrations in another, less verbose way.

In the end, he did neither, only muttering to himself about the unfortunate fact one couldn't choose one's family—or in this case, one's in-laws—before finally resigning himself to his fate. He wanted Alannah to be his wife and Kieran was Alannah's brother, whether he—or she—liked it. Therefore, the two of them would simply have to deal with whatever idiocy Kieran thought up and hope he stayed out of the kind of trouble he'd gotten himself into before. Compared to that, Quin reflected, his current predicament was really quite inconsequential. Yes, Quin's home was a mess, but that was a temporary state of affairs, and he was gaining an obeisance of servants for an understaffed house and an assortment of furnishings for a suite of empty rooms. And while Kieran might take along staff and furniture when he moved out, Quin suspected his departure would be a long time coming. He doubted Kieran had any viable plan to support himself, much less the means and know-how to do so.

In all likelihood, his brother-in-law was here to stay.

"Hmph," he grumbled at the unsatisfactory nature of this conclusion, which nevertheless made him feel better at having reached it.

He could either spend the rest of his days bemoaning Kieran's errant actions, or he could accept the circumstances he found himself in and make the best of them. Choosing the latter option was the way he tended to approach his life, and he'd found this method to be highly effective at reducing frustrations caused by things he couldn't change. This by no means meant he would overlook all manner of bad behaviour from the man—he'd promised him retribution if he ever did anything to harm Alannah again, and he'd meant it—but he would do his best to accept his presence at Glaslearg, and he would not allow him to infringe on his and Alannah's happiness.

Whatever Kieran had done in the past, he was paying for his sins by being reduced to nothing more than a guest in Quin's household—one without a home of his own to return to. Quin would gain nothing from reminding Kieran of his ill fortune at every opportunity, except for the growing unhappiness of his future wife. He would therefore try to hold his tongue and find a place for Kieran on the estate.

How Kieran himself would behave would remain to be seen.

20.

THREE DAYS AFTER their tumultuous return to Glaslearg, Quin called together the tenants in the drawing room, to discuss with them his plans for the estate and their own small plots of land.

A degree of order had been restored to the house, Niall's furniture having been neatly distributed around Glaslearg's manor, which—ironically—lent the house an air of hominess it had been lacking before, the furnishings providing a sense of warmth in the previously stark environs. Niall's servants had also been settled in their new home and were bustling about their business, seeming easily to have made the transition from one homestead to another, with little concern for the change in proprietor, grateful only to have survived with their livelihoods intact.

As for Kieran...

He was making himself scarce, melting away quietly whenever Quin or Alannah appeared—head lowered and looking at the floor—confining himself mostly to his self-appointed room. The man had barely exchanged two words with either of them since his unexpected arrival at Glaslearg, leaving them no wiser as to the circumstances of Niall's sale.

Quin wondered briefly whether Kieran would ever tell them anything—or even talk to them at all—but shook his head briskly to dispel the thought, deciding to turn his attention to the waiting tenants instead.

Having returned from Dublin, Quin had sent a summons to the men who'd been working on neighbouring farms, and most had returned to their homes on Glaslearg. Some, though, would only be back later in the season, as they had to complete the labour agreed upon in order to get their pay. Quin had asked them to come only if they were being paid per day and could leave without indebting themselves to their employers or going back on their word, and he was pleased to see so many of them had made the effort to respond to his request and the recompense he'd promised them.

"They're probably afraid I'll evict them if they don't show up," he'd said to Alannah the day before, when they'd come across a group of returning men as they rode through the estate.

"No, not likely." She'd given him a sideways glance that had made a dark ringlet of hair fall across her face. "It's the Custom of Ulster," she'd added by way of explanation—an explanation that had gone right over his head.

Ulster Custom, he'd been given to understand, was the unwritten agreement between landlords and their tenants in Ulster province that the tenants would not be evicted from their land as long as they paid their rent. Although the custom was not founded in the law and could thus not be legally enforced, the arrangement nevertheless conferred a degree of security to both parties involved, as it was in both the landlords' and the tenants' interests to see the requirements were met. Beyond the matter of evictions, though, Alannah had explained that the Custom of Ulster—which was also known as tenant right— also held that tenants who chose to give up their holdings could sell their rights to the land to incoming tenants, including any improvements they'd personally made to the farm.

Quin had been in equal parts pleased and astounded by this revelation, as he'd always assumed—based on what he'd heard in London and elsewhere—that landlords and their agents could and would evict their Irish tenants at their pleasure. Now, it seemed—and he was happy to hear it—this wasn't necessarily the case, or at least not in the province he found himself in—although it probably did still happen now and then, Quin reflected, thinking about Mr Brennan. What things might be like in other parts of Ireland, where farming conditions were reportedly poorer and the peasants even worse off, he had no idea.

How people could possibly *be* worse off than those currently residing on his own estate, he also found difficult to grasp, looking at the ragged men gathered before him in the drawing room now.

He welcomed them and thanked them for coming, after which Alannah greeted them warmly in Gaelic. Her friendly smile visibly put the men at ease, and he was grateful for her presence. Ulster Custom or no, the men were clearly wary of him—quite understandably—but Alannah seemed able to reassure them without the least bit of effort on her part. Perhaps it was her genuine desire to help others that shone through her friendly demeanour, her willingness to go beyond what others might do that made her promises ring true. It wasn't something that could be learned or practised, but he'd seen it in her the first day he'd met her and was in fact the very reason she was here at all—her readiness to help someone in need, no matter how trivial that need might seem.

237

Quin looked affectionately at her as she turned toward him expectantly, waiting for him to tell her what she should say. Another useful trait, he thought. While several of the tenants could in fact understand and speak passable English, conversing with them in Gaelic through a trusted translator was a far better— not to mention easier—approach that ensured both parties had their say and understood exactly what the other said.

With a smile, he asked Alannah to thank the tenants for awaiting his instructions, which in his opinion had been a long time coming. He'd decided within a few days of his arrival at Glaslearg he wanted to improve the tenants' situation and had promised them as much, a promise they seemed grudgingly to have believed. Several weeks had passed since then, though, and Quin was sure they'd started to question his intentions, no doubt dismissing him as a loud-mouthed Englishman who had much to say but little action to back up his claims. The looks on the faces of the men as they listened to Alannah's translation confirmed as much to Quin, although they stood there quietly enough.

"Tell them," he said to Alannah, wanting to erase the doubtful frowns that adorned numerous foreheads turned in his direction, "that I wish to improve the conditions they are living in and that I intend thus to assist each of the families in building a two-roomed stone cottage, providing what materials cannot be collected—at no cost to themselves."

The men's eyes grew wide even before Alannah had finished her translation, a reaction enhanced by his promise to pay the tenants to start building straightaway, to compensate for any money they might have made working outside of Glaslearg. He folded his arms smugly across his chest as Alannah continued talking, pleased with his plan.

To his surprise, though, a few of the tenants aimed furtive, annoyed glances at him and started mumbling irritably amongst themselves—never directly at him, he was their landlord after all, but their discontent was obvious, nonetheless. He heard a word repeated several times that sounded to his ears like "jerk" and turned toward Alannah in confusion.

"Um," she started, as a look of comprehension bloomed on her face, "they think you're offering them alms."

"But..." Quin stammered, thoroughly confused, "I'm offering to help them...and to pay them for it!"

"I know that." Alannah gave him a crooked smile. "And they probably know that too, but..." She turned her blue gaze on him as she tried to make him understand. "They're proud, Quin. They've had to work incredibly hard just to put the flimsy roof of a mud cabin over their families' heads and put food in their bellies. They don't have much. Not much beyond their pride, pride at not having to beg to survive."

Quin looked at the men before him, seeing them in a new light.

Alannah was right, they had nothing but the clothes on their backs and a handful of measly possessions, and after every long and trying day of back-breaking labour they came home to a sparing, monotonous diet and a tiny hut made of mud.

How would he feel if he were one of them?

Yes, they were poor, but they had a home to live in and food to eat—sparse commodities that were exceedingly hard won. If he were one of them, would he relish the opportunity to live in a bigger, sturdier cabin, given to him by the good graces of his rich English landlord? Or would he feel belittled, denigrated as a man incapable of taking adequate care of his family? Appearances and circumstances aside, he doubted these men were all that different from most other men he'd known, or to himself.

If he were one of them, he knew how he would feel.

"Ask them," he said to Alannah quietly, "if they would agree to accept the materials I am offering them in exchange for a small fee...perhaps from the profits made on the additional acres of land they shall have available to farm."

Alannah repeated his proposal in Gaelic, and the men's expressions of annoyance changed to ones of calculation as they considered Quin's offer. They had known about the extra two acres of land he intended to assign to each of them, although by now they were probably doubtful of the promised land ever materialising, little progress as had been made in this regard. Relieved at having at last made the choice several weeks earlier, Quin had told Denis and Bryan of his plan to double the size of the tenants' plots without much increasing their rent, and the two elderly servants had started spreading the happy news to any tenants they happened to come across. Not wanting the tenants to speculate on the validity of Denis and Bryan's tale, Quin had visited them himself a few days later to confirm his intentions. The news had been met with a reserved enthusiasm not unlike the reaction he was getting now.

"I shall add it to the proposed agreement of tenure," Quin continued, warming up to the idea himself. "Over the five years of their contractual occupancy, they shall be required to pay me a total of...six pounds in return for the building materials for their cottages. If they should choose not to build such a cottage, they need only pay the agreed-upon rent, with no further monetary obligations toward me. In either case, they will be eligible to receive payment for working Glaslearg's fields."

Quin waited a moment for Alannah to translate before continuing.

"Should they choose to accept my proposal and build the cottages under the conditions described, they shall be awarded monetary compensation for the new cottage should they give up their holding at a future date, in recompense for the moneys and time spent on the building thereof...in keeping with the Custom of Ulster," he added softly, looking at Alannah.

She smiled at him, her eyes suffused with tenderness as she held his gaze for a moment before translating what he'd said. He felt his own mouth turn up in a smile in response and was almost—but not quite—embarrassed at how much it meant to him that Alannah was pleased with the solution he'd come up with.

The tenants themselves seemed to be equally content with the proposed arrangement, most of them nodding their approval, either silently to themselves or with muted discussions with their neighbours. Here and there a face continued to show scepticism, with one or two eyeing him with barely concealed distaste.

He shrugged. All he could do was to make good on his promises and hope they came around.

Thinking they would be less likely to doubt his word with legally binding paperwork to hand, he assured them he would have the lease contracts ready for them within the next few days. This statement was met with further approving nods, in what he hoped would be the first real step toward erasing the pervasively negative opinion they seemed to have of him. He knew it wasn't necessarily a particular dislike of his person, but rather a result of the years of hardships they'd endured under British landlords or their agents, who evidently hadn't cared much for their wellbeing. Having been enlightened about the unscrupulous behaviour of Glaslearg's erstwhile steward, Mr Brennan, Quin could hardly blame them for being sceptical of his own intentions, particularly if they'd been unfortunate enough to have had similar experiences before.

The promised paperwork did have the desired effect, though, and the tenants visibly relaxed, allowing Quin to broach the more practical topic of acquiring the materials necessary to build the promised houses. Shyly at first, but with increasing enthusiasm when they saw Quin valued their opinions, some of the men made suggestions as to where the best stone for the building might be collected, how they would go about bringing it to the building sites and when the building might be able to commence. Quin promised to provide the tenants with what means he had for transport and any additional stones that might be necessary, and materials such as nails, hammers and other tools that would make the work easier, as well as the windows he insisted would adorn each new cottage.

Talk of windows caused a wave of excitement to pass through the men, most of whom had evidently never lived in a house with a single window in their lives. The thought made an unexpected feeling of anger well up in Quin, as he pictured the sprawling mansions of the British aristocracy, which stood in such stark contrast to the tiny hovels the tenants currently called home.

Making an effort to suppress his irritation, he brought out the map of Glaslearg he had prepared, which showed the tenants' current plots, overlaid with the proposed division of the land into the bigger four-acre plots. There was some discussion about the positioning of one family over another at particular locations, which seemed to be based on the desirability of being in closer proximity to certain neighbours, rather than any misgivings about specific plots of land.

The Barony of Clogher, where Glaslearg was situated, was home to some of the best farmland in County Tyrone, and indeed Ireland, and none of the tenants would be suffering as a result of the small-scale move the rearranging of their holdings would entail.

It took some time until the map was organised to everyone's satisfaction, but Quin was nevertheless happy he'd thought to discuss the positioning of the new plots with the tenants, rather than simply telling them where they would be moving. He could see they were enjoying the rare opportunity to have their voices heard and to make decisions for themselves on how and where they would live, including the handful of men who expressed themselves content to stay on the two-acre plots they currently occupied.

By the time all the details for the building of the cottages and the move to the larger holdings had been decided on, several of the men wore an unmistakable look of content over their generally scruffy countenances. Quin was pleased to see this change in attitude—which he hoped also extended to himself—and bade the tenants a hearty farewell as they filed out of the room, promising to have wagons and carts waiting for them in the morning, so they could start the laborious process of gathering the stones that would be used to build their new homes.

QUIN TOOK A deep breath and knocked.

"Come in," came the soft reply from inside the room.

He slowly opened the door. As it swung into the room, he caught sight of Alannah, standing in front of the bed and looking expectantly at the doorway.

"Quin," she exclaimed in surprise, but smiled at him as he stepped into the room and greeted her. She glanced at the bed behind her, and a slight blush crept into her cheeks. She averted her gaze and cleared her throat, her eyes lighting up as she looked at him.

"I wanted to thank you for your help with the tenants this afternoon," Quin said as he came to a stop in front of her.

"Oh." She shrugged dismissively. "It was nothing."

"You eloquently assisted me in removing my foot from my mouth," he countered.

Alannah laughed. "In that case, you're most welcome."

They smiled at each other for a moment and their eyes locked. Quin took a step closer to her and pulled her gently into his arms. He kissed her on the lips, and she leaned into him. He held her for a minute or two, enjoying the feel of her in his arms, before extricating himself from her embrace and reaching into his pocket with one hand.

Alannah looked at him in some confusion as he removed a small cylindrical box, the plain wooden surface of which was polished to a smooth gleam. Her eyes widened as she realised what it was, and she looked up at him with a slight intake of her breath. He undid the simple clasp and opened the box slowly to reveal the soft velvet cushion it contained, and the small silver circle nestled therein.

"Oh," she mouthed silently.

"I had hoped you might be persuaded to wear this," Quin said slowly, feeling a little breathless, "as a token of my affection...and my promise to you."

He looked down at her expectantly, his heart thumping steadily. She lifted her eyes from the small wooden box, and he saw they were shining with tears. The sight made his throat constrict and he gently took her by the hand.

"I had meant to give it to you upon our return from Dublin but..." He trailed off, lifting one shoulder. Their arrival at Niall had hardly warranted celebrations.

She shook her head and waved away his concern. "It's beautiful," she said softly, looking down at the delicate ring.

Quin carefully removed it from its casing and held it between his fingers, turning it slowly to catch the light.

"The jeweller in Dublin who sold it to me assured me it was a traditional Irish wedding ring." He looked at her with some apprehension, thinking suddenly he might have been misled, that the man might have lied to him to loosen his pockets.

But Alannah smiled at him before looking back down at the ring, gently running one finger over the intricate silver band to caress the fine tracery that wound its way around the circle within two delicate filigree borders.

"A Claddagh ring," she said. "Two hands joined in friendship, clasping a heart in love. A loyal crown to guide them and an endless knot to bind them."

She held his eyes as she rose onto her toes to place a soft kiss on his lips. He pulled her to him and closed his eyes. When he opened them, he gently took her left hand in his and slid the ring onto her finger—the heart pointing toward her fingertip. He gripped her fingers tightly, suddenly overcome with emotion.

"Love and friendship," he said softly when he felt in control of himself once more. He ran his thumb slowly over the ring, feeling the smooth patterned surface under his skin. Alannah closed her hand around his fingers, her eyes glistening as she looked at him.

"And loyalty," she whispered.

"Always," he ended softly and brought her hand to his lips.

21.

QUIN'S HEART STILLED at last, beating slowly and steadily once more, each thump reverberating through his breast cage with every breath he took.

He opened his eyes.

His gaze fell on the carved cross that stood on a pedestal behind the simple altar, an unassuming reminder of Christ's sacrifice. He let his eyes wander, scarcely noticing the people around him as he sought to quieten his mind along with his heart while he waited.

The parish church of Ballygawley was a small edifice of the United Church of England and Ireland, that clerical establishment that sought to spread Protestantism throughout an Ireland that remained largely Catholic. The humble simplicity of the church did nothing to impair its effect, though. Instead, Quin felt the opposite was true. Here and there, the subtle symbolism of the cross drew the eye, inconspicuous signs of the building's purpose. But by stripping away all pretence, the heart and mind could focus without distraction on the grandeur of God, which no amount of opulent adornment could replicate.

Quin had been raised in far more majestic Protestant churches in England but had never felt himself to be particularly religious, finding it difficult to consolidate the Church's belief in a loving God with Man's brutality in acting out His supposed commands. But as he stood in front of the plain wooden altar— which displayed nothing but a leather-bound bible, a large white candle and a small, gilded chalice—he felt a strange sense of serenity settle over him, as if God Himself were blessing the day with His presence.

A movement at the door attracted his attention and he turned toward it, only for his breath to catch in his throat.

Alannah was standing at the threshold, looking so radiant Quin could only stare at her in wonder. She caught his eye and smiled softly at him, making him feel as though he could barely breathe. He wanted to draw her to him with the force of his will, while at the same time wanting only to look at her and drink in the sight of her.

His eyes slowly caressed the glossy fabric of her gown, which was light blue in colour in the Irish tradition, tapered at the waist and widening at the hip into a full skirt that fell in gentle ripples to the floor, the sleeves falling like soft petals around her upper arms, leaving her neck and an expanse of shoulder tantalisingly bare. Her black hair had been gathered at the sides and a delicate wreath of wildflowers placed at the crown, and he itched to run his fingers through the long dark locks that hung loose down her back.

He swallowed heavily and took an involuntary step toward her, her vivid blue eyes pulling him to her like a magnet.

"Not so fast, old boy."

Quin felt a hand on his arm and turned, startled, in the direction of the amused-sounding voice, finding himself looking at the grinning features of Lieutenant Archibald Bellinger.

Archie had arrived unexpectedly at Glaslearg a few days earlier, to Quin's unashamed delight. Hoping his visit would coincide with Quin and Alannah's wedding—the exact date of which he hadn't known, as Quin himself hadn't been sure of it when they'd met in Dublin—he had contrived to have himself excused from his duties for a week. Having managed to reach the estate in time, Archie had agreed with alacrity to be part of the ceremony.

"No matter how much you may want to," he said to Quin with a humorous glint in his eyes as he slowly shook his head, "you can't touch her until the minister says you can."

Quin smiled wryly at his friend, relishing in his presence on this day—a day where he would be marrying the woman he loved, but one where he was surrounded mostly by strangers.

His eyes passed over the small assembly, flitting from one unknown face to another, lingering briefly on Kieran's curly head, whose face was set in a carefully blank expression as he stared straight ahead. The beaming features of Rupert caught Quin's eye, making him smile as the guests rose from their seats on the wooden pews.

He turned back toward Alannah, his heart skipping a beat as he looked at her, the unfamiliarity of his surroundings fading into insignificance. Her eyes locked with his as she made her way slowly down the aisle toward him, making him forget everything else around him. When she finally reached his side, his heart was pounding rhythmically, and he eagerly took her hands while the curate began the ceremony. The words the man spoke barely registered in Quin's mind, intoxicated as he was by the vision in front of him and the delicate perfume that drifted toward him from her exquisite presence.

Looking at her standing in front of him, Quin could feel his throat constrict as an onslaught of emotions threatened to overwhelm him. He swallowed the lump in his throat, and she smiled at him, her eyes filled with tenderness, reflecting the love he felt for her. She gently squeezed his hand, and he tightened his grip on her fingers, wanting to put her hands to his lips and pull her close. One corner of her mouth lifted in amusement as she obviously read his thoughts, but she darted a glance toward the minister, who was standing between the alter and their linked hands with an expectant expression on his round face.

Alannah's smile widened as Quin's addled mind grasped the fact that the curate was waiting for him to do something. He cleared his throat and shrugged apologetically, but the stoic cleric inclined his head with a knowing look on his plump features and repeated what he'd said.

Realising they'd reached the exchanging of vows, Quin pulled himself to attention. Looking deep into Alannah's eyes, he repeated the words the curate uttered, words Quin meant with his whole heart.

"I, Quinton Fletcher Philbert Williams," he began slowly, deliberately, "take you, Alannah Mary O'Neill, to be my wedded wife and I do promise, before God and these witnesses, to be your loving and faithful husband, in plenty and in want, in joy and in sorrow, in sickness and in health, as long as we both shall live."

He could see Alannah's eyes fill with tears and he gripped her hands firmly as she repeated the same words back to him.

"I, Alannah Mary O'Neill," she started in a shaky voice, before getting herself under control, "take you, Quinton Fletcher Philbert Williams, to be my wedded husband and I do promise, before God and these witnesses, to be your loving and faithful wife, in plenty and in want, in joy and in sorrow, in sickness and in health, as long as we both shall live."

Her lips quivered, and she blinked away tears while he let go of her right hand, taking hold of her left with both of his. Holding her eyes, he gently removed the ring he'd given her only two weeks earlier, before reversing it and replacing it on the same finger, so the incised heart of the delicate circle faced inwards, a sign of their binding commitment to each other.

Alannah smiled at him, and he beamed back, leaning toward her, wanting to take her into his arms at last.

Before he could close the distance between them, though, the curate grasped each of them by the right hand, joining them together in front of him and proceeding to wrap a length of knotted cord around their linked wrists.

"You are bound together before God," the minister said while he lay his own hands over theirs, a benevolent expression on his face as he looked at each of them in turn. "*Go n-éirí Dia is bhur bpósadh libh.*"

Quin glanced at the curate in some surprise, but before he could further ponder the meaning of the Gaelic words or the significance of their bound hands, the cleric undid the cord and uttered a statement in English that required no explanation and elicited no hesitation from the addressee.

Feeling as if he were about to burst with joy, Quin finally pulled Alannah toward him, lowering his head until his lips met hers in a long-awaited, tender kiss. He closed his eyes, aware of nothing but Alannah's soft mouth on his and her hands resting delicately on his waist, his heart thumping steadily under his breastbone as he pressed her closer, relishing in the feeling of holding her in his arms as his wife at last.

A gentle throat-clearing brought him back to the present some time later and he opened his eyes to see the minister's rotund, bewhiskered face looking at him in amusement. Grinning back at him, Quin untangled himself from Alannah's embrace. Keeping hold of her hand, he turned toward the congregation and, among cheers and well wishes from people he barely knew, led her down the aisle and through the door to their joint future.

"*CHA DEOCH-SLÀINT, i gun a tràghadh.*"

"Ah…" Quin looked quizzically at Bryan, the elderly groom, who was peering down into Quin's glass with some consternation.

"Drink…drink," Bryan said encouragingly, motioning vigorously with one hand lest Quin not understand what he meant. "No health…if glass…full," he stammered in his broken English, staggering slightly, having clearly partaken generously of the wedding fare himself. Quin caught the old man by the arm before he should fall onto the scattering of edibles that remained on the table, eyeing him with some amusement.

Quin and Alannah had decided to invite the servants and the tenants to their wedding feast, wanting them to be part of the festivities and having little else in the way of acquaintances in any case. Those acquaintances of Alannah who'd attended the ceremony had been visibly shocked to learn they would be expected to celebrate alongside commoners—although they were far too well-mannered to put their disgruntlement into words. It had probably never occurred to any of them to so much as converse with members of the lower classes, much less invite them to their wedding, even wearing their Sunday best as they were—attire which would no doubt be described as scarcely bearable in any case.

Quin and Alannah had refused to let anyone put a dampener on their day, though, and were simply ignoring the perturbed expressions that appeared on the haughty faces at regular intervals—not to mention Kieran, who wasn't quite able to hide his discontent with his sister's new bridegroom, skulking gloomily around the grounds while the other guests made merry around him. All things considered—particularly seeing the enjoyment on the faces of the servants and tenants—Quin was finding the day to be a roaring success, one that hadn't reached its conclusion yet.

Beaming jovially at the thought of what was still to come, Quin took a healthy gulp from his glass, making Bryan break into a wide grin that revealed the three or so yellowed teeth that were all that remained of his dentition.

"I suppose the lack of teeth does encourage one to focus one's efforts on drink," Quin said merrily under his breath, feeling not a little intoxicated himself. He had no idea how much he'd actually had to drink, as the level of the contents of his glass seemed never to subside, someone always appearing to add "just a little more". Fortunately, it seemed the guests were starting to depart—the room being mostly empty—so his forcible alcohol ingestion was likely to be nearing its end.

Bryan nodded energetically, clearly not having heard or understood what Quin had said. Screwing up his eyes in concentration and making an obvious effort to wrap his tongue around the words he was about to utter, he said something that sounded like, "shlucht shlachta ar shlucht bur shlachta," before turning precariously on his heel and tottering off.

"With the number of times I've heard *that* today, the house will be teeming with children in no time."

Quin turned toward Alannah, who'd come up next to him. His heart skipped a beat at the sight of her and he inclined his head toward her.

"Is that so?" He leaned toward her and looked deep into her eyes, which seemed even bluer than usual above her light blue dress.

"Ah...yes," she stammered, plainly flustered by his penetrating look. She cleared her throat and dropped her eyes for a moment before looking back up at him with renewed assurance. "It means, 'may there be a generation of children on your children's children'...more or less." She cocked her head to one side and smiled mischievously, before adding, "It's better than the gem offered by Mr Moore."

"Oh?"

"*Socraichidh am pòsadh an gaol.*—Marriage takes the heat out of love."

Quin laughed. "Did he really say that to you?"

"No." Alannah gave a mirthful shake of the head. "He was imparting this piece of wisdom to a few of the other tenants as I happened to pass by them. When he saw me looking at him and realised I must have heard him, Mr Moore went bright red in the face and the other men looked terribly abashed."

"What did you do?"

"I smiled innocently at them, pretending I hadn't heard, and continued on my way.—But I doubt any of them will be repeating the saying within hearing of a woman again any time soon."

"Well, let us hope we can disprove the wisdom of Mr Moore!" Quin said with a chuckle. "I have been on the receiving end of a good few proverbs myself.— Let's see now, those well-wishers who were kind enough to translate for me wish for me never to be sent to the gander paddock and hope you will do your knitting for the infants after dark." He gave Alannah a confused look, having no idea what the latter could possibly mean. "Oh, and my favourite," he continued cheerfully, "I was reminded that whoever burns his backside must himself sit upon it."

Alannah burst out laughing, her eyes crinkling into triangles as she held her hand in front of her mouth to stifle the sound.

"Speaking of Gaelic sayings," Quin said, suddenly reminded of something he'd been meaning to ask her, "what was it the minister said at the church? And why did he bind our hands?"

"*Go n-éirí Dia is bhur bpósadh libh.*" Quin recognised the words the curate had spoken and leaned expectantly toward her. "May God and your marriage bring you joy." She smiled tenderly at him and lay her hand on his arm, making his skin tingle. Their eyes locked for a moment before she went on.

"The parish curate thinks he can convince more of the Irish to join his flock by embracing the local culture," Alannah explained, a slight flush to her cheeks. "He knows many Irish people continue to reject the Protestant faith in large part because it's thought of as *English*...a foreign belief pressed upon them by their oppressors." She gave Quin an apologetic look. "The Protestant clergy have oft found themselves to be separated from the Irish by their language and their culture, and the firm belief Protestantism is the belief of their conquerors. Ballygawley's curate is hoping to change that. He delivers some of his sermons in Gaelic and includes Ireland's traditions in his teachings where he can, hoping thus to make Protestantism more appealing to the common folk.—The first since William Bedell to do so, I'm sure," she added with a small frown.

"I see." Quin had no idea who William Bedell might have been but decided to ask a more pressing question instead. "And the tying of our hands during the wedding ceremony, that was one such tradition?"

"Yes. It's called hand-fasting. It comes from a time before Christianity came to Ireland, the ritual by which couples were married then, or later, when clerics were few. Some also say it signified a sort of temporary marriage, by which the couple could separate—if they so chose—within the trial period of a year and a day or be bound together for life thereafter." Quin raised his eyebrows in mingled surprise and amusement. "There's nothing temporary about our marriage," Alannah said softly, holding his eyes, a tender smile on her lips. "Besides," she went on, "it's quite possible hand-fasting never actually had anything to do with marriage at all."

"Oh?" Quin cocked his head in Alannah's direction, intrigued. She nodded animatedly, making Quin smile at her scholarly enthusiasm.

"Although it's generally thought hand-fasting joined a man and a woman in holy matrimony, some people believe the ceremony was originally conducted when a betrothal was announced, not when a wedding was performed, a ritual denoting the couple's mutual consent and their promise to each other."

"And what do you think?"

Alannah paused for a moment, considering. "I think it doesn't matter," she finally responded in a soft voice, tentatively taking Quin by the hand and looking into his eyes. "It's the symbolism that's important. The plighting of a troth, the binding together of two hands...and the hearts and souls of the people they belong to."

Quin leaned toward her and pulled her closer. "You have my heart and my soul," he said softly, gently stroking her cheek.

He could see her pulse beating rapidly in her throat as she looked up at him with wide eyes, her lips slightly parted as her breath came short. His own breathing was becoming noticeably heavier, and he suddenly felt as if he could not wait a moment longer to hold her in his arms. He lowered his head toward her, wanting to kiss her soft lips.

An amused sounding "ahem" behind him stayed his advance.

He turned in some annoyance, only to meet Archie's grinning face. Quin narrowed his eyes at his friend, before breaking into a lopsided smile.

"Impeccable timing, as always, Lieutenant Bellinger."

"I do apologise for interrupting what was clearly an intimate conversation," Archie said with a twinkle in his eyes, making Alannah blush. "I only wanted to bid you farewell before you retire for the night." He raised one brow in a knowing look.

"You're leaving?" Quin asked in some surprise. "Now?"

"In the morning." One corner of Archie's mouth turned up in amusement as he looked from Quin to Alannah and back again. "I thought you might miss my departure, though. I assume you'll be having a late night?"

Quin gave Archie a wry look, making his friend break into a wide grin. Alannah cleared her throat and looked down briefly before turning toward Archie with a saddened look on her face.

"Must you depart so soon, Lieutenant Bellinger?" she asked, the tips of her ears still pink.

"I'm afraid so," Archie responded with some regret, his shoulders drooping at the prospect of returning to the army in Dublin. "But enough of this Lieutenant Bellinger business," he said suddenly, flapping his hand as his good humour returned. "Any wife of Quinton's is like a sister of mine. And my sister calls me Archie...and a few other names, but those aren't suitable for polite conversation." He winked at Alannah, making her laugh.

"I thank you...Archie. And I do hope you will visit us again soon."

"I shall do my best," Archie replied solemnly before turning toward Quin and thumping him companionably on the shoulder. "I'll leave you to return to your earlier pursuits." He grinned at them and bowed to each of them in turn before bidding them farewell and ambling out of the room.

Quin watched him go in amusement, laughing softly to himself. As Archie disappeared through the doorway Quin looked around the room. It was empty. Most of the guests seemed to have left the house. He could hear merriment through the window outside, but that was no matter; the celebrations would continue well into the night, the revellers taking shelter in the barn and stable, or falling asleep where they lay.

He turned back toward Alannah, taking a step closer. She looked up at him with a smile, but her eyes flickered to something behind him, and he turned around in some irritation at having to deal with yet another intrusion on their privacy.

"Denis," he greeted the elderly butler who had materialised at the door, making an effort to rearrange his features into ones of welcome. Denis bobbed his head and made his slow way toward them, wearing a knowing look he was trying unsuccessfully to hide behind a business-like expression.

"Sorry, master," he said once he'd reached them. "I ask...more ale?" He cocked his head enquiringly in Quin's direction, relying as much on body language to communicate his needs as his limited grasp of English.

"Of course, Denis. You may bring out what we have, you needn't ask.—It is a night of celebration after all."

Denis nodded his thanks before breaking out into a gummy grin. "*Mí Lúnasa atá ann, is geall le scíth malairt oibre*," he intoned. He chuckled, as if to himself, and walked away, leaving Quin blinking after him in confusion.

He turned toward Alannah, raising his brows inquiringly, hoping to be illuminated about the latest Gaelic wisdom with which he'd evidently just been imbued.

"It's the month of August, a change is as good as a rest," she translated.

"Ah...I see," he muttered, feeling even more confused than before.

Alannah laughed at his bewilderment. "I believe he was referring to a line from an old Irish wedding song."

He cocked his head in interest and she obligingly recited the words.

"Marry when the year is new, always loving, kind and true.

When February birds do mate, you may wed, nor dread your fate.

If you wed when March winds blow, joy and sorrow both you'll know.

Marry in April when you can, joy for maiden and for man.

Marry in the month of May, you will surely rue the day.

Marry when June roses blow, over land and sea you'll go.

They who in July do wed, must labour always for their bread.
Whoever wed in August be, many a change are sure to see.
Marry in September's shine, your living will be rich and fine.
If in October you do marry, love will come but riches tarry.
If you wed in bleak November, only joy will come, remember.
When December's rain fall fast, marry and true love will last."

"Whoever wed in August be, many a change are sure to see," Quin repeated with a grin. "Based on the adventures we've had already, that seems accurate enough. Although...by the sounds of it we should have waited a few more days until the start of September. We might have spent our lives bedecked in riches and finery instead."

Alannah laughed, shaking her head. "I don't need riches and finery." She took a step toward him. "Only you."

He lowered his head until his eyes were mere inches from hers. "I believe all the guests have gone outside," he said in a husky voice, giving her a long look that made a soft blush creep into her cheeks.

Abruptly, he swept her up into his arms, making her gasp in surprise. He held her tight against his chest and looked deep into her eyes. She swallowed, and he stroked her back, his heart thumping steadily. He lifted one brow and cocked his head in the direction of the stairwell, a small smile on his lips. Alannah nodded breathlessly, her eyes wide and round as she looked at him.

He carried her up the steps, ascending the staircase with ease, barely feeling the weight of her in his arms. On the landing, he turned determinedly toward the sitting room outside his bedroom, a single thought in his mind. He pushed the half-closed door open with his shoulder and walked backwards into the room, still carrying Alannah in his arms, before resolutely heading toward the bedroom door.

"Wait," she exclaimed suddenly, sounding breathless.

"What?" Quin asked explosively, looking down at her in utter bewilderment while he hovered in front of the door.

"I...I need a moment..." she stammered, her cheeks flushed.

Quin narrowed his eyes at her and she dropped her gaze, inclining her head in the direction of the hallway.

"I'll be right back."

Quin growled deep in his throat, wanting to march her into the bedroom this instant, without further delay. He frowned at her but smoothed out his features when she looked up at him with pleading eyes.

"Alright," he said slowly and unenthusiastically, putting her down reluctantly. "One moment." He raised his eyebrows for emphasis.

Alannah started to nod but he pulled her toward him and kissed her thoroughly, pressing her close to him so the lengths of their bodies met, leaving her swaying in front of him when he finally released her. He chuckled, somewhat breathlessly, and nodded toward the bedroom door.

"I'll be waiting."

MY HEART BEAT wildly as I turned away from Quin's grinning face. I rapidly made my way toward my former room, feeling an urgent need for a few minutes' respite. When I reached the room, I quickly closed the door behind me and headed toward the commode. Once the pressure on my bladder that had led me there had been eased, I sat down briefly at my dressing table to remove the wreath of flowers from my hair. I breathed deeply a few times to slow my heart, staring at my flushed reflection as I tried to regain my composure, until I at last felt ready to face Quin once more.

My serenity didn't last very long.

The moment I headed back into the corridor my heart resumed its frantic tattoo. By the time I found myself standing in front of the door to what was now our marital bedchamber, trying to work up the courage to go in, it was thumping ready to burst through my chest.

When I finally opened the door, I instantly caught sight of Quin. He had removed his jacket and was sitting on the edge of the big tester bed that dominated the room. He lifted his head, and the expression on his face made my heart leap into my throat, leaving me trembling with anticipation—and a touch of apprehension. I closed the door and leaned against it for support. Quin rose and came toward me, slowly, like a big cat with its eyes on its prey, green orbs burning with longing. He held my gaze until he stood right in front of me, making me feel utterly at his mercy. He seemed even taller than usual, looming over me in a way that was almost unnerving. He reached out a hand and lightly stroked my cheek, doing something to put me at ease, although my heart kept pounding steadily. He bent his head toward me and kissed me, slowly and lingeringly, gently pulling me close to him and cradling my head with one big hand, leaving me lightheaded and weak at the knees. When he finally released me, he swung me up into his arms and carried me to the bed, where he sat down and held me on his lap, gently stroking my back.

"Are you afraid?" he whispered into the top of my head.

"A little," I admitted, my voice reasonably steady. "But, I do...I mean...I want..."

He grinned. "You want me in your bed?"

"Well, yes...I do," I said with what dignity I could muster, "but that doesn't seem like a very ladylike thing to say."

"You needn't be a lady for me here, Mrs Williams."

I was only slightly shocked at this, and undeniably thrilled at my new title. He was mine. Despite all odds, he was mine.

"You also don't need to be afraid," he said, all humour gone from his voice. "I'm not going to hurt you." He stroked my cheek and looked deep into my eyes.

I swallowed, feeling my heart thump beneath my breastbone while my breath came short.

But I trusted Quin completely.

I shyly ran my hand up his arm, sliding my palm up the snowy white fabric of his shirt, along the curve of his shoulder and up to the cravat at his neck, hesitantly pulling his head down toward me. I kissed him softly, closing my eyes and savouring his touch, wanting to lose myself in his tender embrace. After what seemed like a long time, he gently pulled his head away from mine and stood up still cradling me in his arms. He set me down in front of him and turned me so my back was toward him, holding me steady with a hand on my waist. He swept my hair over one shoulder and kissed the nape of my neck while his deft fingers undid the buttons of my dress, before sliding it slowly down over my hips, followed by my corset and petticoats, leaving me covered only in my shift.

When he turned me to face him again, the naked hunger I saw in his eyes tore straight through me, touching a place inside me I hadn't known was there.

With trembling fingers, I tentatively removed the cravat around Quin's neck, before turning my attention to unbuttoning his waistcoat, slowly working my way through the numerous silver buttons that adorned the cream silk. After a moment, he assisted me in my efforts by simply tearing the waistcoat off, making buttons fly in all directions. I laughed nervously, but he pulled me toward him and kissed me again, while slowly running his hands down my legs to undo my garters, before dispossessing me of my shoes and stockings, caressing me through my shift as he went. He followed suit with his own hosiery and his trousers and smallclothes, holding my eyes as he pushed the latter deliberately over his rump, leaving him wearing only his knee-length shirt, which he pulled off over his head in one smooth motion a moment later. My heart leapt into my throat and started pounding furiously as he reached out his hands to remove my own remaining garment in a similar fashion.

Standing before him, with nothing but my hair covering my naked breasts, I might have felt vulnerable and exposed, except for the fact that he, too, was laying himself bare before me, trusting me with his innermost self, as I was trusting him.

"You are so beautiful," Quin whispered, his voice heavy with emotion.

He pulled me toward him and lay me gently down on the bed. The feeling of his bare skin on mine took my breath away. I remained breathless as he caressed me tenderly with his hands and mouth, exploring every part of me, making my body respond to his in ways I hadn't thought possible. I quivered beneath him, wanting more. He came to me slowly, carefully, wanting to keep his promise not to hurt me, looking searchingly into my face and caressing my cheek. When I at last assured him he could move, he cried out within moments, carrying us both over the edge into the shuddering release of our mutual joy.

WHEN I FINALLY returned to myself, I cracked open one eye, only to see two anxious green ones looking down at me.

"Did I hurt you?"

"A little," I admitted.

"I'm sorry," he said, stroking my cheek, his face creased with concern.

"It's alright. It isn't that bad. And I'm told it's only temporary."

"And who told you that?" he asked, surprised.

"Ah...well...one or two of the servants."

"The servants? And since when does a lady discuss such things with a servant?"

I wasn't sure whether he was more shocked I'd spoken so openly to a servant or that such a topic had been discussed in the first place.

"Well, my mother was dead," I said defiantly. "Who else was I to talk to?" I stuck my chin out boldly, daring him to object. But he only looked at me in astonishment. "You see, I knew how things worked...um...between a man and a woman...at least theoretically..." I could feel heat rising in my cheeks, but I soldiered on. "There's a difference between knowing the mechanics of something and really understanding it. So I decided to ask." I stared at him rebelliously at this further evidence of my unladylike behaviour.

"I see," he said slowly, an unreadable expression on his face. "And what other titbits of information did your...servants...bestow upon you?" He raised his eyebrows questioningly.

"Ah...um..." I stammered as my cheeks started to blaze again.

Quin cocked his head to one side and looked at me expectantly.

"Well...Margaret...ah...she did say that...um..." I lowered my eyes and cleared my throat.

"Yes?"

"She said that...ah...girth...was more important than...um...length."

Quin's lips quivered, one side turning up in amusement. "Is that so?"

"Apparently." I shrugged my shoulders in some discomfort.

"And did you find yourself to be...satisfied in that regard?"

The blush that had only just abated came back in full force, making Quin break out in a wide grin, to my extreme agitation.

"I have been quite satisfied, thank you," I said, making an effort to sound dignified under the circumstances. "As for me being able to make a general assessment about the accuracy of Margaret's observation...I have no comparison and therefore I cannot say." I lifted my chin and looked him in the eye. "But I would say that you are...ah...quite well proportioned."

Quin looked at me for a moment, before bursting into laughter. He laughed and laughed, in great gasping whoops that made his eyes water as he held his straining sides. Finally, he took my head between his hands and kissed me thoroughly.

"Oh, I do love you, Alannah! Here I thought I would have to teach you all about the ways of the flesh, and it turns out you're already an expert on the subject. I shouldn't have expected anything less from a scholar like you."

"I'm hardly an expert! In fact"—I pulled him toward me with growing confidence—"I believe I'm in need of another practical demonstration."

QUIN LOOKED AT Alannah, asleep next to him, with her silky black hair spread out wildly around her head, her skin glowing like polished ivory in the moonlight.

He touched her cheek lightly with his index finger, tracing the line of her jaw and her tender lips. She moaned softly and rolled toward him, making him want to take her all over again.

Instead, he placed a chaste kiss on her forehead and gently stroked her back.

The tenderness he felt at the sight of her was like nothing he'd ever experienced before. He wanted to hold her close, keep her safe, protect her from all that threatened her in the world; and to touch her, every inch of her, to possess her, body and soul. She had been so trusting of him, opening up to him in complete surrender, without reservations, even though she'd been nervous and afraid. But by giving of herself so freely, he had felt at *her* mercy, as she reached into the depths of his soul and bound him to her more strongly than any marriage vow ever could.

His past before he met her paled into insignificance and he knew without question he would spend the rest of his life doing everything he could to make her happy and to keep her safe, hoping only he would do it right and be worthy of her.

22.

WHEN I WOKE up the following morning, I felt utterly content, with a sense of tranquillity I hadn't experienced since I was a child. Quin was nowhere to be seen, which dampened my spirits momentarily until I remembered I would be waking up next to him every morning for the rest of my life.

I jumped out of bed, wincing slightly, and got dressed. As I was sitting at the dressing table, the door opened, and Quin came in, presumably returned from seeing off Archie on his way back to Dublin. My heart jumped at the sight of him, dressed in a fine burgundy morning coat that set off his olive skin, and my hands itched to touch his freshly shaven cheeks and sensuous mouth.

Then I remembered what he'd been doing with his mouth the night before and started blushing furiously.

"Is something wrong, Mrs Williams?" I could see Quin's grin reflected in the mirror as he walked toward the dressing table.

"Um…no…certainly not," I stammered, suddenly feeling inexplicably shy of him and unable to meet his eyes.

"Alannah." He came to stand next to me and lifted my face toward him, making me feel breathless. "Did you enjoy your wedding night?"

"Yes," I croaked barely audibly. "I most assuredly did."

"Good. Then there's no need to be embarrassed. Besides," he added with a smile that showed his dimple, "you'll become more accustomed to our liaisons with a bit more practice. Shall we give it another try this evening?" He raised one questioning brow.

"Um…" I cleared my throat. "Why not now?" I could feel my cheeks start to blaze again but stuck my chin out defiantly.

A wide smile broke out on Quin's face, and he pulled me up from my chair and gathered me to himself. "Alannah, I can't tell you how long I've waited for you to present me with an offer like that."

He nuzzled affectionately at my neck. I slowly slid my hands across his broad shoulders and down his back to his rump, pulling him closer to feel the length of his body pressed against mine.

Quin groaned. "If only I could accept it."

"Why can't you?" I breathed into his ear.

"I promised Mr Smith to travel with him to Augher to meet a potential new employer. I had made some enquiries on his behalf and received a note that an interested party would like to meet with him today. I had assured Mr Smith I would accompany him to the meeting to vouch for him. I'm only sorry about the timing."

I waved away his apology. "What about Kieran?"

The only reason Mr Smith was looking for a new employer was that Kieran had sold Niall without making provisions for any of the farm's personnel. While Quin had found a place for the other servants at Glaslearg, he had no need for an overseer, having already hired someone else to take over the role. The new overseer, Mr Dunne, who'd been introduced to Quin by Constable Ryan, was scheduled to arrive at the estate in a week or so.

Quin sighed. "I asked him what he intended to do with his staff after he sold Niall, but he only shrugged, essentially leaving the matter to me. I also informed him I intended to act as character witness for Mr Smith to ensure he found new employment, thinking Kieran might want to accompany us, but he made no such suggestion...although he did thank me for my efforts."

Quin sounded rather surprised at this sign of civility from my brother.

"I'm sorry," I said, feeling I ought to apologise on Kieran's behalf.

"It's not your fault." Quin's face softened as he looked at me. "I rather think your brother is embarrassed about the whole thing."

"I think you're right. He avoids the topic and looks uncomfortable whenever it comes up.—And he still hasn't said who bought the farm or how much he sold it for." I waved a hand dismissively. "It doesn't matter but..."

"I know." Quin stroked my cheek. "You had hoped for things to be different between the two of you."

I nodded. While Kieran was treating me courteously enough during our limited interactions, his decision to sell Niall without my knowledge had made it difficult to continue on the path of reconciliation that had been cautiously laid out when he'd returned from Omagh gaol. I understood his reluctance to confide in Quin but had hoped he might feel differently toward me, all things considered.

"He'll come around," I said, trying to convince myself as much as Quin. Kieran's choices had been made; he would have to live with them. If he chose to do so alone, there was nothing I could do about it.

Quin took my face in both his hands and lowered his head toward me, kissing me lightly on the lips. I pulled him toward me, and the pressure of his mouth increased, promise of a passion reluctantly held in check.

"I shall try to think of something to keep your mind off such troubling thoughts."

The look in his sparkling green eyes gave me a glimpse of what he had in mind, and my heart began to beat a little faster.

"I'm looking forward to it," I said, all thoughts of Kieran forgotten.

"I CAN'T GET enough of you," Quin whispered into my ear that evening as we lay dishevelled on the bedclothes, limbs entangled.

I kissed his temple, which was damp with exertion. "I feel the same way."

I stroked him gently, running my hand lightly across his chest and down his flat belly to the top of his thigh, and back up again, marvelling at the feel of him.

"How do married people ever do anything else?" I asked.

He chuckled, a sound that reverberated through his deep chest into my hand.

"I don't think it's quite the same for all married people. I've seen plenty of loveless marriages, where the act is no doubt performed purely for procreative purposes, if at all. And by all accounts," he continued cheerfully, "even those that start out passionately enough tend to end in barely concealed disdain. You'll tire of me soon enough."

He grinned down at me, and I narrowed my eyes at him. "No, I won't."

He raised an eyebrow.

"Never," I insisted, pulling his head toward me.

He returned my kiss eagerly and rolled closer to me, so he was half lying on top of me, one hand gently caressing my breast. I ran my hand across his chest and down his side, pausing briefly as I felt the scar from Doyle's sword under my palm. Abruptly, he rolled me onto my back and started kissing my neck, moving slowly from the angle of my jaw to my collarbone and down to my breasts. I shivered as his mouth continued its descent, moving across the sensitive skin of my belly, and lower still.

"Quin," I said breathlessly.

He lifted himself onto his elbows on top of me, his forehead almost touching mine. I wrapped my legs around him and pulled him closer until he sighed with contentment. My mouth found his as we rocked together gently, like the lapping of the water in the ocean, feeling the strength of the wave build until it crashed over us, washing away all consciousness until only sensation remained.

RETURNING TO BED after visiting the commode some time later, my heart gave a slight jolt of excitement at the novel thought of sharing a bed with Quin. I tried to make no noise as I lay back down beside him, but he was fast asleep and clearly hadn't noticed my absence. He was turned slightly toward me, and his chest was rising and falling in peaceful rhythm. An overwhelming feeling of love rose in me as I looked at him, making my throat constrict in its intensity.

He sighed in his sleep and his eyelids flickered, making me wonder what he might be dreaming about.

I knew what I would be dreaming about.

I smiled wryly at the thought, my eyes travelling slowly over Quin's body, drinking in the sight of him. We hadn't closed the curtains before going to bed—being otherwise occupied—and Quin was bathed in the light of the moon coming in through the window. He breathed in deeply, parting his lips slightly. I wanted to lean forward and kiss him but didn't, instead enjoying the opportunity to observe him unobserved.

His dark lashes lay against his high cheekbones, his strong features softened by the sensuousness of his mouth. His body was long and graceful, smoothly muscular like a finely chiselled sculpture. My eyes moved over his even skin, which was lightly dusted with fine hairs on arms and legs, with a darker patch at the apex of his thighs that made me blush as I looked at its sleeping inhabitant. The only blemish to his features was the smattering of scars that dotted his body, signs of battles fought and won—or at least, survived.

My eyes traced the star-shaped scar that marred the right side of his chest, just beneath the collarbone where it joined the shoulder. The centre of the scar was a circular mass, from which tendrils of knotted tissue emanated like spokes on a wheel. Quin had told me the scar had been caused by a bullet wound he'd sustained in China. Seeming frightfully nonchalant about it, he'd informed me the bullet had nicked the large vessel that ran beneath the collarbone, causing him to lose a large amount of blood. Weakened as he was, the wound had festered, leaving him gravely ill and close to death.

Thinking about it now made the blood rush to my head in fear of what might have been, and I quickly tore my eyes away from his shoulder, only for my gaze to fall onto the long line that snaked its way along the left side of his abdomen, from his ribs down to the level of his hipbone. At the top, the scar was thin and barely visible, but lower down, on the smooth flesh of his belly, it was still an angry red. I swallowed the lump in my throat and reached out a hand, tracing the line lightly with my index finger.

Quin opened his eyes, startling me. I tried to pull my hand away, but he took it and held it in his own.

"You're not still worried about him, are you?" he asked softly, stroking the back of my hand.

"No.—At least not most of the time." Since hearing there likely was no royal pardon to worry about—and probably never had been—I *had* felt more at ease. "I just…"

"You don't still think you're to blame, do you?"

"No…" I repeated quietly, looking down.

"At least not most of the time," Quin added with a slight smile.

I shook my head. He gathered me into his arms, kissed my forehead and stroked the back of my head.

"Everything will be alright. Sleep now. I'll keep you safe."

23.

A FEW DAYS after the wedding, I found myself alone in the house with the servants. Quin had left on an errand shortly after breakfast and, as was becoming his habit, Kieran was nowhere to be seen. With nothing else to do, I decided to ride to the Murphys' croft. The tenants had started building their new cottages one or two days earlier, and I thought I would go see how they were faring.

When I arrived at the Murphys' plot, Mary greeted me shyly and, hearing the reason for my visit, invited me to see what the men had accomplished so far.

I was impressed.

Mary's husband, a burly, severe-looking fellow named Robert, and the four men from the neighbouring plots were busy erecting the walls of the new house, which had already risen a good two feet above the ground. The men greeted me courteously but briefly before returning to their work as I circled the growing structure. Over the low threshold of the rising walls, I could see the flat surface of the foundation stones that had been neatly laid out over the cleared soil. There was a gap each in the front and the back of the budding wall where the doors would go, which would open into the main room of the cottage. This would contain the stone chimney and would be the family's main living quarters, with another smaller room adjoining the larger one meant for sleeping. While the structure would be dwarfed by the estate's sizeable manor house, it would nevertheless be a far cry from the tiny, gloomy mud cabin the Murphys had been living in thus far, not least of all because of the addition of two or three windows in the cottage walls.

I smiled at Mary, who couldn't hide her excitement at the growing building, her normally rather stern features transformed with childlike joy.

"Stones," she said with a shy smile, pointing at the pile of rubble from which the men were garnering the building materials for the walls.

"Yes." I returned the smile as Ellen, Mary's two-year-old daughter, started hopping around us repeating the word with glee.

I pointed at the vat that stood next to the stones, which would be used to hold the rubble in place. "Plaster."

Mary repeated the word slowly, trying to commit it to memory. I had no doubt she would. When I'd come to see her the previous week, she had hesitantly asked me if I could teach her a few words of English. I'd been happy to agree and had found her to be a more than able student, seeming to have an enormous capacity to remember long lists of words in a foreign tongue.

"Plaster," she repeated and laughed light-heartedly at the unfamiliar term, making Ellen and Mary's three older children break out in giggles.

I saw Robert glance in our direction at the sound, a frown on his face as he looked at his wife. Perhaps he didn't want Mary to learn English, I thought. Or perhaps he didn't want her to be overly friendly with me.

I had tried my best to make the tenants feel comfortable around me since I'd come to Glaslearg, visiting them regularly and wanting them to think of me as somebody they could turn to—and possibly even a friend—as much as the lady of the manor. While some, like Mary, seemed slowly to be doing just that, for others the divide between landowner and tenant was simply too large to cross and they remained reserved. I could understand this but hoped in time the tenants would realise Quin and I truly had their best interests at heart.

Building all of them stone houses should go some way toward making them think so, I thought wryly.

Quin had been more than generous with his assistance, not only promising to provide each family with any materials that couldn't be gathered from the surrounding countryside for the building of a two-roomed, chimneyed and windowed cottage, but also paying the men to do the building, a fact I still found vastly entertaining. Although he would likely spend less money than he'd initially thought, it was still a good amount to be investing in the tenants in such a short space of time, especially since any income from the estate's crops was still a year away.

I looked back at the building site, watching the men stack the irregularly shaped stones onto the twenty-inch-thick walls that would bear the weight of the family's new home. While building with prefabricated bricks would have been easier, it would have been much more expensive. Although fine brick-making clay could be found throughout most of Ireland, the thin bricks formed from the clay's firing were laboriously produced, a few at a time. Bricks tended to be used only by the rich, or if no other materials were available. Most rural homes were built using earth or, as the tenants were doing now, with rubble, in this case from the limestone that could be found in abundance in numerous locations throughout county Tyrone.

I smiled, remembering how I'd pointed out the merits of using rubble stone to Quin, who'd initially contemplated buying bricks. Although the life he'd lived in London must have been vastly different to the one he was living here, he'd done exceedingly well integrating himself into the workings of the estate and getting to grips with local customs.

Despite the tenants' initial suspicion, they had come to respect him—for making good on his promises and treating everyone with the utmost courtesy, I thought. He never acted as if he thought himself superior to any of his tenants or his servants—as many landowners no doubt did—and he also didn't consider himself above getting involved in the dirty work required on the estate. In fact, he had plans to regularly assist the men with the building of the cottages, and had every intention of lending a hand in the upcoming harvest and the planting of the next season's crops that would follow.

As if my thoughts had summoned him, my eye caught sight of Quin himself riding toward the Murphys' cottage from the adjoining plot. A short distance behind him I could see another rider topping the hill that led down into the Murphys' land. As my eyes adjusted to the sunlight that shone through the wisps of cloud dotting the sky, I realised with some surprise that the rider was Kieran.

"Alannah," Quin said with a smile as he dismounted his horse. "I hadn't expected to see you here."

"Quin." I broke into a broad smile myself, my heart fluttering as it always did when I encountered him unexpectedly during the day.

Without knowing quite how I got there I found myself standing right in front of him, wanting to pull him down to me for a lingering kiss. He inconspicuously shook his head, glancing at the onlookers through the corners of his eyes with his eyebrows raised. I took a quick step back and cleared my throat, embarrassed at having forgotten we had an audience.

Quin broke into a broad grin seeing my discomposure, thoroughly enjoying the effect he was so obviously having on me. I narrowed my eyes at him, but this only made him laugh as he offered me his arm. Quite unable to feign being angry with him, I took his arm with a laugh of my own, relishing in the feel of his sun-warmed skin under my hand. It was a beautiful summer's day and he'd rolled up the sleeves of his shirt to the elbows, exposing the fine muscles of his forearms and the delicate bones of his wrists. My fingertips tingled as I slowly ran my fingers over his skin, feeling the strength of the muscles and bones beneath, and the softness of the light hairs on top.

Wondering whether I would ever stop being completely enraptured by my new husband—a term that gave me a thrill each time I used it—I attempted to clear my mind of the diverting thoughts even the slightest expanse of his bare skin tended to evoke.

Wanting to distract myself I asked him about Kieran's presence at the Murphys.

"He said he wanted to assist with the building," Quin explained with a sense of disbelief.

Since his arrival at Glaslearg three weeks earlier, Kieran had shown no inclination to involve himself in anything to do with the estate, least of all the tenants. He had moped about, barely interacting with either Quin or myself, evidently feeling sorry for himself. Why he should feel that way, I had no idea, as he was entirely to blame for his situation. If he hadn't made the rash—and utterly preposterous—decision to sell his own farm, he wouldn't have to live on Quin's.

Thinking about it still made me puff up with rage. I just could not understand how he could have sold a farm that had been in O'Neill hands for generations, and without even consulting me, his only living relative and sole descendent of Cathal O'Neill's family line besides himself.

I shook off the thought.

I'd promised myself I would not obsess about Kieran and the fate of Talamh na Niall. It was done and there was nothing I could do, nor was there anything I could have done in the first place once Kieran had made up his mind. Whether I was happy about it or not, it *had* been his farm, to do with as he liked, no matter how upsetting his choices might be to me. The only thing that *was* under my control was how I would react to Kieran's continued presence on Glaslearg after his decision had been made. Quin had said he would give him a chance to find a place at Glaslearg despite his reservations about the whole affair, and I would do the same—seeing as I agreed with Quin's assessment that Kieran was likely to be with us for a while. I therefore made a conscious effort to smooth out the frown that had formed between my brows and rearrange my features into ones of welcome as I turned to greet my brother, who was walking toward us from his horse.

"Kieran, how nice of you to come." Suddenly thinking Kieran might mistake the statement for a hidden insult—although I truly *was* happy to see him outside of the manor house at last—I hastened to add, "Quin said you wanted to assist with the building of the cottages. I'm sure the tenants will be pleased."

I smiled encouragingly but he looked at me dubiously as the men continued with their work, with only the briefest of greetings muttered in Kieran's general direction. They would hardly greet him with open arms, I thought—they barely knew him, if at all.

"Give them some time, they'll get used to you," I said, remembering how Quin and I had been received when we'd visited the tenants for the first time.

Kieran shrugged his shoulders and ambled off toward the growing cottage, inspecting the men's work.

"I came to see how the building was proceeding," I explained to Quin as we followed Kieran at a distance. "They've done well, haven't they?"

"Exceedingly well," Quin agreed, smiling down at me, his green eyes sparkling in the sun. "At the rate they're progressing, we might have all of the cabins built before the New Year after all." He laughed, revealing his dimple. "No, that's unlikely." He shook his head. "They won't be able to continue at this pace. Soon the potato crop will be ready for the harvest, and the fields will need to be prepared and the autumn planting begun. They won't have nearly as much time for building with so much additional work to do. Besides, I'll need a bit more time to acquire additional materials. I'm afraid the other tenants will need to wait a little longer for their new homes. Still"—he looked at the growing, solid construction with a sense of pride in his eyes—"it will be worth the wait."

"Like you," I blurted out without thinking and blushed.

Only a few months had passed since the day Mr Quinton Fletcher Philbert Williams had knocked on my door. And yet, I felt as if I had waited for Quin far longer than that, my whole life in fact.

"I waited for you for a long time too," Quin said softly, his voice husky with emotion. He looked down at me with eyes suffused with tenderness, and my heart started thumping steadily beneath my breastbone. He was mine now, body and soul. I leaned toward him, breathing in his musky scent, my body inexorably drawn to his.

"Um..." He carefully straightened up to keep a respectful distance between us. "Perhaps we should join the others?"

"Oh…" I had quite forgotten anyone else existed. "Yes…of course."

Flustered by my reaction to him—when he'd done nothing but smile at me—I self-consciously adjusted my bonnet and patted the tail of my upturned hair before grasping Quin's arm once more and ambling alongside him toward Robert and the other men, who were pausing briefly in their work to take some refreshments. Mary was standing slightly apart from the others, and I went to join her while Quin strode confidently into the group of men, despite the fact they were conversing in Gaelic and throwing the odd nervous glance in his direction.

Respect him they might, but that didn't mean they were entirely comfortable in his presence.

Seeing the men's reaction gave me a curious feeling, and my mind returned to my earlier contemplation of the relationship between tenants and landlords. I understood the tenants' mingled sense of deference and suspicion—I myself had been wary of Quin when I'd first met him simply because he was English—but it saddened me it should be so. In an ideal world, the tenants should be safe in the knowledge that their landlord would see to their welfare—as would have been the case in the days when landlords and their dependants were linked by clan and culture, rather than just financial affairs.

In reality, most Irish peasants would probably find it difficult to feel any sort of warmth toward their proprietors, as their own unfortunate state was inextricably linked with the poor management of Irish land at the hands of the British in the past. The English crown had dispossessed countless Irishmen of the land they'd held for generations and placed it in the hands of the British gentry, many of whom found it easier to rent out tracts of their land to middlemen instead of caring for it themselves. Middlemen—who were often wealthy British countrymen themselves—would sublet these plots to tenant farmers and collect the rent for the landowners, with a share for themselves. Unfortunately, the system was open for exploitation, as any money earned above the landlord's share constituted the middleman's profit, which meant tenants and landless labourers seeking conacre often found themselves paying exorbitant rents for tiny plots of land to satisfy the middleman's greed.

Ironically, though, while the poor Irish smallholders and landless labourers suffered the most as a result of the middleman system, some landlords themselves had started finding the arrangement to be somewhat lacking, as they discovered their divided farmland was earning them less money—and causing them more debt—than leasing out larger tracts of land might have done.

Landlords were required to pay several taxes for their tenants, including the much-fought-over church tax for the upkeep of the Protestant Church of Ireland by the largely Catholic inhabitants of the land, which added up to a not inconsequential sum with the number of tenants that occupied even small tracts of land. Landowners were also in large part dependent on the rent due to them from their tenants for their income, which sometimes proved difficult to collect. And while tenants who were unable to pay the rent could be evicted, this still left the landlords without the season's rent collected, making their own indebtedness grow.

Making matters worse, middlemen were notoriously uninterested in improving the state of the land they were managing—much like Glaslearg's former steward Mr Brennan had been—meaning landlords could find themselves with estates that were subdivided, sublet and in disarray, without much scope for increasing its earnings.

A growing number of landlords had learnt their lesson, turning away from the middleman system and managing their own estates, or hiring land agents to do so for them, in an effort to consolidate their subdivided land, reduce their debt and improve their income. Unfortunately, though, such changes were not easy to achieve after years and years of widespread mismanagement, and the damage to the Irish people had been done. While many tenants who farmed large tracts of land were prospering under the favourable market conditions, small tenants and landless labourers were sliding ever deeper into poverty as they struggled to make ends meet—a plight made more pronounced by a growing population whose demand for land was putting pressure on available resources and steadily driving up the rent, leaving the poorest with little more than the food they could grow to survive.

"Things will be different here," I murmured under my breath as I reached Mary's side. She smiled shyly at me and offered me some ale. I took it with thanks, enjoying the feeling of the cool bottle in my hand before taking a refreshing sip.

I glanced over at the men, who were looking slightly more relaxed. As I watched, Kieran leaned toward Quin, evidently translating something one of the men had said, for Quin smiled broadly, said something in English and reached out a hand to the man who'd spoken in Gaelic. The tenant, who was a short and stringy sort, seemed slightly startled at Quin's gesture, but cautiously shook his outstretched hand, looking undeniably pleased.

My heart warmed at the sight. Quin would do just fine, I thought, language barrier notwithstanding. He was the type of person who drew others to him, who was the centre of attention in a room full of people—not because he wanted to be, but because he couldn't not be. His charisma, his even-tempered nature and his genuine interest in others made those around him want to be in his presence because he made them feel at ease. He'd had this effect on me from virtually the moment we'd met, making me feel like I could talk to him about anything, that he would hear me, that he would listen.

That I was important.

Looking back at the men surrounding him, I could see he was starting to have the same effect on them, as they tried cautiously to converse with him, Kieran translating where necessary. The conversation was brief—there was work to be done—but when they parted ways, some of the wariness in the tenants' eyes had disappeared, and while they couldn't quite be described as smiling, their features wore a note a tranquillity in stark contrast to the thinly veiled suspicion that had greeted Quin before.

He smiled at me when he saw me looking at him, his eyes lightening at the knowledge that a small part of the battle was being won.

ABOUT A WEEK later, I was sitting in the library reading a letter from my former tutor, Mr Henderson, which had arrived that morning, when Quin and Kieran walked through the door, returning from their day assisting the tenants with the building.

To my surprise—and quiet relief—Kieran had gone out again the day after he'd visited the Murphys, and every day after that. Although there was still a noticeable strain between my brother and my husband—particularly on Kieran's part—the two of them had gotten into the habit of traveling the estate together on their rounds.

I knew Quin was grudgingly finding himself feeling almost grateful for Kieran's presence—awkward though he assured me it was—as Kieran's knowledge of Gaelic made it easier for Quin to talk to the tenants. I had offered my own assistance as translator, but Quin hadn't wanted me to have to follow him around all day. Kieran's decision to work alongside him had conveniently solved the problem. Beyond that, though, I also knew Quin was happy to see my brother try to integrate himself into the workings of Glaslearg. Quin hadn't said anything to Kieran about his intentions or asked him about the sale of Niall after he'd moved into the manor house, but I knew Kieran's disinterest and complete lack of transparency bothered him. He was glad, therefore, that Kieran had finally chosen to do something useful with his time instead of living off Quin's good graces—which he'd been doing without asking.

As far as Kieran was concerned, I thought his willingness to be in Quin's company stemmed from more selfish reasons. I had seen how awkwardly he behaved around the tenants, not quite sure what to say to them or how to speak to them. He'd never had a knack for easy social interactions, finding it difficult to start conversations with people he didn't know and always looking slightly out of place, even in groups that were familiar to him. I thought he was using Quin's presence to make his own appearance less conspicuous, riding on Quin's effortless charm to hide his own insecurities.

As they walked through the door now, though, they wore matching expressions of excitement, overlaid with a sense of seriousness that immediately made me drop the letter and sit up straight.

"Doyle's execution has been rescheduled," Quin announced without preliminaries, reaching me in three strides and holding out his hands to me.

My heart gave a sudden lurch and I grasped Quin's hands firmly as he pulled me up from my seat.

"When?" I asked in a shaky voice.

"Three days," Kieran responded, coming up next to Quin.

They glanced at each other, seeming to be in complete understanding for the first time in their tumultuous acquaintance. In this, at least, they'd found some common ground.

"The pardon…?"

"Dismissed," Quin said in a firm voice. "If there ever was one to begin with."

He took a step closer to me and wrapped his arms around me.

"It's almost over," he whispered into my ear and pulled me close.

MARTIN PATRICK DOYLE, convicted traitor and murderer, was hanged three days later on Gallows Hill. The site hadn't been used for public hangings in Omagh since the execution of the highwayman Tom Eccles at the end of the eighteenth century, but it was felt the seriousness of Doyle's crimes warranted a return to tradition. The pens of the cattle market that now occupied the hill had been removed, allowing the spectators to flock in by the dozens. Amid jeers and shouts, the condemned had been brought to the gallows, mouth working incessantly in an unintelligible plea for mercy, frightened eyes flickering back and forth in a face that was bruised and battered, a parting gift from his fellow inmates.

As unpopular as he had been in life, so he would be in death.

As the convicted fell, the rope taughtened, snapping his neck. Death was instantaneous. Though doubtless pleasant for the recipient, the hangman's expertise was lost on the crowd, who had hoped for a more entertaining and drawn-out demise, one that went beyond the stench of voided bowels.

I had no such bloodlust myself and was content to hear about the execution from Kieran, who *had* wanted to see Doyle hang. Quin had asked me cautiously if I wanted to accompany Kieran, but I'd felt no desire to see the man, even to witness his well-deserved death. And whether I'd gone to see him or not, the result was the same—the world was a safer place without Martin Doyle in it, and Quin and I could finally rest assured that the danger he'd posed had passed.

24.

"THAT'S THE LAST one," Kieran said as Thomas O'Reilly placed a medium-sized rubble stone in the last open space in the south-facing wall and added a dollop of plaster with a flourish.

O'Reilly turned around to the other men, grinning broadly, before taking a step back to admire their handiwork. The walls of the cabin were complete, the bumpy stone surface merely awaiting a layer of plaster and limewash for protection. The timber frame for the front door was in place, as were the slender window sashes on either side of the entrance. A further small window sash adorned the rear side of the house, which also featured another door into the main living quarters. The chimney rose above the outer wall of the main room, at the apex of the wall's triangular peak, where the ridge of the roof would be.

Quin shook hands with O'Reilly and the tenants who'd helped him construct the walls for the new cabin, congratulating them on a job well done. Although the men were clearly pleased, their excitement was kept in check. There was still much to be done before the O'Reillys could move into their new home.

Once the walls were plastered, the men would turn their attention to raising the frame for the roof, which would be covered in thatch. Quin had initially hoped to construct the roofs out of more sturdy material but using slate or tiles would have been too expensive—he intended to build fifty cabins after all! Or forty-two, he corrected himself, eight of the families (all with only two or three occupants per home) having opted to stay in their existing huts, with the explanation that it wasn't worth the trouble of improving them, as they only used them to sleep in anyway. Still, the enormity of the task Quin had set himself sometimes staggered him, until he reminded himself Rome wasn't built in a day and continued with his work, one stone at a time. His initial apprehensions about the roofs had also abated, as he'd been informed thatch was a perfectly acceptable, effective and inexpensive covering, being indeed the most commonly used type of roof covering in Ireland. In fact, the tenants had been surprised he'd thought of using anything other than thatch, and it was in large part their consensus that had swayed his decision.

He had, however, insisted on providing them with nails to secure the timber frames, rather than the cheaper wooden pegs that were traditionally used, and had seen to the procurement of numerous pieces of sturdy timber, which had arrived from Dublin the week before. These would be used in combination with any wood the tenants were able to gather from the surrounding countryside—this being in limited supply—to construct the frames. To begin with, the thatch itself would be made up of any materials that came to hand, including the heather and broom that had encroached on the unused farmland on Glaslearg. For future maintenance of the roofs, the tenants would be able to use the stems from the harvested wheat and oats.

"Here," Kieran said, handing Quin a bottle of ale.

Quin accepted it with thanks and drained the contents with barely a pause for breath. Although they'd only needed half the morning to complete the work, it had been an exhausting effort, having to haul the stones to the top of the wall and chimney.

"Will you be helping with the plastering?" Kieran asked.

Quin shook his head. "I was hoping to finish demarcating the lower fields."

He grimaced slightly. In preparation for the upcoming planting of the winter crops, he'd started clearing the existing fields, removing the scraggly vegetation that had started growing there and replacing the boundary walls, some of which had fallen down. Unlike the relatively small stones they'd been using for the cabin walls, the unplastered field walls were made of sizeable rocks, and it would be backbreaking work to lug those about all afternoon.

It needed to be done, though, and so he passed back the empty bottle and bid the men farewell. Kieran followed suit, although Quin hadn't asked his brother-in-law to accompany him.

Quin shrugged. He'd gotten used to Kieran's presence and, in fact, welcomed any assistance he might provide, needing every hand. The tenants were helping with the clearing of the fields, especially the women and children—the men being occupied with the building—but there was much to be done. Between them, they were making good progress and would likely be ready in time for the planting, but they weren't nearly finished yet.

Quin mounted Gambit and rode along the path that led to the fields, passing several of the tenants' plots on the way, pleased to see the progress being made on the other cabins. Quin hoped the next round of building would start soon, so that a good number of cabins would be completed before the winter.

"Have the Moores managed to collect enough rubble stone?" Quin asked Kieran, who'd visited the family the day before. Hugh Moore was assisting with the building of the Murphys' cabin, but his older sons—two sturdy youths of about fifteen and sixteen—had begun collecting stones for their own cabin, which they planned to start building once the Murphys' home was complete.

"Near enough, I think," Kieran said thoughtfully. "There've got a big pile up on the building site. They may need to go back for more, but it's a good start."

"Good." Quin nodded. "We won't need to visit Benburb just yet then."

Although the limestone the tenants were using was found in abundance across County Tyrone, Quin didn't think they'd be able to collect enough for all the cabins. There was a limestone quarry at Benburb, though, where he meant to obtain any additional stone they might need. This, of course, would come at a cost, whereas anything they collected required only time and effort.

"I'm sure we'll collect a lot more when we start churning the fields," Kieran said, breaking in on Quin's thoughts.

"You're right. The soil seems to abound with limestone gravel. Enough for a few more walls at least, I hope."

He grinned, and Kieran chuckled briefly, before they both lapsed into silence. Conversation between them tended to be limited.

They rode along silently for several minutes, ignoring the light rain that had started to fall. It wouldn't last long. A few rays of sunshine were already breaking through the thin layer of clouds spread over the sky, the sunlight making the distant green hills glow like emeralds.

Whatever the English may say about Ireland, it is beautiful, Quin thought.

"I didn't recognise him," Kieran said suddenly, so softly Quin wasn't sure he'd meant to be heard. He glanced at his brother-in-law, who looked at him with a surprised expression, evidently realising he'd spoken aloud. He lowered his eyes and Quin thought he would say no more, but to his surprise, Kieran started speaking again, slowly and softly.

"It was drizzling when Doyle was hanged. When it was over, the sun came out just like this, falling right on the gallows...like a sign..." Kieran's voice faded, and he was quiet for a while. "When they brought him out, I didn't recognise him. His face was bruised and swollen...and he looked half wild with fear. I thought...I suppose I expected him to face his death differently, shouting to the end. It made me wonder...what I would have done, in his place..."

276

Quin had no idea what to say in response, so he stayed silent.

After a moment, Kieran shrugged. "I suppose I won't find out now."

"I suppose not." Quin frowned, not sure how to take Kieran's remark. Did he sense a feeling of regret in his voice? Was he disappointed his days as a rebel were over, that he no longer faced the danger of being hanged as a traitor fighting for his cause? Quin shook his head. His mind was running away with him. Surely, Kieran had changed. He was here after all, living the life of a farmer.

Quin made an effort to smooth out his features as they reached the tumbled down wall. A few women and children were collecting the long stalks of the wild grasses growing on the fields, gathering them into bundles to be used on the roofs of the new cabins. Quin and Kieran greeted them briefly before hobbling their horses and getting to work. Conversation was sparse as they heaved the heavy rocks into place, settling into a rhythm as the hours passed by. Wiping the sweat off his brow some time in the afternoon, Quin glanced at Kieran, who was breathing heavily after manoeuvring a sizeable boulder into a large gap in the wall.

That should keep him out of mischief, Quin thought, flexing his arms before picking up the next heavy stone that awaited his attention.

QUIN RETURNED HOME elated but aching in every muscle.

"You look exhausted," Alannah said as she greeted him at the door. "I saw you walking toward the house from the upstairs window and had my doubts about whether you would make it up the steps to the door." She smiled at him, blue eyes crinkling into triangles. "I would offer to carry you upstairs but as it is..." She offered him her arm and he laughed.

"I may be exhausted but I'm not entirely decrepit just yet. If anyone is carrying anyone upstairs, it'll be me."

He swung her up into his arms and kissed her thoroughly before placing her back on the floor and grinning down at her. She looked beautiful, with slightly flushed cheeks and a few strands of dark hair coming loose from its coil. He raised an eyebrow and cocked his head toward the staircase.

A knowing look grew on her face. "Let's get you fed first. You must be starving."

As if in agreement with this observation, his stomach gave a loud growl, making them both laugh.

"Come," she said and took his hand, leading him into the dining room, where their supper had already been laid out by Mrs O'Sullivan.

His mouth watered at the sight of the laden platters on the table. He quickly looked down at himself to make sure he'd managed to remove most of the grime from the day's labours in the trough outside and, feeling himself to be reasonably presentable, sat down and helped himself to a generous portion. He sighed happily at the delectable flavours that crossed his tongue—roasted lamb slathered with rich gravy, accompanied by boiled potatoes and young carrots.

"Where's Kieran?" Alannah asked, looking at him with amusement as he devoured his meal in the briefest of time.

"He wanted to have a dip in the stream before heading home," Quin said between mouthfuls. "He should be along shortly.—Mmm, this is delicious."

He helped himself to some more meat. They ate in silence for a few minutes, Quin wolfing down his second portion almost as speedily as the first.

"How is the building progressing?" Alannah asked when they'd both finished eating.

Quin leaned back comfortably in his chair, tired but content. "The O'Reillys have finished the walls. The Murphys aren't far behind, and the others will be done within the week."

"That's wonderful. And how are you getting along with your tenants?"

Quin nodded thoughtfully before answering. "The men seem to be less suspicious of me than they were, and the women are looking less like startled deer when I'm around them. So...I'd say we're making progress." He grinned, making Alannah laugh. "Some of them have even worked up the courage to talk to me in English. They seem to have only a basic understanding of the language, but they still know far more than I would have suspected when I first met them...enough for rudimentary conversation, at least. If I'd been a bit more patient with them at the start, I might not have needed you to translate for me." He winked at her.

"How fortunate for me that you're not a patient man," she said wryly.

"Oh, but I am," Quin countered, narrowing his eyes. "I just know what I want...and I make sure I get it."

Alannah raised an eyebrow at him but didn't say anything.

"You were meant for me, and nobody else," he said softly, holding her eyes. "As far as the tenants are concerned, their initial reaction to me didn't match my

278

expectations. I had thought they might be a bit more vocal upon the occasion of our first meeting and when they weren't, I assumed them not to understand any English. When I think about it now, I realise they probably didn't say anything because there simply wasn't anything *to* say, particularly not in the limited English most of them speak. After all, it's unlikely they would have argued with me, no matter what plans I had for the estate, as long as I didn't threaten their existence…which I didn't."

"You might have heard a choice word or two if you had. No doubt they've picked up a few of *those* in English."

"I don't doubt it," Quin responded dryly. "Although I wouldn't imagine they would use them in hearing of their landlord.—It is interesting, though," he added thoughtfully, "with all the effort the British Crown has made to exterminate the Gaelic language, that it's still so widespread."

Quin knew that to the British, the use of Irish Gaelic was seen as a sign of disloyalty to the Crown, to the extent that Gaelic speakers had in the past been threatened with seizure of their property, and at times even death, if they didn't replace their native tongue with English. The Gaelic language, and the culture and religion that generally came with it, was believed to be a threat to the English conquest of Ireland, with continued use of the language seen as an attempt by the locals to maintain their own identity rather than accept defeat, infecting the purity of Englishness with their barbarous tongue and outlandish traditions.

"It's not as easy to eradicate a language most of the inhabitants of the nation speak," Alannah said with a frown. "It's simple enough for the English to tell the Irish to turn their backs on their traditions, but they *are* traditions…and not as easy to ignore. And it's not as easy to *teach* all Irish people English either. Most of them are poor and illiterate. Who would teach them? Where would they learn?"

"It's different for the upper classes, though, isn't it?"

Alannah nodded. "Many affluent Irish people believe Gaelic to be the peasants' language. They don't speak it even if they can, and won't teach it to their children, because they want to believe they're better than the rest. It's quite ironic considering it's still the preferred language of most of the people living in the land they call home…" She was silent for a moment before going on. "I think that's changing, though."

"What do you mean?"

"I think more and more people will turn their backs on Gaelic...or at least not speak it exclusively. Even now, many can speak at least some English. The labourers we employed at Niall used to tell us they got paid more by English landlords if they could speak the English language. And there are those who dream of leaving Ireland and starting a better life elsewhere...in America, or even in England itself. How will they do that if they can't speak English? It's almost inevitable that they'll learn, whether they want to or not."

"They'll have to," Quin agreed, wrinkling his brow.

Although he was an Englishman himself, he'd never quite agreed with the annihilation of other cultures simply because they were different. And to persecute people because of the language they spoke? Quin shook his head.

"How is it you and Kieran speak Gaelic?" he asked, the question having suddenly occurred to him. "You're hardly poor and illiterate."

"True," she said, smiling at him. "Although we're hardly as rich as some.—My father spoke Gaelic, but my mother didn't. Her family lived in Dublin, where Gaelic speakers tend to be frowned upon by the better-off. My father didn't actively speak Gaelic for years but when he took over the farm, he was confronted with the language of his youth...spoken by the servants, the labourers and people he met on the street, not to mention my grandmother, who'd been born into a Gaelic-speaking family herself. Many of the people who came into my father's courtroom were also Gaelic speakers, some exclusively so.—I think it reminded him of his roots."

"And so he decided to teach his children?" Quin guessed.

"Yes, with encouragement from my grandmother, who believed no language should ever be lost. My mother wasn't always best pleased to hear us speaking Gaelic, but she never directly forbade us from doing so."

"She did make sure father and nana knew how unseemly she thought it was, though," Kieran said, walking in through the open door, his hair still damp from his swim. Mirroring Quin's own demeanour, he looked happy but tired, collapsing gratefully onto his chair.

"Well, it has come in use now," Quin said, nodding to Kieran in greeting. He passed him the platter of sliced lamb, contemplating whether he should have some more himself. Eating meat wasn't a daily event and he was savouring the opportunity. "I wonder how other landlords converse with their tenants and labourers," he added, helping himself to one more slice. "It must be rather a laborious business without the benefit of a translator."

Kieran shrugged. "Many landlords probably know some Gaelic themselves, their families having lived in Ireland for generations. As for the rest...people make do. Most Irish likely know enough English to discuss pay and rent. I don't think there's usually much more conversation than that."

"You're probably right," Quin conceded, thinking how peculiar it was that he'd never thought to keep the relationship with his own tenants so restricted.

"You're an anomaly." Alannah smiled, making the corners of his own mouth turn up in reflex as she read his mind.

"You are that," Kieran agreed under his breath, surprising him.

Quin inclined his head toward Kieran in appreciation, feeling undeniably pleased, while Alannah observed the two of them with interest, a small smile on her lips.

Although Quin wouldn't go as far as calling Kieran a friend, the hostility between them had waned, replaced with a reluctant acceptance of each other that had grown over the long hours spent together trudging across the estate and hauling rocks. Aside from his brief reference to Martin Doyle that morning, Kieran had made no mention of his past wrongs, and had shown no signs of wanting to repeat them either. Once he'd made the decision to assist the tenants, he'd been committed and focused, working long hours to help where he could, including on the fields. He'd been quiet but civil, seeming to make an effort to accept his changed circumstances. Quin still watched him cautiously to see if he might revert to his old habits but aside from the odd grumbled complaint when he thought nobody was listening and his peculiar comment about Doyle's hanging earlier, nothing in his behaviour suggested he had ever been anything but a respectable citizen.

Most importantly, he had made no false move against Alannah since his return from Omagh. Besides the selfish decision not to tell her about his intentions to sell Niall, he'd been nothing but courteous toward her, and Quin knew Alannah was slowly starting to trust him again. Looking at them now, he could see the growing affection between them, as they reminisced about their childhoods and remembered their shared past.

Quin hoped Kieran wouldn't disappoint her again.

25.

"ARE YOU COMING?"

Quin's voice reached me from the entrance hall as I descended the stairs, the dark blue skirts of my dress rustling with each step. I smiled. Quin was far too polite to show any irritation openly, but his question had been just a bit more forceful than it might have been had he simply been enquiring about my arrival out of interest.

"I'm here," I said when I reached the bottom of the stairs. He stopped his pacing and offered me his arm. "I told you I only needed a few more minutes." I lifted my brows at him and cocked my head.

He cleared his throat, before grinning sheepishly and inclining his head toward me with exaggerated courteousness. "Shall we?"

"Indeed," I answered with a similar gesture of my own.

We both laughed and made our way to the stable yard where the small carriage awaited us. Quin jumped up to the platform and gave me a hand, pulling me up to the seat next to him. He took the horse's reins from Bryan's gnarled old hands and, with a lift of the reins and a touch of his hat as the elderly groom bade us farewell, led the horse down to the road, the wheels of the carriage clattering on the cobblestones as we crossed the courtyard.

"Perhaps we'll acquire a dairy cow," I said as we turned onto the dirt road that led to the larger thoroughfare heading toward Ballygawley.

"Perhaps," Quin agreed, his eyes slitted against the wan sun that was making its way up the eastern sky in front of us.

"The market at Ballygawley does tend to have every possible provision on offer so we may be in luck."

Quin nodded absently as he led the horse around a patch of washed-out ground, a remnant of the heavy rain that had fallen a few days earlier. I glanced up at the sky, which was covered in scattered clouds that looked harmless enough for the moment. A sudden gust of wind tugged at my hat, and I lifted my hand to hold it in place, narrowing my eyes as I did so, hoping the wind wasn't a portend of further imminent downpours.

"I had hoped to have acquired a cow by now but somehow something else always seems to crop up just when I decide to purchase one," Quin said once we'd passed the obstacle. He gave me a wry grin. "It appears I should simply leave the task to someone else, as I myself am having no luck in this endeavour."

I smiled at him, trying not to laugh. While Quin had no difficulty asking others for help when he needed it, such requests tended to be rare. He was a man who was confident in his own abilities and, indeed, relied on them almost exclusively when dealing with matters he considered to be of any importance. Apparently, the acquisition of a dairy cow was one such matter.

"What are you smiling about?" Quin gave me a suspicious sideways glance.

My smile broadened until I burst out laughing, making Quin look at me in some confusion while one corner of his mouth turned up in grudging amusement.

"I was wondering who you might entrust with the important endeavour of purchasing your new cow."

Quin narrowed his eyes. "You're not suggesting I'm stubborn, are you?"

"Of course not." I batted my eyelashes, feigning innocence.

"Hmph." He turned back to the road in front of us. "I suppose," he started slowly after a moment's silence, "I could delegate a few more tasks."

"I suppose you could." My heart filled with warmth as I looked at the self-assured set of his shoulders and his strong back. "Just because you *can* do everything yourself doesn't mean you *should*."

He chuckled, taking the reins into one hand and reaching out the other to take hold of mine. "I thank you for your confidence in me. But I can hardly do everything. I simply find it difficult to trust others to do things for me that I *know* I can do myself...including purchasing a suitable cow, apparently." He laughed. "You do have a point, I will give you that. I do need to learn to be a little more trusting of others...at least when it comes to trivial matters."

"Things will be easier once the new overseer arrives," I said, giving Quin's hand a gentle squeeze.

He nodded but frowned in some irritation.

Mr Dunne, the overseer Quin had hired to assist him, had not yet arrived at Glaslearg despite his promise to do so at the beginning of September, a date that was by now three weeks overdue. While a few weeks' delay wasn't necessarily a cause for concern—being quite a common occurrence—the man's failure to appear on the advertised date irked Quin.

He shrugged now, though, making an obvious effort to set aside his annoyance. "Things *will* be easier...whenever he might arrive." He shook his head slowly in resignation. "I have sent a letter asking after his whereabouts.—But I suppose he shall simply appear when he deems the time to be right."

"You could always ask after him in Ballygawley," I suggested.

While Mr Dunne didn't live in Ballygawley, the estate he'd been working on was situated only an hour or so's ride from the town. It was reasonable to assume he would have had dealings there, including the occasional attendance at the Friday market we were visiting today.

Quin nodded. "I shall do so. In the meantime..." He looked at me and grinned broadly, his eyes twinkling with mischief. "I shall leave *you* in charge of acquiring a cow."

"NO COWS?" QUIN asked in surprise.

"Not one," I responded cheerfully. "It seems every last available animal was sold at the fair last week."

"Huh." Quin shook his head briefly in disbelief, before shrugging his shoulders and offering me his arm.

"And have you had any luck?" I asked as we ambled through the market square, which was filled with stalls offering everything from pottery items and balls of wool to pails of buttermilk and live chickens.

"Not exactly." Quin manoeuvred me past a group of men in a heated discussion around a tub of ale. Wares from the town's brewery, I assumed, wondering whether the men would wait until after noon to sample the malt whiskey produced at Ballygawley's distillery. "One or two people were familiar with the name of Mr Dunne, but none could tell me anything about his whereabouts. I did manage to track down Constable Ryan, though, who assured me all was in order and that the man was simply a little tardy in his arrival."

Quin frowned in annoyance but soon regained his usual good humour as we walked slowly through the market, inspecting the merchandise on offer, stopping here and there for a closer look.

"I suppose we shall remain overseer-less and dairy-free for the foreseeable future," he said with a grin as we reached the edge of the marketplace and started ambling up one of the town's three streets by silent consent.

I laughed. While the matter of the overseer remained to be resolved, our dairy needs had thus far been met quite adequately with produce purchased at

Ballygawley's weekly market. Having our own dairy cow at the estate would simply be more convenient, not to mention less expensive.

I was about to speak when a movement ahead caught my eye. We were walking through a residential area of the town, one that looked to be of the poorer variety. Although some of the houses seemed to be well built, the overall impression was one of dilapidation—while it wasn't quite a slum, the people who lived there seemed to be part of the lower end of the social scale.

Quin followed the direction of my gaze and narrowed his eyes to peer into the dark doorway that had caught my attention. The door was set some two feet back from the wall of the house, the lintel above throwing the entrance into deep shadows. I suddenly caught sight of two blinking eyes that seemed to be floating bodiless above the ground. I started and emitted a surprised squeak. Quin put me behind him but unclenched his fists when the head and body belonging to the eyes emerged from the deep recesses of the dark entrance.

Slowly, a young man unfolded himself from the shadows until he stood on the threshold, looking at us with a vacant expression on his face. Quin drew in his breath sharply at his appearance and I looked at him quizzically. He shook his head briefly and turned his attention back to the apparition before us. He was probably no more than sixteen but short and thin for his age, dressed all in black and with his face and hands smeared with soot.

"Hello," I said cautiously.

He bobbed his head briefly but made no further acknowledgment of my existence, his eyes roaming slowly from side to side, unfocused.

"Is he alright?" I asked Quin under my breath, frowning in worry.

I'd heard that chimney sweeps, one of which this youth appeared to be, could suffer ill effects from the soot breathed in when climbing down into chimneys to clean them—if they didn't get stuck in the tight flue or suffocate beforehand, I thought with disgust. The life of climbing boys, as they were called, was notoriously hazardous and several attempts had been made to regulate at least the age at which such labour could be expected from children, some of whom were reportedly as young as six.

I suppressed my revulsion at the thought of small children dying an agonising death in the service of the rich, making an effort to smile at the grimy youth before me.

"It's not the soot," Quin said quietly in a voice that made me turn my head to look at him.

His expression was strangely blank, but his eyes were filled with sadness—and perhaps something else. He tore his gaze away from the boy and looked down at me, a frown between his brows.

"It's not the soot," he repeated with more conviction and a shake of the head, "it's his mind."

I turned back to look at the young chimney sweep and suddenly realised what Quin meant. While his occupation was unlikely to be doing his health any good, what ailed this particular climbing boy was not his forays into the claustrophobic interiors of the town's chimney pipes. The vacant expression, the vague acknowledgement of our presence and the unfocused eyes all pointed to some form of mental retardation, an impediment in his development.

"Oh," I said, my heart feeling heavy.

Quin gave me a crooked smile and started rootling around in his pockets, coming up with a few small coins. He handed these to the youth, pressing them into his hand and wrapping his blackened fingers around them lest they should fall. The boy stared at the shiny discs with an open mouth before breaking into a slow smile that quite transformed his features, despite the stained and crooked teeth thus revealed. He gave a surprisingly deep chuckle and turned back toward the door, calling in an unintelligible tongue as he opened it. A young woman appeared on the threshold at the racket, looking wide-eyed at Quin and me standing in the dooryard.

The boy showed her the coins, making her eyes widen even more as he disappeared into the house behind her. She looked at us uncomprehendingly, but Quin merely doffed his hat and bowed to her, making her look thoroughly flustered as a red hue crept into her cheeks in her obvious confusion.

"Madam," Quin said politely as he offered me his arm.

I took it and smiled at the young woman before turning back onto the street.

"Thank you," she whispered as she closed the door softly behind us.

We walked in silence back to the marketplace, each absorbed in our own thoughts. My heart was filled with pity for the young man and the life he must lead, one filled with hardships caused as much by his circumstances as by his very existence. Then again, I mused, his circumstances were no worse than those of countless other people in Ireland, despite his dangerous profession. And in some ways, perhaps, he was better off, unable as he must be to fully grasp his situation. And he evidently had somewhere to live and someone to care for him, someone who had seen him employed as best as possible and allowed him to live in relative freedom, when others might have had him locked away in a lunatic asylum, shunned from the rest of the world out of shame or despair.

I sighed, knowing there was nothing I could do to change the young man's fate.

I glanced at Quin, who looked deep in thought, his expression turned inwards, as if he were seeing something in his mind's eye. I gently stroked his arm, and he shook himself, coming back to the present. I raised one brow enquiringly, making him smile tiredly in return. We looked at each other for a long moment, his eyes reflecting the sadness my own must show. Finally, he took my hand and brought it to his lips, kissing it lightly and squeezing it gently before tucking it into the crook of his arm and leading me back toward the square.

The market had filled up in our absence and we made our way slowly through the thronging masses, sampling the fresh produce on offer and purchasing what items we didn't produce on the estate.

"Is that everything?" I asked some time later as I tucked a wrapped length of linen cloth under my arm.

"Yes." Quin nodded, before suddenly heaving up the heavy basket he carried to avoid colliding with a young girl who came hurtling in our direction, followed by a small and grubby-looking boy. A heavy-set, red-faced woman appeared a moment later, evidently in pursuit of her errant offspring. Seeing the angry look on her face, I rather hoped the children managed to escape. I laughed at the thought.

"She'll catch them eventually," Quin said with a grin as he looked after the delinquents, who had disappeared into the horde of marketgoers, their mother in hot pursuit.

I smiled at him, wondering suddenly how Quin and I might behave around our own children. The thought was immediately followed by a deep sense of warmth and happiness that I might one day find out. Quin caught my eye, holding my gaze as I looked at him, a small smile appearing on his lips.

"Begging your pardon."

The impatient voice made me tear my eyes away from Quin's face, only to land on a short and squat man with eyebrows as prominent as his sideburns, who was looking up at us with poorly concealed irritation. He had a large barrel in front of him, which he was evidently trying to roll to a stall behind us, being blocked in his attempt by our presence in the middle of the aisle.

"I do apologise," Quin said smoothly, doffing his hat and giving the man a brief bow before pulling me out of the way and ushering me back to the carriage that stood at the edge of town.

He stored our purchases under the seat, helped me onto it and turned the horse in the direction of Glaslearg as the afternoon sun threw long shadows from a clear sky, the earlier clouds having been blown away by the gentle breeze.

HE WOKE UP with a start, the dream that had roused him vivid in his mind.

"Quin?"

Alannah turned sleepily toward him and reached out a hand to stroke his arm.

"It's alright," he said softly as his heart started to slow, "go back to sleep."

He gently caressed Alannah's hair and kissed her forehead. She wrapped herself around him and lay her head in the crook of his neck, her chest rising and falling lightly as it resumed its peaceful rhythm. Quin breathed in deeply for several minutes, inhaling her sleepy scent and pulling her close, trying to quell the images the dream had awakened in him.

"What is it?"

Alannah's quiet question startled him, her soft voice breaking into the darkness of his thoughts.

"I thought you were asleep."

"Something's troubling you." The words were spoken slowly, cautiously, as if she were unsure of his response.

"It's..." He bit back the denial that had sprung automatically to his mind. He didn't have to pretend with her. "Yes," he replied simply.

"Tell me."

He started talking softly, haltingly, struggling to describe the reality behind the nightmare, until the words started spilling out of him like water flowing out of a dam that had burst its banks, the relief of having someone to talk to loosening his tongue.

"The war was all but won," he was saying while stroking Alannah's arm. "Despite their large numbers and unwavering ferocity, the Chinese were no match against the British, armed with modern rifles and with steamships at their backs. We had taken Shanghai and Chinkiang in little over a month. Their greatest strongholds were in British hands and their capital was open for the taking. We knew their resistance couldn't last long, Nanking was all but ours.— It had always been only matter of time until they would succumb." He shook his head and shrugged one shoulder at the inevitability faced by a weaker foe. "Victory was upon the horizon, spirits were high. And yet...abhorrence for the Chinese ran deep in some."

Alannah lifted her head and looked at him quizzically. He drew in his breath and clenched his jaws.

"The Chinese don't believe in surrender," he said slowly, closing his eyes briefly at the memories the speaking had evoked. "They would rather die than submit to their enemies...and kill their own children to prevent them from falling into the hands of their foes."

Alannah gave a start and reflexively tightened her hand on his arm. He lay his own hand over hers and gave it a gentle squeeze.

He should stop talking, he thought, spare her the horror he had been subjected to. But he could no more stop himself from speaking than he could change the course of history.

"We found them. Women, children. Strangled, poisoned, their throats slit...their pitiful corpses littering the buildings of the conquered towns. A horror made all the more unbearable knowing our own presence was the cause of their death."

Alannah breathed in sharply and he stroked her cheek, feeling wetness under his fingertips. He wrapped his arms tightly around her, his own eyes filling with tears and his throat constricting. He was silent for a moment, reliving the desolation he'd felt at the sight of the innocent, slain by men who'd sworn to protect them.

"The British..." He shook his head, unable to put into words the depth of shock that had pervaded the camp. "We considered ourselves civilised. Warfare was conducted with etiquette and rules, between men." He snorted at the irony, the thought that anything about war could be civil. "This...this was murder, murder of the most vulnerable."

He closed his eyes, trying to dispel the memory of the sights he had seen—the lifeless bodies of those who'd barely begun to live; boys and girls scarcely old enough to walk, babies swaddled in their dead mother's arms, looking for all the world asleep. He swallowed the bile that had risen in his throat and breathed in heavily.

"Some of the soldiers took out their anger on Chinese prisoners, maiming and torturing them...in recompense for the ghastly acts of their fellows." Quin lapsed into silence, feeling suddenly as though he'd been hurtled back into the past, into the midst of violence.

"Did you...?" The words were barely a whisper. Alannah lay stock-still against him, hardly breathing as she awaited his answer to her unspoken question.

"No," he responded after a long moment, slowly shaking his head. He pulled her closer and she gently stroked his cheek. "I felt it in me, the need for violence, fuelled by horror and disgust. I managed somehow to hold onto my humanity. Others..."

He clenched one of his hands into a fist and breathed in deeply before speaking again. "When we took Chinkiang, the celebrations began...even though the war wasn't officially at an end. One night, some of the younger officers found their way into one of the colonels' private liquor stashes."

Quin ran his hand slowly up and down Alannah's arm while he talked, the touch of her skin linking him with the present while his mind threatened to sweep him into the past.

"There was a Chinese prisoner in our camp, barely a man...more like a boy. He'd shown up in our midst some months before, unarmed, not uttering a word. When he was apprehended, he made no move to defend himself, only looking utterly surprised at his circumstances. He was...soft in the head," Quin said quietly, thinking of the soot-covered youth they'd encountered that morning, the vacant expression that had sparked the dream, the memory of a face that had looked just the same—unfocused and distant. "He wasn't quite aware of what was going on around him. He barely responded to others and lived in a world of his own, although he was remarkably self-sufficient for all that. There was some debate about what to do with him, with a few of the British arguing he should be...disposed of." Quin snorted in derision and anger. "In the end, it was decided his mental faculties prevented him from posing much of a threat. And so, he was allowed to walk the camp and perform menial tasks; watched, but only in a half-hearted attempt to prevent him from wandering off."

Quin looked up at the ceiling, remembering the young Chinaman's face— unfocused slanted eyes beneath a shock of unruly black hair, a look of emptiness on his smooth features that nevertheless lent him an air of innocence as he ambled around the camp, stuck in a mind that could find no common ground with those around him.

"The officers were well into their cups. I had joined them for the celebrations but was still reasonably clearheaded myself. The Chinese prisoner—we called him Chinee, not knowing his name or where he had come from—he stumbled into the tent." Quin paused for a moment, letting his breath out slowly through his nose. "He picked a bad time for it," he went on with a humourless laugh. "The men had been entertaining themselves trying to outdo one another insulting the Chinese. What had started as disparaging comments about their appearance soon deteriorated into a diatribe against their customs...and their very existence. When Chinee entered the tent, they started taunting him, mocking him relentlessly on behalf of his countrymen. He didn't respond, *couldn't* respond, unable as he was to react to anything but the most basic instructions and with no capacity to understand the men's hatred."

Quin shook his head in remembrance.

"They started to get physical in their attack on him, trying to provoke a reaction out of him—prodding him in the ribs and pushing him off balance until he would grunt in protest...to his assailants' utmost satisfaction." Quin gave an angry snort. "It wasn't long before the first blow fell. I tried to stop them, but it was too late. I was up against six seasoned soldiers whose reason had been drowned by the contents of the whiskey bottle."

Alannah lay her hand against his neck, stroking him lightly.

"He hit his head on the corner of a chest as he fell," Quin murmured, vividly recalling the sickening thump, the slow slide of the Chinaman's body onto the floor, and the pool of blood that had formed under him while he'd laboured for his last breath. "The officers...they were surprised, surprised they'd been deprived of their foe. They showed no remorse or shock at his death, wanting only to hide their own involvement in his fate."

"Did they?"

"Yes. It was easy enough to explain. An accident, nothing more. Had I said anything to the contrary, my accusations would have been brushed off—had they even been heard at all."

They were quiet for a moment, the silence broken only by the light sound of their breathing.

"Is that why you resigned your commission?" Alannah asked softly after a while, her hand still caressing his neck.

Quin nodded. "For most of my life I had felt born to two separate worlds. That of my father, who believed in England and imperialism...and that of my mother, who believed in tolerance and respect for all. I had thought for a time the two might be combined, that *noble England* might help advance the citizenry of primitive nations." He gave a humourless laugh at his naiveté. "Those men...the officers who killed a simple-minded youth...they bought their way into high-ranking positions within the army through the time-honoured tradition of purchasing one's commission, a tradition meant to ensure that honourable upper-class gentlemen lead England's military ranks, representing England's interests and her moral pursuits." He shook his head and compressed his lips before going on. "Those *noblemen* acted no more honourably than the Chinese whom they so despised, killing an innocent...for no reason other than to still their anger and their hatred."

Quin sighed deeply and turned onto his side to face Alannah.

"The British Army prides itself on its traditions and its defence of the British Empire, an empire supposedly built on Britain's industrial and moral superiority." He snorted irritably, unable to hide the contempt in his voice. "In fact, it was built on prejudice and derision, a hatred for all things non-British...and all people who are not like us. I could no longer be a part of the army that defended it."

Alannah gently stroked his cheek, a concerned look on her face. "What did your father say?" she asked softly.

Quin laughed without humour. "He was furious," he said slowly, remembering the rage his father had flown into when Quin had come home, not even waiting to hear why Quin had left or asking after his welfare. "He said I was a failure...an embarrassment to him and his forefathers. He berated me for days, giving me no chance to explain...until I stormed out of the house one day and never returned. Things got better after that." Quin emitted a snort before breathing in slowly through his nose. He shook his head, contemplating his relationship with his father. "He never spoke of it again after that and hasn't enquired to this day why I resigned my commission. When people asked why I'd returned from my duties, he brushed off the question, mentioning I'd been injured and leaving others to draw their own conclusions. I let them think what they liked." Quin was quiet for a moment before continuing. "I was..." He shrugged his shoulders, unable to explain the sense of detachment that had accompanied him on his return to England. "My mind was occupied with more important things than worrying about what others might think of me."

"I would suppose so," Alannah said quietly, a worried frown appearing between her brows as they lapsed into silence.

"But I should count myself lucky," Quin said suddenly, making Alannah look at him in confusion. He smiled at her as best he could and lifted a hand to caress the back of her head, running his fingers through her silky black hair. "If I hadn't experienced what I did I might never have come to Ireland...and I might never have met you."

One corner of Alannah's mouth lifted briefly in an attempted smile that had disappeared before it had even begun. She frowned, her eyes still troubled. "Was it worth it?" she asked, placing her hand lightly on the scar on his chest.

He took her hand and brought it to his lips. "It was all worth it," he said quietly, his throat feeling tight. "There is no price I wouldn't have paid for you."

Alannah's eyes glistened with tears, and she leaned toward him, cupping his face between her hands. Her soft lips met his in a tender caress and he closed his eyes, shutting out the harsh world that surrounded them until only her touch remained, making him feel anchored and whole once more. When she pulled away from him at last, she rolled onto her back and gently drew him toward her, laying his head down on her breast.

"Sleep now," she said softly while she stroked his head. "You're home."

26.

"WHERE IS THE blasted man?" Quin asked several days later as we sat down to breakfast, an irritated look on his face.

"Mr Dunne?"

Quin nodded and frowned in my direction. "It's nearly the end of September. He should have been here by now."

"I'm sure it's only a temporary delay, a few loose ends to tie up perhaps."

"Hmph," Quin grumbled, unconvinced. "He's agreed to act as overseer on a large estate. The least he could do is send word."

"True," I said, unable to argue with Quin's reasoning.

Mr Dunne had meant to come to Glaslearg in the first week of September. His arrival was several weeks overdue, and Quin was getting impatient, to say the least.

"It doesn't bode well for his administrative skills that he hasn't arrived, or so much as responded to my letter of enquiry." He gave an irritable shake of the head. "A simple note of explanation would have quite sufficed, one that shouldn't have proved difficult to send, he having resided at no great distance from Glaslearg with his former employer."

I lifted my shoulders noncommittally. Mr Dunne had been introduced to Quin by Constable Ryan from the Irish Constabulary; I had never met the overseer myself.

"Was there something in particular you needed him to do for you right away?" I asked Quin, who was still frowning in annoyance.

"No." He gave me a crooked smile. "We are managing quite well even without an overseer. I do, however, severely dislike having to run after people."

He reached for the toast Margaret had brought to the table, depositing a slice on his plate. Not waiting for it to cool, he slathered on some butter, which melted instantly on the hot bread.

"There is the harvesting to complete and the planting to prepare for," he said after he'd swallowed the first bite. "I had hoped for Mr Dunne to at least have had some time to familiarise himself with Glaslearg before the start of the busy autumn schedule."

I nodded as I took a slice of toast myself. It had cooled enough by now for the butter to remain mostly on top of the bread rather than dissolve into it.

"Between Mr Brennan's uselessness and Mr Dunne's tardiness, I'm starting to wonder whether all stewards in Ireland are somewhat inept," Quin said with a grin as I lay down my knife.

"Your experience is limited.—Although it has been rather unfortunate," I added with a laugh. "There *are* good overseers to be had here...or at least one I know of."

"If I'd known beforehand Mr Smith would soon be available, I never would have hired Mr Dunne in the first place. But I suppose it's done now, and we shall simply have to wait and see."

He sighed in resignation and turned his attention back to his plate. While we chewed in companionable silence, I contemplated the presumably imminent arrival of Mr Dunne.

Although Quin and I were very ably managing Glaslearg on our own, Quin had wanted to hire a factor who could assist in the day-to-day running of the estate as it expanded and see to affairs in our absence. I knew Quin intended to remain heavily involved in Glaslearg's management even after Mr Dunne's arrival and wanted me to do the same, which meant the overseer's job would be largely restricted to ensuring Quin's commands were carried out. While this was a reasonably normal state of affairs for the average steward, many overseers in Ireland took on a much greater role as they essentially took over the estate in the landlord's absence. I wondered what Mr Dunne's previous experiences had been like and whether he would find himself content in the role Quin had in mind for him.

"Nobody's moved in yet."

I looked up at the sound of Quin's voice and was met with a set of puzzled-looking green eyes that made me raise one eyebrow quizzically in his direction.

"Niall," he explained with a nod in the farm's direction as he helped himself to some more toast.

"Oh... Yes, you're right," I said, passing him the butter dish. "It's been weeks since Kieran sold it and it's standing empty still."

"After he was told by the new owner to move out immediately..."

We lapsed into silence once more, each occupied with our own thoughts. Kieran had hardly mentioned Niall since he'd moved to Glaslearg, much less told us who'd bought the farm or how much he'd sold it for. While Niall was a small farm, Kieran should still have made a good bit of money from its sale. The fact he hadn't said anything about it and wasn't flaunting his newly acquired riches struck me as odd.

"Perhaps he didn't get as much as it was worth," I speculated under my breath.

At the same time, Quin muttered, "he probably gambled it all away."

We looked at each in some amusement. Evidently, we'd both been thinking about the same thing.

"It is possible, you know," Quin said, raising his eyebrows at me.

"I've never known Kieran to gamble," I countered, unconvinced.

"At least not with money," Quin muttered.

I narrowed my eyes at him but let the comment pass.

"Perhaps he's invested the money," I suggested, trying to put a positive spin on things.

Quin looked at me sceptically. Such sensible behaviour in connection with my brother was obviously not something he found believable.

"He has changed," I insisted softly.

"Hmph."

"He probably just doesn't want to talk about it. Perhaps he's embarrassed..."

"I'm sure he is that."

A gentle throat clearing at the door caught our attention. Kieran was standing in the doorway, his cheeks flushed and looking uncomfortable.

"Good morning," he said awkwardly, not looking either of us in the eye.

He sat down in his accustomed spot and started buttering a slice of toast. Margaret scuttled into the room and poured each of us some tea.

"Did you sleep well?" I asked Kieran hesitantly once she'd left, wanting to lighten the mood.

"Well enough."

When he offered no further conversation, we all lapsed into silence again. Suddenly, Quin frowned and sat up straighter.

"Enough of this," he grumbled and leaned toward his brother-in-law. "Kieran, your sister and I have just been discussing the strange circumstance that the new owner of your father's farm has not yet moved into his lodgings...despite the fact he insisted you vacate the premises immediately upon its sale."

He looked at Kieran expectantly while I felt my cheeks start to blaze. Kieran's mouth had visibly compressed at Quin's description of Niall as his father's farm. Now he sat stock-still, staring straight ahead of him at the bowl of apples that stood in the centre of the table. I gave Quin a stern look. He lifted his eyebrows, making me sigh. He was right, it was better to have it out in the open, instead of speculating behind Kieran's back.

"He must have his reasons," Kieran responded with a shrug.

"And what might those be?" Quin pressed him.

"How should I know?" Kieran huffed, looking at Quin with annoyance. "And why do you care?"

"I find the situation...peculiar," Quin said slowly, narrowing his eyes.

Kieran returned the favour and they stared at each other for a moment.

"Kieran," I said into the awkward silence, "perhaps you could be kind enough to tell us the name of the man who bought the farm?" I looked at him expectantly.

To my surprise, a red hue crept up his cheeks and he clenched his jaws visibly. I darted a glance toward Quin, who was looking at Kieran with interest, a small frown between his brows. He shrugged when he saw me looking at him.

"Kieran?" I asked, confused by his behaviour.

He looked down, concentrating on buttering his toast.

"Kieran?" Quin repeated in a sterner tone of voice.

"Why can't you just leave it alone?" Kieran erupted suddenly, glaring at Quin and me in turn. "The farm is gone.—Who lives there now is of no interest to anyone."

Quin and I exchanged surprised glances.

"They'll be our neighbours, Kieran," Quin said patiently. "That might be of interest to some."

"Hmph." Kieran lowered his eyes back to his breakfast.

"And have you decided what to do with the money you earned?" Quin asked in a conversational tone.

Kieran banged his knife onto his plate in irritation. "My money is my business," he snapped in Quin's direction.

Any warmth that might have started growing between the two of them had clearly dissipated.

"That may be so, Kieran," Quin said, his tone quietly menacing, "but you are living on *my* estate, under *my* roof and eating *my* food. And you're not paying so much as a farthing for the convenience.—Nor did you ask if you were welcome."

"Are you telling me to leave?"

"No, Kieran, I am not. I am, however, telling you that if you wish to stay, you should have the decency to explain the circumstances that led you to be here in the first place, instead of avoiding the topic at every turn." Kieran opened his mouth to object, but Quin silenced him with an angry look. "If not to me, then at least to your sister!"

Quin glared at Kieran, who stared back without blinking. Finally, after a long moment, Kieran dropped his gaze and turned his attention to the remains of his buttered toast. Quin gave him a disgusted look, shook his head and continued with his own breakfast. I looked helplessly from my husband to my brother, unsure what to do. Silence descended around the table, and we ate quietly for several minutes.

"There is no money," Kieran said suddenly, so quietly it was barely audible.

"What?" Quin looked up at him in confusion. He glanced at me, but I shrugged.

"There is no money," Kieran repeated slowly, forcing each word out of his mouth.

"But..." I started.

"You gambled it all away," Quin said with a knowing look.

"No, I did not." Kieran narrowed his eyes at Quin, who continued to look at him sceptically. They were both quiet for a moment.

"There was never any money to begin with," Kieran said finally, looking down onto his plate.

"But..." I stammered, unable to come up with anything else to say.

"You *gave* the farm away?" Quin asked in total disbelief.

"No!" Kieran slammed his fist onto the tabletop, making the dishes rattle. "I didn't give the farm away...it was taken from me."

"Wha..." I began but got no further, as Kieran suddenly jumped up from his chair, grabbed the bowl of apples from the table and threw it against the wall. The pottery shattered in a thunderous crash and plump red globes scattered around the room. I sat motionless, staring at Kieran in astonishment, before looking at Quin. He seemed to be as surprised as I felt but had a calculating look in his eyes as he observed his brother-in-law standing fuming beside the table.

Margaret's round-eyed face appeared at the door, but I waved her away.

"What do you mean, Kieran?" Quin asked in a calm voice, with no hint of condescension in his tone.

"It...was...Andrews," Kieran said through clenched teeth, staring down at his fists.

My heart jumped into my throat at mention of the name. I glanced at Quin and could see the same comprehension dawn on his face that must have been showing on my own.

"He blackmailed you." Quin leaned toward Kieran, all anger and irritation suddenly evaporated. "Is that what happened?" he asked softly, while Kieran continued to avoid looking at either of us.

"Yes," he finally whispered, slumping back down on his chair. "He said he would have me convicted of treason if I didn't vacate the premises immediately."

Quin and I exchanged a quick look. Andrews had threatened to testify against Kieran when he spoke to me outside the courthouse the day after the trial. My heart constricted, and I felt tears welling in my eyes.

"Oh, Kieran," I said, my throat feeling tight. "Why didn't you tell me?"

He looked up at me with eyes filled with sadness and regret. "I couldn't. After everything... I'd rather have you think me heartless than know I lost the farm because I..." He waved his arm, the gesture encompassing all the choices that had led him to his fate—his hatred of the English, his acquaintance with Doyle, and their scheming and plotting.

I took his hand and squeezed it gently. "It's alright now. Everything will be alright now," I said, trying to infuse the words with conviction. It *would* be alright. Niall was gone but Andrews had gotten what he wanted, and Kieran was free. He would build a new life for himself here, with me, and with Quin. I glanced at Quin, who bore a look of concern on his face but gave me a small encouraging smile when he saw me looking at him.

"Thank you for your honesty, Kieran."

Kieran looked startled at Quin's words but shrugged dismissively. He cleared his throat and fiddled with the tablecloth, evidently feeling uncomfortable.

"You know," I said, "I believe this may call for another early morning foray into the whiskey decanter."

Quin grinned. "I believe you may be right, Mrs Williams." He got up and collected the decanter and three glasses from the sideboard.

"We haven't even finished breakfast," Kieran objected, trying to sound shocked while one corner of his mouth lifted in grudging amusement.

"By all means, do continue." I waved my hand. "I think I'm quite done with the edibles myself."

Quin laughed and handed me a glass containing a generous portion of amber liquid. The smell alone made me feel slightly intoxicated.

"To new beginnings," Quin said once he'd handed Kieran his glass and poured some whiskey for himself.

"To new beginnings," Kieran and I echoed the toast, raising our tumblers in unison.

Kieran caught my eye and gave me a lopsided smile. "*Sláinte,*" he said and drained the contents in a single gulp.

He came up coughing and sputtering.

I sipped my own whiskey demurely, savouring the taste of the sharp liquid before it snaked down my throat, dulling my senses in a not unpleasant way.

"I believe I'm starting to enjoy the water of life," I observed in some surprise, looking down into my glass.

"I'd say you were beyond enjoying it if that's what you call it," Quin said with a grin.

I looked at him quizzically until comprehension dawned.

"Oh…" I nodded slowly. "The water of life is what whiskey is called in Gaelic."

"Well, that would explain why the natives like it so much." Quin laughed before draining his glass.

"No doubt you're right," I said, "I don't know many Irishmen who wouldn't rise from their deathbeds for a drink of *uisce beatha.*"

"Ishke beha?" Quin tried to get his tongue around the unfamiliar sounds, making me laugh.

"Not bad. We'll have you speaking the Gaelic before you know it."

Quin snorted and reached for the whiskey decanter once more. He cocked his head toward Kieran, who held out his glass for another dram. I put my hand over my own glass and shook my head, one was more than enough for me.

"I'm sure my father will be delighted," Quin said once he'd helped himself. "Having been so enraptured at the news of his only son settling in Ireland with an Irish bride."

He gave me a long look. He'd told me about the blistering letter he'd received from his father after our wedding. I knew it had upset him, but I also knew he didn't regret his decision to marry me one bit. My heart warmed at the thought.

"Do you think he'll disown you?" Kieran asked somewhat hesitantly. Conversation didn't flow easily between him and Quin, even at the best of times.

Quin waved his hand dismissively, a small smile still lingering on his lips. "I rather think not. I'm his only heir and I suspect he would die of shame if anyone were to hear I had done anything scandalous enough to be disowned. I doubt anyone else in England even knows I'm married...and if they do, I'm quite sure my father would have conveniently neglected to tell them my wife is Irish. He's probably hoping I'll come to my senses, have the marriage annulled and come running back home to London as if nothing had happened—and re-join the army forbye." He frowned, his irritation with his father getting the better of him. "Hmph."

"He did at least leave you Glaslearg," I reminded him, trying to lift his mood.

A copy of the deed to the estate had been included in his father's letter. Although he clearly hadn't approved of his son's choice of bride, he had at least honoured his promise to pass Glaslearg's ownership on to Quin once he was married.

"He did that," Quin said shortly, making an obvious effort to smooth the frown between his brows.

"At least one of us owns some land," Kieran murmured, staring into his empty glass.

Clearly, the whiskey was having an effect. He would never have made a comment like that otherwise.

"True," Quin agreed, seeming likewise affected.

They were both quiet for a moment.

"I wonder..." Quin started, before snapping his mouth shut and looking at Kieran and me in speculation, slightly tinged with embarrassment.

"Yes?" I asked encouragingly, while Kieran looked expectantly at him, eyes only slightly crossed.

"I wonder...what Andrews wants with Niall. I mean you no disrespect, Kieran, but what would a man like that want with a farm that size? He owns several estates across Ireland, and no doubt some in England, and has more wealth than he can ever spend in a lifetime.—Why would he want to purchase a small and inconsequential farm that is highly unlikely to make a noticeable contribution to his income?"

"I don't know," Kieran said, shaking his head.

I shrugged, none the wiser either. While I had loved Niall dearly and had been greatly upset by its loss, Quin was right, it *was* a small farm. Large enough to sustain its inhabitants but hardly of a great enough size to offer much in the way of expected earnings from the sale of its produce. The crops grown and livestock raised on Niall had been sufficient to see us and the servants comfortably fed and clothed, with any earnings collected at market providing the money necessary to pay the farmhands and buy what items the farm didn't produce. We had scarcely been sitting on a goldmine.

"I don't know," Kieran said again, "I wasn't privy to the details." He snorted in irritation and compressed his lips in a tight line.

"Did Andrews himself come to see you?" I asked, as the question suddenly occurred to me.

"No."

Kieran looked up at me and I could see the pain and humiliation he felt at reliving the event, although I also sensed he was relieved to be able to talk about it at last.

"He sent a note," he explained. "A very polite note, asking me to follow the instructions of his servant to the letter. He said that he wished our mutual acquaintance had been able to join us and that he hoped I wouldn't be inflicted with the same ailment that had seen him indisposed." He breathed heavily out of his nose. "I understood the hint."

"I would imagine so." I glanced at Quin, who was frowning into his empty whiskey glass. "Would you like some more?" I asked.

He looked up at me in surprise. Seeing the direction of my gaze he shook his head.

"No...certainly not," he responded distractedly. "It's not even midmorning yet." He turned back to Kieran. "So Andrews had his servant tell you to leave the farm immediately?"

"Yes." Kieran's shoulders slumped. "He handed me the note and informed me his master required me to vacate the premises without delay.—Although he was kind enough to allow me to take the contents of the farmhouse." He snorted in derision, and a sense of self-loathing, I thought.

Seeing his reaction as he told the tale, I thought I could imagine the anger, fear and humiliation Kieran must have felt that day, mingled with the certain knowledge I would blame and berate him for Niall's loss.

"I'm sorry I was angry with you, Kieran," I said with a heavy heart.

"Don't be." Kieran sighed as he turned toward me. "You had a right to be angry after all.—Whether I sold it or not, the farm is gone because of me." He took a long, deep breath, letting the air out slowly again through his nose while he braced his hands on the tabletop. "All I can do now is try to make up for it," he said and rose from his chair. He gave me a tired smile, wished Quin and me a good day and walked slowly out of the room, his head hanging in shame.

"IS THAT THE end of it?" I asked Quin later that day as we prepared for bed.

He turned away from the wardrobe, where he'd been hanging his coat, and came toward me.

"I think so."

He gathered me to himself, and I wrapped my arms around him, laying my head against his chest and savouring the feeling of his strong arms around me.

"Doyle is dead, and Andrews seems to have what he wants." He stroked my back. "I should hope that would be the end of it."

"But Andrews might try to blackmail Kieran for something else."

"He has nothing else."

I was quiet for a moment.

"You're right," I finally said, a sense of sadness coming over me at the thought.

Quin gently kissed the top of my head. I closed my eyes and leaned against his chest, breathing in his musky scent as his heart thumped steadily beneath my ear. I ran my hands slowly up and down his back, wishing we could stay like this forever. Quin lightly stroked my hair and caressed my neck, until I sighed in contentment, wanting to purr like a cat. I turned my head to place a gentle kiss into his palm. I opened my eyes and looked up at his face. He smiled at me and ran his hand softly along my cheek.

"You are so beautiful," he whispered, his eyes filled with tenderness.

I pulled his head down toward me and kissed him, wrapping my arms around his neck. He leaned into me, his hands sliding down my body and pulling me close. Still kissing me, he slowly undid my dress while I slid my hands under his shirt, my fingers tingling at the touch of his naked skin. He pulled the shirt off

303

over his head, and I kissed his neck and ran my palms lightly across his chest, making him shiver. He took a small step away from me to undo his trousers, holding my eyes while I let my dress slide to the floor.

"Come closer," I whispered in a breathy voice as the silky fabric of my shift slithered down my legs.

One side of his mouth turned up and his arm snaked around my waist to pull me close. His mouth found mine while his hands caressed me, my own hands similarly occupied. He drew me with him as he lay down on the bed and I gasped as he pulled me on top of him. I moved slowly at first, hesitantly, but with increasing vigour until I soared above him, borne on the wings of the love that joined us, 'til at last his arms enfolded me in welcome as I collapsed on his heaving chest, our two hearts beating as one.

QUIN CRAWLED QUIETLY back into bed, trying not to make a sound. Alannah was lying on her side, the blanket tucked under her arm. She had fallen asleep almost immediately, worn out from the day's revelations.

His own mind had been unwilling to grant him the same peace.

He'd kissed her cheek lightly and stroked back her hair before sliding silently out of bed and covering her with the blanket. Then he'd crept out of the room and made his way into the abandoned drawing room, there to mull over everything he'd learnt.

In some ways, he was relieved. Relieved Kieran hadn't selfishly sold his family's farm without thought of his sister's welfare. This observation did seem to indicate Alannah's brother wasn't as inconsiderate and foolhardy as Quin had thought, and that he *had* changed for the better after all. But the fact Kieran had been blackmailed into giving up ownership of his estate did present its own problems. For one thing, he'd been left with virtually nothing. Beyond the furniture and other household items scattered throughout Glaslearg's manor house, Kieran hadn't a thing to his name and was entirely dependent on Quin's good graces for his survival.

But while this was an unfortunate state of affairs for all concerned, a far greater problem was the blackmailer himself. Herbert Andrews seemed to have gotten what he wanted—for whatever reason he wanted it—but that didn't necessarily mean he was done collecting. What Quin had told Alannah was true, Kieran had nothing else left to lose.

304

But they did.

There was nothing stopping Andrews from using the threat against Kieran to blackmail Quin. The man knew Kieran was Alannah's brother and that she would presumably want to protect him. By inference, Andrews was sure to assume Quin would give in to his threats to see Kieran safe, for his wife's sake.

What Quin didn't know was what Andrews was after. His acquisition of Niall—if one could use such a term to describe the act—made no sense to Quin; unless it was done out of pure vindictiveness, in which case there was probably not much stopping the man from using the same tactic to attain whatever Quin was willing to give up to protect Kieran from his past.

Quin didn't know what sort of evidence Andrews had against Kieran—or what he would fabricate—nor whether it would hold up in court and lead to Kieran's conviction. But would Quin be willing to risk Andrews' testimony by refusing the man if he came knocking at his door?

He didn't know, even after spending the past two hours contemplating just that.

Quin frowned and stroked Alannah's cheek.

She sighed in her sleep and turned onto her back, the blanket slipping down to reveal one breast. The sight sent a pleasant jolt through Quin's body despite their earlier encounter, and he ran his hand gently over the exposed skin, making her nipple tighten in response. Unable to resist, he bent his head and flicked his tongue lightly over the hard nodule, making her moan softly and arch her back.

He closed his mouth around her nipple, and she drew in her breath sharply, placing her hand on the back of his head and pressing him to her while he ran his palm slowly along her side, down to her hip and along her leg. He gently caressed the inside of her thigh, his hand inching its way languorously up the tender skin, making her gasp as he touched her sensitive flesh. He stroked her lightly until she cried out suddenly, pressing his head against her chest with one hand so he could hear her heart thumping beneath his ear.

He chuckled lightly to himself and gently kissed her breast, before pulling the blanket back over her and wrapping himself around her.

Nobody can take this from me, he thought fiercely, as he finally drifted off to sleep.

27.

"WELL...THAT IS...unexpected."

"What is?"

Quin looked up from the letter he'd been perusing to see Alannah standing at the open study door, a look of curiosity on her face as she peered into the room. He beckoned her inside and waved at the yellowed paper in front of him.

"I've received word from Ballygawley."

"About Mr Dunne?"

Quin nodded absently, frowning down at the slanted writing.

"What does it say?"

"It appears...that our would-be overseer has been arrested for drunken assault. He's been imprisoned for six months...with hard labour," he added with a pointed look at Alannah.

"Oh." She raised her brows, a look of disbelief on her features.

"Indeed."

"No wonder you couldn't track him down before."

Quin nodded absently. Having heard nothing from the man for the past month and his letters and enquiries at Ballygawley having gone unanswered, Quin had ridden to Mr Dunne's former place of employment, only to be told the overseer had been gone for several weeks.

"I did have a stern word with Constable Ryan on my return, he having assured me previously Mr Dunne was simply delayed. But it seems"—he tapped the pages in front of him—"that the constable was covering for the man."

"Why would he do that?"

"It appears the two are related. Cousins, by the looks of it." Alannah's eyes widened in surprise and Quin pursed his lips as he frowned down at the letter. "Ryan assures me he had no inkling of Mr Dunne's...bothersome conduct, as he calls it, but..."

"That seems unlikely," Alannah finished Quin's thought with a scowl. "Surely he would have known something of his cousin's character when he recommended the man to you."

"I would think so. But...I imagine he was trying to help him. Perhaps he thought he would change his ways..."

Alannah opened her mouth to respond but snapped it shut suddenly. She looked at Quin and he could see she was thinking of Kieran.

"I would have given him a chance," Quin said. "He did make a good impression on me when I met him. I wouldn't have hired him otherwise. As it is though..." He spread his hands in resignation. There wasn't much he could do for Mr Dunne when the man was behind bars and set to stay there for some time. "Perhaps it's for the best. Who knows what mischief he might have gotten up to here."

"We'll find somebody else."

"I suppose.—But speaking of problems that need solving...have you had any luck with the labourers?"

"Some..." Alannah moved her head slowly from side to side in contemplation. "I have managed to locate most of them at least. The others will show up soon enough. The potatoes must be more than ready for the harvest by now."

"True.—One can only hope the labourers who show up for the reaping are in fact those who rented the land in the first place."

Quin snorted in annoyance, making Alannah emit a humourless laugh.

The land under discussion was the fifteen acres Glaslearg's former overseer, Mr Brennan, had rented out as conacre, unbeknownst to Quin or his father. Quin had discovered this feat quite by accident when he'd come across the large, subdivided section of farmland on one of his early excursions around the estate. Having seen the tiny parcels of land and the potato vines that grew there, he'd instantly understood the purpose of the arrangement.

What hadn't been nearly so clear was to whom the land had been rented, nor what price had been agreed upon.

After days of digging through the estate's sparse records, he'd finally come across a carelessly scribbled note that had included nothing but the underlined heading 'conacre', followed by the brief notations '15 acres' and '£9/acre'. Quin had immediately grasped the note's significance, his eyebrows nearly reaching his hairline at the ludicrous price the man had demanded. Try as he might, though, Quin could find no other paperwork relating to the leased conacre land and was thus none the wiser as to the names of the poor people who would be arriving in the autumn to be collecting their preposterously expensive crop.

"That's why the man was uninterested in farming the land...it's so much easier to rob the poor," Quin muttered under his breath. Turning back to Alannah he said, "Most of the labourers have evidently been working on other farms, and they certainly don't live here. Have you had any indication of whether the conacre rent has already been paid?"

The rent for rood parcels was traditionally collected before the harvest was in, with the labourer who'd leased the land legally required to pay the full rent even if it turned out the crop had failed or wasn't worth the money paid.

"It isn't entirely clear," Alannah answered slowly. "Several of the men who have thus far come to tend their crops told me Mr Brennan demanded the rent several months ago, presumably shortly before he left. But others said they were expected only to pay before the harvest, at an unspecified date, with no money having passed hands yet." She lifted one shoulder. "It looks to me like Mr Brennan accosted any of the labourers who happened to cross his path once he heard of your coming. With no intention of awaiting your arrival and knowing he would be unable to collect the rent after his departure, he likely tried to amass as much money as he could before making his escape."

"You're probably right. But what are we to do now? We can hardly expect the labourers who claim to have paid Mr Brennan already to pay the rent again...nor can we simply cancel the debt owed by those who say they have not paid. It's hardly fair on those who have."

Alannah nodded, her eyebrows drawn together in thought. Finally, she smoothed out her features and looked up at Quin.

"You'll have to take their word for it," she said, "and collect the rent from the labourers who say they have not yet paid. If some of them should lie about having paid already..." She waved her hand. "We shan't get the money back from Mr Brennan in any case."

Quin grumbled in dour agreement. Mr Brennan was unlikely ever to show his face at Glaslearg again.

"I doubt any of them *would* lie, though," Alannah continued, making Quin cock his head at her in interest. "The labourers are so dependent on conacre for their survival that they're unlikely to do anything they think might jeopardise the system. Every rood of conacre land is hotly contested, allowing the landowners and large tenant farmers to charge exorbitant rents...amounts that must surely be beyond the labourers' grasp, but which they are willing to pay nonetheless." Alannah shook her head slowly. "They wouldn't lie about having paid the rent, out of fear of having no ground to lease the following season if they were ever found out."

308

"Hmph," Quin grumbled, finding himself at a loss for words at the unjustness that seemed to be accosting him at every turn. Finally, he sighed and placed the letter from Constable Ryan into one of the drawers of the large desk that was gracing his study—an acquisition from Niall, Quin remembered with a slight frown.

"So it shall be," he said as he shut the drawer with a dull thump, looking up at Alannah with raised brows. "We shall collect what conacre rents the labourers are willing and able to pay...with moneys earned through the labour they have provided on this very estate." He snorted at the irony as he got up from the desk. While the tenants would be assisting in the upcoming harvest and autumn planting, he still needed extra hands to complete the work—work that some of the labourers who'd rented conacre would provide.

Quin blew out his breath slowly through his nose, before shaking his head and plastering a smile to his face. He offered Alannah his arm and led her out of the room, determining to pay the men a fair price for their labours. While he might not agree with the way things were done—and at times feel helpless in the face of the plight of Ireland's poor—the least he could do was to ensure all who lived and worked at Glaslearg were treated justly.

Even if his efforts amassed to nothing more than a drop in the ocean.

A SUDDEN FLASH of lightning startled me, and I glanced outside the window. A steady sheet of rain was falling in the darkness, accompanied by a distant rumble of thunder. I relaxed back into the soft padding of my chair, picking up my book off my lap, glad of the fire's warmth on a blustery night.

We had retired to the drawing room after dinner at the end of a day that had provided nothing worth mentioning besides the letter from Ballygawley. Quin and Kieran were engaged in a game of chess, the two of them bent low over the chequered board. While Kieran wore a look of gritty concentration, Quin's mind was clearly not on the pieces in front of him. Kieran was no match for his brother-in-law, and it was only a matter of time before his king would fall.

I smiled and turned back to my book.

I was engrossed in the fourth and final part of *Travels into Several Remote Nations of the World*, more commonly known as *Gulliver's Travels*, that satirical tale of Man's peculiar nature and absurd social practises, which had proved to be both wildly popular and deeply offensive—depending on who was asked—since its first publication more than a hundred years ago.

I myself was finding it to be quite entertaining, despite the fact I'd read it a few times before, and nestled cosily into my seat, pleased at being able to spend a little longer in Gulliver's company.

With a sigh of contentment and a sense of regret at having reached its conclusion, I closed the book a short time later, feeling some sympathy with Gulliver, who'd elected to spend his time with his horses, rather than his family, after his return home from the Houyhnhnms—there had been days when I too had preferred the company of horses to that of humans. I laughed softly to myself as I placed the book on the table, glancing at the chessboard, which now lay unused, the white king toppled, lying helpless in the face of defeat, the pitiful remains of his army scattered around him.

Quin caught my eye as I looked at the carnage on the playing field. He shrugged, darting an apologetic glance toward Kieran, who was reclining in his seat with a slight scowl on his face. I stifled a laugh. Kieran had never been any good at admitting defeat.

"I see you've finished another book," Quin said with a crooked smile, looking pointedly away from Kieran.

"I have."

"At the rate you're going I shall have to send for the entire contents of the London Library to keep you occupied."

I smiled at him, detecting a hint of pride in his voice. He had told me the library contained over thirteen-thousand volumes, in spite of the fact it had opened its doors only three years before.

"That would be wonderful," I said, "although I doubt I should be able to manage quite so many books in my lifetime, despite my best efforts."

"Pick an author then," Quin suggested, inclining his head toward the book on the tabletop. "That should keep you busy for a time."

"That would depend on the author."

Quin looked at me with some consternation and I laughed.

"I've heard it said that the author of *this* tale"—I tapped a finger on the cover of *Gulliver's Travels*—"spent five years or more compiling its contents. If that's the rate at which such narratives are produced, it's unlikely the works of any one author will keep me occupied for long."

Quin gaped at me, before shaking his head slowly in disbelief. "Five years?" He picked up the leather-bound book, staring at the compact tome with some astonishment. "Five years to write a few words?"

"It's rather a lot more than a few words."

"No doubt," he agreed absently, still shaking his head and gawping at the book.

"Have you never wondered why even well-known authors aren't more prolific?" I asked in some amusement.

"I suppose." He lifted one shoulder noncommittally. "Still...to spend five years writing a book that can be read in five days? It hardly seems worth the effort."

"I would say it's very much worth the effort, for the pleasure it gives the reader."

"But what if the reader dislikes the book?" He raised his brows, making me shrug.

"Not everyone has the same taste in literature. The writer can only write as he is led, be that to the amusement of some or the disappointment of others, and at whatever speed he so can write."

"Hmph," Quin grumbled, unconvinced. "Perhaps it's simply a lack of diligence on the part of the author."

"A lack of diligence?"

"Yes. Surely, setting oneself to a task allows for speedier completion, no matter what that task may be. It's a matter of focus."

I narrowed my eyes at him but tried a different tact. "What about paintings and sculptures?"

Quin looked at me in confusion. "What about them?"

"Paintings and sculptures are just another expression of Man's creativity, much like writing down stories. Are these not worth the effort it takes to make them? Should Michelangelo not have bothered to pick up his chisel or his paintbrush for fear he might require years to complete artworks people might not like?"

"Of course they're worth the effort!" Quin objected. "He created priceless pieces of art that can be admired for generations."

"And if it should take a lifetime to create a single such piece? Would that be a lack of diligence on the part of the artist?"

Quin shook his head. "Each brushstroke, each strike of the hammer must be placed just so, to ensure the harmony and beauty of the whole. One can hardly rush such work.—And the time it takes to complete each piece is hardly relevant when one gazes upon the final masterpiece."

"And perhaps," I said slowly, cocking my head in his direction and smiling at his enthusiasm, "each word in a novel needs to be placed just so, each sentence phrased and each paragraph constructed with care so that the tale compels the reader, drawing him into a world unknown with a subtleness that masks months and years of thoughtful construction."

Quin blinked at me, evidently taken aback.

"And much like a sculpture can be viewed and appreciated for generations, a book can be read and enjoyed by many, for many years to come," I continued. "Writing is simply a less visual expression of the arts. But one that doesn't require any less care in its application, nor any less effort."

"Hm...I suppose you're right," Quin said at last, "I hadn't thought of it that way. It's only that the efforts of the artist seem so much more apparent when looking at a sculpture or a painting, rather than words printed on paper."

He placed the book on the table before turning back toward me. He looked at me for a moment, a slow smile growing on his lips.

"Speaking of efforts...it's a shame you didn't have the opportunity to become a lawyer. Your skills at winning an argument are unparalleled...even when you're the one who started it."

"I shall choose to take that as a compliment," I replied dryly, unconvinced I had started anything, nor that we'd even had an argument.

"Of course."

I narrowed my eyes at him. "I am not stubborn," I insisted with dignity, making him break out in a wide grin. "At least not nearly as stubborn as you," I amended with a laugh.

"Fair enough."

"You know," I said, raising my brows at Quin, who was still grinning, "Irish women were allowed to practice law in the past."

"Oh yes?" Quin's voice was tinged with disbelief.

"Yes, under Brehon law.—That's traditional Irish law," I explained, seeing his confused look. "I've heard it said that in the old days, men and women were treated almost equally." I paused for a moment, quite unable to imagine such a thing. "Not least of all because women could also become Brehons...the judges who enforced the law."

"How remarkable," Quin said in some surprise. "And how progressive."

"Indeed. How ironic to think ancient Gaelic customary law could possibly be more advanced than modern English law."

"You see," Kieran spoke up suddenly, startling me. I had almost forgotten he was there, silent as he'd been for the last several minutes. He leaned toward me, face intent. "That's just one more thing that was taken from the Irish by the Eng...lish." He trailed off as he looked at Quin out of the corner of his eye. "Ah..."

Quin cleared his throat and eyed Kieran askance. After a moment, Kieran returned the look and shrugged his shoulders.

"Just because I've learnt to tolerate *you* doesn't mean I'm any more fond of your countrymen," he muttered.

"I suppose not." One corner of Quin's mouth turned up in amusement.

"It does prove a point, though," I said suddenly, seizing on the abrupt change of topic.

"What does?" Quin asked, while at the same time Kieran said, "What point?"

"That not all Englishmen are the same...nor all Irishmen."

The two of them eyed me with identical looks of impatience, evidently waiting for me to explain myself.

"The English," I began, "believe they have brought a degree of enlightenment and progress to the primitive nation that is Ireland, while the Irish believe the English have brought little more than oppression and misery."

Quin and Kieran both nodded. Seeing each other's reactions, they both scowled, making me laugh.

"My point is," I went on quickly, "that both viewpoints have merit. Furthermore, both viewpoints are held by both English and Irish people...depending on who you ask."

Quin raised a sceptical eyebrow at me, while Kieran wrinkled his brow.

"There are some Englishmen," I said, looking at Quin, "who do not agree with the forceful methods the English employ when attempting to civilise other nations." Quin nodded reluctantly, although he still looked somewhat cynical. "There must be more than one of you, not so?" I asked, making him give me a lopsided smile.

"You can't say the same thing about Irishmen," Kieran objected before I could continue. "What Irishman believes the English have ever done us good?" He glanced at Quin and shrugged his shoulders apologetically, but Quin only looked curiously at me.

"When the English first arrived in Ireland, some Irish lords looked to them for protection from their Irish foes. And," I went on before Kieran could protest, "even now, many Irishmen look to their English landlords for the same. Large tenant farmers are reaping the benefits of the landlord system through the expansion of commercial agriculture to the British market, even as the poor peasants are getting poorer."

Kieran shook his head. "That doesn't necessarily mean they're *supportive* of English rule!"

"Perhaps not," I agreed, "but the farmers who have themselves become wealthy under English reign are presumably less likely to be *against* it."

"But it's more complicated than that," Quin said with a frown, evidently warming to the topic. "It's not just the farmers who might have a sense of mixed loyalties. Most landowners in Ireland are not originally Irish, but they don't necessarily identify themselves as being non-Irish, either, having lived here for generations."

"Exactly." I nodded toward Quin. "Englishmen have been settling in Ireland for centuries...and the Old English who arrived before the plantations were Catholics—they had as much reason as anyone to lament Protestant English rule, particularly as the penal laws saw Catholics being increasingly excluded from administrative and political offices, while their properties were threatened and more."

"And the Anglo-Irish of more recent times may also have divided loyalties," Quin said. "While most of them likely enjoy the benefits of the Union with Great Britain, there must be some who think Ireland would be better off as an independent state."

"I would think so," I agreed. "It would be difficult to live in Ireland and not see the plight of the poor Irish people and think that something needed to change."

We lapsed into silence for a moment, each absorbed in our own thoughts. The longcase clock in the corner ticked rhythmically while the rain continued to fall.

"Does that mean you support the idea of Irish independence?" Kieran asked quietly after a while, looking at me curiously while studiously ignoring Quin. "At least in theory," he added as an afterthought.

I looked at him for a moment before speaking, trying to decide how to respond.

Finally, I shook my head. "I don't know. English occupation of Ireland has been fraught with violence and tyranny...I can hardly argue with that. But would a free Ireland make a difference *now*? Even if Ireland were free and able to govern itself, would it reduce the animosity between the Catholics and Protestants who live here, between the poor peasants and those who control them, between those who believe they belong here and those who claim that right for themselves? Would it make a difference to the thousands of Irish people who are struggling to survive?" I sighed. "I am Irish, I have lived in Ireland my whole life. To think of an Ireland free from British interference... I could wish for such a thing," I said softly and looked up at Quin, holding his eyes with my own. "I believe we should no longer be oppressed...but I'm not convinced the Irish people would be better off even so."

Quin gave me a tender look and gently squeezed my hand. Kieran wrinkled his brow and pursed his lips in thought.

"If Ireland were free and able to govern itself," Kieran said in a determined voice, "the lives of the Irish people *would* be improved."

"How?" I lifted one shoulder. "Would our independence from Great Britain provide more work or better pay for the thousands of labourers who are struggling to make ends meet? As much as the English have greatly contributed to bringing us to our fate, it's more than English occupation that's to blame for the plight of Irish peasants today."

"But..." Kieran started to say but stopped, aiming a sideways glance at Quin.

"She's right, Kieran," Quin said, making Kieran glare at him and compress his lips in irritation. Quin spread his hands out in front of him, trying to subdue any impending outbursts. "I can understand your sentiments...at least to a point." He gave Kieran a long look. "But what sort of impact could Irish independence possibly have on the state of the poor? Even with a reduction in trade restrictions and taxes imposed by the British, Irish farmers and labourers are trapped in a circle of dependence that will not be easily broken, not even by Irish liberty."

"Hmph." Kieran crossed his hands in front of his chest as Quin continued.

"The farmers need the labourers to work their fields, and the labourers depend on that work for their very survival. But most farm work is seasonal, and there will never be enough of it to support the vast number of labourers looking for employment."

"There must be a way," Kieran insisted.

"I'm sure there is," Quin agreed. "But it's not an easy one to find. Even farmers who *want* to change things find it difficult to do so.—The very nature of Irish farming makes it more labour-intensive, but while that means more hands are needed, it also means the farmer's money is spread amongst a greater number of people, thus keeping individual wages low. And while some farmers may want to increase the labourers' pay, there's only so much they can do without putting themselves at a disadvantage...especially the large number of farmers with only small plots of land at their disposal."

"And the conacre system doesn't help either," I said, remembering my earlier conversation with Quin. I looked across at Kieran, who was frowning into his lap. "With so many labourers competing to grow potatoes on these tiny patches of land, the rent has been pushed up to exorbitant levels the labourers can hardly be expected to pay."

Quin nodded. "Nine pounds per acre," he said, making Kieran's eyes grow round in astonishment. "That's what Mr Brennan was charging. And I hear that's the norm."

"But"—Kieran shook his head—"the labourers must be able to pay the rent, otherwise the tenant farmers and landowners would stop leasing out conacre land."

"You're right of course," I said. "They manage if they're able to find enough work to assure themselves of a steady income, and if the potato yield is sufficient to allow for profitable sale at the market. There's no guarantee, though. And if they don't find enough work or the potato harvest fails, they still have to pay the rent.—That's why father stopped letting conacre. He felt it was an exploitation of the poor, one that often led to conflict. And yet...he knew the labourers depended on conacre for their survival and so he also felt a sense of guilt for not providing some of them with such land.—There is no simple solution for Ireland's problems, whether the Irish are bound to the British or not."

Kieran didn't respond for a few minutes, instead looking down with a frown between his brows.

"Maybe..." he began at last, raising his blue eyes to meet mine. "I..." He shook his head irritably before trying once more. "I want Ireland to be free," he said softly, spreading his hands in a simple gesture. "Free to rule itself, free to look after its own people, but..." He paused once more, compressing his lips. "I always thought...that the Irish people would be better off without the British. But...from what you've said..." He trailed off and lowered his eyes, looking downtrodden.

"The Irish probably *would* be better off without the British," I admitted quietly, aiming an apologetic glance at Quin, "but not everyone to the same extent. There are always those who seek their own advancement above all else. Would Irishmen ruling Ireland care more about the common man than the British who have ruled until now?" I shrugged. "I just don't know."

"Me neither," Quin said, shaking his head. He stood up and went to stand in front of the window. The rain was still falling but had slowed to a gentle patter that drummed softly on the patio.

"I *do* know it is our moral duty to take care of those who depend on us, no matter who may govern the land we find ourselves in." He turned back toward Kieran and me, giving us a small smile. "And I for one intend to fulfil that duty, even if those in power may not." He paused for a moment, coming to sit down next to me once more. "Kieran," he said softly as he gently took my hand and looked across at his brother-in-law, who still had a dejected expression on his face. "I know you want Ireland to be free...and perhaps it will be...one day. But while that dream may be a while away yet, I hope you find other ways to help those who are suffering...as you have already done, on this estate. The tenants of Glaslearg are grateful for your efforts, as am I."

Kieran looked up at Quin with a startled expression on his face.

"I mean it," Quin insisted. "These people here, the smallholders and the labourers...they don't care whether Ireland has its own parliament or who sits on the throne of England. They want a roof over their heads and food in their bellies. They want to be secure in the knowledge that they can take care of their families and that there is someone to turn to when times are tough. They want a fair chance, nothing more.—And you can help give them that, Kieran, even while you hope for something more."

"I..." Kieran looked down as he visibly tried to control his emotions. He took a deep breath before speaking. "Yes," he said simply in a soft voice as he looked up at Quin.

He nodded once, as if to himself, and got up from his seat. He inclined his head toward Quin and me and headed out the door without another word. We watched him go, lapsing into silence as the fire in the hearth crackled companionably, the sound merging with the steady pattering of the raindrops outside.

When I finally turned toward Quin, I could see my own thoughts reflected in his green eyes.

"He needed something to believe in…" Quin said.

"A purpose," I agreed.

"He has spent so much time vilifying the English, convincing himself only Irish freedom would improve the lives of the Irish people, that he never realised he had the power to effect change himself…even if only on a small scale."

I nodded. "And by acknowledging his longing for independence, you've lifted a burden off his shoulders. The burden of pretending to be someone he's not. He wants Ireland to be free…he's not going to change his mind about that. But you've given him a way to work toward the change he wants without having to deny his beliefs or falling back into destructive old habits."

"Perhaps he'll go to London and campaign for Ireland's independence instead of attempting to start another rebellion at home." Quin smiled, and I could feel the corners of my own mouth turn up at the thought of Kieran addressing the houses of parliament.

"Perhaps. But for now, I think he will continue with the work he started here…with a lighter heart, thanks to you."

I lifted my hand and stroked Quin's cheek, feeling an overwhelming sense of tenderness come over me.

"You're a good man, Quin," I said softly.

"You think so?" he asked in some surprise.

"Of course. Why would you think otherwise?"

Quin wrinkled his brow for a moment before answering. "Some people would disagree with your assessment."

"It doesn't matter what anybody else thinks."

I looked at him for a long time, wanting him to read the truth of my words in my eyes. Finally, he lowered his face toward mine until our foreheads were almost touching. He took both of my hands in his and held them tight.

"You're right." He brought my hands up to his mouth for a gentle kiss. "It doesn't matter what anybody else thinks. With you by my side, I have everything I need."

28.

"I'M FAMISHED," QUIN said with feeling.

Kieran's stomach rumbled loudly, as if in agreement with Quin's statement, and both men laughed as they made their way along the path that led to the manor house.

They had been working on the fields all day, bringing in the last of the potato crop. It was backbreaking work but had been well worth the effort. Although Glaslearg's former overseer had neglected most of the estate's crops, the few fields that had been cultivated had yielded a good-sized bounty, and the newly collected potatoes were a welcome addition to the small quantity of oats that had been harvested a month or so before.

"You could hire a few more hands to do the work for you," Kieran suggested with a sideways glance at Quin.

Quin narrowed his eyes at Kieran but realised he'd spoken in jest.

"I could," he agreed with a grin, "but then what would I do all day?"

Kieran shrugged his shoulders. "Whatever it is aristocrats customarily do."

"Hmm...If only I could remember what that was." Quin rubbed his chin as if deep in thought, making Kieran laugh.

"Whatever it may be, it probably doesn't include doing farm work."

"Probably not. I doubt most landlords ever get their hands dirty, thinking themselves far too good for that sort of thing."

"Not you, though." Kieran's voice held a note of admiration that made Quin pause in his step.

Kieran gave him a shy smile but quickly dropped his eyes and continued on his way. They walked in silence for several minutes. Although aching in every muscle and ravenously hungry, Quin found himself to be content. More than content, actually, he thought with a satisfied sigh. The estate's crops had been harvested and the new fields were ready for the autumn planting, which would begin in a day or two. The tenants' own bountiful harvests had also been collected, and the first stone cottages were complete.

Quin himself had assisted the Murphys in laying the last bundles of thatch onto the roof and securing the ropes that held them in place. Robert Murphy had triumphantly driven in the nail to anchor the last rope Quin had pulled taught over the newly laid covering, making the men break out in spontaneous cheer. Quin smiled at the recollection, a spring in his step.

"I..." Kieran started suddenly, making Quin turn toward him.

They stopped walking, but Kieran looked away from Quin, fidgeting with his sleeve and shuffling one foot back and forth in the dirt. Quin raised one eyebrow and looked at him expectantly but didn't say anything.

"I...I wanted to thank you," Kieran murmured without meeting Quin's eyes. "For taking me in...when I..." He shook his head slowly and waved his hand toward the East, toward Niall. "I had nowhere to go," he said, finally looking up at Quin, "and no one to turn to. You had no reason to help me...in fact, the opposite was true. And yet...you did..." He compressed his lips and dropped his gaze once more. "I didn't deserve your help...but I'm grateful for it."

"Oh," Quin responded, feeling at a loss for words.

He looked at Kieran for a moment, his mind replaying the events of the last few months—the pain he'd caused Alannah and the anger Quin had felt. And quite suddenly, Quin realised his anger was gone, that he had forgiven Kieran for what he'd done, the mistakes he had made; that he accepted him for who he was and what he believed in.

Somewhere in the toils of daily farm life Quin had found absolution—and evidently, so had Kieran himself.

"You're welcome," Quin said softly, gripping Kieran's shoulder and looking him in the eyes, "brother."

DOING THE LAUNDRY was hard work and took the better part of the day. It was almost suppertime now and my back was aching with the strain. I had insisted on my involvement, though, despite Margaret and Mrs O'Sullivan's best efforts. The lady of the manor was not to burden herself with such chores, they'd argued—as they did every time I attempted to take on domestic chores, including the laundry, which I had assisted with on numerous occasions. I had told them in a firm voice that I had no intention of twiddling my thumbs while there was work to be done, especially not while the lord of the manor himself was off reaping the fields with his own bare hands. The two women had given me identical looks of disapproval but had finally relented.

The three of us had been fortunate enough to have acquired four additional helpers, in the form of two-year-old James, three-year-old twins Samuel and

Jacob, and five-year-old Robert, whose mothers had come to the house that morning to make use of the big tubs for their own washing, limited though their material possessions were. Although the boys had been happy to assist where they could—this being restricted to carrying the dirty laundry to the tubs—the actual assistance had lasted for less than five minutes, the attention span of small children being what it was. Before long they'd abandoned all pretence of helping and were entertaining themselves gleefully by playing in the mud, while the women went about the laborious business of washing and rinsing the clothes in the large cauldrons, heaving out the dripping wet masses and hanging everything up to dry—while hoping the rain would stay away long enough for the latter to occur.

Within a short time, the boys had been covered in mud from head to foot. They'd played to their hearts' content all afternoon, but now that their mothers were ready to return to their homes, it was time for a wash. The ablutions provided further entertainment, though, as the children started dousing one another with water the moment their muddy clothes had been removed, squealing with joy while the women watched, shaking their heads in amusement.

I stood a short distance away, watching the boys dash about, small round buttocks gleaming in the late afternoon sun. I couldn't help but smile to myself at their pure and innocent joy—and their complete lack of regard for social niceties, I noted, espying two-year-old James, who was standing somewhat apart from the others, studiously involved in examining his anatomy.

As I stood there laughing, Quin appeared around the corner of the house, looking tired but pleased after the day's work in the fields. I smiled at him in greeting.

"Naked boys are a sight to behold," I said as he reached my side. "Why do we even bother getting them playthings? They're obsessed with the one attached to them, every last one of them."

He turned in the direction of my gaze and gave a deep chuckle. "I believe you're right. And it doesn't really change with age.—Although we do generally prefer somebody else to play with it when we're a bit older," he added with a twinkle in his eyes.

I laughed, enjoying the spectacle the little boys provided. Quin came up behind me and put his arms around my waist. He affectionately nuzzled my neck, making me shiver.

"With the way little boys yank on their parts I marvel at the fact that any grown man ends up with working equipment!" I observed.

"Well, it does require regular attention and tender loving care to keep it in good working order," Quin whispered in my ear with a smile in his voice. He pulled me closer, making it evident there was nothing whatsoever wrong with his own equipment. "Perhaps you would be kind enough to have a look at mine a bit later?"

"Gladly." I turned around to face him. "You look happy."

"I am." He dimpled at me while his eyes crinkled into dark green triangles of delight. "The harvest is in, a good number of cottages is complete...and I'm married to the most wonderful woman in the world. What more could a man possibly want?"

"A mud-covered cherub of our own, perhaps?"

I cocked my head in the direction of the little boys, who had at last been subdued by their mothers and were disappearing into the folds of the large towels I had brought out for them. I raised one eyebrow enquiringly at Quin.

"All in good time," he said with a tender expression on his face as he pulled me close. "In the meantime, I am more than happy to keep practising."

I laughed and kissed his cheek. "So am I. But first, let's get you fed.—You'll need your strength!"

"YOU ARE SO beautiful," Quin murmured as they lay dishevelled on the covers that night.

Alannah smiled at him and stroked his cheek.

The candlelight flickered, making shadows dance over her naked skin. He ran his hand lightly along her shoulder, down to her waist and along the swell of her hip, enjoying the feeling of her smooth skin under his fingertips, and the shiver his touch evoked.

"I can scarcely remember what life was like before this."

"Me neither," she said as she gently caressed his back. "Before, I used to wonder...what it would be like..."

He grinned. "And have I met your expectations?"

"You've exceeded my expectations...in every way," she said in a tender voice, making his throat constrict.

"It's not just this." She waved a hand at the big tester bed. "Although this is wonderful. But...it's so much more. I feel safe with you...and whole. Like I am enough."

"You're more than enough," Quin said, swallowing the lump in his throat that had only just disappeared. "So much more." He stroked her cheek and looked into her eyes, which glistened in the darkness. "You have filled a place in my heart I hadn't known was empty. You are...like a mirror to my soul. You bear my weaknesses as you uplift my strengths, making me stronger by the love that you hold for me."

Quin could see Alannah's eyes fill with tears as she gently ran a hand over his head, stroking his hair and cradling the base of his skull. He closed his eyes, his heart overflowing with tenderness.

He felt her lean toward him, and her soft lips touch his. He pulled her closer, savouring her touch.

"I bear your weaknesses as you bear mine," Alannah whispered as she lay her head on his chest. "I don't have to pretend with you. I can just *be*.—And know you will love me just the same."

Quin stroked her back and kissed the top of her head, the subtle perfume of rose water floating up from the soft mass of her hair.

"I do love you," he whispered with a catch in his voice. "More than I ever thought I could love anybody."

"I love you too," she said softly, pressing closer to him.

Quin tightened his arms around her, wishing he could be locked in her embrace for all eternity. He closed his eyes and, with her head resting on his chest and their limbs entwined, drifted off to a deep and peaceful sleep.

29.

"WE SHOULD PREPARE for the festival of Samhain," Alannah said as they sat down to breakfast several days later. "It's the end of October, the harvest is in, and the planting is complete. The tenants will want to celebrate."

She smiled at Quin enthusiastically. He smiled back automatically but wrinkled his brow at the unfamiliar term.

"*Sow-in?*" he exclaimed suddenly, having just realised what she meant. "Isn't that a little...pagan?" he asked cautiously, replacing his unused cutlery on the tabletop beside his untouched plate as he contemplated what Alannah was suggesting. Although he'd never found himself to be overly zealous in his religious beliefs, the idea of participating in the pagan festival of the dead gave him a rather peculiar feeling in the pit of his stomach.

Alannah looked at him with raised brows, one corner of her mouth turning up in amusement.

"Most Christian festivals have their origins in paganism, you know.—It's true." She nodded earnestly. "Christmas is celebrated at the time of the pagan festival of Yuletide. Easter derives its name from a pagan goddess. Even Samhain is celebrated elsewhere in a Christian guise...known as All Saints' Day."

"Hm..." Quin had heard something of the kind before but wasn't quite sure what to make of the information.

"It's only that the early Christian missionaries found it easier to convert the pagans to their faith by incorporating their teachings into some of the existing traditions.—It doesn't take anything away from the Gospel itself, nor the Christian belief."

"True," Quin agreed slowly, raising his chin slightly as he looked at Alannah's eager face across from him. "Still...the festival of the dead?"

"It's a festival marking the end of the harvest as much as a celebration of the dead."

"That makes it sound so much better," Quin grumbled under his breath, shaking his head and exhaling heavily.

Alannah laughed. "How is All Saints' Day any different? It celebrates the spiritual bond between those in heaven and those still bound to the Earth. Samhain does much the same."

"With the addition of a few Unchristian rituals I would expect," he muttered.

Alannah pursed her lips for a moment before responding. "We'll dispense with the human sacrifice to spare your sensibilities."

Quin blinked at her once or twice, until she broke out in a wide smile that made him laugh. He had known she was only teasing him but had been carried away in the moment.

He grinned sheepishly. "You're right. I am being a little..."

"English," Alannah concluded for him with a sparkle in her eye.

He narrowed his own eyes at her in mock consternation. "Cynical, is what I was going to say.—But I will admit that the differences in our cultures are more apparent at certain times than others." He shook his head briskly and gave a small sigh, before looking back at Alannah, making an effort to sound entirely pragmatic. "What did you have in mind?"

"Nothing extravagant. The tenants would ordinarily celebrate among themselves, each family bringing along some of their harvest to share at the feast. I thought we could do much the same, except to hold the celebrations here, at the manor house and grounds, with a few additions from our own harvest."

She looked at him expectantly, her blue eyes observing him patiently while he contemplated his response.

"That sounds...agreeable," he said, inclining his head toward her while trying not to think about any pagan ceremonies he might be expected to participate in when the day came.

"I'm sure you'll find it to be *most* agreeable." Alannah's eyes softened. "You'll see."

"THINK OF IT as a harvest festival," I said, catching Quin's eye in the mirror as he adjusted his cravat.

He narrowed his eyes at me while he completed his ministrations, taking a moment to smooth down his jacket before responding. Satisfied with his wardrobe, he turned around to face me.

"I shall be on my best behaviour," he promised. "I may not agree with some of the sentiments expressed by my staff and tenants—or even my own wife—however...I have never believed in persecuting anyone for their beliefs, outlandish though they may be." He chuckled and, winking at me good-naturedly, offered me his arm to lead me downstairs.

As we crossed the entrance hall on our way to the drawing room, we passed a small table set in a nook in the panelling, which was laden with food and several lighted candles. Quin paused in his step, eyeing the edibles and reaching out a hand to one of the small savouries.

"No! Don't touch that!" I exclaimed, laying a hand on his arm in restraint.

He looked at me in surprise but dropped his outstretched hand.

"It's the food for the dead," I explained. "It mustn't be touched by the living."

"The food for the..." His brows rose in astonishment as he looked back at the laden table with wide eyes, before turning back toward me. "Of course, it is." He cleared his throat, making an obvious effort not to say anything else. "Shall we?" His features were carefully blank as he offered me his arm once more.

"It's nothing sinister, Quin," I insisted, taking his arm but turning him to face me. "It's believed that on the night of Samhain, the dead come to walk unseen among us." I could see his eyes widening again at this and pressed on. "Not to harm us," I said, trying to think of something to say to make him understand. "To reconnect with us, to see how we are faring in their absence. It's believed that on this night, the boundary between this world and the next becomes thin, allowing the spirits of those we have lost to return to us for a short time. We can talk to them, tell them what's on our hearts, share a meal with them." I waved at the small table. "Tell them how much we miss them," I added softly, my throat suddenly feeling tight, "and know they will hear us."

Quin blinked down at me, his green eyes softening as he examined my face. He wiped away the tear that had fallen unnoticed down my cheek.

"I see." He turned toward the table once more, gazing at it silently for a moment, a faraway look appearing on his face as the candlelight flickered across his features. When he turned to face me again, he wore an expression of contentment, mingled with a sense of sadness.

I knew without asking he was thinking of his mother.

I reached out a hand to stroke his cheek, smiling up at him as I did so. He smiled back at me and took my hand, squeezing it gently in acknowledgement.

We turned away from the table in silence as Margaret and Mrs O'Sullivan came bustling out of the kitchen, carrying baskets of freshly baked bread. I watched them disappear rapidly in the direction of the drawing room ahead of us but had to stop my own progress suddenly as Quin came to a halt, looking perplexedly in the other direction.

"I suppose," he said cautiously, "that there's a perfectly plausible explanation for the doors and windows to have been left open?" He raised one brow at me, inclining his head toward the front door, which was indeed standing open, alongside the windows in the dining room across the hall.

I nodded. "It's to allow the dead to enter unhindered."

"Of course, it is," Quin muttered with slightly glazed eyes as we finally made our way across the entrance hall and out of the house through the large double doors that opened onto the portico and demesne from the drawing room.

Outside, the sun was hanging low in a sky covered in shredded clouds. It had rained most of the morning and the ground was rather muddy, but I was happy to see the evening looked likely to remain dry—at least for now. Not that a downpour would impede the celebrations in any way. Even if the revellers were inclined to be distracted from their merriment by something as insignificant as a drizzle, they could simply continue their gaiety underroof, where much of the feasting would be conducted in any case—the drawing room, several other rooms in the house and even the barn offering ample opportunity for the celebrants to escape any inclement weather that might spoil their night.

For now, no such weather threatened, and the long rays of the afternoon sunshine were keeping autumn's cold bite at bay. The trestle tables set up on the porch were filling up with food, both from our own pantry and that brought by the tenants, who were beginning to trickle in from their small farmsteads at the other end of the estate. The women greeted me shyly, some looking wide-eyed at Quin, who smiled encouragingly at them as their husbands came forward to shake his hand.

I smiled to myself, seeing the warmth with which Quin was receiving his tenants—all of whom he knew by name—and the genuine liking they seemed for the most part to return, remembering the suspicion that had greeted his arrival at Glaslearg only a few months before.

No such misgivings were evident now as I wandered slowly through the growing crowd, which comprised a host of content-looking faces, freed for this one night of the constant burden carried by those who must toil long and hard to survive—a night where they might find relief in the season's successful harvest and comfort in the unseen presence of their yearned-for dead.

Among the happy faces were those who looked around the grounds with big eyes, having never been to the manor before. While most of the men and several of the women had had occasion to see Quin or me up at the house, others had never made the trip, especially the youngsters, who stood together in small groups, observing their unfamiliar surroundings with interest. I nodded toward one such assembly as I passed, receiving a smattering of shy smiles in return.

A giggling group of children suddenly came hurtling in my direction and I quickly skipped out of the way as they bounded past me onto the lawn, where they started chasing one another and rolling on the soggy grass, coming up mud-streaked and squealing in delight, not a care in the world. I looked after them, laughing, but turned in some startlement when I felt a hand on my waist.

"Mrs Williams," Quin said, beaming down at me.

He handed me a cup of cider, which I accepted with thanks. As I took a sip there was a sudden shout as some of the children ventured too close to the centre of the lawn, where a bonfire was being set up. As we watched the children scuttle away, four or five men came forward, each carrying a piece of turf, which they placed onto the growing pile before walking away. Quin turned toward me in some confusion, one brow raised enquiringly, just as another man arrived on the heels of those lately departed, repeating the same process with a piece of wood.

"Each family contributes to the bonfire fuel," I explained. "It's tradition.—No doubt as much from a practicality point of view as any sacred meaning. They will have extinguished their fires at home and will relight them with brands taken from the bonfire tonight."

"I see."

"It symbolises the end of one season and the beginning of the next, a rebirth of sorts if you will. The extinguishing of the fire as the darkness of winter approaches...and the reigniting of the flame as a promise of summer's return."

Quin nodded slowly to himself. "I had always assumed such rituals to be slightly more"—he paused, evidently searching for the right word—"sinister," he concluded with a grin, settling on the same term I'd used earlier.

"Well, festival bonfires once held great significance for the banishing of evil spirits. In fact"—I pointed my chin toward the mound of turf and wood—"to some they still do."

As we watched, an elderly woman came forward holding a lumpy piece of peat in her right hand, the fingers of her left hand clasped in the ancient horned sign

328

against evil, index and little finger raised, her lips moving incessantly as she muttered something to herself. She placed the peat on the pile and, straightening up slowly, suddenly spat onto the ground beside her, before turning from the bonfire and walking away without looking back, crossing herself as she did so.

Quin blinked after her in some surprise but was distracted in his contemplations by the sudden appearance in front of us of a man bearing a burning brand in one hand. I recognised Mr Connell, a stocky, middle-aged tenant who'd become something of a leader of the families living on the estate. Quin had been pleasantly surprised to learn Mr Connell was able to speak more than tolerable English, although he'd been rather annoyed at how long it had taken the man to reveal this feat about himself, considering how difficult it had been for Quin to converse with his tenants at the start. After a little observation, I'd come to the conclusion that Mr Connell had simply needed time, being a pensive sort who didn't seem to be in the habit of making any rash decisions— or trusting people without good cause.

"It's time, sir," he said now in a determined voice, nodding briefly toward me before turning his head to the west, where the sun was hovering just above the horizon.

"Of course, Mr Connell." Quin straightened up and inclined his head toward the older man. "Please." He extended his hand in invitation for him to proceed.

Mr Connell gave Quin a curt bow, before turning resolutely toward the waiting pile of fuel as the other tenants flocked onto the lawn, gathering around him in anticipation. Quin and I followed at a distance, watching the proceedings from the edge of the crowd.

Mr Connell positioned himself next to the bonfire, holding the burning brand at arm's length while waiting for the noise of the spectators to subside to his satisfaction. Once a level of silence had descended, he closed his eyes and raised his free hand to the heavens.

"*Altú a thabhairt do Dhia ar son beannachtaí an fhómhair,*" he intoned in a strong and clear voice that carried easily across the small park.

"Thanks be to God for the blessings of the harvest," I translated to Quin in a whisper as the onlookers echoed the sentiment in murmured voices while Mr Connell opened his eyes.

"*Is lá machnaimh agus cuimhnimh é,*" he continued, looking intently at the crowd, which had fallen silent once more. "*Agus muid ag machnamh ar an saol, cuimhnímid ar ár gcairde ionúine atá ar shlí na fírinne.*"

"It's a day for reflection and remembrance. As we reflect on life, we remember our dear departed friends."

He paused briefly, holding a gaze here and there as the other tenants stared solemnly back at him, the burning brand flickering impatiently in his hand, eager to set the waiting pyre alight.

"*Go mbeirimíd beo ar an am seo arís,*" he said suddenly in a loud voice. "*Níl dada cinnte ar an saol seo ach an bás!*"

"May we be alive at this same time again next year," I translated quietly as Mr Connell lowered the flame to the waiting kindling. "The only certain thing in this life is death!"

The onlookers held their breaths while they waited for the fire to take, giving a collective sigh as the first tongues of flame spread across the pile of turf and wood. I looked to the west, where the sun had just dipped below the horizon, coinciding perfectly with Mr Connell's well-timed performance.

"He's something of a showman," Quin mused as he followed my gaze, echoing my own thoughts.

"So it seems."

"It *was* impressive," he admitted as we turned away from the growing bonfire and made our leisurely way back to the porch and the tables laden with food, which were rapidly disappearing from view under the onslaught of hungry revellers.

"I can't say I've seen anything quite like it before," Quin continued as we patiently waited for a gap to appear in the crowd. "Everything in England seems to be so much more..."

"Civilised?" I suggested in amusement.

Quin chuckled. "Utilitarian, I was going to say. The Irish do seem to have a flair for the dramatic...even the landscape is captivating, beckoning the observer with untold secrets." He looked into the distance in some wonder, at the gentle hills that could just be made out in the dying light. He turned back toward me with a wry smile. "Or perhaps I'm simply mesmerised by the alien language that rolls so elegantly off native tongues, when those who can't understand it struggle to speak even a single word."

I laughed as I finally reached the edge of one of the tables. I espied a large bowl of colcannon Margaret had just brought to the table and eagerly helped myself to a generous portion, adding a thick slice of black pudding to my plate before turning back toward the lawn.

Quin emerged a moment later, holding a steaming bowl of stew in one hand and a large boxty in the other. He nodded in approval as he took a bite of the fried potato cake, chewing contentedly as we walked to the edge of the porch. In mutual agreement, we sat down on the step that led down to the demesne, choosing to join the other celebrants outside rather than to eat a more civilised dinner indoors.

We ate silently for a few minutes, observing the dancing flames of the bonfire that lit the night, which had by now descended in full.

"Mmm, that was delicious," Quin said a while later as he scraped the last few drops of stew out of his bowl. "I may need to go back for more."

"Please do. There's plenty more." The tenants had been more than generous with the food they'd brought along to the feast, which—alongside our own plentiful addition—was making for a bountiful spread.

Quin replaced the spoon in his empty bowl. "It reminds me of our wedding feast."

I nodded as I swallowed the last of my colcannon, savouring the flavour of the buttery potato and cabbage mash. "Me too."

I thought back with fondness on the day. It had been an unpretentious feast, plentiful in quantity but simple in its tastes, catering for those who didn't require fanciful banquets to have a good time—without too much concern for those who did.

"Come to think of it," Quin went on, "I'm not sure I wouldn't prefer an unassuming feast such as this one to London's most lavish of dinner parties." He gave me a wry grin and I laughed, having just reached a similar conclusion myself. "They certainly seem to be enjoying themselves far more than I ever did at a stuffy banquet." He nodded toward a group of youths, who were making their way across the demesne, laughing and cajoling as they went.

"They'll be heading to the barn," I said as the group disappeared around the corner of the house, picking up a few stragglers on the way. "There'll be music and dancing there."

"I'm of a mind to join them. Although," he added with some amusement, "would it be seemly for a landlord to dance with his tenants?"

"I don't know about seemly, but it would no doubt be unusual."

I turned around to see Kieran grinning down at us, having come up unheard behind us.

"Don't listen to him," I told Quin, lifting my chin and narrowing my eyes good-naturedly at Kieran. "The tenants would be happy to dance with you."

"I never disputed that." Kieran raised his hands defensively, palms out toward us. He sat down next to Quin and looked across the park, where groups of revellers were standing around the fire, smiling and laughing. "They wouldn't be having such a good time if they weren't halfway comfortable in your company." He chuckled and clapped Quin familiarly on the shoulder.

"I shall take that as a compliment," Quin muttered dryly, making Kieran laugh out loud.

"Come along then." Kieran jumped up from the seat he'd taken only moments before. "Let's go join them." He cocked his head in the direction of the barn and raised his brows expectantly.

"Alright." Quin got up himself and offered me his hand. "If you two are sure the merriment won't cease abruptly the instant I cross the threshold." He winked at me as he pulled me up and tucked my hand into the crook of his arm.

Snatching up a large chunk of crusty bread as we passed the food tables—including another small one laid for the unseen visitors of the night—Quin towed me across the porch, down onto the lawn and around the house to the narrow trail that led through the hedgerow surrounding the park. We emerged at the top of the courtyard and followed the path toward the outbuildings, from where the sounds of merriment were drifting in our direction.

As we reached the barn, a group of adolescent girls came bursting out through the door, giggling and looking flushed. One of them cannoned into Quin, who caught her by the elbow before she could fall. Looking up at her rescuer, a deep red blush sprung up on her freckled cheeks, almost matching the colour of her hair in its intensity.

"Sorry, sir," she stammered with big eyes, fidgeting nervously with her hands.

"No harm done. Ladies." Quin inclined his head toward the girls as they scuttled of.

I watched them for a while, smiling as they made their way down toward the house along the lighted path, tittering among themselves and throwing furtive glances behind them as they went.

Inside the barn, the air was warm and inviting. A group of musicians had taken up position in one corner and was playing a lively tune. The sounds of fiddle and flute mingled with the rhythmic thrum of a bodhran that made me tap my foot on the floor in time to the beat.

"Come on!" Kieran called, towing Quin and me into the middle of the barn, where several revellers were dancing a sprightly jig. Quin paused long enough to deposit his jacket on the bales of hay that lay against one wall, where a few red-faced women and men in shirtsleeves were reclining as they caught their breaths. With the rest of the hay stored in the stable's loft for the horses' use, the barn was mostly empty, leaving plenty of space for even the most energetic of dancers.

Quin took my hand and spun me expertly into the open space, laughing as I looked at him in some surprise.

"Even Englishmen are known to dance on occasion," he said with a grin.

This particular Englishman evidently *did* dance on occasion—and not just the odd one at that—Quin having no trouble keeping up with the Irish dancers. Laughing light-heartedly alongside his tenants, he whirled me across the floor and into their midst, giving himself over to the music's irresistible pull.

Stepping and turning, and leaping and twirling, we danced until my sides ached and Quin's face was flushed with exertion. Seeing me panting for air, he pulled me toward the hay, where I collapsed gratefully, breathing heavily as I waited for my heart to slow. Quin was puffing noticeably himself as he leaned back onto his elbows and closed his eyes for a moment, breathing in deeply a few times. When he looked back at me his face was suffused with happiness, filling me with happiness in turn.

"It's been a long time since I've had so much fun!" he said with feeling.

"Me too! Although"—I raised one brow—"I can't say the last few months have been entirely *without* fun."

One corner of Quin's mouth rose slowly, and he gave me a deep green look that made me want to pull his head toward me for a lingering kiss.

"Not at all.—But, come to think of it, why was there no dancing at our wedding?"

"There was, but you were too busy fending off whiskey-proffering well-wishers to pay much attention.—In either case, you were probably otherwise occupied by the time the dancing really got under way."

Quin broke into a wide grin, his eyes sparkling with amusement. "No doubt I was. And I wouldn't have had it any other way!" He laughed softly to himself. "Ah," he sighed a moment later, an expression of nostalgia appearing on his face, "but I haven't danced like this in years."

"Neither have I," came Kieran's breathless voice as he flopped down onto the hay next to us. His cheeks were glowing, and his hair was dishevelled, damp brown tendrils sticking to his forehead in disarray. He sighed in contentment as he pulled his shirt away from his chest, flapping it vigorously in the hopes of generating a cooling breeze. He stopped suddenly as he caught sight of something across the barn. I turned in the direction of his gaze, spotting a young woman who was looking coquettishly across at him. When she noticed me looking at her, she quickly lowered her eyes and turned away.

"Excuse me." Kieran jumped up from the hay and made his way rapidly across the barn to the door, where the young woman had disappeared.

"Well, that was a brief exchange of words," I said as I watched Kieran's departure.

Quin chuckled. "I'm inclined to follow his example."

"His example?" I turned toward Quin in confusion.

He raised his eyebrows and gave me a knowing look.

"You mean..." I sputtered, looking back at the barn door. "Kieran...and... The two of them...?"

Quin shrugged. "It's been known to happen." He cleared his throat as a slight flush came to his cheeks. "In any case, I believe there may be more pleasant amusements than even dancing to be had here tonight." He cocked his head toward me and raised one brow enquiringly.

I looked at him for a moment before answering, making an effort not to think about what trouble Kieran might be getting himself into.

At least he wasn't likely to be plotting rebellions under the circumstances.

"No," I said slowly. Quin's eyes widened in surprise, making me laugh. "Not until we've danced a little more."

I got up from the bale of hay, making Quin grin and jump up next to me. He offered me his arm as he led me back to the open floor, where a few more merrymakers had arrived in our absence.

Around and around we went once more as the music continued unabated. We danced and danced, smiling and laughing with unbridled joy, until we were both drenched in sweat and gasping for breath. When I at last couldn't take another step, we bade the remaining revellers a good night and burst gratefully through the barn door into the welcome coolness of the night.

I breathed a sigh of relief as I leaned against the cold stone of the wall, closing my eyes as my heart slowed and the spinning sensation in my head abated.

When I opened my eyes, Quin was looking down at me with a tender expression on his face.

"You were right," he said softly.

"I was?"

He laughed at my startled response but nodded earnestly. "The festival *has* been most agreeable. Now, I wouldn't go as far as saying my life in England was all bad but here...I feel...more free. Even with all the challenges I'm presented with." He shook his head ponderously for a moment before going on. "Perhaps it's simply the distance from my father's suffocating presence." He gave me a wry look. "Or the beauty that surrounds me here." He ran his hand slowly along my arm. "But it's been some years since I've been able to enjoy myself so freely...and so completely."

"I'm glad you can do so now." I reached out a hand and gently stroked his cheek.

"Shall we go back to the house?" he asked with a twinkle in his eyes, which shone a deep green in the near darkness.

"We shall." I pushed myself off from the wall and took Quin's arm.

We walked slowly down the path back to the courtyard, meeting a few people heading in the other direction along the way.

"They seem in no hurry to get to their beds," Quin observed in amusement as we passed a large group of tenants making their way to the barn, singing and whistling in anticipation of what was to come.

"Unlike you?" I asked with a smile.

Quin raised one brow at me good-naturedly and gave me a speculative look. A sudden breeze came up, making the light of the torches that lined the path flicker wildly. He reached a hand toward my face and brushed away a lock of hair that had blown across my cheek.

"I shan't deny it." He pulled me suddenly toward him. "Seeing you with flushed cheeks and gasping for breath..." He pressed me closer. "It makes me think of other activities that might have a similar effect." He closed his teeth gently around my earlobe, making me shudder. He gave a deep chuckle before releasing me, just as the sound of voices became audible from the end of the path.

"Mr Williams," called a youth of about sixteen as the group of new arrivals came up alongside us. He beamed at Quin and energetically pumped his hand, while his equally youthful comrades looked at him with some awe, clearly impressed by the ease with which he was addressing his landlord. One or two of them threw a few quick glances in my direction but looked away before I could meet their eyes.

I lowered my face to hide my amusement.

"Mr Moore," Quin said, inclining his head toward the youth. "Mr O'Reilly, Mr Connell...and the younger Mr Moore. There's fun to be had in the barn yet. I wish you all a good night." He gave the four of them a curt bow, making them puff up in importance and repeat the gesture somewhat awkwardly.

"Good night, sir," said the youth Quin had addressed as Mr O'Reilly, glancing at me while the others echoed the send-off. They turned away jovially, and we continued along the path back to the house.

"Oh," Quin exclaimed suddenly and stopped, "I've forgotten my jacket. Wait here while I fetch it quickly."

He gave my hand a brief squeeze and was off, loping toward the barn before I'd uttered a word. I laughed as I watched him go, coming to stand next to one of the torches at the edge of the path. The flame flickered in the breeze, and I shivered. Outside the warmth of the barn the night was getting cold.

"Winter is on its way," I murmured, rubbing my upper arms briskly as the wind picked up. While I'd been sweating with the exertion of dancing only a short time before, the thin fabric of my dress was doing little to keep out the growing chill now, long-sleeved though it was. And I was feeling the absence of my shawl, which I'd left inside the house—not to mention the absence of Quin, who always seemed to be warm, no matter the weather.

I looked up at the sky, where a sheet of clouds was billowing, hiding the stars. It was a new moon, and the night was dark, the grounds lit only by the torches that had been placed at regular intervals around the estate.

A good night for ghosts, I thought with a shudder, my mind flitting briefly to Martin Doyle.

For despite what I'd told Quin about the benevolent nature of the night's visitors, there were also plenty of tales of evil spirits coming to Earth on the night of Samhain to exact their revenge, and fairies looking for offerings and sacrifices to appease them and ward off their wrath.

A sudden gust of wind blasted into my face, snuffing out the torch that stood beside me. I hugged myself in the cold air. Looking at the tendril of smoke rising from the extinguished flame, an overwhelming feeling of premonition came over me, making my scalp prickle and a cold shiver run down my spine. I shook myself, trying to shrug off the sense of evil that had come over me so abruptly.

"On we go."

I jumped at Quin's voice. I hadn't heard him come up behind me and turned toward him, holding a hand over my pounding heart.

"Are you alright?" he asked with a look of concern, reaching out to stroke my arm. Noticing me shivering, he placed the jacket he was carrying around my shoulders.

"Yes, of course," I said with a slight nod. "You just startled me." I gave him a small smile. "On we go," I repeated his statement, making an effort to sound cheerful.

With Quin's solid presence by my side, my unease soon abated. By the time we'd reached the welcoming lights of the house I was once more thoroughly composed, laughing under my breath at my ridiculous fancies.

On the lawn that fronted the manor, the bonfire was still burning brightly, its light reflected in the windows of the house, which were shadowed with the people moving around inside. While some of the tenants were still huddled around the bonfire or gathered on the porch, picking at the last scraps of food remaining on the tables, most had moved inside, seeking the warmth of house or barn on what was turning into a breezy night.

I rubbed my cold hands together as Quin led me across the porch and into the house through the large doors that opened into the drawing room. I sighed with relief as I came to stand in front of the fireplace, letting tendrils of warmth caress my arms and face, and creep under my skirts and into my shoes.

Thawed at last, I turned away from the fireplace and into the room, taking note of the people around me, whose presence I'd barely registered in my rush to get to the fire's warmth. I nodded to Mary Murphy, who was sitting on the far side of the room with several other women. They glanced shyly at me, flashing quick smiles before turning back to their conversation. A group of men was reclining not far away, looking bleary-eyed and dazed, eyes glazed over with the effects of copious amounts of liquor.

With what little they had, the tenants weren't accustomed to the regular consumption of strong alcohol, generally being unable to afford it and having to make do with less potent drinkables for day-to-day use. When such concoctions were on hand, though, they weren't shy to indulge.

I laughed softly to myself as I looked at Mr Connell, who was staring unseeing into the fire, his earlier showmanship forgotten.

A movement at the hearth attracted my attention.

A group of adolescent girls was kneeling in front of the fire, giggling and whispering among themselves while staring intently at something at the fire's edge. I recognised the freckled, red-haired girl who'd collided with Quin on our way into the barn. She glanced up suddenly and, seeing me looking at her, started chattering animatedly with her friends, the lot of them peeking at Quin and me through lowered lashes, eyes flitting from us to the hearthstone and back again in unconcealed interest.

"What are they looking at?" Quin asked, seeing the direction of my gaze.

"Besides you?" I laughed, getting a raised brow and impatient look in response. "Hazelnuts.—They're trying to divine their future," I elaborated, seeing Quin's confused expression. Remembering playing such games myself as a child, I smiled. "The nuts are placed near the fire to roast, to determine if the person one desires might make a good match." As I was speaking the girls emitted a series of oohs and aahs, eyes intent on the ground before them. "One takes two hazelnuts at a time, one to represent each person of the intended pair. A good match is foretold if the nuts roast silently side by side but..." The girls suddenly erupted in sounds of dismay as one of the hazelnuts rolled away from the fire, coming to rest at the edge of the hearthstone. The red-haired girl glanced in our direction, a dejected look on her face as she eyed Quin. "...if one of the nuts rolls away from the fire, it's a bad omen."

"I see." Quin chuckled, looking toward the girls, who'd lost interest in their game following their recent disappointment and had gone to stand at the window to look outside.

From where I stood, I could see what had attracted their attention.

In a pool of light on the edge of the porch, a group of young men was standing around a tub filled with water. As I watched, one youth, his hands held behind his back, dunked his head into the tub, coming up dripping a few moments later, a large red apple held between his teeth. The sight was greeted by cheers from his fellows, and he jumped up, brandishing the apple victoriously—oblivious to the rivulets of water running down his face—to further shouts and roars of encouragement.

Shuddering at the thought of immersing my own head in cold water, I espied two more youths a short distance away, on the lawn. They were engaged in a similar game, one holding aloft a stick from which an apple was suspended on a string, which he was dangling in front of the other adolescent, who was attempting to catch the apple in his mouth without using his hands. As the catcher was about to close his teeth around the bobbing globe, it was jerked away from him, making him lose his balance and topple clumsily onto the grass.

His friends, including those on the porch who'd seen him fall, roared with laughter, pointing their fingers and slapping their thighs in hilarity at his misfortune. The fallen youth got up hastily, his cheeks blazing even in the dim light, and tried to brush off his companions' quips at his expense.

"Oh dear," I exclaimed, feeling somewhat sorry for the lad, who lowered his head against the relentless banter.

Next to me, Quin shrugged. "Boys." He gave a dismissive wave of his hand.

"They're almost men," I objected.

"Those are even worse!"

We both laughed as the hilarity outside finally subsided and the youths disappeared around the corner of the house.

I turned back toward Quin, looking around the room as I did so.

The group of women had left and the girls who'd been observing the boys' antics were making their way into the entrance hall. Two of the men were engaged in a low-voiced conversation, while Mr Connell was snoring softly in his chair. I smiled at the sight. It wasn't often any of the tenants could simply let go and give themselves to the moment so completely—there were always things to do and things to worry about, mouths to feed and debts to pay.

My eyes drifted to the longcase clock that stood against the wall. It was well after midnight. By the sounds emanating from the rest of the house, a good number of tenants was still awake and likely to stay so for a time, but the celebrations here were more subdued than in the barn.

A few families had left—taking along a burning brand from the bonfire to relight the fires in their homes—but others were making the most of the celebrations, staying awake long past the time they would normally have gone to bed. I smiled as a small girl staggered into the room, yawning hugely, before collapsing onto the hearthrug, rolling herself into a ball and falling fast asleep.

Quin chuckled softly at the girl's slumbering form, his eyes soft as he looked back at me. I took a step closer, drawn to him. He inclined his head toward me and offered me his arm, one corner of his mouth turned up knowingly.

As we walked toward the door, a woman came hurrying to the threshold, a look of concern on her face. Her eyes scanned the room and, seeing the small girl asleep in front of the fireplace, her features relaxed, flooded with relief at seeing her daughter safe.

She smiled shyly as she passed us, making her way to the little girl's side, kneeling next to her and gently running a hand over her small blond head.

I looked at Quin, who was wearing a tender expression on his face as he watched the peaceful scene. He caught my eye and took me by the hand. Quietly, he led me out of the room, leaving mother and child to their rest as we ascended the staircase in search of our own.

I SLOWLY RAN my hand down Quin's naked back, along the smooth line of muscle that lay beneath the skin. He lifted his arm to wrap it around my waist, pulling me close so we lay face to face, our noses almost touching. He ran his palm along my arm, and I shivered, making him pull up the blanket that was tangled around our bare legs, wrapping us in a warm cocoon.

"Better?" he asked.

"Much."

I nestled into him, savouring the feeling of his warm skin next to mine.

He could probably do without a blanket, I thought in amusement, grateful he'd pulled it up, nonetheless. Despite the banked fire, I found the air to be decidedly nippy.

I adjusted my position, making Quin change his as we settled down for the night. It was very late and yet, I didn't really feel tired.

The events of the day kept running through my mind, keeping me awake. I smiled to myself, thinking about how much we had enjoyed ourselves—and Quin's surprise that such a festival could in fact be enjoyable at all. But, as Mr Connell had said, Samhain was also a time for reflection and remembrance, and it had it always been so for me, the memory of those I had lost more vivid on this night than any other.

I turned onto my back, swallowing a sudden lump in my throat and taking a deep breath to keep my emotions at bay.

Quin lifted his hand and gently stroked my cheek. "Are you alright?" he asked softly.

"Yes," I whispered. "I thought you were asleep."

"My mind is not letting me sleep."

I turned back onto my side to face him. "Neither is mine."

His eyes shone in the darkness, a faraway look lingering in the deep orbs as a tender expression appeared on his face. "I've been thinking about my mother.— It's this business of celebrating the dead..." He waved a hand and gave me a lopsided smile.

"You miss her." It wasn't a question.

"Yes." He was quiet for a moment, his eyes unfocused as he looked at something I couldn't see. "You always think there will come a day when the pain will have disappeared but...it never does."

"No. You just learn to live with it."

We lapsed into silence.

"How did she die?" I asked gently after a few minutes, finding Quin's hand under the blanket and holding it tight.

"She..." he started but stopped, looking troubled. "I don't really know." His brows drew together in a frown, making me look at him quizzically. "I was with the army in China when it happened. My father sent a note..." He snorted irritably. "A few words telling me my mother had died, no more. No words of condolence, no description of the circumstances of her death, or even its

341

means." He had a look of disbelief on his face, one which I was sure was reflected on my own. He'd mentioned his father's one-line account of his mother's death before, but I hadn't realised just how callous it had really been.

"Later," he went on slowly, drawing my attention to him once more, "I received word that...she had died peacefully in her sleep." He looked bewildered, disbelieving. He shook his head and closed his eyes briefly. When he opened them, they were filled with sorrow. "She was too young to die like that, the picture of health...always smiling, always happy."

"Do you think...?"

"Do I think someone is to blame for her death?"

I nodded, unable to put the thought into words.

Quin sighed deeply before answering. "I thought about it, obsessed about it for a while. I simply couldn't believe she had been snatched away from us like that.—But do I have any proof of any wrongdoing?" He shook his head. "No. And I have no reason to doubt my father's account of events. Except a simple refusal to believe it. I've had to learn to live with it"—he squeezed my hand gently—"letting the past rest and remembering her for the person she was."

"She sounds wonderful." I wrapped my arms around Quin and pulled him close.

"She was," he said softly, his breath tickling my ear. His heart thumped steadily next to mine, and I closed my eyes, tightening my embrace.

Suddenly, he chuckled, making me look up at him in surprise.

His eyes were crinkled with amusement and heavy with memory. "My parents couldn't have been more different." A small smile formed on his lips as he looked at me unseeing. "I often wondered how my mother could possibly have endured my father for as long as she did. But she loved him...and he loved her." His eyes cleared, holding mine as he gently stroked my cheek. "That counts for a lot."

"It does.—Or it should." Quin gave me a curious look. "I'm not so sure my own parents loved each other in the end, although they did seem to start out that way."

Quin gathered me to himself once more. "What happened?"

I nestled my head into the crook of his shoulder, my hand gently caressing his chest. "Resentment, disappointment. My mother...she had expectations. Expectations my father couldn't live up to, no matter how hard he tried."

"Did it have to do with the farm?"

I nodded. "She never wanted to live at Niall. She had pictured herself living in luxury in Dublin, married to a successful lawyer who would move up the ranks, allowing her to mingle with the elites. Instead, she found herself to be little more than a farmer's wife—as she put it—and having to live with a mother-in-law she never quite got along with."

"Did she not voice her concerns before they came here?"

"I don't know. She never told me." I shrugged. "Perhaps she agreed to come here initially to make my father happy, thinking he would tire of farming and return to Dublin after a few years."

"Except that he didn't."

"No.—He came to love the farm and immersed himself in his duties and his surroundings, doing what he could to aid the people around him." I smiled in remembrance, recalling my father's passion for his work. "But I'm afraid my mother resented him in the end...and not only for bringing her to Niall."

"Oh?"

"She was raised Catholic but converted to Protestantism when my father asked her to marry him." I paused briefly before going on, gathering my thoughts. "She loved him then. She did it for him.—Although he never asked her to," I added, lifting up onto one elbow to look at Quin. "I heard them arguing about it a few times. And my mother's opinion was clear enough. Her parents were furious at her decision to convert, continuing to berate her about it until their deaths...a fact she was happy to throw into my father's face later on, forgetting she was in fact the one who had made the choice." I compressed my lips at the memory. "As for my father...he couldn't understand why she was so unhappy. He believed they had made their choices together, had built their lives together in mutual consent. He expected her to be content." I sighed. "I suppose he had unreasonable expectations of her too...that she would give up on her own dreams so he could follow his."

Quin ran his hand gently up my arm. "My mother once said expectations are the death knell for any relationship."

"There's some truth to that, I think."

Quin nodded absently. "I wonder if my mother was talking about my father when she said that. I often wondered how she could stand his temper...and how two people who were so utterly different could ever have found any happiness at all. But she never tried to change him, accepting him for who he is, the good and the bad.—Perhaps that's what made the difference."

He was silent for a moment, a pensive look on his face.

"Are you afraid I'll try to change you?" I asked with a small smile.

He chuckled, looking me in the eye. "I'd like to see you try. I'm afraid I'm rather set in my ways by now."

"At the ripe old age of twenty-five?" I quipped. "For what it's worth," I added, running a hand along his cheek, "I wouldn't want to change you anyway."

Quin pulled me close, before looking down at me in amusement. "Not yet at least."

I laughed. "Perhaps you'll be the one who'll want to change me," I suggested with raised brows.

"Not yet," he said with a broad smile.

We snuggled close and lapsed into silence, until we drifted off to sleep at last, secure in the knowledge that each of us was enough.

30.

"HOW MUCH IS missing?" Quin asked with a frown.

On the other side of the desk Mr Connell drew his bushy brows together in thought. "Not much, sir," the stocky man answered slowly. "We only noticed something was wrong when a bucket of buttermilk disappeared. My son asked around and"—he shrugged—"a few others said some of their food also disappeared." He cleared his throat, looking a little uncertain, but squared his shoulders as he looked expectantly back at Quin. "I told them I'd speak to you about it, sir."

Quin nodded. "You were right to come to me, Mr Connell." He paused for a moment, considering. "Have any of the tenants noticed anything else amiss? Somebody who shouldn't be there lurking about their plots, perhaps?" he elaborated when he saw the look of confusion blooming on Connell's stern face.

"No, sir. Only the missing food."

"I see. And when did the others first notice some of their food was missing?"

"A week or two ago."

"And...none of the tenants themselves can account for the missing food?" he asked with a raised brow.

"No, sir." Connell looked rather offended at the suggestion.

"I had to ask," Quin said with a small shrug.

Connell made an irritable sound at the back of his throat but didn't say anything else, only looking at Quin with a sullen expression on his face.

"Well, Mr Connell," Quin addressed the man pleasantly, ignoring his bad-tempered countenance, "thank you for coming to me. I shall make some enquiries, see if I can find out what's happened to your food.—In the meantime, please do ensure the other tenants that I'm sure they have nothing to worry about." He smiled confidently at the man, wanting to impress upon him that his concerns would be addressed.

One side of Connell's mouth turned up ever so slightly in what could by no means be called a smile, although it was no doubt intended as such. After a moment, he nodded and inclined his head toward Quin.

"Thank you, sir." He gave Quin a quick bow and disappeared out the door.

Quin's brows drew together in a frown as he looked after Connell's receding form, thinking about what the man had told him.

Evidently, somebody was stealing the tenants' food. Not large amounts, only small bits here and there, but enough that they'd taken notice.

Despite Connell's clear objections to the suggestion, Quin wondered once more whether it was perhaps one of the tenants who was to blame, supplementing his own stores with those of his fellows. That would explain why only small amounts of food had disappeared sporadically over a span of some weeks and that nobody had seen anyone suspicious. Surely, if it was a matter of a common thief, then a greater amount would have been taken on just one or two occasions. And if a vagrant were lurking about the estate and regularly helping himself to the tenants' fare, then surely somebody would have seen him.

"Hmph."

Quin would make the enquiries he'd promised Connell, but he wondered what he would do if he found out it was indeed one of his tenants who was to blame.

Although some were more likeable than others, he'd come to respect all of the people who lived on his estate and found the thought of having to see one of them charged with theft disagreeable, particularly so as he'd tried to impress upon them that they could come to him if they needed anything or had any concerns—there should be no need for any of them to steal anything.

He sighed, looking around for something to distract him.

His eyes fell on the letter he'd received that morning, which he'd been about to open when Mr Connell had appeared at his door. With a smile at the seal that adorned it, he eagerly tore open the envelope and leaned expectantly over the missive.

Sitting back in his chair a few minutes later, he chuckled heartily to himself.

"What's so amusing?"

He looked up to see Alannah standing at the open study door, peering at him curiously. He waved her inside and she sat down at the desk across from him.

"I've received a letter from Archie." He paused briefly, considering. With a shrug, he slid the paper across to her.

She raised one brow but quickly scanned the page, a broad smile blooming on her face as she did so. She laughed softly to herself when she reached the conclusion of the missive.

"Your friend Archie has a way with words," she said as she looked up at Quin, her eyes twinkling with amusement.

"He does that," Quin agreed with a grin.

Although the letter was short, confined to a single page, it was filled with puns and innuendos, the likes of which few people but Archibald Bellinger could produce. Alannah was right, Archie *did* have a way with words, not so much because of any particular linguistic skills, but rather because of his ability to see right through all manner of pretence. Archie saw what was in front of him and dealt with it accordingly—he wasn't one to shy away from embarrassing questions just because they might make someone uncomfortable.

In short, Archie was brutally honest. He hid nothing from anyone, nor did he allow anyone to hide anything from him.

It was this candidness that gave him a unique perspective. While others may skirt around an issue, thinking it indelicate or inappropriate to discuss, Archie dealt with it head on—a trait that was no less conspicuous when it came to his friends.

One particular friend, in this case.

According to Archie, Ollie had fallen in love—desperately so. His inamorata, it seemed, was a young Anglo-Irish woman from Dublin, who—by Archie's evocative description—was something of a buxom lass, likely to smother slight Ollie in her ample embrace. This—if Archie was to be believed—wasn't at all a bothersome prospect to the lovesick Ollie, quite the opposite, he by all accounts being barely able to eat or sleep in his besotted state, but unable to work up the courage to confront the object of his affection in the flesh. The drooping, pining countenance that had resulted from Ollie's inaction had evidently become too much for Archie, who'd threatened—with only a hint of humour—to march to the woman's door and confront her himself.

Quin chuckled at the thought of the sizeable Archie appearing unannounced on the unsuspecting woman's doorstep. Even more entertaining, though, was the thought of Ollie head over heels in love. Quin had only ever known his friend to be logical and calculated in his actions, giving only the barest hint of any sentimental propensities, even when it came to the fairer sex.

"You've known them for a long time, haven't you?" Alannah asked, pulling him out of his reverie.

Quin nodded. "Since I was eighteen." He laughed, remembering that first encounter. "We met at officers' training. We were all so proud and arrogant, our noses up in the air at our own importance.—We soon found out joining the army wasn't quite as romantic as we'd thought!"

"Hard work was it?"

"It was. Up at dawn and collapsing into bed at dusk, aching in every muscle and knowing the next day would bring more of the same." He peered into the distance, his mind flooded with memories. "In times like that you need a friend! I was lucky enough to find three."

He smoothed down the letter in front of him, looking at Archie's familiar hand. "Archie and I got on immediately. He sat down next to me in the mess hall one day and, quite without preliminaries, asked me if I'd cried since I'd arrived at the army. I said that I had. He nodded to himself, and that was that. We've been friends ever since."

He chuckled and Alannah laughed softly.

"Archie introduced me to Ollie, who he'd taken under his wing. Ham joined us later. Despite his aristocratic looks and aloof demeanour, he was no more fond of the conceitedness of some of our fellows than the rest of us.—But I forget, you haven't met him," he said, realising Alannah had met neither Hamilton Wolstenholme nor Oliver Penhale when they'd gone to Dublin, only making Archie's acquaintance by chance when he'd come upon them at the inn they'd been staying at.

"I would like to."

"And I'm sure you will. Just be sure not to mention any of this," he added wryly, lifting the letter and waving it in the air.

Alannah shook her head as he folded up the sheet of paper and placed it back in the envelope. He was about to slide the letter into one of the desk drawers when he remembered his earlier conversation with Mr Connell.

He wrinkled his brow.

He would tell Alannah about it later, he decided, not wanting to spoil the light-hearted mood.

"I've never had friends like that," Alannah said suddenly, making Quin raise his head to look at her.

"Never?" he asked in some surprise.

Alannah shook her head. "I had friends as a child of course. Kieran for one..." She gave Quin a long look. "The children of my parents' acquaintances for another. But...as we got older, we drifted apart." She lifted one shoulder in a gesture of inevitability. "The girls started spending their time speculating who they might be lucky enough to marry one day and what estates they might find themselves living on, what titles they might acquire. I had no time for such things."

Quin raised one brow at her and cocked his head.

She gently lay her hand on his. "I wanted more.—As for Kieran..." She drifted off. There was no need for her to explain how she and her brother had drifted apart. Quin had seen the evidence thereof himself. The two of them were only now beginning to repair the rift that had started growing between them so many years before.

"I never much regretted the lack, though," she continued. "While the other girls couldn't quite understand me, and the boys were no doubt bewildered by my lack of what they would consider normal pursuits, I enjoyed pitting my wits against my father's acquaintances, some of whom—strangely enough—seemed to be more tolerant of my unladylike views than my agemates."

"They didn't seem to be particularly tolerant of your views on appropriate wedding guests, though." Quin grinned, remembering the shocked faces as they'd realised they were expected to feast alongside Glaslearg's servants and scruffy tenants.

Alannah laughed. "No, certainly not.—But do you know what?" She leaned toward him. "I wouldn't have changed a thing."

Quin raised himself from his chair to place a brief kiss on her lips. "Me neither. But perhaps," he added as he sat back down, having suddenly had an idea, "we should invite those same acquaintances again...to show them we haven't quite forgotten how to entertain the upper classes after all."

"You mean...a dinner party?"

Alannah gave him a quizzical look, a thoughtful frown appearing between her brows. They'd been invited to a few such affairs since their wedding, lavish soirees as much designed to entertain the guests as to show off the host's prosperity. While they both enjoyed the company on offer on such occasions, Quin knew the wasteful abandon on display bothered Alannah, in plain view of Ireland's wretchedly poor masses as it was.

She pursed her lips, considering. "Why not? It will give them something else to talk about, at the very least."

The unusual nature of their wedding feast continued to be a frequently discussed topic, even some months after the event—although it was always discussed in entirely civil terms in their hearing.

"Oh, I doubt even the most lavish of dinners will completely erase the shock of having to share a bottle of wine with a groom."

"No doubt you're right." Alannah gave Quin a wry look. "We can always call Bryan and John to join us if the evening becomes too dull."

Quin chuckled. "That would probably be more of a shock for the poor grooms than our esteemed dinner guests."

Alannah nodded slowly, a sudden look of annoyance blossoming on her face. "They can be rather conceited, can't they?"

Quin waved a dismissive hand. "It's nothing unusual. You should see the haughtiness that abounds in London society!—It comes with all those titles," he added with a wink. "Dreadful burden to bear. It's a good thing you didn't have time for such things when you were growing up, otherwise you might have been similarly afflicted."

He grinned at her as she raised one brow. "Then it's a good thing, too, that you don't have any titles yourself! I wonder if your demeanour will change when you become a baron one day."

"Hm…it might, you know. Perhaps that's what happened to my father. I don't think he was always as miserable as he is today.—In fact, I recall my mother telling me she heard him laugh once." He chuckled at the jest.

"That bad, is it?"

"Not quite," Quin admitted, "but he is possessed of a rather foul temper, not to mention a pervasively sour dispossession. Most days it's a right challenge simply wishing him a good day." Quin snorted with mirth, before giving a deep sigh. "My father is"—he lifted his shoulders, temporarily at a loss for words—"a man unto himself."

"Do you think I'll ever meet him?"

"I would think so. I want to take you to London one day, to show you the sights, where I grew up." He reached across the desk to take her hand. "As for what sort of reception we might receive from my father…" He spread out his hands, palms up, and gave Alannah a long look.

She was aware of his father's displeasure at their marriage, having read the letter he'd sent shortly thereafter, in which he'd berated Quin for marrying a minor Irish noblewoman he barely knew. All subsequent missives had made no mention of Alannah at all, except for curtly worded well-wishes to be passed along to Quin's wife—unnamed at that—added for form's sake rather than any particular feelings of affection, Quin was sure.

He shook his head, making an effort to erase the frown he felt forming between his brows. "Any such meeting is likely to be a long way off," he said, feeling his usual cheerfulness return. "Let us instead turn our attention to some other dour faces—those that reside a little closer to home."

"Let's," Alannah agreed. "I'll speak to Mrs O'Sullivan about the preparations. Early December?" She raised one dark brow at Quin as he got up.

He nodded and gave her a hand to rise from her seat.

"I shall pick a suitable date and see to it that the invitations are sent." He pulled her toward him briefly, before looking out the window, where a steady rain was falling. "Let us hope the day will dawn a little drier than this!"

31.

WHEN THE DAY of the dinner party arrived a few weeks later, the sun shone brightly in a cloudless sky on an unseasonably warm morning.

I looked outside the bedroom window, enjoying the view of the estate below me. I could make out Quin's form at the edge of the small park that fronted the house, giving instructions to Finnian the hall boy about the placement of torches around the lawn. I smiled. In the few short months I'd lived here, Glaslearg had become my home, more so than Niall had ever been while I'd lived there with Kieran.

Here, I felt free, that I could live the life I wanted to with the man I loved.

I sat down at the dressing table, glancing at the wardrobe where Rupert had hung Quin's fine evening coat. Thinking about Quin filled me with an overwhelming feeling of tenderness. His presence in my life was like a shining light, a beacon leading me home when obstacles threatened to throw me off course. His faith in me never wavered, and his belief in me made me believe in myself.

I closed my eyes, wanting suddenly to feel his arms around me, my body hungering for his touch. The joy he'd shown me these past months was like nothing I'd ever experienced before, more than I could ever have imagined. A simple kiss could make me weak at the knees and with a touch I was at his mercy.

I opened my eyes and looked at the mirror, which showed a pale face with large blue eyes and dilated pupils, lips slightly parted, wearing a look of such undisguised longing as to make my desires quite clear to the most casual observer. I smiled at the thought, wishing suddenly the day was already over, and we were preparing for bed.

"There's a bit to be done before then," I said and raised an eyebrow at my reflection as I began to prepare myself for the day.

AFTER BREAKFAST, I spent some time overseeing preparations in the house, before deciding to look into affairs in the kitchen. The smells emanating from the feast being prepared made my mouth water, but I was told firmly by Mrs O'Sullivan that I could offer no assistance and, further, that I was not to set foot in her kitchen again on this day under any circumstances.

I laughed and scuttled hastily out of her way, before wandering around the grounds looking for something else to do. As I neared the stable, I heard a sound that attracted my attention. Curious, I poked my head through the door and saw Quin, who was bent over his sorrel, stripped to the waist, evidently inspecting the horse's hoof.

I stopped where I was, taking the opportunity to admire his strong back, muscles neatly indented around the spine. Broad shoulders and smoothly muscular arms promised a strength held in check only by the self-possession of the owner, unleashed strictly when necessary.

He suddenly turned toward me and, seeing me standing in the dooryard, put down the horse's hoof and broke into a wide smile that revealed the small dimple in his left cheek. His bright green gaze went straight through me, and I found myself on my feet and in his arms before I'd made a conscious decision to move. I ran my hands along his naked back, up his neck and through his russet hair, cradling the skull beneath.

He swept me into a tight embrace, kissing me ardently, making me feel light-headed.

I pressed closer to him, wanting more.

"Not here," he breathed into my ear with some reluctance.

"You can't kiss me like that and offer nothing else," I protested.

He chuckled. "Later," he whispered, sending shivers down my spine. "There's a bit of work to be done before the guests arrive."

"I see." I disentangled myself reluctantly while looking at his horse.

"Gambit's shoe came loose and one of the nails got lodged in the sole. I thought I'd see to the hoof straight away."

I looked at the sorrel's leg in concern, but he seemed to be having no difficulty bearing his weight on the affected foot and was showing no signs of discomfort.

"The nail bent at an angle and doesn't seem to have done any damage. I'll keep an eye on him over the next few days, though, and let him rest." He stroked the horse's neck affectionately.

"You do realise it's the beginning of winter," I said, looking appreciatively at his bare chest.

"Is it? Some summer days are not as warm as this."

I laughed. He reached for his shirt and pulled it over his head, catching my eye as his head popped out of the snowy white fabric.

"I wouldn't want my state of undress to be the cause of any impure thoughts on your part," he said, his eyes crinkling into triangles of amusement.

"They're only impure out of wedlock."

"You have a point, Mrs Williams." He chuckled and pulled me close. "Later," he whispered as he nuzzled affectionately at my neck and gave a lower part of my anatomy a gentle squeeze.

I smiled, administered a squeeze of my own and left him to his horse.

STILL SMILING, I returned to the house, where I inspected the arrangements that had been made in my absence. Nodding approvingly some time later, I made my way to my room to contemplate the evening's wardrobe. This didn't take very long as I'd already decided beforehand I would wear the dark green satin dress with the lace trim—the only one suitable for the occasion in any case, besides my wedding dress. Looking through the meagre selection again did nothing to change my mind.

"Well, that settles that then," I said aloud and called Margaret to assist me.

Dress changed and hair tidied, I wondered what I should do next, with about an hour or so left before the first guests were likely to arrive.

Quin evidently had something to do. What that was exactly, I had no idea. But perhaps I could assist him, I thought brightly, heading to the door.

He wasn't inside the house and so, as I'd last seen him in the stable, I decided to look for him there. As I got nearer, I thought I could hear voices, and so I was not surprised to see Quin had company that was not equine in nature. What did surprise me, though, was that this company was female and presently engaged in a tight embrace with my husband, lips locked in what was clearly a passionate kiss.

I was so shocked that I gasped audibly.

Quin released his grip on the woman and looked up. When he saw me looking at him his expression changed—to one of dread, I thought. I didn't wait around to hear his explanation. I ran to the house and flew up the stairs to the bedroom.

My cheeks were burning, and my blood was boiling. I could hardly comprehend what I had seen. Just a few hours ago, he'd kissed me with that same passion, promising a romantic dalliance at the earliest convenience.

How could he now be embracing somebody else?

I stared at the big tester bed that had been witness to our shared joy. The bed where he had covered me with his body, promising me care and succour in every way he could supply.

And I had believed him!

I sat down at the dressing table, feeling unable to stand in my shock.

The first guests must be arriving by now, I thought. Quin was presumably occupied in their reception and unlikely to come and find me, which was some relief under the circumstances. I slumped back into the chair, wanting nothing more than to let my emotions have free reign in the privacy of my bedroom.

Unfortunately, though, that wasn't an option. No matter what had happened and what I'd seen, I would be expected to make an appearance at the dinner party.

I shook myself, took a deep breath and plastered a dreadful smile to my face, before preparing to meet my guests.

I WANDERED AIMLESSLY around the drawing room where the guests were milling before dinner, greeting people along the way but barely noticing who I was speaking to. My mind kept replaying the sight of Quin with the other woman, making me seethe with anger.

How could he do this to me?

I had trusted him, given him everything, all of myself, held nothing back. I had thought he loved me the same way, was sure of it by the way he looked at me and the way his body responded to mine.

How could it all have been a lie?

"What a lovely dress, my dear," the elderly Mr Docherty was saying to me as I stared vacantly at him.

I shook myself to attention, forcing myself to smile at him.

The Dochertys were Ulster Scots who owned a moderate estate to the south-east of Glaslearg. Despite the fact that the family must have lived in Ireland for at least a hundred years, Mr Docherty still retained something of his native accent.

"If I may say so, that shade does become you," he said, admiring the green fabric.

I inclined my head in his direction. "Thank you."

"My dear wife now...she would never wear a hue like that. At least not anymore."

"Oh?"

The man's aged face took on a look of surprise. " 'Twas the strangest thing. She was standing by the fireplace wearing her pretty new dress.—It looked just like yours," he added, waving his finger in the air lest I disagree with this assessment. "The fire crackled, and a few small sparks went up the flue...and suddenly." He looked at me intently, eyes round with remembered astonishment. "Whoosh," he exclaimed loudly and lifted his arms in imitation, making several heads turn in our direction. "Burnt the eyebrows right off her face! Luckily, I was able to douse the flames.—There was a large vase of roses on the occasional table, ye see?"

He paused for a moment, looking around conspiratorially. Spotting his wife on the other side of the room, he leaned toward me and lowered his voice. "One of her eyebrows never quite grew back." He raised his own bushy brows for emphasis. "If I were you...I wouldna mention it in her presence."

"Ah...no, I would suppose not."

"The grey is becoming, though, isn't it?"

Mr Docherty nodded approvingly as he looked at his wife, whose small stocky frame was swathed in a mass of dark fabric that made her look rather severe. I nodded noncommittally, but Mr Docherty had already been distracted by the dry sherry that had made its appearance in the company of Denis. I looked after him in some amusement as he made his way toward the decanter, picking up a small savoury from the tray Finnian was carrying as he went.

I continued to walk slowly around the room—making sure to keep my distance from the fireplace—exchanging pleasantries here and there.

Quin was nowhere in sight.

I hadn't seen him since I'd come back downstairs, nor had I seen the woman he'd been with in the stable. The thought of the two of them together somewhere made me fume with anger and I turned to face the wall and breathed heavily a few times to get myself under control.

Turning back into the room, I suddenly knew he was there.

I lifted my head toward the door that led to the entrance hall, where he was just coming in. Our eyes locked across the room and the background faded into insignificance as we stared at each other. As if drawn by a magnet, he came toward me and pulled me to him against my will.

"I'm sorry." I stood stock-still, not daring to move, barely daring to breathe. "Please. Just let me talk to you. Let me explain."

I continued to stare at him, unable to look away but unwilling to let him see how much he'd hurt me. "Let go of me, everybody's staring at us."

"I don't care!" he growled under his breath, looking around defiantly but letting go, nonetheless. "Let them look, then they'll hear the truth...that I've done nothing wrong."

"Nothing wrong?" I sputtered, barely able to contain my growing rage. "How dare you say that?"

We were standing nose to nose and had attracted a sizeable audience, with a number of hostile looks aimed in our direction. Such marital disputes were best conducted in private, the haughty glances said—they, of course, would never have such arguments, in private or otherwise. That's because you never talk to each other, I fumed mentally. Rather difficult to argue with your spouse if you spend no time together and couldn't care less what the other does.

Quin took me by the arm and drew me none too gently to the nearest exit. He led me out of the drawing room, through the entry hall and outside the front door. The moment the door had closed he pulled me close and kissed me with such fervour I momentarily forgot to be mad at him. This was remedied speedily, though, when his ardent kisses reminded me of other kisses I'd seen him bestow, upon lips that were definitely not mine.

"You bastard," I growled and pulled away from him. "How dare you pretend nothing's changed between us?" I suddenly felt close to tears and turned away from him, heading toward the closest building—which happened to be the stable, of all places!

"I didn't..." I heard him say behind me as he crossed the courtyard to catch up with me.

"I saw you with my own eyes," I yelled, spinning around. "How can you deny it?"

"Alannah, please. Listen to me."

"What is there to say? I should have expected something like this.—No man can stay true to just one woman, much less his wife. Why should I expect my own husband to be any different?"

"Because I am different," he shouted. "Alannah, I love you. And only you!"

He tried to grab me by the arm, but I pulled away.

"Don't touch me!" I hissed.

"She means nothing to me."

"Oh, yes? I'm sure no man has ever uttered those words before.—Did you lie with her?"

"If you mean today, then I did no such thing," he roared. "If you mean have I in the past, then yes, God damn it, I have."

I stared at him, shocked into silence.

"Alannah, if you would just let me explain…"

"Explain then, if you think it will make a difference," I said, without the least bit of effort to hide the hostility in my voice.

"Her name is Sarah…" he started but got no further.

"Sarah?" I asked in disbelief. "Your friend Archie…he thought I was someone called Sarah when he met me in Dublin.—I am such a fool."

I turned away from him once more, but he caught up with me in two strides.

"Alannah, please…just listen to me." He grabbed me by the arm and turned me roughly to face him.

His eyes burned into mine and I stared back at him for a moment, before having to look down as my eyes filled with tears. Quin let go of me and dropped his hand.

"Sarah…" he started again, "she…our families have known each other for years and…well, it was expected we would marry. Everyone thought we would do so in the new year."

"I am so sorry to have gotten in your way," I said sarcastically, crossing my arms in front of my chest and lifting my head to look at him, my face barely under control.

"I didn't love her." He lifted his hand as if to touch me but dropped it when he saw the expression on my face. "I love only you, Alannah. Only you. Always."

My vision began to blur but I blinked away the tears that threatened to fall. Quin pulled me into a tight embrace, stroking my back and pressing me to him. I stood motionless, unable to move, unable to speak through the sense of betrayal that continued to envelope me.

"She caught me unawares," he said softly as he stroked my hair. "I didn't know she was here. If she sent word of her coming, I never received it. When she came upon me in the stable, I was completely unprepared. She flung herself on me and I caught her by reflex before she kissed me."

I remembered that all too clearly and stiffened in his arms.

"Alannah, I pushed her away the moment it began," he insisted in a rising voice as he put me at arms' length to look into my eyes. "You have to believe me when I tell you it meant nothing!"

He searched my face, desperate to find the reassurance I could not give him, as I stubbornly hung onto my hurt pride.

"She's the reason I left London," he said suddenly, his voice soft and filled with sadness. "Or at least one of them. I had known for some time I didn't love her, never had. But I still felt a sense of obligation toward her, and I did at least genuinely like her and didn't want to hurt her."

"So you abandoned her without a word?" I asked, utterly astonished at the thought.

"No, I did not! Despite what you may think of me now, I am not that sort of man!" His eyes blazed at the insult, but he got himself under control.

"We talked. I told her how I felt, that I knew I could never be the husband she deserved. To my surprise she said she felt the same and that we should go our separate ways. Now that she's here, though…" He ran his fingers through his hair, looking puzzled. "I didn't get much of a chance to talk to her earlier." He gave me a sideways glance. "I ran after you as soon as I realised you'd seen us. Unfortunately, I was intercepted in my efforts by the arrival of the first guests."

He reached a hand toward me, tentatively, lest I push him away. I didn't, and he gently caressed my cheek.

"Alannah, I never knew love until I met you. From the moment I laid eyes on you there could never have been another for me. Please believe me."

His eyes held such desperate longing that I finally unlocked my heart and stepped into his embrace.

"You should have told me," I whispered into his chest as I clung to him.

"I know. I'm sorry. It was stupid.—I was afraid of how you might react." He gave me a wry smile, indicating I'd exceeded his expectations in that regard. "And I hadn't wanted to hurt you with my past," he added, looking crestfallen. "It seems I failed on that account. I really am sorry."

"I know. I'm sorry too. I shouldn't have been so quick to doubt you." I looked up at him. "But Quin...I couldn't stand the sight of you with another woman. To think of you with somebody else..."

"Hush." He lay a finger over my lips before drawing me close. "That part of my life is over. My future holds no one but you."

"WHAT A DELECTABLE feast you have prepared for us, Mrs Williams."

I looked over at Mr Byrne and smiled at him, doing my best to ignore Sarah, who was seated a little further down the table from him. She'd appeared in the drawing room not long after Quin and I had returned ourselves, having evidently changed her gown. Quin had introduced her to me, looking uncharacteristically stiff and uncomfortable, while I had tried to smile jovially at my uninvited guest and forget the vision of her wispy arms wrapped around my husband.

"Thank you, Mr Byrne. My cook, Mrs O'Sullivan, has outdone herself."

"She has indeed," Mr Byrne agreed around a mouthful of roast pork. "I haven't feasted like this in ages." He closed his eyes dreamily, plump chin wobbling as he chewed, but suddenly frowned and looked around the table accusingly. "Not that I haven't been able to, of course. I just haven't had the opportunity, with so many of our fellows residing across the Irish Sea..."

"Hmph." Sir Spencer grumbled something next to me, making Mr Byrne aim an irritated glance in his direction.

"Mr Byrne," I said quickly to distract him, "I do hope your sons are well?" I looked at him enquiringly while he continued to frown at Sir Spencer.

"Oh yes," he finally replied, looking back at me. "They are quite well, thank you. They are currently residing in Dublin. Hoping to make their fortunes there...or find suitable brides."

He winked at me, and I laughed. Although Mr Byrne was wealthy, he was a tenant farmer, and his sons were largely dependent on their inheritance for their own wealth—unless they could find themselves a bride with a sizeable dowry.

"And how are things faring on your farm?" I asked him.

Next to me, Sir Spencer gave a condescending snort.

"*My* farm," Mr Byrne responded edgily, frowning toward my neighbour, "is doing exceedingly well. We have increased the export of oats and barley, and have made a very handsome profit, with which I've purchased several additional dairy cows to add to my growing stock." Mr Byrne gave me a conspiratorial look. "Butter," he said, nodding animatedly, "it's the business to be in, I say."

I cocked my head. "Will you not have to give up some of your corn acreage for the dairy farming?"

"Indeed. I shall have to relieve several farmhands of their duties as well. It is regrettable, of course, but..." He sighed and lifted his hands in a gesture of inevitability.

"It's more profitable," Sir Spencer ended the sentence for him.

Mr Byrne narrowed his eyes but nodded, nonetheless.

"It is," he agreed, sticking out his voluptuous chin. "In any case, they'll find something else. Business is booming. If a labourer can't find any work, it's his own laziness that's to blame."

I opened my mouth to respond to this preposterous statement but caught Quin's eye. He was sitting across from me and had been engaged in conversation with Mr Docherty but had evidently heard some of the exchange with Mr Byrne. I frowned at him.

"Do you not think," I said slowly to Mr Byrne, ignoring Quin's warning look, "that the divide between the wealthy and the poor is simply too large for the poor to cross, no matter how much effort may be put in on their part?"

"Of course, it is. Shouldn't it be?"

"And do you not feel yourself in any way obliged to care for the people under your charge?" Quin asked. Seeing me looking at him in surprise, he shrugged.

"They're hardly under my charge." Mr Byrne gave a dismissive flick of the wrist. "They're in my employ. That's an entirely different matter."

"I see," Quin said. "And to increase your own profit you simply won't require their services anymore."

"Precisely," Mr Byrne responded, completely oblivious to the fact Quin had infused the statement with some scorn.

"At least in that we can agree," Sir Spencer piped up, nodding toward Mr Byrne. "That is exactly how I deal with affairs on my own land." He emphasised the last two words to underline the vast difference in status he clearly saw between himself, a landowner, and Mr Byrne, a wealthy—but in his eyes clearly lowly and unimportant—tenant farmer.

"Of course, Sir Spencer," I said with feigned understanding. "And if you were to decide to increase your own profits by turning more of your land to pasture, it would be entirely logical for you to evict the tenants who now reside there."

I batted my eyelashes in Mr Byrne's direction as I awaited Sir Spencer's response. Mr Byrne scowled at me but quickly dropped his eyes and frowned onto his plate. I looked across at Quin, who was wearing a wide grin on his face. I smiled at him—until I caught a glimpse of Sarah, who was looking down the table at us with interest, being herself watched attentively by Kieran, who sat alongside her, eyes shining with unconcealed admiration.

I grumbled something uncomplimentary under my breath and turned back toward Sir Spencer.

"Indeed, Mrs Williams," he said. "While it would involve something of a legal brouhaha, that would be the precise course of action I would employ. In fact"— he gave me a conspiratorial wink—"I am contemplating just such a venture." He raised his eyebrows importantly, before nodding approvingly in my direction. "I always knew you to be an intelligent woman, Mrs Williams."

"Intelligence in a woman is a dangerous thing," Mr Byrne muttered with a sour expression on his rotund face.

"Only to those whose own intellect pales in comparison," Quin said cheerfully, making Sir Spencer break out in gales of laughter, the ends of his moustache quivering in delight.

The other dinner guests turned toward him in astonishment, while Mr Byrne sat slumped and scowling in his chair, arms crossed over his ample midsection, his head glowing bright red.

Fortunately for Mr Byrne, his discomfort was soon relieved by the arrival of the dessert, which consisted of so many cakes and puddings I thought we could scarcely make a dent in the numerous creations on offer. The guests set themselves to the task, though, and tucked in heartily, despite the fact we'd already consumed two different kinds of soup, broiled and baked fish, and several types of roast meat—along with an enormous variety and quantity of side dishes—in succession. My own sides ached with the effort and my head was starting to throb, but I couldn't help accepting a small portion of plum pudding, nonetheless.

I closed my eyes and savoured the delectable morsel.

Mrs O'Sullivan truly had outdone herself. Having been deprived of the opportunity to cater for quite such a lavish occasion since my father had passed away, she'd pulled out all the stops. Each dish was better than the last, in presentation as much as taste. And there was plenty of it. Contemplating the quantity of food we'd been presented with during the course of the evening, I mused it must come close to the amount prepared for our wedding feast, although that had comprised much simpler fare.

With the food left over after the dinner party, we would no doubt be able to host a similar banquet for the tenants. I smiled at the idea and determined to do exactly that. While Mr Byrne could easily afford an extravagant lifestyle with the money he earned off his large plot, Glaslearg's tenants were in no way so lucky, living on tiny pieces of land with minimal income and hardly a thing to their names.

I compressed my lips in irritation, contemplating for the thousandth time the inequality that pervaded our land. Even people who were in a position to rent land to farm could differ greatly in their circumstances, depending on the size of the plot they held and the capital they had at their disposal, with some living lavishly off the financial benefits of Ireland's trade with England, while others were little better off than the landless labourers the farmers employed to tend their crops.

I shook my head and glanced across at Quin. He looked up and smiled at me but was distracted by Mr Docherty, who was having a vigorous discussion with two or three of his dinner partners and was evidently under the impression Quin would side with him on the topic of interest. I saw Sarah turn toward them as the men's voices rose, an overly attentive look on her face as she caught Quin's eye. He gave her a small smile in response.

I frowned.

Things were not quite settled between Quin and me just yet.

"IT'S BEEN SIX months, Quin. It's time you came home."

Quin looked at Sarah, perched on the settee in the drawing room, looking like a tulip in her pink dress, with her blonde hair piled high on top of her head.

He rubbed a hand tiredly across his face. "I am home, Sarah."

It was late. The guests had gone home, and Alannah had gone to bed citing a headache. He'd wanted to follow her straight away but had been obliged to

363

entertain the lingering O'Malley brothers, who hadn't seemed to realise they were overstaying their welcome, being too preoccupied prostrating themselves in front of Sarah to notice everyone else had left.

"Oh, Quin," Sarah said with a pitiful look on her face, "we both know you're not meant to live on a farm.—And certainly not one in God-forsaken Ireland." She compressed her lips and wrinkled her small nose in a moue of distaste.

"You're welcome to leave if that's your opinion of the place," Quin said, hovering at the door in the vain hope she would let him go to bed.

She gave a slight laugh. "I'll leave tomorrow if I can persuade you to come with me, Quin." She lifted one eyebrow enquiringly.

"I am not leaving," he insisted, narrowing his eyes at her.

"Suit yourself, Quin. The evening was very pleasant and all but…if you'd rather be in the company of Ireland's idle peasants for the rest of your days instead of London society…"

"They're only idle, as you put it, because there isn't enough work for them to be permanently employed." Quin took a step closer to her, feeling irritated. "And what makes you think you're so much better than anyone else, in any case? The Irish people are no different to you or me. We're only separated by circumstance. All anyone needs is a chance."

"Oh, Quin, always trying to save the world. Is that why you took up with your little Irish girl? Did you rescue her from a ghastly fate?" She tittered mockingly and placed her hand on her chest in feigned shock.

Quin's nostrils flared in anger, and he breathed out heavily through his nose before he thought it safe to open his mouth. "You will speak of my wife with respect, or you will not speak to me at all."

"Oh, all right, Quin." She sighed. "There's no need to get upset."

"Must you insist on using my name in every sentence?" he hissed, thoroughly annoyed at her casual dismissal of his anger.

She laughed briefly before going on. "Quin," she began with a mocking smile on her lips, getting up from the settee and walking toward him, "we've known each other long enough to be honest with each other, wouldn't you say?"

He didn't respond, only glaring at her with narrowed eyes.

"You've made your point." She emphasised the last word as she came to a stop in front of him. "It's safe to come back to England now."

"What do you mean?"

Sarah sighed once more and gave Quin a long look he couldn't quite read.

"You made your feelings for me clear. There's no need for you to hide in the backwoods of Ireland any longer."

Quin cocked his head to one side, looking at her in speculation. "I was under the impression we had parted ways amicably."

"We did, of course. But there was talk...naturally. Everyone assumed we would be married, so when you left..."

Quin had been aware of the talk, of course. It was one of the reasons he'd left. Sarah's family had been less than thrilled at the severing of their betrothal—or what everyone had assumed to be a betrothal, there never having been an official agreement—not least of all because she would no longer rise up to his higher social rank.

In their circles, though, the undoing of an intended match must perforce be the result of an impediment on the woman's part. For weeks, people had tittered about the possibilities behind Quin and Sarah's backs, speculating whether she'd displayed some defect in character he'd found intolerable. Rumours had started to spread, including the inevitable conclusion that she was a loose woman and had played him false.

Quin had tried to defend her virtue where he could, only to discover that none of the gossips cared one bit about the truth, only wanting some reprieve from their dull and meaningless existence. And the truth wouldn't have helped Sarah's predicament, in any case—whether or not they'd loved each other would have been irrelevant, as Sarah had in fact displayed what would be called loose morals, although only with Quin himself. While such behaviour was perfectly acceptable, and almost expected, from a man—both prior to and within the confines of a marriage—any woman found to have acted thus would be disgraced.

"They're not still saying that you..."

Sarah waved her hand and shook her head. "Of course not...at least not to my face." She pursed her lips for a moment before turning her eyes on him. "Nobody will ever know."

"But...what about...?"

"I can *pretend*, Quin," she said irritably. "And there are ways to fool a man..." Her mouth compressed in a hard line. "I'll not go into that with you," she snapped.

"I'm sorry, Sarah, I never meant for any of this to happen."

She shrugged her shoulders while her face hardened. "I only have myself to blame. I did invite you to my bed after all…"

She had, when Quin had returned from the war in China. They'd known each other all their lives and had had their hands on each other a time or two even before Quin had been called to duty, but it had never gone that far before. Quin had been hesitant at first but she'd been persistent and so he'd given in— without too much resistance, he was honest enough to admit to himself— believing, like everybody else did, that they would one day be married anyway.

But as he'd settled down in London and contemplated a life with Sarah as his wife, he'd felt like something was missing.

She was attractive, could hold an intelligent conversation and came from a good family—one with close ties to his own—and yet…

It was only once he'd admitted it to himself that he'd realised he simply didn't love her. Unfortunately, by the time he'd come to this realisation half of London society had thought they were already betrothed, despite the fact only a few months had passed since his return to England. And even though she'd declared her own feelings to be the same, their public separation had been almost scandalous.

"Hmph."

"In any case," Sarah went on, "nobody's talking about us anymore. So it's quite safe for you to come home." She looked at him expectantly, one blonde brow raised.

Quin blew out heavily through his nose. "I am not coming home," he insisted. "I've told you so before. This is my home now." He emphasised each word to make her understand.

"Suit yourself." She gave a small shake of the head. "If you change your mind your father will be delighted to hear about it."

"My father?"

"Yes, Quin, your father, The Baron Williams of Wadlow. Had you forgotten about him?"

She smirked and he frowned at her.

"Don't be facetious, Sarah.—Since when are you in my father's confidence?"

She sniffed. "Things changed when you left."

Quin looked at her askance. Although his father had tolerated Sarah's presence in their lives, he'd believed her to be beneath Quin's station and thus not worthy of his extended interest. Despite their families' long-standing connection, there'd never been any particular warmth between the two of them, and their conversations had tended toward the civil rather than the personal—spiced with the occasional disparaging remark from his father that everyone did their best to ignore.

For Quin's father to admit to Sarah even casually he wanted Quin to come home would have been utterly out of character.

His father's public demeanour never changed, no matter what was going on in his personal life. Acerbic and cynical at best, he would never admit to any difficulties of a private nature, much less discuss his emotional state with a woman he barely tolerated—he was not the type of man to air his dirty laundry for others to see, even those closest to him.

Quin shook his head irritably, suddenly unspeakably annoyed with the entire affair, including Sarah's presence on the estate.

"What are you doing here, Sarah?" he asked her bluntly. "If you thought you could appear on my doorstep and drag me back to England, you are very much mistaken."

A surprised expression bloomed on her face. "Can I not visit an old friend?"

He gave her a sceptical look.

"Think what you will, Quin. I've only come to assure myself of your welfare.—Now, if you would be kind enough to show me to my room, I believe I shall retire." She extended her hand to him expectantly.

Grumbling under his breath, he tucked the proffered appendage under his arm and led her to the room Margaret had hastily prepared following her unexpected arrival. The house was quiet. He'd sent the servants to bed once the O'Malleys had finally left, expecting Sarah also to retire upon their departure. He got an unpleasant feeling walking with her through the silent corridors, as if he were betraying Alannah in some way. He stopped in front of the door to the guest room and gave Sarah a curt bow in farewell, before turning away.

"See you in the morning," she called after him, making him frown and pause in his step. He waved back to her noncommittally and continued along the hall and down the stairs, to the interview with his wife.

367

"IT WAS A mistake," he said quietly to Alannah as she lay with her head on his chest, nestled under his arm. "I never should have..." He waved his hand and sighed, wishing he could change the past. "When I came back from China, I was..." He stopped, struggling to find the words to explain.

Alannah stroked his cheek, and he took her hand and gave it a gentle squeeze in acknowledgement.

She had been asleep when he'd arrived but had woken when he'd crept into bed next to her, wrapping her arms silently around him as he began to talk.

"I felt like...like I was living outside of myself...like my mind and my body no longer fit together...like I was an empty shell. I had lived through war, seen men torn to pieces in front of my eyes, screaming and dying. I had killed men, men with whom I had no personal quarrel.—And the sight of the murdered women and children..." He shook his head in remembrance. "You train for it, of course, but no amount of training can prepare you for the brutal reality of warfare."

"I can barely imagine such a thing." Alannah gently passed her hand over the scar on his chest.

"My father had no time for my sensibilities. He told me to get on with things." Quin clenched his jaws and breathed out heavily. "I wanted to feel alive again. When Sarah came to me...she was very persuasive...and I didn't need much persuading." He glanced at Alannah to gauge her reaction, but her eyes were filled with sadness, not reproach.

"I wish *I* could have been there for you," she whispered.

He tightened his arms around her, his throat constricting at the overwhelming love he felt for her.

He had been afraid she would turn away from him, that what lay between them had been irrevocably damaged by the day's revelations. Sarah's appearance in the stable had been so unexpected that he'd barely grasped her presence at Glaslearg by the time he'd found her arms wrapped around him and her mouth on his. Snapping suddenly out of his stupor he'd been horrified to see Alannah's shocked expression greet him as he disentangled himself from Sarah's embrace, the hurt in Alannah's eyes tearing through his soul.

And yet here she was, giving him comfort, when he was the one who should be comforting her.

"I'm sorry." He touched his lips to the soft mass of her hair. "I never meant to hurt you."

"Hush. You don't need to apologise for your past."

"But I do," he said, his heart heavy with regret. "My mother did not raise me to take advantage of vulnerable young women...no matter what state of mind I might have been in.—When I realised I didn't love her I was fully prepared to marry her, nonetheless. I had kissed my share of women...but what sort of callous man would lie with a woman and not offer to wed her?" He breathed out heavily as a sense of self-loathing crept over him. "But she said she felt the same...and that she wouldn't want to marry a man who didn't love her. She relieved me of the burden of responsibility, but I felt it just the same."

Alannah raised herself up on one elbow and looked down at him, her eyes filled with sorrow. She bent toward him and gently kissed his lips, cradling his head with one hand. He pulled her closer, feeling some of his guilt fade away with her touch.

"It's in the past," she said softly as she lay her head back down on his chest. "You have to forgive yourself."

He wrapped his arms around her and held her tight, kissing her forehead as he swallowed a lump in his throat. They lay silently for several minutes, Alannah gently stroking the side of his neck.

"There was one other," he whispered into the silence some time later.

Alannah's hand froze, and she lay stock-still.

"It was in China, after I was shot. I lay fevered for days, hovering between life and death, hallucinating...sure I could see my mother, whose death I'd learned of only a few days before. The surgeons had all but given up on me.—There was an Indian woman who had travelled to China with the army. She took care of me, wiping my brow and feeding me what food I would take, until it looked like I might survive. She came to me one night when I was still so weak I could barely lift my own arm..."

He remembered only glimpses of that night—bare coppery limbs and thick wavy hair that was dark as night, a rustling of fabric as she lowered herself onto him, floating over him until he sighed in pleasure and lapsed into a deep sleep.

"The next day she was gone. And I went back to the army to regain my strength for the rest of the campaign."

He looked at Alannah lying motionless beside him, wishing he could have spared her the day's pain.

"I have made mistakes," he said quietly, stroking her hair, "and I regret the pain I have caused.—But I would make them all over again if it meant finding my way to you."

Alannah slowly lifted her hand and placed it on his cheek, and he turned to face her. He looked into her eyes, wanting her to see into the depth of his soul, to know there would never be another for him.

"I love only you, Alannah. Only you."

She pulled him close, and he kissed her roughly, overcome with emotion. He ran his hands over her—shoulders and breasts, belly and thighs—offering her restitution with his body for the pain he'd caused her, until at last they lay entwined, secure in their union once more.

32.

BREAKFAST THE FOLLOWING morning was an awkward affair.

Quin hadn't been sure whether Sarah had been aware of my presence in the stable when she'd kissed him, as her back had been toward the door and he'd left her standing there without a word when he'd run after me. None of us had made any reference to the event, of course, and none of the guests at the dinner party had mentioned Quin's and my abrupt departure, but the three of us had exchanged occasional awkward glances when our eyes had met unexpectedly.

The dinner party had proceeded without further incidents, though, and I'd found myself enjoying the company of long-neglected acquaintances. I'd kept my eye on Sarah during the course of the evening—lest she show any signs of wanting to throw herself at Quin once more—but she'd been nothing but courteous and charming to all those present, talking animatedly and laughing with anyone inclined to join her. I myself had barely spoken to her aside from the few words exchanged when we were introduced to each other, but I'd known I wouldn't be able to avoid her forever, when she would be spending the night under our roof.

I'd told myself to treat her with the same curtesy and respect I would bestow upon any guest but was finding the task to be exceedingly difficult.

Despite Quin's assurances he'd been an unwilling participant in the scene I'd witnessed, and that whatever relationship they might have had was in the past, I just could not find it in myself to feel any warmth toward her, even though she was being nothing but polite toward me.

"I must apologise again for my unannounced arrival, Mrs Williams," Sarah said to me as she replaced the napkin she'd been using in her lap, "and thank you most heartily for the hospitality which you have shown me in spite of it."

She smiled at me, showing her small white teeth, seeming genuinely grateful for her reception. I inclined my head toward her by way of acknowledgement.

"Would you like me to show you around the estate, Miss Alford?" Kieran asked with a shy look at Sarah as a soft blush crept up his neck.

"Why, yes. Thank you, Mr O'Neill, that would be wonderful."

I looked from Kieran to Sarah in some astonishment before glancing at Quin, who shrugged his shoulders noncommittally. I looked outside the window, where the blue sky from the day before was being replaced with smatterings of grey clouds.

"You should leave now to avoid getting wet," I suggested, only to realise that under the circumstances, the statement might have sounded like an eager dismissal of my guest. I was trying to think of something more intelligent to say when Sarah herself came to my rescue.

"An excellent idea, Mrs Williams," she said and placed the teacup she was holding onto its saucer.

She picked up her napkin again and delicately dabbed her mouth before making to rise from her seat, causing Kieran and Quin to leap up from theirs. I watched her covertly as she got up and swept out of the room in Kieran's company, holding her nose ever so slightly in the air.

She was lovely, I had to admit with some annoyance. Not so much beautiful in the typical sense. Her brows and lashes were a little too pale and her nose was just the tiniest bit rounded, but she held herself with a confidence that radiated to those around her, making her more attractive the longer you looked.

I emitted an unladylike snort, trying to suppress the stab of jealously that had made itself felt in my heart. I glanced at Quin to see if he'd noticed my discomposure but found him to be frowning down onto his empty plate.

"Um...Quin..." I cleared my throat. "How long is...Miss Alford intending to stay?" I looked at him demurely, trying to keep any hint of irritation out of my features.

He wrinkled his brow and ran a hand through his hair. "I don't know," he admitted with a sigh. "She didn't apprise me of her particular plans."

"I see. And...ah...what exactly might she be doing here?"

"I don't know," he said again, this time with a distinct air of annoyance. "I asked her that.—She said she'd come to visit an old friend. I find this explanation to be highly doubtful. Sarah is not..." he started and glanced at me. "She is not the type of woman to go out of her way for others. She's helpful enough when it's at her convenience, but anything that requires a bit more effort..." He flapped his hand dismissively. "She would hardly go to the trouble of travelling from London to the sticks of Ireland for an old friend." He emphasised the last three words scornfully. "Not unless there were something in it for her..."

And that something was likely to be Quin himself, I thought.

He had told me she'd asked him whether he would be returning to England. Evidently, she'd come here to try to lure him back. I rubbed my temples, feeling a return of the headache from the night before.

"Are you alright?" Quin asked with a worried look on his face.

"Yes." I gave him a weak smile. "It's only a headache."

"Perhaps you should go lie down," he suggested, reaching out a hand toward me.

I nodded, feeling suddenly very tired. "I think I will."

He got up and came to stand next to me, giving me a hand. As I rose from my chair I was overcome with dizziness and had to lean against him for a moment until I could stand unassisted. He looked at me with concern, green eyes searching my face for further signs of faintness.

"I'm alright now," I assured him. "I'm sure I just stood up too quickly." I smiled at him, but he continued to frown at me.

"I'm sorry about all of this," he said softly and stroked my cheek.

I shook my head and leaned against him. "It's not your fault. And I'll feel better after a rest."

AFTER I MADE my way upstairs, I spent the morning lounging on the chaise longue in the bedroom—an activity that was turning out to have more than one benefit. Lying there with my eyes closed while the headache slowly subsided, I found myself reflecting on the previous day's events.

I'd known before Quin and I were married that I wouldn't be the first woman he would lie with. I had accepted his past but his revelations about Sarah and the woman in China had nevertheless come as a shock. I had at first felt anger, and even a sense of betrayal, at his words but had realised quickly these emotions were entirely unjustified as the events he'd described had occurred before he'd met me.

Part of me wondered, therefore, why he'd felt the need to tell me.

In the peace and solitude of our room, I realised he simply didn't want any secrets between us. Having kept his history with Sarah from me before, he'd wanted to tell me everything there was to tell, to prevent any misunderstandings in the future.

I also thought, though, that part of his honesty came from a need to bear his soul.

373

From what he'd said, it was clear he'd been berating himself for his past actions, which he believed to be roguish and cowardly. Thinking about Sarah and the other woman myself, though, I came to the realisation that—right or wrong—Quin had taken what he'd needed to survive in times when he'd been desperately lonely and afraid. The thought filled me with sadness but also an overwhelming feeling of love for a man who tried to bear everyone's weaknesses while thinking himself weak for having his own.

Feeling at peace once more, I drifted off to a restful sleep.

When I opened my eyes, the headache was gone, and I made my way downstairs for afternoon tea, having slept through the midday meal. I found Kieran and Sarah in the drawing room, engrossed in conversation while sheets of rain were falling outside the window.

"Mrs Williams," Sarah greeted me when she saw me at the door, "I do hope you are much restored?"

I looked at her closely but could read nothing but concern in her face.

"Yes, thank you, Miss Alford," I responded with a nod. A moment's silence descended on us, no one knowing quite what to say next. "Um...did you get a chance to visit the grounds before the downpour?"

Sarah smiled. "Yes, I did. Your brother was kind enough to give me a small tour." She turned toward Kieran and gave him an appreciative glance—one that seemed a little too familiar for my liking. "I was surprised at the ferocity of the storm, though," she continued, looking back at me. "It came upon us quite suddenly, releasing buckets of water within moments, when I had expected nothing but a gentle rainfall."

"The only thing predictable about Irish weather is its unpredictability," Kieran said with a grin.

"That seems true enough." Sarah laughed. "The estate seems...quite well established." Evidently, she was searching for something nice to say.

"Yes, it is," I agreed. "Mr Williams has worked very hard to see it reach its full potential."

"We aren't quite there yet," Quin himself said behind me as he came through the doorway.

He came to stand next to me and touched me lightly on the arm. His eyes met mine and he raised his brows at me enquiringly. I gave a small nod and smiled at him in reassurance, causing him to smile warmly in turn. Turning back toward

Kieran and Sarah, I thought I could see her looking at Quin with an expression that could only be described as envious. It was replaced almost immediately with one of courteous interest, but I was sure I'd seen it, nonetheless.

"There are a number of fields standing empty still," Quin explained to Sarah as he led me to one of the empty chairs. "The estate's previous overseer saw fit to focus his agrarian efforts on exploiting the tenants and labourers rather than doing much in the way of actual farm work. The few fields he cultivated were used to grow mostly potatoes, while the others stood empty...to be overgrown with wildflowers." He shook his head as he always did when contemplating Glaslearg's erstwhile steward. "We managed to clear a good number of them and plant the seeds I purchased, but we could hardly manage all of them in such a short time."

"We'll still have a good bounty come next season," Kieran said with a hint of pride in his voice.

I noticed his use of the term *we* and suppressed a smile. Kieran had assisted in the clearing and planting of the unused land and was evidently feeling himself to be part of the estate's machinery—in a way he'd never managed to achieve on his own farm.

"Yes," Quin agreed. "By the looks of the seedlings, we should get a good harvest from the winter wheat and oats. And we'll use a good number of this season's potatoes for the spring planting, so the potato yield should increase too."

Quin looked at me and a feeling of warmth flooded through me at how much he'd been able to achieve in such a short time. The estate had been close to ruin, and he'd managed to see it steered back on the right course, using every resource at his disposal to fulfil the promise he'd made the estate's inhabitants, and himself. While the monetary recompense for his efforts would be collected at the next harvest, I knew seeing the gratification in the tenants' eyes was already reward enough for him.

He had promised to take care of them, and he had—and in the process, he had made the estate our home.

Our eyes locked for an instant, making everything else in the room fade momentarily into the distance.

"And don't forget the sheep," Kieran said, making me tear my eyes away from Quin, who laughed at Kieran's comment.

"They'll hardly bring us much of an income," he quipped. "Although we may be lucky enough to make each of us a nice new cloak."

Kieran smiled, although his expression was tinged with a sense of regret. He and Quin had collected the sheep from Niall a few days after Kieran's hasty departure from the family farm. It hadn't been established whether Niall's sheep had meant to be part of the agreement of sale—or the pretence thereof—but they had in fact meant to be part of my dowry. When nobody had appeared to take care of them, Quin had decided to take things into his own hands, thinking he could always address the matter if the new owner should come looking for them—or the chickens he'd collected along with the sheep.

Nobody had come to claim them, though, and so Glaslearg now boasted a small herd of Cheviot sheep, whose handsome woolly bodies ambled picturesquely along the pasture that was their new home. While they would undoubtedly produce enough wool to contribute to the estate's textile needs, they were hardly going to make us rich.

"Still," Kieran went on jovially, "Glaslearg does have livestock."

He grinned at Quin, who shook his head in amusement. "Six sheep, a handful of chickens and one cow...with such riches we'll be able to turn the farm to pasture in the new year."

Sarah raised her brows. "*One* cow?"

"It's *his* cow," Quin said, nodding toward Kieran.

"And what a sorry sight it is," I added, making Kieran jump to the animal's defence.

"Ah, now, all sweet Maggie needs is a bit of love and attention."

"And food," Quin said. "She's skin and bones," he added in Sarah's direction.

"I saw the lass at the market last week," Kieran said. "She looked at me with her big brown eyes...and I had to take her home."

He grinned and we all laughed.

"Big brown eyes, you say?" Sarah batted her lashes and turned the force of her own brown orbs on Kieran. He stared at her, mesmerised, and I exchanged a glance with Quin, who was wearing a slight frown.

"Speaking of cows," Quin said, making Kieran jump, "I thought we might keep Maggie in the barn, the stable being rather full at present."

He cleared his throat and avoided my eye, the thought of the stable having evidently triggered a memory from the afternoon before. I compressed my lips but didn't say anything.

"Yes...yes, of course." Kieran was slightly pink around the ears as he turned toward Quin, trying to put on a serious expression. "I'll prepare a pen for her and move her there myself.—If you will excuse me. Miss Alford." He bowed toward Sarah before making a speedy exit.

"It's pouring with rain," I observed, glancing out the window.

"A good downpour will do him some good," Quin muttered under his breath with a sideways glance at Sarah, who was looking after Kieran's departing form.

She turned back toward Quin and me, a small smile on her lips. "Mrs Williams," she said, "I wanted to thank you for including me in the banquet last night. Both the food and the company were most enjoyable." She glanced at Quin, and I narrowed my eyes slightly but relaxed as she continued. "More so, in fact. The food was simply exquisite.—And so much more varied than the Irish potatoes one only ever seems to hear about in England." She laughed, a light musical sound.

"Hardly," Quin said dryly in response to her jest.

"Oh, but you must agree it is a popular crop. You said yourself it's the main crop grown on your own estate."

"Yes," Quin agreed shortly, evidently no longer in a conversational mood.

"It is a popular crop," I said to Sarah, making her turn toward me and raise one pale brow in interest. "Potatoes are the staple food of a large portion of Ireland's population—the labourers and those with only small plots of land to farm."

"I wonder why that is?"

"Because the vines yield a large number of potatoes even on small fields," Quin explained, seeming to make an effort to engage his guest, "enough to feed whole families."

"I see." Sarah looked intently at Quin.

"They're also easy to grow," I added, making Sarah turn her eyes away from Quin and back toward me—reluctantly, I thought. "Once they're planted, there's not much to do until they're ready for the harvest, the timing of which also doesn't need to be as precise as for other crops such as oats.—It gives the labourers and small farmers time to earn their wages on other fields without neglecting their own crops."

"Hmm." Sarah gave a small nod, evidently losing interest in the topic. "I suppose it's better than eating stale bread." She flapped a hand dismissively.

Quin frowned at her but smoothed out his features as the conversation returned to trivialities. After a few minutes, Sarah mentioned someone Quin knew from London and the two of them spent the rest of the afternoon discussing shared acquaintances.

Quin glanced at me apologetically—and somewhat guiltily, I thought—on a few occasions and tried to include me in the conversation as best he could, but I waved away his concern—he had few opportunities to speak to someone from his home after all. I inconspicuously picked up a book I'd left lying on the table to entertain myself while listening with half an ear. Once the discussion of their mutual acquaintanceship had at last been exhausted, the talk tapered off and Sarah excused herself before dinner, calling her maid—who'd travelled with her to Glaslearg from London, along with her footman—to assist her.

When we converged in the dining room not much later, Sarah having changed her gown and freshened up and Kieran having re-stabled his cow, everyone seemed more at ease. With a lessening of the tension that had marked the earlier parts of the day, conversation flowed more easily and, after the food had been cleared away, I found myself laughing alongside Sarah as Quin described his failed attempts at conversing with the tenants of Glaslearg when he'd first arrived on the estate.

Wishing one another goodnight after a pleasant evening some time later, my leave-taking from Sarah went a touch beyond simple civility.

While I didn't quite like her, I didn't exactly *dis*like her either. She was polite and polished, attractive and astute, but underneath her shiny exterior I sensed a loftiness that wasn't quite in keeping with her wholesome façade, although she did her best to hide it. I also wasn't entirely convinced she thought of Quin as only a friend, the occasional glances she threw in his direction telling a rather different tale—which made me all the more interested to learn the reasons for her presence at Glaslearg and how long she was intending to stay.

Neither topic had been broached once.

33.

QUIN THOUGHTFULLY RUBBED his chin, wondering how long Sarah was intending to stay at Glaslearg.

She'd been with them for over a week now, accepting their hospitality with grace and gratitude but avoiding all talk of her proposed departure. Not that one would necessarily discuss such a thing in polite company, it being considered rude to ask one's guest when he or she was planning to leave, but under the circumstances...

Alannah hadn't said anything to Quin after her first cautious enquiry into Sarah's affairs, treating her with nothing but courtesy and respect, but Quin could hardly blame Alannah if she would prefer Sarah not to linger on the estate.

He shrugged his shoulders, resigned. "I suppose she'll tell us sooner or later when she wants to leave...and what she's doing here in the first place."

He looked out the window, where a steady, icy rain was falling from a reluctantly waking sky. After the unseasonably warm weather that had greeted them on the day of the dinner party, winter had set in. While Ireland's winters were reportedly mild, they did seem to bring with them plenty of rain—of course—and a noticeable chill in the air.

And a steady reduction in daylight hours, Quin thought, tapping a finger thoughtfully against his lips.

In pleasant contemplation of conjugal activities that might be conducted during the long winter nights ahead, Quin walked across the sitting room to the bedroom, where he found Alannah sitting at the dressing table, absently brushing her hair. She looked startled when he came up next to her but smiled when he gently touched her shoulder.

"Good morning," he said softly, holding her eyes. "Sleep well?"

"Not as well as one might hope," came her surprising response.

"Oh?" Quin frowned and gently ran one hand along her upper arm. "Are you not feeling well?"

She had told him the headache she'd experienced at the dinner party had made itself felt on a few more occasions since then.

"Not exactly," she replied, making him raise an enquiring brow. "I...I think...I think I may be pregnant," she stammered, sounding utterly bewildered at the possibility.

Quin broke into a huge smile. "But that's wonderful!"

He pulled her off the chair and gathered her into his arms, kissing her thoroughly as his heart filled with joy, and an undeniable sense of pride. They came apart smiling and laughing, making Quin embrace her once more, lifting her off the floor as he held her tight.

"That's wonderful," he repeated, nuzzling her ear.

When he finally put her down, he beamed at her, wanting to shout the news from the rooftops.

"But what do you mean, you *may* be pregnant," he asked as the wording she'd used suddenly came back to him. "I thought it would be reasonably clear...it being rather difficult to hide a growing baby." He winked at her, bolstered by his jovial mood.

"Well, yes," she admitted, shaking her head and laughing at his attempted jest. "I simply meant that I am not *certain*...at present..."

"Have you missed your courses?" he asked, matter of fact.

"Ah...yes," she admitted and blushed.

Quin narrowed his eyes at her good-naturedly. "Alannah, I think we're on intimate enough terms that we can discuss such things without discomfiture, wouldn't you say?—Besides," he added practically, "I've shared your bed for some time now. It's not as if I wasn't aware of them before."

He *was* aware, but not counting the days—except to know when his advances might be accepted once more.

He grinned at her.

"I suppose so," she said, one side of her mouth turning up.

"So?" He cocked his head.

"Yes, I've missed my courses." She looked him in the eye. "But it's only been a week. And they have been irregular at times in the past..." She trailed off and frowned.

"I see. And how do you feel?" Quin stroked her cheek, looking searchingly into her face.

"Fine," she answered with a shrug, sounding almost cross at the observation. "Besides the odd bout of headache, I feel absolutely fine."

"But...that's good...isn't it?"

"Yes, it is, Quin." She smiled in response to what was undoubtedly a bewildered expression on his face. "It's only that I've heard it said pregnant women feel terribly ill..."

"So...you think you're not pregnant because you're not ill?"

"I don't know." Alannah laughed, shaking her head.

"Well," Quin said, pulling her close once more, "I suppose we shall see soon enough. If there's a baby on its way, it will make itself felt...in a few months at the latest." He lowered his head to hers so their faces were almost touching. "I would be thrilled.—But if perchance you should not be pregnant after all...then we'll simply keep working on it until you are."

She ran her hands slowly down his back to his rump.

"That sounds like an excellent idea," she said softly, her eyes dark blue pools as she pressed his hips toward her and sealed his mouth with a kiss.

QUIN CAREFULLY RAN his hand down Gambit's leg before lifting his foot and peering at his hoof. The horse stood still, taking the inspection stoically, only twitching his ears in response to Quin's voice.

"Good lad." He lowered Gambit's foot and slapped the horse lightly on his flank. "Good as new."

Gambit blew out noisily through his nostrils and jerked his head toward the stable door.

Quin smiled. "You'll go for a ride soon enough," he promised as he patted the horse's sturdy neck, feeling a sense of relief come over him.

Although the injury had at first seemed slight, a few hours after the horseshoe nail had been driven into his hoof, Gambit had started lifting his foot off the ground in discomfort and treading carefully on the affected leg, making Quin worry that the nail had lodged deeper in the hoof than he'd initially thought. Seeing the horse limp slowly out of his stall the morning after the dinner party, Quin had been concerned the nail had pierced the bone or punctured the soft flesh nestled inside the hoof's protective casing, driving in dirt and impurities that could so easily cause the wound to fester, leading to permanent lameness and even death.

Quin had watched Gambit anxiously and had doggedly cleaned and bandaged the hoof, inspecting it daily for signs of infection.

But aside from the horse's awkward gait, he'd found nothing amiss. There had been no swelling, and gentle inspection of the site had led to no greater reaction than a swish of the tail, nothing like the violent response one might have expected if the hoof had been seriously damaged.

And yet, Gambit had continued to hobble on three legs for several days after the incident.

Quin and the two grooms, Bryan and John, had been just about at their wits' end when suddenly, one morning, Gambit had pulled his hoof out of Quin's grasp, stomped on the affected foot, walked through the open door of his stall and headed resolutely toward the stable's entrance, no limp in sight. Quin had gaped after him in astonishment before breaking into a broad grin.

Evidently, the patient was feeling better.

"You were just vying for my attention, weren't you?"

Quin stroked Gambit's velvety nose. He'd continued to keep an eye on the erstwhile invalid, but the animal was showing no signs of his recent troubles, which was making Quin wonder in amusement whether he'd been putting on something of a show. The horse bobbed his head energetically, making Quin laugh.

"You do have a point," he said as Gambit whinnied softly and butted his shoulder, "I've been neglecting you."

With the harvest collected, the planting concluded, and the season's building completed, Quin was spending less time outdoors. His horse, apparently, was feeling the lack of exercise this change in lifestyle entailed.

"We'll go for a nice long ride as soon as I'm able," Quin assured his companion. "If only a certain someone were out of my hair…"

He had said this under his breath but suddenly felt sure someone had heard him. He looked around slowly, with the distinct feeling he was being watched. He eyed the dim confines of the stable and peered at the patch of light at the open door, but he could see no one. He was alone with the horses, which were shuffling around in their stalls, not visibly upset. He shook himself, trying to rid himself of the feeling of someone's eyes boring into the back of his neck.

"You're just feeling guilty for voicing your uncharitable thoughts," he muttered to himself.

He checked his surroundings once more but, finding nothing untoward, bid Gambit farewell and headed back toward the house, trying to shake the sense of unease that continued to cling to him.

When he reached the manor, he could hear voices coming from the dining room, where he presumed the midday meal was about to be served. As he neared the open door, he could see Alannah and Sarah standing beside the long table, evidently engrossed in conversation.

"You invited your *servants* to your wedding feast?" Sarah was asking, wearing a look of utter astonishment that Quin could discern even in profile. "As *guests*?"

"Well, they did assist with the preparation and some of the work on the day...but yes, we did.—And our tenants too," Alannah added, darting Quin an amused look as she espied him at the door. Sarah turned so her back was toward him and Quin waited at the threshold, wanting to hear her response.

"But...what...I mean...there are so *many* of them."

"It was a simple feast, everyday fare for everyday people. People we like to think of as friends."

"I see..." Sarah's voice was filled with a dubiousness that made it clear she didn't see anything at all. Quin knew she herself would never consider inviting anyone not of the aristocracy to any social gathering, much less her wedding, no matter the circumstances.

Alannah, evidently feeling Sarah needed some respite from the present conversation, looked up at the doorway, where Quin now entered, pretending he'd only just arrived.

"Quin." Alannah's eyes lit up in amusement. They'd forgone the formality of addressing one another with their last names in Sarah's company, she herself having invited the use of her Christian name instead.

Quin smiled, trying not to laugh at the conversation he'd overheard. Suddenly remembering the news Alannah had shared with him that morning, his smile broadened, and he looked at her tenderly, wanting to pull her into his arms. Her eyes caught his and her lips turned up in a secret smile, understanding crossing her features.

"Alannah, Sarah," Quin said, managing to tear his eyes away from Alannah momentarily and bowing to each of them in turn.

"Quin." Sarah inclined her head in his direction. She cleared her throat, probably trying to recover from the shock of hearing about her hosts' peculiar social habits. "Has your horse quite recovered?" she asked after a moment, a concerned frown forming between her blonde brows.

"Yes, thank you, he has." Quin nodded as Mrs O'Sullivan bustled into the room carrying a large serving dish, from which emanated the delectable smell of pork casserole. She clicked her tongue disapprovingly and gave the three of them a disparaging look.

"Sit, sit," she ordered none too gently, before depositing the bowl on the tabletop and hurrying back out to the kitchen as Margaret entered with a basket of bread.

Quin laughed but followed Mrs O'Sullivan's instructions, while Margaret started ladling stew onto their plates. As he waited to start eating, a thought suddenly occurred to him. "Was either of you at the stable earlier?" he asked, looking from Alannah to Sarah and back again.

"No," Sarah said as Alannah shook her head.

Alannah wrinkled her brow in confusion. "Why do you ask?"

"Oh…no reason." Alannah gave him a sceptical look. "I thought there was someone there," he conceded with a shrug. "I felt like I was being watched." Saying it out loud made his earlier apprehensions sound ridiculous, and he lowered his head and set himself to his meal.

"I've felt it too."

Quin looked up to see Kieran walk through the door, a slight frown on his face.

"In the stable?" Sarah sounded shocked as she gaped at Kieran while he took his seat. Seeing Quin eyeing her, she quickly averted her gaze, a red hue creeping into her cheeks.

"In the barn," Kieran said as he reached for a slice of bread. "I've felt it a few times when I've gone there to tend Maggie."

They all chewed in silence for a minute.

"Perhaps there's a vagrant about," Alannah suggested at last, looking expectantly up at Quin.

"Hmph. Could be."

He found the notion puzzling, as he'd seen no signs of anyone having made the outbuildings their home, nor had the servants mentioned any such thing. He paused suddenly, remembering what Mr Connell had told him about the tenants' missing food.

That had been several weeks ago, though, and he'd heard of no other incidences since then. He frowned as a sudden thought occurred to him. When no more food had been reported missing, he'd assumed whoever had been stealing from the tenants had disappeared—or, if it had been one of the tenants themselves, that the guilty party had simply stopped, following Quin's renewed assurance they could come to him for any assistance. But perhaps the culprit had simply become more cautious, leaving no further signs of his presence as he continued to lurk about the estate.

Quin compressed his lips slightly for a moment before making an effort to clear his features, looking back toward Alannah's expectant face as he did so. "We'll search the grounds this afternoon."

Kieran nodded his consent, looking around the table in apparent self-assurance.

If there *was* a vagrant lurking around the estate, they would find him.

"THERE'S NOTHING TO worry about," Kieran declared as they convened in the dining room once more for their supper.

Quin could see Sarah visibly relax at the news, while Alannah only nodded.

Kieran looked intently at Sarah. "We searched every corner of every outhouse and found no signs of any disturbance."

"Good," she said softly, "good."

Quin frowned. "You were never in any danger." He found Sarah's reaction rather irritating, when she barely left the house.

"Of course not." She glanced at Kieran, who was looking rather pink around the ears as he watched her. He cleared his throat and lifted his eyes.

"No doubt Quin and I were simply imagining things," he said, looking expectantly at Quin.

"No doubt," Quin agreed, making an effort to smooth out his brow. He smiled reassuringly at the women, who soon relaxed and dropped into casual conversation as they all tucked into their dinner.

Quin ate mostly silently, only nodding here and there when a comment was addressed to him, thinking all the while that he hadn't imagined a thing.

34.

QUIN STIFLED A yawn, feeling the aftereffects of a long night.

It was a new year, and Sarah had wanted to celebrate its birth. The others had declared themselves eager to join her, but Alannah had started nodding off in her chair before the clock had struck twelve. Quin had carried her to bed before returning to the drawing room, not wanting to leave Sarah and Kieran alone.

His brother-in-law had been following Sarah around like a lost puppy since she'd arrived at the estate, and the way they looked at each other bothered Quin. He wasn't entirely sure *why* it bothered him—and he tried hard not to think about the reasons—but bother him it did. He'd been half tempted to tell Sarah about Kieran's dubious past to keep her away from him, until he'd realised how spiteful such an act would be. Kieran had done nothing to arouse Quin's suspicions since he'd come to live at Glaslearg—in fact, the opposite was true—and Quin had developed a genuine liking for the man. Contemplating what it must have taken for Kieran to turn his back on his misguided former existence and embrace the life of a farmer, Quin had concluded he perhaps ought rather to focus his efforts on keeping Kieran away from Sarah, who had after all exhibited rather loose morals in the past.

Since he, Quin, had been the beneficiary of this wanton behaviour, though, this line of thought had done nothing but provide Quin with a list of his own shortcomings, leaving him feeling rather deflated, and cruelly vindictive to boot. He'd therefore decided he'd best leave Sarah and Kieran to their own devices. It was highly improbable, after all, that anything would come of any romantic involvement between the two of them—Sarah was exceedingly unlikely to settle in Ireland to be with Kieran, nor was she likely to encourage him to follow her back to London.

Quin wasn't entirely sure, though, whether that would stop them from doing anything foolish.

And so, he'd gotten into the habit of acting as something of a chaperone whenever he could, which had prompted him to re-join the two of them in the drawing room the evening before, after having tucked Alannah into bed. Despite the occasional suggestive glances between Sarah and Kieran—and the awkwardness his own presence had provoked in those moments—they'd spent the night in pleasant conversation in the company of a good few bottles of wine, staying awake long past the chiming of the longcase clock at midnight.

Feeling the lingering effects of the wine and the lack of sleep now, Quin realised in some amusement that he sensed no discernible difference between the end of one year and the beginning of the next, concluding that the new year's celebration was simply an excuse to eat and drink.

"Like so many other celebrations," he said to himself with a laugh, thinking with fondness about the various festivities he'd thus far enjoyed in his new home, including the Christmas dinner they'd partaken of the week before.

It had been a muted affair at the end of an ordinary day, a simple celebration in honour of a humble King. Alannah had laid some evergreen sprigs on the table, and they'd sat down to their meal, giving thanks for their Saviour's birth. Quin had declared himself entirely satisfied with an ordinary meal, but Mrs O'Sullivan had had other ideas. While not nearly so opulent as the feast she'd prepared for the dinner party, their Christmas fare had nevertheless been more than generous.

Feeling grateful for the abundant blessings in his life, Quin had carved the roast goose, running the knife through the crispy skin to the tender meat below, cutting generous slices that would be slathered with the rich gravy waiting in its boat and accompanied by the steaming potatoes and carrots standing alongside. He'd smiled tenderly at Alannah, who'd sat next to him looking lovingly up at him, imagining their life together with the child she may be carrying—while doing his best to ignore the presence of his former lover, who'd sat across from him, gazing adoringly at his wife's recently reformed, Anglophobic and traitorous brother.

Quin shook his head at the absurd circumstances that had marked his first Christmas as a married man. If his marriage could survive this test, it was likely to survive anything, he thought wryly.

A gentle throat-clearing caught his attention, pulling him out of his musings.

"Sir," Denis said cautiously, hovering at the doorframe.

Quin waved the butler into the room. "Yes, Denis?"

"Ah..." He stopped in front of Quin's chair, looking a little uncomfortable.

"What is it?" Quin nodded encouragingly. The man's spoken English had improved a good bit since Quin's arrival at Glaslearg—and he could understand the language well enough—but he still tended to be a little shy in its use, preferring to relay anything complex to Alannah in Gaelic.

"A man come, sir," he started hesitantly. "Today."

"A man came to Glaslearg today," Quin repeated in confirmation, making Denis nod. "Was he looking for me?"

Denis shrugged uncertainly, moving his head from side to side in thought. "I not know. He not...knock."

Quin drew his brows together in confusion. "But he came to the manor house...?"

"I see man," Denis explained, pointing at his eyes, "through window."

"Oh?"

"He stand...outside house. I go open door but..." He waved one arm. "He gone."

"I see. And did he see you?"

"No." Denis gave a determined shake of the head. "He stand outside and look...at house. I inside parlour...dark inside, no fire. I go to parlour...to close door, see man outside through window."

Quin nodded in understanding. The entrance to the small parlour was directly across from the room's window, from which the front of the house was easily visible.

"So the man arrived after sundown," Quin muttered to himself.

Denis nodded, thinking the comment addressed to him. "Not long after."

Quin frowned. Although the sun set early in winter and an arrival after sundown could still fall well into normal visiting hours, this particular visitor's behaviour was peculiar, to say the least.

"What did he look like?" Quin asked suddenly as the thought occurred to him, cocking his head in Denis' direction.

"I not sure, sir. He had cloak and...hat...pulled down." He gestured with his hand, drawing a figure hunched inside obscuring coverings. "I not see more." Denis shrugged his shoulders, looking at Quin apologetically.

"That's quite all right, Denis." Quin made an effort to smile at the older man. "Thank you for telling me.—Go ahead and seek your bed if you wish. We won't be needing you anymore tonight."

"Sir." Denis bowed his head before turning around and making his slow way out of the room.

"Hmph."

Quin contemplated the meaning of the butler's tale in light of the other peculiarities he'd been confronted with of late, including the tenants' missing food. He suppressed a shudder as his mind flitted briefly to Martin Doyle and his promised vengeance, but he dismissed the idea. The man had been hanged, for God's sake, and there had been no signs of any impending retribution from any quarter either before or after Doyle's execution.

In all likelihood there was nothing to worry about, Quin told himself.

Anyone could have stumbled across his land, and anyone could have stolen the tenants' food—this was Ireland, after all, where poor and desperate souls were easy enough to find. No doubt it was simply a destitute man who'd come to the estate looking for help but had been struck with fear and shame at the thought of asking for it.

Yes, Quin decided, that must be it. The more he thought about it, the more it made sense.

It wouldn't be the first time somebody desperately hungry had turned to thievery to ward off starvation. And seeing the condition of the tenants and the relationship they had with their landlord, the man had thought he might be able to get some help from Quin himself but had been afraid to ask. Lurking around the estate trying to work up the courage to speak to Quin, he'd found himself at the house after dusk one day, only to be struck with doubt before rapping his knuckles on the door, causing him to fade into the night once more.

Quin nodded to himself, content with his analysis.

He would search the grounds once more, to see if he might be able to locate the man who so obviously needed his help. He took a deep breath, letting it out slowly through his nose as he made an effort to erase the lingering frown from his face.

"And why are you looking so glum?"

Quin looked up in startlement, his eyes travelling to the door, where Sarah was just coming in. She was eyeing him with some amusement, having spoken in jest.

"No reason." Quin gave a brief shake of the head. "Ah...where's Kieran?" he asked to change the subject.

"Asleep, I presume. Alannah too?" She raised her brows.

"Yes. She went to bed about an hour ago." Quin stifled a yawn and ran his hand over his eyes, feeling suddenly rather tired. "I'm not sure why I didn't do the same."

Sarah laughed, giving Quin a mocking look before glancing at the clock. "Because it's still early. I've never known you to be in bed by ten-thirty."

"Hmph," Quin grumbled, feeling annoyed at the familiarity with which Sarah was discussing his habits, even though she was entirely correct. No doubt lingering irritation from his conversation with Denis, Quin told himself. Still...

"Since we're both here..." Sarah inclined her head toward one of the padded chairs that stood around the low table, ignoring Quin's scowl.

"Of course." Quin made a conscious effort to smooth out his brow and extend an inviting hand. "Sherry?"

"Thank you, yes."

He poured her a glass and, upon some reflection, topped up his own. A slight dulling of the senses might be quite desirable under the circumstances, he decided.

They sipped quietly for a few minutes, each absorbed with their own thoughts.

"I hear Kieran had to give up his land," Sarah said suddenly, making Quin look up at her. She had a slight frown on her face and was pursing her lips in thought.

Quin made a noncommittal noise in his throat in response, not knowing what story Kieran had told her about the loss of his farm. If he hadn't told her the truth, Quin didn't want to be the one to explain that Kieran had been blackmailed into giving up Niall out of fear of being otherwise condemned for treason.

"He said there were better opportunities elsewhere, that he hadn't wanted to hold onto a farm that might have led to his ruin."

Quin gaped at Sarah for a moment. That was one way of putting it, he thought. Before he could respond Sarah continued.

"What opportunities might there be for him, do you think?" She looked at him expectantly, absently running her fingers through a long strand of her blonde hair.

"Ah..." He searched for inspiration. "I suppose he might invest what money he has...get into a different line of business altogether."

"Hm..." Sarah nodded to herself, chewing on her lower lip as she smoothed down the strand of hair and flicked it behind her shoulder. She swirled the last of her sherry around her glass, before swallowing it in one healthy gulp and holding out her tumbler for more. Quin raised one brow in surprise but obligingly topped up her glass. She was silent for a moment, focusing her attention on the light amber liquid.

"There seem to be an awful lot of poor people in Ireland," she said as she placed her sherry on the table, giving him a penetrating look with her brown eyes and wrinkling her forehead.

"There are," Quin agreed slowly, seeing no point in denying the obvious, but wondering what she was getting at. A thought suddenly occurred to him. "If you're worried Kieran might become one of them..."

"Oh no." Sarah flicked a hand in a dismissive gesture. "He's part of the gentry. He would never descend to the level of a *commoner*." Quin blinked at the contempt with which she'd infused the last word. "I only wondered about his prospects."

"I see."

"He and I encountered some beggars on the way to the town this morning," Sarah continued, clearly unaware of Quin's growing irritation. "They're rather unsightly, aren't they?"

"I'm sure they're not begging solely because they wish to offend your sensibilities!"

Quin looked at Sarah's sherry glass, noticing that it was almost empty once more. She didn't seem noticeably intoxicated but perhaps her sherry consumption was to blame for her current behaviour.

Sarah pouted her lips and sniffed disdainfully. "Still, one doesn't want to see such things."

"And what do you propose should be done with them?"

She shrugged. "I'm sure I wouldn't know."

"But you'd rather not lay eyes on them." He didn't phrase the comment as a question, her answer was clear enough. "Out of sight and out of mind, is that your solution?" He frowned and leaned toward her in his chair, wishing he could shake her to her senses.

She raised her brows and lifted one shoulder, making it clear this was precisely what she thought. "There are simply too many of them."

"Beggars?"

"Those," she agreed with a nod, as if Quin had been looking for a genuine answer to his rhetorical question, "and the indolent peasants from whom they must derive." She paused for a moment, her mouth turning down in a moue of

391

distaste while Quin could only gape at her in disbelief. "When I arrived in Dublin harbour, an entire boatload of them was just leaving. Every last one of them dirty and bedraggled, and dressed in rags.—And with passage on a vessel bound for *England*, I was told!" She compressed her lips and wrinkled her small, round nose before going on. "If they wouldn't breed like rabbits, then they wouldn't have to leave their own land to take over ours!"

Quin shook his head slowly back and forth, stunned into silence. "It's not that simple, Sarah," he said once he'd recovered something of his wits at last.

She looked at him with indifferent eyes, clearly uninterested in an explanation. He exhaled heavily through his nose before continuing, meaning to give her an explanation even so. The words that had eluded him over the shock of the past few minutes were rapidly coming back to him, colliding in his mind in their urgency to cross his tongue.

"Ireland produces vast quantities of grain for the insatiable British market," he began slowly as he tried unsuccessfully to contain his temper, "so people like *you* can eat their cake!" He narrowed his eyes, but she continued to look disinterested, making him snort irritably before going on. "Who do you think works the land and plants the seeds...and harvests the produce that ends up being shipped to England?" His voice was rising but he didn't care. "The peasants! Farmers want to sell more and more produce and so they're using larger tracts of land for more intensive farming. And that requires labour. Lots of it! Especially in Ireland, where much of the tilling is still done by hand."

"They should buy some ploughshares," Sarah said with a haughty expression on her face.

"Not everyone has the capital to purchase large quantities of modern equipment, or the horses necessary to operate it. Small farmers virtually ruin themselves for the simple pleasure of having land to farm in the first place."

Quin shook his head angrily and clenched his jaws.

While the Ulster Custom of tenant right did provide a sense of security for existing tenants, preventing them from being unfairly evicted or losing the investments they'd made in their farms, it made it exceedingly difficult for new tenants coming in. Having to pay for the right to occupy an outgoing tenant's land meant many small farmers had to borrow large sums of money, often at excessive interest rates, leaving them with little or no capital to spare once they'd secured their plot.

"Besides," Quin added in a muted voice, making a renewed attempt at civility, "much of the land in Ireland doesn't lend itself to the practice of modern ploughing and simply requires manual labour. And the peasants you so look down upon are the ones who provide that labour!"

Sarah raised her chin slightly but didn't say anything, making Quin flare his nostrils in frustration.

"A prospering peasant population is a perfectly natural response to an increase in market opportunities," he went on with an exasperated sigh. He was starting to feel like a teacher trying to educate an inattentive pupil but couldn't seem to stop talking. "With a greater demand for Irish produce on the British market, Irish farmers inevitably try to increase their productivity to enhance their profit, including a greater number of smallholders who lease land at increasing rents...which they can nevertheless afford to pay with their increasing income.— All of this entails the hiring of a greater number of labourers to work the land, who themselves flourish under the favourable market conditions as the opportunity for employment grows."

He paused for a moment and Sarah raised one enquiring brow. "So why don't they just stay here?"

"Because we're reaching a point of saturation. Because some of them have no wealth to begin with and can't afford to rent even the tiniest patch of land to live on. And, because, despite the great need for labourers to work the farms, there are only so many who can in fact *be* employed...to perform the labour that by its very nature keeps them poor."

Sarah looked at him in confusion.

"The labourers are hired for planting and harvesting," he explained with exaggerated patience that took every ounce of willpower he could muster, "both of which are seasonal occupations. With no work in between, there is no income in between." He took a deep breath before going on. "Some of the workers hope to find better opportunities elsewhere, including in England. As for them taking over our land, as you put it..." He gave Sarah a long look. "The small influx of Irish people into England is unlikely to greatly dilute the purity of the English populace...this being considerably larger than the Irish equivalent to begin with—and, as I'm sure you well know, also largely composed of *peasants*." He spat the last phrase with considerable irritation, a sentiment that seemed largely lost on his audience.

"And how do you know so much about it?" Sarah asked with some contempt, ignoring his irate countenance.

Quin ran a hand vigorously through his hair before responding.

"Because I used my mental faculties of deduction," he said, making Sarah narrow her eyes at the implied insult that she wasn't capable of the same feat. He didn't care. "And because I chose to educate myself about matters here when I chose to settle in Ireland."

"I thought your wife had made that choice for you."

Quin stared at Sarah for a long while before he finally felt he could speak. "What happened to you, Sarah? When did you become so bitter?"

She pursed her lips and took a deep breath, glaring at Quin as she blew the air out through her nose. "I'm exactly the same as I've always been, Quin. It's *you* who's changed." She got up abruptly and held his eyes for a moment before turning away.

Quin watched her disappear through the door, staring after her for a long time until he finally realised he was standing in the middle of the room, having risen from his seat automatically when Sarah had gotten up from hers. He walked back to his chair and sat down, closing his eyes and leaning his head against the back rest.

Was Sarah right, he wondered? Had he changed so much since he'd left England?

He didn't think so. And if he had, he felt like he'd changed for the better—since Alannah had come into his life. She had given him a focus he was lacking before, something to live for, something to strive for, and he was a more compassionate man for it.

And Sarah? Had she changed?

He tried to remember the time he'd spent with her in London before he'd come to Ireland and earlier, before he'd gone to the army. He'd known Sarah for most of his life, he couldn't clearly remember a time when she hadn't been there. Now that he thought about it, there had been moments throughout their acquaintance when she'd made disparaging comments, often about people of a lower social class or different background. Most of his friends had done it, of course, thinking it all in jest, but Sarah's remarks had often held a sharper note, as if she truly believed what she was saying.

Quin hadn't thought too much about it at the time, as a good portion of the British aristocracy *did* believe themselves to be superior to just about everyone else. And so, he'd overlooked Sarah's bigotry, enjoying her company for other reasons, not least of all its familiarity when he'd returned from China.

But now, it seemed he could no longer turn a blind eye to what was an unfortunate flaw in her character.

"I suppose I *have* changed, then," Quin muttered to himself, "since it never bothered me before."

He'd always thought of himself as a caring man, someone who could empathise with those less fortunate, somebody who didn't believe himself to be better than anybody else simply because of his birthright.

And yet, he'd never gone out of his way to call out those who did hold such opinions, restricting his criticism to a stern expression or a disapproving shake of the head. But Sarah's thoughtless comments on this night—about people who were struggling to survive on a daily basis, for no reason other than the unfortunate circumstance of having been born into the wrong social class in a land that could not support them—had infuriated him, to the point he'd felt the need to educate her on her ignorance in a vain attempt to let her see the error of his ways, knowing full well no such insight would ever come.

Sarah was right, *she* hadn't changed, *he* had.

And he could only be grateful for it.

35.

"I'VE DECIDED TO head home," Sarah announced at breakfast the next morning, studiously avoiding Quin's eye.

"Oh?" Alannah looked at her in some surprise, while Kieran's head snapped up.

"Must you leave so soon?"

"I've been here for almost a month," Sarah responded with some astonishment and a hint of irritation, making Kieran look crestfallen. "I've made use of your hospitality for long enough, Kieran," she added in a conciliatory tone, "Alannah." Sarah nodded her thanks in Alannah's direction but made no mention of Quin.

"Hmph," Quin mumbled under his breath, more irritated with his annoyance at her petulance than the behaviour itself.

"But...it's winter," Kieran had another try, shaking his head slowly back and forth, his light brown curls bobbing along as he tried to convince Sarah to stay.

"Ships sail between Ireland and England throughout the year," Quin said cheerfully before Sarah could answer, making her turn toward him at last, bearing a distinct look of dislike. "Sarah will have no difficulty getting off our shores at her earliest convenience," he added, unable to help himself.

Sarah narrowed her eyes at him. He raised his brows in response, looking at her in mock surprise. She scowled and turned away from him, making one corner of his mouth turn up as he tried to suppress a grin. He caught Alannah's eye and shrugged his shoulders inconspicuously. She gave him a brief smile before rearranging her features into something more suitable and turning back to their guest.

Quin had told Alannah about the altercation with Sarah the night before. Alannah had declared herself saddened but not terribly surprised by Sarah's views, despite the fact Quin himself had been shocked by her blatant disregard for people she considered beneath herself—particularly as he hadn't noticed the tendency in her before.

Quin was only too glad he hadn't been tied down to her by marriage.

Darting an appreciative glance at Alannah, he popped a crispy piece of bacon into his mouth and chewed contentedly, followed by a creamy forkful of poached egg. Looking forward to the scones that were to come, he glanced at the gloomy sky outside the window to gauge the time, tempted to start counting down the hours until this farce of a visit was finally over.

"When were you planning on leaving?" Kieran asked, making Quin turn his attention back to the table.

"As soon as possible," Sarah replied shortly, darting a quick glance at Quin.

"I see…"

Sarah rolled her eyes as she looked at Kieran's downtrodden face. "I suppose I could wait out the week."

"That would be wonderful!" Kieran piped up happily but stopped talking abruptly as Alannah and Quin turned curiously in his direction. A slight blush crept up his cheeks, but he continued to beam at Sarah, who in turn raised her chin and pouted in Quin's direction.

"If that would be agreeable, *Mr Williams*?"

"Miss Alford," Quin said dryly, "I can't think of a single thing that would be *more* agreeable."

SARAH LEFT THREE days later, in the company of her maid, her footman and Kieran, who'd insisted on seeing her to the harbour despite her most vehement objections.

It was raining steadily when she left, as it had done for the better part of a freezing week. The ground was soggy and muddy, with scattered murky patches covered in slick ice. It would be a hellish ride to Dublin, but Sarah had refused to stay another day. Nor could she be persuaded to travel to England via Belfast, insisting on returning the way she'd come—which was the same route Quin had taken himself.

Quin shrugged as he watched the carriage pull out of the courtyard.

Stubborn or not, her reasoning for continuing her journey was sound. It would likely make little difference to wait an extra day or two. Conditions were unlikely to change much, certainly not past the point of a few short minutes' reprieve from the incessant rain or an inconsequential rise in temperature. And if Sarah took the shorter route to Belfast, a lengthy journey overland would probably still ensue once she'd made it across the sea. For while vessels leaving Irish ports could be bound for almost any other harbour in Britain, those departing from Belfast were most often destined for Glasgow, and there might be no ship heading toward England available for weeks. Departing from Dublin, Sarah would likely be able to obtain passage to Holyhead or Liverpool, which, while still some way from London, were nevertheless considerably closer than Glasgow.

"Are you at all sorry to see her go?" Alannah asked, coming up behind Quin and wrapping her arms around his middle.

"I'm not sure," he said, darting a glance behind him. "Sarah has been part of my life for as long as I can remember. It would be peculiar for me to feel no inkling of sadness at her departure. And indeed...a part of me shall miss her." He looked back at Alannah's upturned face but, seeing nothing but genuine interest in her expression, he continued. "It's to do with familiarity, I think. The comforts of home.—God knows I shan't miss the conceited side of her she revealed to me over the past month!"

Alannah tightened her arms around him, and he ran a hand lightly along her upper arm. They were silent for a while, looking out at the dreary courtyard as the rain continued to spatter against the window.

"I don't think you should let the past month cloud your view of her entirely," Alannah said after a few minutes.

"What do you mean?" Quin turned around to face her.

"I mean...that you shouldn't vilify her because of her insecurities."

"Insecurities?" Quin sputtered, gaping at Alannah in complete astonishment. "Sarah? Insecure?" He couldn't think of a less apt description of the woman. Wherever she went, Sarah had men falling at her feet and women swarming around her in admiration, and she carried herself accordingly.

Arrogant would be a far more fitting term, he thought.

Alannah cocked her head as she looked at Quin, her blue eyes intent. "Have you ever considered it may all be a front?" She raised one dark brow. "That she needs the attention to feel she's worth something? That she puts down others to feel better about herself?"

"But"—Quin shook his head—"that doesn't make it right!"

"I am not trying to excuse her behaviour, Quin, only to establish its cause."

Quin looked at Alannah for a long moment.

For all the years he'd known Sarah, she'd always seemed more than comfortable in her own skin, confident—in herself and in getting what she wanted—and secure in her rightful place in the world.

"I don't know, Alannah," he said, shaking his head slowly back and forth. "It seems rather unlikely she's anything except arrogant and selfish...but...I would hardly presume to know her mind, despite the fact we knew each other well...once."

"I'm sorry, Quin, I didn't mean to upset you." Alannah lay her hand on his arm, her eyes searching his face.

"You haven't," Quin assured her. "But it has been...an interesting few weeks!" He lay his hand gently on her abdomen and raised one brow.

Alannah smiled tenderly at him but lifted one shoulder cautiously. "I think it's likely. Although...I still can't say for certain...yet."

Quin felt the corners of his mouth turn up in a smile and pulled her toward him. "That's good enough for me."

SEVERAL DAYS LATER, I opened the bedroom curtains and was greeted by the sight of snowflakes drifting down from the morning sky, gently dusting the grounds below.

"Quin," I called excitedly as he emerged from the screen that hid the commode, "it's snowing!"

"I see."

He smiled sleepily and came to stand next to me as I continued to stare out the window in wonder. While I had of course seen snow before, its enchantment never seemed to fade, particularly as snowfall in Ireland was relatively scarce.

"It's so beautiful," I said quietly, looking at the soft white peaks that covered the shrubs and blanketed the hills.

"It is that," Quin agreed with a faraway look in his eyes. "At least until it starts to melt and turns the ground into a quagmire," he added as he turned toward me with a grin.

I narrowed my eyes. "Well, it isn't going to melt just yet, so I'm going to enjoy it while I can!" I lifted my brows in defiance, making him laugh.

"And I want you to." He bent his head down toward me and kissed me gently on the lips. I leaned into him, the snow temporarily forgotten as he wrapped an arm around my waist and pulled me closer.

"And what's this then?" I asked somewhat breathlessly, pushing my nightgowned hips toward him in illustration.

He smiled against my mouth and pressed me closer to him with a hand on my lower back.

"I may not be as picturesque as snowfall from the heavens," he whispered into my ear, "but I believe I can provide you with some entertainment nonetheless."

He gently closed his teeth around my earlobe, making me shiver. I tilted my head back and he kissed my neck, running his mouth from the angle of my jaw to my collarbone, while one hand caressed my breast. I sighed, and he picked me up and carried me to the bed. He lay me down gently on the rumpled sheets and kissed me lingeringly on the lips, while he slowly loosened my nightgown with one hand. When he finally pulled his mouth away from mine, he replaced it again on my neck, where it began a slow downward trail that followed the path of my nightgown as he pushed it down my shoulders, over my breasts and past my hips.

I shuddered beneath him until I could bear it no longer and pulled him up to lie next to me, removing his nightshirt in the process. I ran my hands over him, my fingertips tingling at the touch of his skin, while I kissed down the side of his neck. My lips gently skimmed his chest and belly, and he tightened his fingers in my hair as I continued my descent. After a moment, he drew in his breath sharply and pulled me up, rolling me onto my back and pinning me under him.

Breathing heavily, he lowered his forehead to mine, his eyes filled with raw hunger as he looked at me. I pressed his rump toward me, pulling him into me as his mouth met mine. He moaned against my lips, and I wrapped my legs around him, drawing him closer. He ran one hand up my thigh, pulling my leg up, his rhythm meeting mine stroke for stroke. I could feel the wave building as the urgent need of our joining obliterated everything else from my mind, until it crashed over me with such intensity that I arched my back and cried out, even as he lost himself within me with a cry of his own.

FEELING THAT ALL was right with the world after the pleasant start to the morning, I went down to breakfast, after which I settled in the drawing room while it continued to snow.

When it finally stopped around midday, I wrapped myself in my cloak to take a turn around the grounds. I wandered around the demesne, my feet crunching softly on the fresh snow and my breath steaming lightly in front of me, delighting in the sight of my surroundings. Draped in a soft white blanket, the park looked almost ethereal as it glowed mutedly in the soft winter sunshine that had emerged after the snowfall.

"You're right," Quin's voice came from behind me, making me turn around to face him, "it is beautiful."

I smiled at him as he came up next to me and took my hand. His hand was wonderfully warm, and I sighed in contentment as he enveloped my frozen appendage. In my eagerness to go out into the snow I'd left without gloves or a muff. Noticing how cold my skin was, Quin took both my hands in his and rubbed them vigorously, before pulling me close.

"Better?"

"Yes," I said and leaned into him as we looked at the wintery scenery.

We started walking across the lawn, our footprints leaving soft dents in the fresh snow as it gave way reluctantly. The air was fresh and crisp, making me feel almost giddy as we ambled along side by side. We didn't talk much, the white sheath that covered the landscape engendering silence as it smothered all sounds.

By mutual consent, we walked around the house to the courtyard once we'd traversed the demesne. The usually hard lines of the quad and its central fountain were softened by the light layer of snow, giving the courtyard an enchanted air. I smiled at Quin with childlike glee, making him grin back at me.

He looked around at the pastel scenery as we walked toward the frozen fountain but suddenly cocked his head in surprise. Following the direction of his gaze, I could see hoofprints in the snow on the far side of the courtyard, leading toward the stable.

"It seems we have a visitor," Quin said and turned in the direction of the outbuildings.

Just then, a figure emerged from the stable.

"Kieran," I exclaimed, recognising his tousled hair even at this distance. I hurried toward him. "You're back!"

"Alannah," Kieran greeted me as I reached him. I threw my arms around him, squeezing him tight. "Oof."

He patted my back somewhat awkwardly but smiled at me readily enough.

"It snowed," I said joyfully when I let him go, unable to help myself from pointing out the obvious in my delight.

Kieran chuckled. "I can see that."

Suddenly, something white came flying in our direction and hit Kieran on the side of the head. I squeaked and took a quick step back as bits of snow spattered my face.

"Argh!" Kieran hunched his shoulders as the snow slithered down into his shirt.

He shook his head and turned toward Quin, who was standing a short distance away, grinning from ear to ear, another snowball held at the ready.

"Is this your idea of a suitable welcome?" Kieran asked as he wiped his face and bent down to scoop some snow into his hands. Quin's missile hit him in the chest as he straightened up, but Kieran brushed it off with a laugh, advancing on Quin.

"In some cultures, it's considered most fortuitous to be met with a sprinkling of snow upon one's return," Quin said as he circled Kieran.

"You just made that up! As for it being a sprinkling..." He let fly but Quin ducked, and the snowball whizzed past him.

"It stopped snowing before you arrived..." Quin lifted one shoulder in resignation. "Besides," he added as he picked up some more snow, "this is more fun."

He fired at Kieran, who turned his back to avoid being hit in the face. Quin laughed but stopped suddenly as a good-sized snowball hit him high in the chest.

"What?" he yelped in disbelief and turned in my direction.

I smiled at him and batted my eyelids innocently.

"Is that how it is?" One corner of his mouth lifted as he gathered some more snow.

I quickly scooped up some more of my own but before Quin could throw, a snowball exploded against his neck. He yelped in surprise and redirected his aim at Kieran, who was heaving with laughter. Slow to respond, Quin's missile hit Kieran on the head, dusting his hair and eyebrows with smatterings of white that made him look like a jovial old leprechaun leering out from beneath his snowy mane through two astonished-looking blue eyes. I laughed out loud but squealed in alarm as two snowballs came flying in my direction, hitting my side as I tried to turn away.

With the abandon of children, we ran around the courtyard, roaring with laughter and pelting one another with snow until all three of us were covered with fine white flakes. Before long, my cuffs and collar were soaked with melted snow, my hands so cold I could barely move my fingers.

Grinning with mirth, I took aim once more.

36.

A FEW DAYS later, I was sitting in the drawing room reading an ancient copy of Moll Flanders that had been my mother's. Contemplating the numerous pregnancies described in the convoluted tale, I marvelled at the number of babies a single woman could bear—and started wondering about my own pregnancy.

If there was such a thing.

I was reasonably sure by now but still had some doubts. I hadn't bled in two months or so, which should have been sign enough—except it had happened before. While some women's bodies might work like clockwork, mine evidently did not, my cycle never having been predictable to the day. Then again, thinking about it now, I realised my courses had last gone *drastically* awry around the time of my father's death, which made me wonder whether my mental state might have had something to do with it.

The thought intrigued me, and I spent some time pondering the possible connection between one's emotional state and physical health. Being anxious or nervous could evidently have physical effects, from sweaty palms to nausea and stomach complaints. But did it go further than that? Could emotional distress upset a woman's natural rhythm somehow, or cause other physical symptoms?

I didn't know and wondered if I ever would.

What *did* by all accounts cause physical symptoms was early pregnancy. I remembered my mother telling me—in response to my endless questions—how dreadful she'd felt when she was pregnant with Kieran and me, a sentiment repeated by Mrs O'Sullivan. If their stories were to be believed, pregnancy seemed to be little more than a curse, made worthwhile only by the baby that would eventually be born.

And yet, if I was indeed pregnant, I was in no such ill health myself. In fact, aside from the occasional headache or bout of tiredness, I'd rarely felt better—physically or mentally.

"That must surely mean that I *am* pregnant," I muttered, having weighed up the options and come to a logical—or so I thought—conclusion.

I put down the book I'd still been holding and got up to find Quin, intending to tell him what I thought I knew. He'd gone to check on the horses and see to some chores. I should probably wait until he returned but felt unable to sit still. I had to speak to him now, I thought with some excitement, and a touch of apprehension.

I put on my cloak and headed to the door. As I stepped outside, a cold shiver suddenly ran down my back, making me stop in my tracks. My heart started racing and my breath came short, and I gripped the doorframe as a feeling of overwhelming dread came over me. I bent forward and gasped for air until at last the moment had passed. Shaking in reaction, I straightened up and swallowed the bile that had risen in my throat.

I turned toward the outbuildings, anxious to find Quin without delay.

QUIN HOISTED UP the bale of hay and carried it to the barn. Unable to see his feet, he walked slowly over the uneven ground, trying not to slip. The thin blanket of snow from the week before had melted, but it had rained and sleeted heavily the day before and getting to the outbuildings was like crossing an icy swamp.

He'd seen to the horses, which were healthy enough but suffering from a lack of exercise. Or rather, a lack of varied exercise. While John and Bryan made sure to lead them around the paddock every day, the horses much preferred to carry riders across the countryside instead of running in circles at the end of a rope.

Weather permitting, he would persuade Alannah to go for a long ride with him tomorrow, Quin decided, shifting the hay to get a more comfortable grip. He'd taken the bale from the stable where it had been stored for the horses, meaning to bring it to Kieran's cow, which was still housed in the barn. The poor creature had recovered well since its arrival at Glaslearg, polishing off large quantities of hay as it chewed incessantly throughout the day.

"Making up for lost time, no doubt," Quin said in some amusement, wondering how much the animal was likely to contribute to the estate's neglected dairy requirements in the future.

As he walked further along the path, Quin suddenly felt a prickling sensation sliver down his spine. He stopped abruptly and his heart skipped a beat, making him shudder in apprehension as he looked around. He could see nothing amiss, though. After a moment or two, he shook himself and continued on his way, a sense of uneasiness following in his wake.

When he reached the barn, Quin cursed softly under his breath. The doors had been left wide open. Hoping the cow hadn't escaped—or frozen—and that the barn hadn't been flooded from the rain, Quin hurried inside, hauling his heavy burden across the threshold.

He stopped dead.

It was gloomy in the barn but not nearly dark enough to dispel the horror of the scene he'd come upon. Kieran was lying on his back a few steps away from him, a pool of blood spreading on the stone floor beneath him, his cut throat gaping hideously open. The expression on his waxen face was one of extreme surprise.

"Quin?"

Quin shook himself and tore his eyes away from the gruesome sight. He dropped the hay and turned toward Alannah, who'd come up behind him. He took her by the shoulders and turned her back toward the house before she'd reached the door—but not before she'd had a glimpse of her brother, lying murdered before her.

"Kieran?" she shrieked. "Kieran?"

She tore at Quin's shirt, trying to get past him, screaming in anguish. Quin held her tight, shielding her eyes from the dreadful reality her mind could not face, from the lifeless body of the brother she'd held dear.

"Kieran...Kieran."

The anguish in her voice broke Quin's heart and he pressed her closer to him.

"You can't help him," he whispered into the top of her head.

"No!" she screamed. "No! No!"

She started pounding him on the chest with her fists, each thump a blow to his heart for the pain he could not save her from. He held her tighter until the anger finally went out of her, and she slumped against him, tears running down her face, her body shuddering in agonising cries.

He picked her up and carried her to the house.

The servants gaped at the sight, but he brushed off their questions and went into the drawing room, where he sat down on the settee, holding Alannah on his lap. She cried out her anguish in great gasping sobs, wailing in agony, shaking in his arms as terror and fright overwhelmed her.

Quin pulled her closer, wanting to draw her into himself to shield her from her despair, knowing it was too late, that he'd failed her already. He wrapped his arms tightly around her as his own shock and fear overcame him, desolation at the loss of a brother-in-law he'd come to love, and the crushing sense of failure that he hadn't been able to prevent his death. His tears fell unnoticed into Alannah's hair, leaving no trace of their existence in her thick, dark locks as he fought to find the strength she would need from him.

He continued to hold her long after his own tears had dried, until her trembling finally waned, and she lay spent in his arms, the large wet blotches on his shirt a testimony to the outpourings of her soul.

"Doyle," she whispered at last as another tear rolled down her cheek.

Quin's heart gave a sudden lurch at the name and a creeping feeling scuttled down his back. "It must be," he said, tightening his arms around her. "Somebody who knew him...who wanted to avenge him." He didn't want to believe it, but he knew in his heart Kieran's death was no random act, had known it the instant he'd laid eyes on him in the barn. "Who else would want to..." He let the rest of the sentence hang in the air. He wasn't sure how much Alannah had seen of Kieran, but it was enough.

There was no need to apprise her of the details of his fate.

"He was doing the right thing...he was turning his life around..."

"Hush," Quin said, his heart aching, "hush."

He stroked her hair, her back, wanting to take away the pain she was feeling but knowing he could never make things right, that he could never bring Kieran back—or make up for his own failings.

"He'll come after you next."

Alannah's barely audible voice made the hairs on the back of Quin's neck stand on end.

"I know," he responded quietly, pulling her close.

There was a sudden screech outside that made Alannah flinch. One of the servants had discovered the body.

"I'll think of something," Quin promised as he gently moved Alannah from his lap onto the settee and wiped the tears from her cheeks, clenching his jaws tightly at the sight of the desolation that marred her face, hoping he could keep his promise—this time.

He had failed when he'd last uttered those words, when Martin Doyle had first come into their lives. He hadn't believed Doyle when he'd promised them his vengeance and said he didn't work alone. And now Kieran had been murdered, and both of them were likely in danger of the same fate. For Quin knew whoever had come on Doyle's behalf wouldn't stop at Quin's death. Alannah had been complicit in Doyle's capture and conviction, and whoever had killed Kieran was likely to know that.

"I'll think of something," he repeated, hoping his voice conveyed a conviction he didn't feel, as he rose to face the storm that awaited him.

"WHAT'S HAPPENED?"

"Mr O'Neill's been *murdered*."

"What?"

"I heard he was..."

"Shhh! Mrs Williams..."

I turned my head toward the voices, feeling slow and distant, as if I were moving under water. The servants were huddled at the door. As I lifted my swollen eyes toward them, they quickly looked away from me, but I could see them throwing furtive glances in my direction as they continued to whisper amongst themselves.

"Let me through please."

A man I dimly recognised stopped in front of me. I stared at him, making no move to offer him my hand or acknowledge his existence.

"Mrs Williams, I'm Constable Ryan from the Irish Constabulary.—I realise this is a difficult time, but I must ask you some questions about your brother's death."

I flinched.

"If you will allow me..."

"Constable Ryan!" Quin came into the room and advanced toward the settee where I sat, looking furious. "You can ask *me* anything you need to know. In my study. Across the hall."

"But Mr Williams..."

"Now!" Quin stared at the constable with an expression that should have turned the man to stone.

"Yes...ah...certainly..." the constable stammered, looking away from Quin. "Mrs Williams..." He bowed awkwardly in my direction before leaving the drawing room.

Quin glared after him for a moment before turning toward me. He searched my face anxiously with tired eyes. I tried to smile at him, but my lips quivered, and a tear rolled down my cheek instead. Quin compressed his mouth in a hard line and swallowed. He stroked my cheek and dropped a gentle kiss on my forehead, before turning to follow the constable out of the room.

"Will you be needing anything, mistress?"

I looked up at Margaret, who'd appeared in front of me, her eyes red-rimmed and her cheeks blotched with tears.

"No...thank you," I said slowly, the words an effort to get out.

"Some tea? A syllabub? A drop of whiskey?"

"No!" I repeated harshly, shaking my head.

"I'm sorry, mistress." Margaret stopped her babbling and looked down, her eyes filling with tears.

"It's alright," I forced myself to say. "But please..."

I waved her away as politely as I could, wanting only to be left alone.

She curtsied and scuttled off, ushering the other servants out of the room before her. The door closed behind them with a gentle thump, a sound that echoed the painful beating of my heart. I stared ahead of me in the welcome silence that descended on the room—a silence that just as suddenly became too much.

Left by myself after an afternoon of turmoil, a crushing feeling of grief came down on me, making me gasp for air as my throat constricted in pain. I clenched my jaws and clasped my hands into fists, digging my nails into my palms to keep from crying out. I wrapped my arms around myself and lowered my head, rocking back and forth in an agony that seemed to find no end.

QUIN RAN HIS hand tiredly over his face. He'd told Constable Ryan what he knew, little as that was. The man had said the police would investigate, follow what leads there were, trying to sound confident in the Constabulary's success. Quin hoped his confidence was justified, and that the murderer would be found.

If he was not...

Quin drew in his breath sharply through clenched teeth.

Somebody had been watching them. They'd all felt it over the past few weeks, a sudden cold shiver running down the spine, the feeling of someone's eyes on them. They'd searched the estate and found nothing, and so they'd thought they were being foolish, that they were imagining things.

But they'd been wrong—and Kieran had paid the price for their mistake.

And his death might not be the last.

Quin curled his hands into fists and let his breath out strongly through his nose. He had been keeping his emotions under tight control, but a sliver of fear was snaking its way into his heart, even as his mind struggled to come to terms with Kieran's death.

Surely, he'd only imagined it, the scene his mind kept replaying over and over again—Kieran lying lifeless on the floor of the barn in a congested pool of coppery blood. Surely, Quin would wake from this nightmare, sweating and trembling but none the worse for wear.

He stopped in front of the door to the drawing room, thinking for a moment it would open to reveal Kieran's smiling face as he and Alannah laughed about some childhood escapade. Instead, he opened the door to the sight of Alannah curled up on the settee and staring ahead of her with unseeing eyes, eyes swollen from crying in a face streaked with grief.

Quin swallowed the lump in his throat and walked slowly toward her. She gave a sudden start as she saw him, sitting up in a rustle of fabric, her eyes wide with fright.

"It's alright," Quin said softly, kneeling in front of her. "It's only me."

She took a deep breath and let her head hang tiredly.

"Are you...?" He stopped.

He was going to ask if she was alright, but the question seemed ludicrous. He compressed his lips into a tight line and clenched his jaws. He gently took both of her hands in his and she lifted her head to look at him. Her blue eyes were filled with sorrow but underneath the bone-deep grief he could see the trust she had in him. Trust that he would be there for her and that he would see her safe.

He pulled her roughly to him, not wanting her to see the doubt and fear that must mask his face. He wrapped his arms tightly around her as she clung to him, knowing he was no longer worthy of that trust.

I STARED AT the open casket, dry-eyed.

Kieran's hair had been neatly combed and brushed back, which gave him a strangely well-ordered look, not in keeping with the bouncy curls I was used to.

I reached out a hand to ruffle his hair but stopped myself, his pale face staying my touch with its alien, unlifelike appearance. His throat had been carefully bandaged; to my exhausted mind the white cloth seemed to be shining brightly, almost pulsating, like a beacon leading the eye to the cause of his destruction.

I tore my eyes away and looked back at his face.

A flurry of memories flitted through my mind. A snub-nosed Kieran rolling in the dirt shouting for me to join him; laughing good-naturedly as I tried unsuccessfully to mount my pony by myself; his adolescent cockiness as he informed me about the ways of the world; looming over me, fist raised, face suffused in anger; and, at the last, forgiveness and repentance as he wept in my arms in remembered shame and regret.

My knees buckled as grief flooded through me, a physical ache that robbed me of my breath. I leaned on the casket, bent over in agony, gasping for air.

Strong arms circled my waist and pulled me up, holding me upright as I staggered to my seat, tears rolling down my face in a flood of heartache. The mourners filed past me, and the funeral mass began, a blur of words and music that held no meaning for me, my mind going numb with shock, hiding behind its protective shell. I felt detached, as if I were watching myself, my body going through the motions without conscious thought.

I found myself at the graveside, staring at the coffin as it slowly disappeared into the frozen earth, while my mind retreated further into itself with every handful of dirt thrown into the gaping hole in the ground.

A swirl of dark-clad people moved around me as I sat in the drawing room, with no knowledge of how I'd come to be there. A few spoke to me, touched my shoulder, took me by the hand. I responded mechanically, with words I forgot as soon as they crossed my lips.

"They're gone now," I heard Quin's voice through the haze.

I looked around slowly. We were alone.

Quin's face loomed in front of me as he knelt before me. His eyes searched my face, worry etched into his features. He took my hands and squeezed them tightly, before gently stroking my cheek. I stared at him, unblinking, unfeeling, not daring to think for fear it might lead me over the edge into the abyss. Quin tightened his jaws at sight of my expression and pulled me to him, stroking my back, murmuring things of no consequence.

I let him but lay limp in his arms, unresponsive to his touch.

He picked me up und carried me upstairs, where he gently undressed me down to my shift and tucked me into bed. He knelt next to me and stroked my head.

"Try to get some rest," he said softly and kissed my forehead.

He stroked my cheek and looked at me searchingly for a moment before turning to go.

I stared after him as he left, feeling nothing.

QUIN CLOSED THE bedroom door with a heavy heart. He had hoped Alannah would let him comfort her on this dreadful day but instead she'd shut him out. Since her breakdown at Kieran's casket, she hadn't spoken a word to him, shown no emotions, barely registering his existence. He knew it was her mind's way of protecting her, but she'd always found comfort in his arms before and her complete lack of response when he'd held her frightened him.

All the more so because he was afraid that by shutting him out, she would come to realise he was to blame for Kieran's death.

She'd come to him after Kieran's release from gaol fearing her actions would place them in danger. He'd promised her he could keep her safe, could keep them all safe.

And he had failed.

He'd selfishly taken what he'd wanted and given no thought to the consequences, arrogantly believing he was capable of dealing with all manner of danger that might present itself, blinded by his desire for her.

He swallowed the lump in his throat and poured himself a sizeable drink.

Then he made sure the front door was locked and checked that every other possible entrance to the house was barred. He was taking no chances of a repeat visit from Kieran's murderer. Quin had guards situated around the grounds and the police was out looking for the man, but Quin would give him no opportunity to get close to Alannah.

The thought of anyone of Doyle's acquaintance anywhere in the vicinity of his wife gripped him with fear, followed immediately by rage. A rage that suddenly threatened to overwhelm him in its intensity, as the terror of the last few days came crashing down on him in a blinding fury.

He turned, eyes blazing, wishing Doyle himself—hanged or not—would walk through the door this instant, wanting urgently to ram his fists into his face, to feel the crunch of bone and cartilage as Quin obliterated him with his bare hands.

He struck the door to the dining room a solid blow that split his knuckles. Oblivious, he struck it again and again, until at last he leaned against the thick wood, panting with exertion, his efforts affording him some reprieve from his feelings. He wiped his brow, noticing the blood stains on his knuckles but paying them no mind.

"Sir?" Rupert's cautious voice came from behind him.

He turned toward his valet, whose round eyes magnified his shocked expression at sight of his master. Quin tried to smile at him but gave it up as a bad job. Rupert slowly came toward him, watching him carefully for signs of further violent outbursts. When he at last stood in front of Quin, he produced a large white handkerchief from his pocket, with which he dabbed at Quin's abused knuckles, before leading him gently back to the drawing room.

Quin let himself be seated and attended to, too tired and drained to object.

Without asking for permission, Rupert poured a generous portion of whiskey and placed the glass in Quin's unresisting hand. Quin drained the contents in a single gulp, coming up sputtering and gasping as the liquid burned down his throat while the fumes wafted up his nose.

"Thank you," he said weakly as the whiskey started having its effects.

"Sir," Rupert responded with a bow. "Is there anything else you might need, sir?"

"No, thank you, Rupert. I wish to sit here for a while. You go on to bed."

As Rupert disappeared Quin leaned his head back, the whiskey's sweeping tendrils dulling his senses until he was engulfed in a pleasant fog. He lay there for a while, not thinking, just breathing with his eyes closed, a swirl of colours dancing behind his lids. When he came back to himself, he opened his eyes and sat up, swaying slightly.

He carefully made his way upstairs, holding onto the banister for support, and crept into the bedroom. There was no sound. He undressed quietly and slipped under the sheets beside Alannah, his heart filling with tenderness, and the utmost sadness, at the sight of her. He had an overwhelming urge to pick her up and hold her close, but he contented himself with lightly stroking her cheek.

She needed to sleep. He would try to do the same.

QUIN WOKE UP suddenly, instantaneously alert, springing to his feet and reaching for his weapons. Slowly, belatedly, he became aware of his surroundings, as the cry that had awoken him brought him to the realisation he wasn't facing an enemy attack.

"Kieran! No!"

The anguish in Alannah's voice cut through him and he climbed back into bed and gently pulled her toward him as she continued to murmur in her sleep. He stroked her back, and she woke up with a start, instinctively trying to push him away from her.

"Hush, Alannah, it's me," he whispered, holding onto her.

He could feel her heart thumping against his chest as her tears trickled onto his neck, and he wrapped his arms tighter around her. She slumped against him in defeat and his heart contracted painfully as she trembled in his arms.

"I'm sorry, Alannah. I'm so sorry," he murmured as he held her, knowing the words wouldn't help but having nothing else to give.

He stroked her hair and her back, and as her tears dried, she pressed herself into him.

"I need you, Quin," she whispered suddenly, urgently.

He froze, not sure he'd heard her right.

"Please," she said and pulled his hips toward her.

"Alannah..."

"Quin, please!"

Her voice was filled with desperation and the same urgent desire suddenly overcame him. He pulled her shift up over her hips and buried himself inside her in one thrust. She cried out and wrapped her legs around him, and he lifted her hips to meet his urgency.

It was over in moments, as their overwrought minds sought the oblivion that could only be found in their joining.

He lay on top of her, breathing heavily, and a lone tear rolled down her cheek. He rolled away and looked at her in despair, the ecstasy from a moment before forgotten.

"I'm sorry Alannah," he said, his throat feeling tight. "I'm sorry for putting you through this."

"What do you mean?" she asked, confused. "I wanted you to."

"Not this." He indicated their nakedness with a sweep of his hand. "For Kieran," he whispered, barely audibly.

She looked at him for a long moment and he braced himself for the anger he knew must come. She opened her mouth to speak but no words came out as she struggled to contain her emotions. She held his gaze in the moonlight and he could see the pain in her eyes, clear as day.

"Quin," she finally said and reached out a hand to stroke his cheek. "You can't blame yourself. It wasn't your fault."

"Was it not?" he demanded, suddenly filled with rage and self-loathing. "I knew there was somebody lurking around the estate...watching us and stealing the tenants' food. And what did I do about it? Nothing!"

"You did everything you could, you couldn't have known."

Quin shook his head angrily in denial. Unable to lie still, he got up in a heave of bedclothes and started pacing the room. "I promised I would keep you safe! When you came to me frightened and in doubt, I promised you Doyle would be no threat to us, that he had no one who would act on his behalf, that I would take care of you...that we wouldn't have to live in fear. And look what's happened...your brother murdered and you in danger of the same fate." He looked at her with anguish in his heart. "I wanted you so much that I didn't pause to think what consequences my selfish actions would have." His voice broke and he turned his eyes away, unable to face the reproach he knew would come, the loathing he knew she must feel for him.

"Quin." Alannah crawled across the bed toward him. She knelt in front of him and took his face in her hands, forcing him to look at her. She wiped away the tears that were trickling down his cheeks, her own eyes glistening with moisture.

"I wanted you just as much," she whispered, stroking his cheek. "If you want to blame someone, then blame me." Her face crumpled. "If I hadn't defied Kieran's orders, had gone along with Doyle's plan...then Kieran would still be alive."

"No!" Quin pulled away from her in his anger at her words. "Don't ever think that! *You* are not to blame for any of this!"

"Am I not?" she asked, tears running down her face. "*I* chose for us to stay here. Doyle told me he didn't work alone...I knew we would be in danger if we stayed in Ireland. But I chose to stay anyway. I was a coward...afraid to leave...even to see us safe."

Quin stared at her in utter bewilderment, overcome with despair. "No!" He reached out a hand toward her. "No. You can't ever think this was your fault. You couldn't have known. You are not to blame."

Alannah looked at him for a long moment, her eyes reflecting his own anguish. "And if I am not to blame, then what makes you think that you are?" Another tear rolled down her face and she pulled his head toward hers until their foreheads were touching. "Quin, I love you," she said softly, stroking his cheek. "And you loving me back is not selfish and it's not the reason Kieran is dead."

She swallowed and was quiet for a moment.

"We both made choices, choices we felt were right. Perhaps...perhaps things might have turned out differently if we had each chosen differently. But...Kieran made choices too. And as much as it pains me to say so"—her voice shook as she struggled to get herself under control—"Kieran brought this on himself. He got involved with the wrong people and...he lost himself." A few more tears rolled down her cheeks. "By the time he recognised the error of his ways it was too late. Whether you had married me or not, whether we had moved to England or not...Doyle would never have forgiven his betrayal."

Quin wanted to believe her but couldn't stop feeling himself responsible for Kieran's death. If he hadn't shown up on the O'Neills' doorstep, none of this would have happened.

"Kieran was mixed up with Doyle long before you met me," Alannah said, as if divining his thoughts. She sat back on the bed and looked up at him with sad eyes. "If it wasn't because of me, they would have clashed about something else. Kieran...he didn't have the heart for violence. He wanted to believe otherwise, tried to convince himself and everybody else...with his threats and his loud-voiced opinions, but...he was never cut out for rebellions and bloodshed.—He should have politicised for Ireland's freedom...become another Daniel O'Connell." She smiled a tired smile. "Things might have been different if he'd recognised that about himself sooner."

Quin kneeled next to her on the bed and took her in his arms, stroking her hair.

"It wasn't your fault," she said quietly into his chest, wrapping her arms around him, "no more than it was mine."

Holding Alannah in his arms, Quin slowly started to feel the weight of responsibility lift off his shoulders, as he dared to believe he was not to blame. But as the guilt over Kieran's death lessened, he suddenly remembered something else, something that had gone quietly unnoticed in the chaos that had surrounded them over the past week.

"How are you feeling?" he asked, gently running his hand over Alannah's abdomen. "I hadn't thought to ask..."

Her face fell, and she shook her head. "I...I'm not... I started bleeding..."

"What? Why didn't you tell me?" He looked at her in shock, his heart heavy at this further burden, one she'd felt she had to bear alone.

"It was just after Kieran..." She swallowed and looked up at him with tired eyes. "I was..." She shrugged, and he stroked her cheek.

"I understand. But I wish you would have come to me."

She nodded slowly, looking down. "I'm not sure that I was ever..." She let the rest of the statement fade away. "I thought I was...but now..." She lifted one shoulder in doubt, a look of defeat on her face.

"Hush." Quin pulled her close once more, wishing he could ease her pain.

They lapsed into silence, holding each other up.

"I love you, Quin," Alannah said after a long time, sounding almost asleep.

Quin lay her gently down on the bed and covered her with the blanket. He kissed her forehead as her eyes closed.

"I love you too," he said and crawled in next to her, wrapping them together like a cocoon, wishing they could wake up changed the next morning.

37.

"WE HAVE NO suspects, sir."

Quin narrowed his eyes at Constable Ryan and took a step toward him, so he was menacing over him. "How can that be?"

The constable puffed out his chest and pulled himself up to his full height—which nevertheless fell several inches short of Quin's own.

"Because there were no witnesses. Because nobody on your estate or the surrounding estates reported anything suspicious before or after the murder. And because we have no clues to go by." He tugged importantly on the hem of the bottle green jacket that formed part of the Irish Constabulary's uniform and raised his chin. "We are doing everything we can.—Now, if you will excuse me, sir." He gave Quin a curt bow and spun on his heel, disappearing before Quin had uttered another word.

Quin growled deep in his throat in irritation.

It had been two weeks since Kieran's murder and the police had made no progress in solving the case. Everything Constable Ryan had told Quin was true. There were no suspects, no witnesses and no clues.

It was almost as if the angel of death had swept down to Glaslearg, knife in hand, only to disappear again once the job had been done.

"Don't be absurd," Quin berated himself for his fancies.

He ran a hand angrily through his hair, making it stand up in all directions. He caught sight of his reflection in the window and scowled.

He knew there was a culprit, had seen the work of the man with his own eyes. But where was he?

He was sure it had been an acquaintance of Martin Doyle, but the police had searched high and low, questioning anyone who might have had ties with the man but had come up empty-handed—a state of affairs that seemed not to have altered one bit since Quin's last conversation with the constable.

Quin breathed out heavily through his nose and clenched his hands into futile fists.

He knew what he had to do.

"I'M TAKING YOU to England."

Alannah looked up from the chaise longue but didn't say anything.

"It's not safe here. Until Kieran's murderer has been caught..."

"Yes." Alannah nodded slowly. "Of course." She took a deep breath. "I just wish..."

Quin kneeled down in front of her and took her hands in his, looking searchingly into her face. She looked tired, and her blue eyes were filled with an unutterable sadness, as they had been since Kieran's death.

"I'm sorry, Alannah. I know you don't want to leave.—But it's not safe for you to stay."

"I know."

Alannah looked down into her lap, visibly struggling to control her emotions. Quin's heart contracted painfully at the sight, and he gently stroked her cheek. She looked back up at him and gave him a sad smile.

"When will we go?"

"As soon as I've made the necessary arrangements. I have to ensure the estate and the tenants are taken care of until our return."

He stopped talking and they lapsed into silence, neither of them wanting to utter the words they were both thinking.

If Kieran's murderer was never caught, they would never return.

I WAS SITTING in the drawing room, listlessly staring out the window. I had a book open on my lap but had given up on reading, incapable of taking note of a single word.

Quin was on his way to Ballygawley, leaving me alone with the servants. Once he'd decided we would go to England he'd wasted no time in preparing for our departure. In the space of two days, he'd informed the house staff and tenants of our plans, ensured all was in readiness for the upcoming spring planting and had given strict instructions on the care of the estate's livestock, fields and manor house in our absence. He'd also called on numerous acquaintances in the hope of finding a suitable factor to act in his stead to oversee the estate's running until our return.

Should we ever return.

I sighed and went to stand by the fireplace. I looked into the dancing flames as the fire's heat gently caressed me, wishing for the thousandth time I could change the past. The fire crackled, pulling me back to the present. A large piece of turf collapsed, making sparks sail into the air, and I took a hasty step back, remembering Mr Docherty's tale about his wife's burning dress at the dinner party only a few weeks before.

It seemed like a lifetime ago.

It had been the day Sarah had come to Glaslearg. I had been so angry at Quin for his perceived betrayal of me. I would give anything to replace the sorrow and fear I felt now with the needless anger I had felt then.

"Mistress?"

I turned toward the door with a start, my heart beating rapidly. John the groom was hovering at the threshold, his eyes darting around uncertainly.

"What is it, John?" I asked somewhat breathlessly as I walked toward him.

"I apologise for coming into the house, ma'am," John said, lowering his eyes.

I waved away his apology as my heartrate slowed. Although all of Glaslearg's servants slept in the manor's attic, the grooms and outdoor staff generally didn't come into the house, usually going up to their rooms using the servants' entrance at the back. John's presence in the drawing room didn't bother me in the least, though.

"I did debate with Bryan and Denis about coming...we decided I'd better tell you...in case..."

My heart gave another painful thump. "Tell me what?" I looked around nervously. Quin had instructed the servants to keep the house locked and stay watchful, but suddenly I felt vulnerable.

"It's Milly, ma'am," John said, wringing his hands.

"Milly?"

"Yes, ma'am. She's fevered."

"Fevered? How bad is it?" I looked at John anxiously, but he shrugged his shoulders.

"Bad enough," he answered unhelpfully, making me frown at him. "It's hard to say, ma'am," he defended himself. "There don't seem to be much else wrong with her but... We'll have to keep watch. We found her so on our rounds of the stable. We went and made her comfortable. Now we wait."

John stopped talking and darted a glance at the entrance hall behind him, obviously wanting to escape my scrutiny.

"I see," I replied with reasonable calm. "Thank you for telling me, John." I smiled at him as best I could. "I'm sure Milly will be quite all right."

"Yes, ma'am."

John cast another uncomfortable look around him and I waved him away.

When he'd left, I went to stand at the window, looking onto the lawn that sprawled in front of the house. It was drab now, nothing like the bright green colour that would emerge in the spring. I looked in the direction of the stable, which lay across the dull, wind-blown hedges that lined the edge of the small park, wishing I could check on Milly myself. Quin had given strict instructions for me to stay indoors, though, and in truth, the thought of going outside made my palms go sweaty and my breath come short. I tried to convince myself there was nothing to worry about in any case.

Except there might be.

I had to check on her, I decided. My heart leapt into my throat at the thought, but I hurried to get my cloak.

I would be away for only a few minutes, I told myself, just enough to convince myself of her welfare. I would be back before anyone had missed me and no harm would be done.

I left the house quietly and walked quickly, crossing the courtyard in a few strides as the wind blew dark grey clouds overhead. Being out in the open made me feel exposed and vulnerable, and I entered the warm sanctuary of the stable with relief. Quin would be furious I'd left the house, but I'd simply had to come.

A fever could mean just about anything, from a short-lived illness that would blow over in a day or two, to sudden collapse and death a brief time later, as had been the case with Niall's cows. Thinking about cows made a sharp pain stab through my heart as I thought of Maggie, the cow that was still housed in the barn where Kieran had been killed.

I swallowed heavily, trying to suppress the panic that had risen abruptly in my throat at the thought of Kieran's murderer.

A murderer who was still on the loose.

The police hadn't found a trace of him, not knowing who he was and what he looked like. He could be anywhere.

He might be watching me right now, I thought, feeling suddenly lightheaded.

I held onto the doorframe until my heart started to slow, before walking down the stable's central isle, toward the far stall where John and Bryan appeared to have put Milly. I would have a brief look at her and then I would return to the safety of the manor, I decided.

I quickly walked past the other horses, noticing with relief that all of them seemed to be in good health. As I neared Milly's stall, I could hear her laboured breathing, but when I reached her, she tiredly lifted her head in greeting. She came slowly toward me and leaned heavily against me as I put my arms around her.

"My poor girl," I murmured, stroking her neck.

She whickered softly in response, a sad sound quite unlike her usual jovial communiqué. She was warm to the touch, clearly fevered but not burning. And her eyes were clear, not glazed with illness, although she certainly was ill.

"You'll be alright," I said softly as we leaned against each other for support.

I stood quietly for a few minutes, listening to Milly's heavy breathing and the rustling of the horses in the other stalls. I closed my eyes and let the comforts of the stable surround me.

When I opened my eyes, a sudden cold shiver ran down my back. I turned toward the stable door, feeling eyes on the nape of my neck.

There was nobody there.

I stood motionless, looking around while my heart pounded in my chest. But all seemed peaceful, the horses standing quietly in their stalls.

I took a deep breath and patted Milly's neck in farewell, before walking up the central isle toward the exit. When I got to the open area in front of the foremost stalls, the stable's large wooden door suddenly swung shut amidst a loud rustling noise, plunging the building into semi-darkness, the only light coming in through the narrow window slits high in the walls.

My heart leapt into my throat, and I yelped in alarm while the horses whickered and pranced nervously.

"It was just the wind," I whispered to myself as I stood frozen in fright.

"I'm afraid not, sweetheart," came a voice from the darkness that made cold sweat break out on my brow and my legs tremble in fear.

I made an incoherent sound as I watched a dark shadow detach itself from the wall next to the door, my eyes adjusting to the darkness but my mind refusing to believe what they saw.

"Miss O'Neill," Martin Doyle sneered, slowly coming toward me. "Or should I say...Mrs Williams?"

"But...you...I..."

"Never seen a ghost before, have you?" Doyle gave a nasty laugh as he watched me struggle for words.

I stared at him, the blood roaring in my ears but my body frozen in shock. "You were hanged..." I whispered. "Kieran saw it."

"Oh, your poor pathetic brother. That was no more me being hanged than he was ever fit to be a rebel." He shook his head and grimaced in distaste.

"But..."

Doyle laughed once more. "It was another prisoner. Looked much like me to begin with and had any differences beaten out of him.—I did that," he added with evident pride. "Ah..." he said with a dreamy smile, "what a night it was."

He took a few steps closer to me and I plastered myself against the wall of the nearest stall.

"Here I thought my luck had run out when a kindly visitor came to my lonely cell the night before the hanging. Told me my...replacement"—he winked at me—"was waiting for my attention. I had a good bit of rage built up, so I was happy to oblige. Mind you," he added with a frown, "it took a fair amount of restraint on my part not to kill the fellow. Wouldn't have done any good, though."

"But..."

"The guard was bribed, of course. To keep his mouth shut...and see me safely on my way."

"Who...?"

Doyle shrugged. "I told you I have associates. Which one it might have been I couldn't say. I was led to a wagon and told to keep my mouth shut until we got to where we were going.—I thought I would obey." He chuckled and smirked at me. "Before long I found myself deposited on the outskirts of Newtownstewart, a free man once more."

"Kieran..." I whispered.

Doyle narrowed his eyes at me, his face contorting into a grimace of anger. "He got what he deserved! He shouldn't have interfered with my plans. And neither should you...or your Englishman."

He suddenly lunged toward me and grabbed me by the arms, pulling me into an unwelcome embrace.

"I've been watching you," he said as he held both my wrists with one hand and stroked my cheek with the other. I squirmed and tried to escape his grasp but couldn't loosen his vicelike grip.

"I had to move at night and steal my food. I don't much mind such things in general, but it does make for slower travel." He snorted and pulled me roughly against him, his rank odour creeping up my nose. "You can imagine my delight when I came here a few months ago and found all three of you living merrily together on this here farm.—I did wonder what happened to Kieran's own farm." He looked at me expectantly but when I didn't respond he shrugged. "And to think you'd married your Englishman. And you and your brother reconciled.— It warms the heart, doesn't it?" He smiled a smile that didn't touch his eyes.

I tried to pull away from him, but he tightened his grip, making me cry out in pain.

"And dear Kieran looked so content," he continued, ignoring me. "Living the life of a farmer." He shook his head in astonishment. "And such a lovely lass on his arm.—I waited, you see. Waited and watched...watched them frolicking in the hay."

He licked his lips lasciviously and I felt the blood rush to my cheeks. I didn't know whether he was lying, but Kieran and Sarah *had* seemed inordinately close.

"It almost made me sorry to have to end it," he said in a melancholy tone and sighed. He was quiet for a moment, an almost dreamy look on his unshaven face. "But not quite," he hissed suddenly in a hard voice, turning his black eyes on me with menace.

I screamed and struggled against his grasp, trying to get away from him. I thrashed and kicked with all my might but couldn't budge him.

"Scream all you want, lassie," he breathed heavily into my ear. "Nobody will hear you."

I noticed then it had started to rain, the downpour thrumming on the roof of the stable, drowning out all sounds. Doyle was right, nobody would hear me from the house.

And nobody would miss me.

I had told no one I was going to the stable, intending to return within a few minutes. The servants would assume I was resting in my room, as I had been doing much of late, since Kieran's death. And John and Bryan had seen to Milly a short while earlier, they were unlikely to return so soon—not until it was too late.

I felt panic rise within me, constricting my throat and making my heart pound in fear as I continued to struggle.

"Kieran's end was unfortunately quick," Doyle murmured as he started dragging me across the floor.

I jerked at his restraining arms and scrabbled with my feet to find some footing, but he lifted me off the ground and threw me roughly onto the pile of hay that lay in the corner by the stable door. My head was dealt a glancing blow against the wall, and I cried out as I landed heavily on my elbow.

I edged back against the wall, trying to disappear, my breath coming fast and ragged as Doyle advanced on me. He looked down at me with menace in his eyes and a leer on his face. Licking his lips, he lifted the hem of his shirt and took a step closer.

"I'll take my time with you," he hissed and tugged at the waistband of his breeches.

QUIN WAS FEELING edgy.

He didn't like leaving Alannah at the best of times and leaving her while there was a murderer on the loose made his skin crawl. He had to get her out of Ireland until it was safe to return. But he couldn't leave the estate unattended. After everything they'd worked for, he couldn't let it fall back into neglect.

He breathed out heavily through his nose as a sudden feeling of anger overcame him—anger at himself for having ignored Doyle's warning and at whoever had acted out his commands. And deep down inside himself he felt a dark tendril of anger toward Kieran himself, for having put all of them at risk with his actions.

He shook his head irritably, berating himself for having such thoughts about a dead man.

He would ride to Ballygawley to meet with the overseer Sir Spencer had recommended and then he would take Alannah home. It had been a while since he'd thought of London as his home but with everything that had happened, Glaslearg was feeling less and less like home by the day. He hoped the unknown overseer would be up to the task of looking after the estate in Quin's absence and that he could take over immediately, so he and Alannah could get on the next vessel heading toward England.

He spurred on Gambit, wanting to get the job done and get back to his wife.

Quin had told Alannah to stay indoors and keep the house locked while he was away and had instructed John and Finnian to keep watch until his return. But he was starting to get a creeping feeling it wasn't enough. While John was a burly, capable-looking fellow, he was a groom and unlikely to offer too much resistance if a knife-wielding killer came upon him. As for Finnian...he was eager enough to defend his mistress, but a ganglier, clumsier youth could scarcely be found.

"Nobody can get into the manor house unannounced," Quin said to himself to calm his nerves.

He spurred on his horse once more. If he hurried, he could be back by the afternoon. He rode on for a few minutes, trying to look ahead to the upcoming meeting, but his mind kept wandering. He kept thinking about Alannah, sitting at home waiting for him—alone, without him there to protect her.

He tugged on the reigns and turned Gambit in the direction they had come, giving the horse his head before he'd made a conscious decision to return to Glaslearg. Suddenly overcome with an overwhelming need to assure himself of Alannah's safety, he urged the horse to a gallop, cursing himself for having left her behind without proper guards.

How could he be so stupid? If something happened to her, he would never forgive himself.

He bent low over the saddle as Gambit flew over the rough ground. Quin's heart was pounding ready to burst through his chest, as doubt and fear nagged at him while his rational mind kept insisting she was safe. He had to get to her, no matter what. If all was well, he would not leave her side again until the murderer was caught.

And if not...

Quin shook off the thought and urged the horse on to even greater speed, desperately afraid he would come too late.

DOYLE'S STALE BREATH was hot on my face. He was pushing me into the hay while I struggled against him. I clawed at his face with my nails, landing a long scratch on his cheek that made him screech. He pinned my arms above my head, scraping my knuckles against the wall, and got hold of both wrists with one hand. With the other he hit me across the face, hard enough to make my ears ring.

Keeping my arms trapped, he pulled at my skirt with his free hand, trying to push it up above my hips. I thrashed at him with my legs in panic, screaming for help even as the rain drowned out my cries, twisting and kicking, desperate to get away. He suddenly let go of my skirt and reached behind him, pulling out a knife he must have had tucked into the back of his waistband.

I froze as he brought the blade up to my face, swallowing the bile that rose in my throat at sight of the knife that had killed my brother.

"That's better," he panted into my ear as I lay motionless beneath him.

He lay the knife down next to my head, patting it reassuringly as he glared at me. I understood the hint. The knife was within his grasp. He wouldn't hesitate to slit my throat if I continued to fight him.

With one last murderous look at me he released the knife's handle and pulled up my skirt and petticoats as I lay unresisting beneath him. He fumbled one-handed at the waistband of his breeches, and fear and revulsion rose within me as I felt his erection against my thigh, followed with panic as his fingers probed me intimately.

He pushed at one of my thighs with his free hand, trying to open my legs, but I pushed back against him, unable to comply. He growled deep in his throat, slapped me hard across the face and jammed his knee into my thigh, making me cry out in pain as he tried to force my legs apart.

I could not keep still.

I could see the knife out of the corner of my eye, but I could not have lain unresisting had I tried. I bucked and turned beneath him as he rained blows upon me, screaming at the top of my lungs, tears and mucus running down my face, knowing I was only delaying the inevitable and spurring him on to even greater violence.

His fist hit my cheekbone with a dull thump, and my vision began to blur. Through the haze, I could see him reaching for the knife that lay next to me, lifting it in a wide arc that left his intentions in little doubt.

As I gasped for breath and cried in anguish beneath him, he placed the blade against my neck.

WHEN QUIN FINALLY reached the estate, he was sweating despite the heavy rain that had fallen along the way.

He rode into the courtyard fearing the worst but could see no signs of disturbance, the manor lying quietly, with the doors and windows looking as he'd left them. He dismounted, deciding to tie Gambit's reigns temporarily to the fountain instead of taking him to the stable, so he could go into the house without delay. Once he'd assured himself Alannah was safe, he would see the horse properly stabled.

The rain had slowed while he'd ridden into the courtyard, with no more than a drizzle remaining of the downpour that had gushed from the sky just moments before. As he bent down to sling Gambit's reigns around the brass loop on the edge of the fountain, he thought he heard a sound coming from the direction of the outbuildings.

He froze, listening.

He was about to bend back to his task when the sound came again. The hair on the back of his neck rose in response, leaving him in no doubt as to the nature of the noise he had heard.

"Alannah," he yelled and dropped the reigns.

He ran up the path that led toward the outbuildings, his arms pumping and his chest burning, while his ears were filled with Alannah's terrified screams. He slowed as he reached the stable, unsure exactly where the sounds had come from.

Alannah screamed again, and he dashed toward the stable door, his heart pounding in fear of what he might find. As he reached the entrance, the screaming cut off abruptly and his head spun in terror as he burst through the door.

The gloomy confines of the stable reminded him all too unpleasantly of the darkness that had enveloped Kieran's lifeless body on the floor of the barn. It wasn't a lifeless body that greeted him this time, though, but a heaving and cursing one that was writhing on the pile of hay in the corner, trying to control a pair of bared legs Quin recognised instantly as those of his wife.

Quin reached the man in two strides, picked him up by the back of his shirt and flung him violently against the wall. Alannah was lying bruised and motionless on her back in the hay, her skirts rucked up and her neck covered in blood.

428

Quin's breath caught in his throat but a noise behind him made him tear his eyes away from the sight. He spun toward Alannah's assailant, who was picking himself up off the floor, the front of his breeches hanging open obscenely. He lifted his head as he heard Quin approach.

"Martin Doyle," Quin exclaimed in disbelief, staring at the monster he had thought safely dead.

Doyle sneered. "At your service, Englishm…"

He got no further, as Quin leapt at him, suddenly overcome with a furious rage as the despair and dread of the last few weeks came crashing down on him. His hands closed around Doyle's neck as he lifted him off the floor and pinned him against the wall, crushing his windpipe while Doyle's own hands scrabbled at his neck, trying to loosen Quin's grip. He squealed and bucked, but Quin didn't budge, only glaring at Doyle in hatred as he tightened his grasp.

Doyle's eyes started to bulge, and his tongue protruded from his lips, but still Quin didn't loosen his grip, until at last, with a final rasping sound, Doyle's arms slid to his sides, and he slumped in Quin's restraining hands.

Quin dropped Doyle's body in disgust and turned toward Alannah.

She was sitting in the corner with her skirts pressed down around her ankles, her eyes huge with shock.

Quin crawled across the hay toward her and pulled her into a tight embrace.

"Alannah," he said as she lay motionless and silent against him. "Oh God, Alannah."

He ran his hands over her, to assure himself she was whole. Her face was a mass of bruises, the skin on her cheek split and oozing blood, and there was blood running down her neck. The cut ran along the angle of her jaw, from just below her ear to the side of her throat. While it was bleeding, the blood wasn't spurting, the large vessels of the neck seemingly unharmed.

Quin swallowed heavily, trying not to think about how close she had come to being killed.

"It was a warning," Alannah said in a scratchy voice, her eyes unfocused as she lifted her hand to her neck, stopping just short of touching it. "To stop struggling…"

Quin looked at her helplessly, his throat constricting in anguish.

"He didn't…" she began, shaking her head and looking down.

"Hush." Quin pulled her against him, stroking the back of her head. "It's over now. Martin Doyle is dead...for good."

38.

"NO!"

Quin's voice came out in a strangled moan as his knees buckled beneath him, his body crumpling into a heap on the cold stone floor.

Alannah was lying motionless on the hay before him, her thighs slick with another man's pleasure, her spilled blood cooling beneath her bruised and battered body. Her mouth was agape, forever frozen in an unanswered call for help. Her lifeless eyes stared at the ceiling, seeking a deliverance that had come too late.

Quin woke up with a start, bathed in sweat, making an incoherent sound as his eyes flew open. His heart was pounding, and bile rose in his throat. He turned his head to the side and breathed heavily into his pillow, swallowing the rankness of the remembered dream.

A nightmare that had almost become reality.

His breath still coming short and ragged, he turned toward Alannah, who was lying next to him. She mumbled in her sleep, her eyelids flickering while a frown formed between her brows. Quin gently stroked her head and murmured softly to her until her features smoothed and the steady breathing of rest resumed as his own heart began to slow.

He looked at Alannah's sleeping form and felt his throat constrict at the sight. He clenched his jaws, the bruises on her face and neck burning themselves into his memory and cutting deep into his heart.

He had come in time. But he had been too late, nonetheless.

Tears started spilling down his cheeks and he wept. He lay soundlessly beside her as he poured out his soul, his body trembling with sorrow, his heart aching at the pain she had suffered—and breaking at his own failure to protect her.

MARTIN DOYLE WAS dead.

I told myself so every morning. Since his attack on me I had felt jumpy and jittery, tensing at every sound. I knew this to be irrational and cursed myself for idiocy, even as my heart would leap into my throat at the sound of the kitchen door slamming shut. My bruises had all but faded and I was in good physical health. There was no reason for me to be acting thus.

431

Doyle was dead, and the danger had passed. Quin had seen to that.

After Kieran's murder, my every waking moment had been consumed with grief for his loss and fear for Quin's safety and my own, expecting at any moment the killer to return and grant us the same fate he had bestowed upon Kieran. With Doyle's reappearance and subsequent death, the overwhelming dread for our own safety had abated, leaving my mind free for other pursuits, fixating on what might have been.

I had started obsessing about that day in the stable, overcome with anxiety and shame as my mind replayed over and over again the helplessness I'd felt in Doyle's presence, the certainty he would not let me leave the stable alive—and the crushing desolation of knowing I had survived when my brother had not. While reminding myself Doyle was dead allayed my fears about the future, it did nothing to change the past.

As the days dragged on, I felt myself sliding ever deeper into despair.

My surroundings faded away as my mind shut out the outside world, focusing instead on the gloom that was starting to consume me. I stopped caring about what I wore and what I looked like, I ate mechanically or not at all, and I barely spoke to those around me. Quin tried to engage me in conversation but would soon tire of my disinterest, leaving me to my own devices with a sigh.

I wanted to reach out to him but felt incapable of the task.

I had nothing to offer him.

I sat in the bedroom or lounged in the drawing room, staring into space, cloaked in a misery I couldn't seem to shake.

Wandering aimlessly through the house one day I returned to the bedroom, only to be confronted with a sight that temporarily dragged me out of my stupor.

Mary Murphy was bent over my dressing table, industriously rootling through my mother's jewellery box.

"What?" I said, dumbfounded, as I came to a stop in the doorway.

Mary screeched and spun around, so quickly the box toppled, spilling its glittery contents across the tabletop. Seeing me standing at the door, all colour drained from her face, her mouth opening and closing like that of a landed fish as she struggled to speak.

"What are you doing?" I asked her in Gaelic, barely able to form the words myself.

"I...I..." she stuttered, wringing her hands.

I walked toward her, coming to a stop in front of her. "Mary," I addressed her softly but sternly, "what are you doing?"

She looked up at me and I could read her fright plain in her eyes as she suddenly dropped to her knees in front of me, clutching my skirt. "Oh, please, mistress...please," she wailed, tears streaming down her face, "don't tell my husband."

"I..."

"Please don't tell him," Mary begged once more, in a voice so filled with dread that I gently pulled her to her feet, led her to the chaise longue and bade her to sit.

Once she had stemmed her tears, the words slowly started bubbling out of her, until they flowed like a waterfall that could barely be stopped.

Mary's husband Robert, it seemed, was in debt. To make the tenant right payment that was required to secure the small plot of land they farmed, he'd had to borrow heavily from a local money lender. While this was a fairly normal course of action for most tenants, as few had large amounts of free capital at their disposal, Robert Murphy was several months behind on his payments—and the usurer was coming to collect.

"He was relying on the conacre potatoes for his income," Mary explained as she pleated her skirt nervously between her fingers, looking down into her lap. "He rented an acre from Mr Docherty." She looked up at me and her eyes filled with tears. "The crop didn't take...there was hardly enough to sell. But he had to pay the conacre rent. And now Mr Driscoll..." She snapped her mouth shut, compressing her lips, which quivered as she tried to control herself.

I patted her hand reassuringly.

"It's not enough," she cried as a tear rolled down her cheek. "It's never enough." Her voice was so filled with despair I felt my own heart constrict in pain for her. "We work the land here, the conacre land there, Robert sells himself as labourer wherever he can, and I weave until my fingers bleed...but it's still not enough." Her voice cracked, and the tears spilled down her face unabated, her chest heaving as she sobbed.

I looked helplessly at her for a moment, struggling to find anything useful to say to her, a woman whose circumstances were in such stark contrast to my own, despite the fact that we lived on the same estate, just a short distance away from each other.

I swallowed the lump in my throat and gathered her into my arms. "It will be alright," I promised as I patted her trembling back. "We'll think of something."

QUIN WAS STARING forlornly out the window at the rain falling incessantly outside.

He should get up, he thought, do something useful. Go check on Alannah.

He sighed, not getting up.

Thinking about Alannah made his heart feel heavy, like a weighty burden was trying to drag him under while he struggled to keep his head aboveground. The sight of her in the stable when he'd pulled Doyle off her would never leave him. It had carved itself into his heart, leaving him with a crushing sense of despair—and guilt.

He couldn't blame her for keeping her distance, of course. The events of the past few weeks had been a shock for all of them. They had thought themselves safe. They had been happy, happy with the home they'd made for themselves and the improvements they'd made on the estate, happy that Kieran had found a place for himself and shut the door on his former life.

And then, in one dreadful swoop, their contentment had been ripped away, only to be further eroded as the days went by, as Doyle's reappearance slashed viciously at the bond that joined Alannah and Quin. He could feel it weakening under the strain, like a strong rope fraying as it was pulled over a sharp rock.

One last tug and it would snap.

"Quin?"

He turned toward the door in surprise. Alannah was hovering in the doorway, looking uncertain.

"Alannah."

He got up and walked slowly toward her. She held his gaze for a moment but dropped her eyes as he reached her. He swallowed heavily at the sight.

"I... There's something I need to speak to you about."

Quin's heart jumped into his throat. She would tell him she'd come to realise he was to blame for all that had happened, that he had broken her trust, that her faith in him was spent.

"Yes?" he breathed softly, the word barely audible.

"It's about Mary."

"Mary?" Quin blurted, taken aback.

"Mary Murphy," Alannah said in some irritation, as if he ought to have known who she meant.

"What about her?" The words came out harshly as he struggled to find his footing.

"The Murphys are in debt."

"Oh?"

"I thought you might..."

"You thought I might pay their debt for them?" he interrupted her, thinking he knew what she would say. He felt suddenly annoyed. Why should he have to solve everyone's problems?

"No, I..."

"I couldn't take care of my own family, so you thought I should make amends with somebody else's?"

"What?"

"I know that's what you think," he snapped as she looked at him with big eyes.

"I don't..."

"Alannah, please. Stop pretending." He shook his head as the doubt and self-loathing of the past weeks suddenly overwhelmed him. "You've barely spoken to me in weeks.—You can barely look at me."

Alannah lowered her eyes, confirming his suspicions. He clenched his jaws in anger and disappointment.

"It's got nothing to do with you," she said suddenly, raising her eyes, only to glare at him angrily.

"And I'm supposed to believe that?" he demanded. "I know you blame me."

Alannah looked at him with a sense of disbelief, but Quin could see uncertainty flitting across her features.

"I..." She stopped, shaking her head. "My brother was murdered," she said after a short pause, evidently trying to get herself under control as she forced the words out between her teeth. "And I nearly met the same fate...and worse." Her mouth snapped shut and she compressed her lips. When she looked up at him her eyes were glistening with tears, but her features were hardened with scorn. "I'm so sorry I haven't been able to shower you with attention under the circumstances."

She stared at him for a long moment, with a look of such desolation on her face that he wanted to slit his own throat for the pain he had caused her.

435

"I blame myself," he said, ignoring her last remark. "I should have protected you.—I should have protected Kieran."

"You had nothing to do with Kieran's death," she snapped. "I already told you so. And you couldn't have known Doyle was still alive."

"And does that change the fact that Kieran is dead?" he asked, making Alannah flinch. "Does that change the fact that I allowed his murderer to come within an inch of violating you and laying you dead at my feet?" His throat constricted at the thought, and he clenched his fists as the rage he'd felt that day resurfaced. "I knew there was a murderer on the loose. And I let the same man lay violent hands on my wife not once but repeatedly. What sort of husband does that make me? What sort of *man* does that make me?—There is no excuse for my behaviour!"

"It's not about you!" Alannah hissed, glowering at him.

"It is my responsibility to keep you safe."

"What do you want me to say, Quin?" Her lips quivered as she tried to contain her emotions. She shook her head and started turning toward the door. "You shouldn't have left me!" she cried suddenly, turning back to Quin. Her face cracked, and tears started trickling down her cheeks. "Is that what you want to hear? Is it?"

Alannah's eyes were filled with the accusation Quin had known was there all along. He had been berating himself for the same thing she was condemning him for but hearing the words coming from her mouth was like a physical blow to his heart.

"Alannah..."

"I needed you...and you weren't there."

"I..."

"You should have known..."

She trailed off and Quin's anguish suddenly disappeared, the heartache from a moment before being rapidly replaced with irritation—and something more.

"What should I have known?" he demanded, suppressed anger bubbling to the surface. "That a violent criminal was lurking around the estate? I *did* know...that's why I told you to stay inside the house!" His voice was rising rapidly, and he took a step toward her, wishing he could shake her to her senses. "You shouldn't have left the house!" he roared, looming over her and taking hold of her upper arms. "I told you not to leave the house!" He emphasised each word

436

as rage overcame him—rage at Alannah's refusal to follow his orders and at his own deplorable attempts to protect her. "You would have been safe if you had done as I said!"

"And do you always expect me to do as you say without complaint?" Alannah asked scornfully, pulling against his grasp.

"When it comes to your safety, yes, I do!" He breathed out heavily through his nose, before releasing her arms.

Alannah stared at him with barely concealed disdain, and he thought of the promise she'd made him shortly after they were wed—that her feelings for him would never change.

He felt a pain in his heart seeing the look on her face now.

"Have I not asked for your opinions?" he asked quietly, his shoulders slumping as he suddenly felt utterly defeated. "Have I not enquired after your welfare and included you in every decision I have made?—Have I not put you first at every turn?" He swallowed heavily as tears welled in his own eyes. "I don't want you to concede to my every command without complaint...but I want you to be able to trust me, to trust that I can look after you and provide for you...and keep you safe."

"I do trust you," Alannah whispered, "with my life."

She came into his arms, and they clung to each other, each holding the other up as they struggled to find a way through the gloom that had enveloped them since Kieran's death.

"I'm sorry," Quin murmured into her hair.

"I'm sorry too."

"I shouldn't have left you."

"I should never have left the house."

Their words collided, and they were silent for a moment.

"I don't blame you for anything, Quin," Alannah said after a while. She pulled away from his embrace to look into his eyes. "What I said before... I spoke in anger. I didn't mean it."

Quin shrugged his shoulders and gave her a defeated smile. "You needed me, and I wasn't there."

"But you *were* there," she protested, looking searchingly into his face. "If you hadn't listened to your instincts and returned when you did..."

"If I hadn't left you in the first place..."

"And if *I* hadn't ignored your instructions..." She shook her head. "We both made mistakes...but we're both still here."

She took his head between her hands, pulling his face down toward her. Her eyes were filled with tears and a bone-deep sadness that cut through Quin's heart to see it.

"I am lost, Quin," she said softly, a single tear running down her cheek. "All around me there is darkness, and I cannot find my way out. Not alone.—I need you."

He looked into her eyes, his throat constricting with pain at everything they had lost, at the despair he could see in her face—a despair he felt himself responsible for. He looked at her for a long moment, trying to find the man he'd once been in her eyes.

Seeing his own reflection in the shiny surface, he finally felt a glimmer of hope. He was part of her, as she was part of him. He would be her beacon of light, as she would be his.

"I am here," he whispered, "for as long as you will have me."

"Always," she said and pulled him into her arms.

39.

SPRING HAD COME to Glaslearg, and the land was shaking off its winter gloom. The hills were erupting into every imaginable shade of green, dusted with delicate blossoms that shyly peaked their colourful heads above the jade carpet. The air was filled with birdsong as the jovial creatures flitted across the azure sky, diving toward the bubbling streams and sprouting shrubs that dotted the landscape, rejoicing in the pleasure of being alive.

The people of Glaslearg were busy; the spring planting had begun.

Across the fields of farm and tenants, women and children were dropping myriad seed potatoes onto the ridges prepared in the soil, to be covered by the sod the men dug from adjoining trenches with their spades. Lying in their lazy beds, the seeds would steadily take root, only to burst into the light as the vines emerged, the new season's crop hidden safely underground.

I looked across the estate, feeling my lingering despair slowly begin to fade. I closed my eyes, letting the sun's soft rays gently caress my cheeks. When I opened them, I caught sight of Quin, who was making his way home after the day's planting. He waved to me, and I smiled at him.

We, too, would take root once more.

Ripped from safety by circumstance and left exposed, we had both been adrift, kept from being washed away only by the other's force of will.

But as the earth warmed and nurtured its creatures back to life, so would we be sheltered in each other's warm embrace until we emerged, at last, firmly anchored and full of life again.

"THAT'S EVERYTHING FROM the wardrobe, mistress."

"Thank you, Mary."

I turned to Mary Murphy and gave her a small smile. After I'd told Quin about the Murphys' plight, he'd agreed to employ her as a house maid to ease the Murphys' financial burden and assist Margaret in her duties, with an upfront payment of her wages to assist her husband in settling some of their debt.

Mary returned my smile shyly but with a slightly worried look in her eyes. I reached out a hand to her and clasped hers tightly, erasing the frown between her brows.

We were clearing out Kieran's room. It was the first time I'd set foot in his quarters since his murder, and I'd braced myself for an onslaught of emotions.

I hadn't been disappointed.

Seeing his spare clothes and personal items had momentarily robbed me of my breath as grief overwhelmed me. I'd had to lean against the doorframe for a few minutes before working up the courage to go in. I had myself under control now, but my emotions were still all too near to the surface.

Looking at the items Mary had laid out on Kieran's bed awoke in me a mingled sense of sorrow and regret, one I'd become all too familiar with in the past few months. Sorrow at Kieran's death and regret at the circumstances that had led to it, and the life he might have lived if he'd chosen differently.

I sighed as I gently ran a hand over the soft fabric of Kieran's evening coat. Besides the clothes he'd been wearing when he was killed, he'd owned only a handful of additional items, including three shirts, two pairs of breeches and one pair of fine trousers, as well as the evening coat and two waistcoats.

"I shall distribute them amongst the servants," I said to Mary, pointing at the clothes.

She nodded and started gathering everything into a bundle.

"And take these," I added, picking up the cravats and top hat that lay on the dressing table.

I looked at the comb and shaving implements, and other similar items that also adorned the table, unsure what to do with them.

"One of the men will take them, mistress," Mary suggested, seeing me hesitate.

"Yes, I suppose so."

"If the master doesn't want to keep them for himself, of course." She looked at me anxiously lest she had overstepped her boundaries.

"No, not at all," I assured her. "Why don't you go ahead and take them for your husband?"

"Oh no, mistress, I couldn't! Not after everything you've already done for us."

I waved away her objections. "It would please me if you would take them, Mary."

I picked up the comb and pressed it into her hand. She stammered her thanks, and I could see tears forming in her tired brown eyes. She quickly turned away and busied herself with carefully placing the items into her apron, before picking up the clothes and heading toward the door. I sent her on her way with instructions to see the clothes suitably allotted to the staff. I closed the door after she left, wanting to spend some time alone in Kieran's room.

I walked slowly around the space he'd inhabited for the last few months of his life, where he'd finally broken free of his disillusionment and hatred. Where he had found himself at last, only to be snatched away by the fate he hadn't been able to outrun.

I sat down on the bed and closed my eyes for a minute to still my heart and clear my mind, wanting to replace the image of Kieran as I'd last seen him with ones from happier times. It took a moment, but at last, Kieran's curly head bobbed in front of my mind's eye, his blue eyes crinkling into triangles as we laughed together, revelling in the joy of life's simple pleasures.

A feeling of peace settled on me at the memory, and I opened my eyes as I gently ran my hands over the thick quilt that covered the bed. I felt a small bump under my palm and pulled the coverlet aside curiously. On the untouched white sheet lay a small black stone I recognised instantly although I hadn't seen it in years. The stone was shaped like a heart, with such perfect proportions it looked like it had been sculpted by an artist. I had found it one summer day playing in the stream as a child and had given it to my best friend.

My brother.

A tear escaped my eye, and I gripped the stone in my palm.

"I can't believe you kept it all this time," I murmured.

Of course, I did, came the unexpected answer in my mind.

My throat constricted and a few more tears rolled down my cheeks. And quite suddenly, as if the key to the final shackle had been turned, I finally found it in myself to let go of the last vestiges of anger I had felt toward Kieran for the wrongs he had done. The tears ran soundlessly down my face as I wept for the brother I had lost, clutching the heart-shaped stone to my chest, a solid reminder of a bond that had buckled and bent, but in the end, had survived even death.

When I at last got up and headed toward the door, I felt lighter than I had in months.

Standing at the threshold, I turned back into the room one last time.

"Goodbye, Kieran," I said quietly. "Go in peace."

40.

THE DAYS PASSED, and the seasons turned, spring's bright colours giving way to summer's luscious greens, before fading into autumn's more subdued hues. As Glaslearg flourished around me, I once more immersed myself in its duties, discovering a forgotten joy in seeing an estate well tended and its people well cared for. I still thought of Kieran every day, sometimes with remembered happiness, sometimes with unutterable sadness, but always with a sense of regret.

His loss was like a dull ache, one that never left, but one I could push aside so I myself could go on.

It was harvesttime and it was a season of plenty. The estate's crops and livestock had thrived, and the last of the cottages were almost complete. It was only a matter of weeks before the remaining tenants would at last move into their new homes.

It warmed my heart to see how the lives of Glaslearg's residents had improved since Quin had arrived at the estate. As a result of his dogged determination, their demeanour had changed—markedly in some, only subtly in others—from one of subdued misery to a sense of contentment with their lot in life. They still had very little, of course, but having a landlord who genuinely cared for their wellbeing and considered their needs and wants had removed some of the insecurity that had plagued their existence before. They had come to trust in Quin's ability to assist them where they needed him to, and to follow through with the promises he had made them.

I lifted my eyes from the ledger open in front of me, a feeling of tenderness coming over me as I thought of Quin.

He had done so much for them, and for me.

As I looked back down at the desk a shadow suddenly fell across the open doorway. Looking up, I found myself peering at a short and slight man I was sure I'd never seen before. He was probably in his late thirties, with a rather weather-beaten, bewhiskered face and slightly thinning, brownish hair, and round eyes that darted back and forth nervously above a small nose. My overall impression was one of a mouse that had been cornered and was looking for a way to escape.

I suppressed a smile at the thought and turned toward the man.

"May I help you?"

"Um...yes, ma'am...at least I...I hope so," he stammered, darting me a brief glance before looking down at his feet as he took two or three cautious steps into the study.

"Yes?" I nodded encouragingly as I got up from my seat, thinking he might feel a little more at ease facing me at eye level.

"Ah...um...I'm Mr Dunne, ma'am." He had phrased this in the way of a question rather than a statement and was looking at me expectantly, as if the name should mean something to me.

"Mr Dunne," I repeated slowly, before comprehension suddenly dawned. "Mr Dunne? The overseer?"

He nodded briefly, and I gaped at him in unconcealed fascination.

So this was the overseer Quin had hired, who'd been arrested and imprisoned for drunken assault. Quin hadn't described Dunne to me, but the timid-looking man standing in front of me fell far short of what I had imagined. He hardly looked like the sort to assault anyone, drunken or not.

But appearances could be deceiving, I thought to myself.

"I see."

I blinked at the mouse-like man, unsure how to respond. Dunne must have served his time in gaol months ago. What was he doing here now? I was trying to think of something to say when the doorway darkened again, this time revealing the taller and broader form of Quin. He caught sight of my visitor and his eyes went wide.

"Mr Dunne?" He glanced at me, but I shrugged. I certainly hadn't invited the man.

"Mr Williams." Dunne gave Quin a quick bow before pulling himself up to his full height, which, nevertheless, barely allowed him to reach Quin's shoulder. "I...ah...I have come to Glaslearg." He was making an obvious effort to sound confident but was falling rather short.

"I see," Quin said dryly, narrowing his eyes at him.

"I realise my arrival is...somewhat delayed..."

"You might say that.—But only by a year or so." Quin flipped his wrist in mocking dismissal.

The overseer cleared his throat. "I apologise, sir," he said, spreading out his hands in supplication, his head slightly bowed.

Quin looked at Dunne in some surprise, before inclining his own head ever so slightly in acknowledgement. "How can I assist you, Mr Dunne?"

"I...ah...I had hoped to take on the position of overseer on your estate, sir.—As we had agreed," he added hesitantly, his hands clasped in front of him. With the tips of his ears and his nose still pink, he looked even more like the mouse he'd reminded me of when I'd first seen him.

"I see," Quin said slowly, rubbing his chin in thought as he assessed the slight man. "And what makes you think the overseer's position has not already been filled? Your delay is...considerable, after all."

Dunne swallowed visibly at Quin's words but squared his shoulders before responding. "I have no such assurance, sir, only hope. But...I thought it right to present myself...regardless." He paused briefly before adding in a soft voice, "I am an honourable man, sir." He looked up at Quin as he spoke, his eyes round and guileless, the picture of sincerity.

I felt a stirring of compassion in my heart for the man and was hard pressed to remind myself not to welcome him with open arms. I glanced at Quin to see if he was similarly affected, but his face gave nothing away, showing little more than courteous interest.

"As it happens, Mr Dunne," Quin said, "Glaslearg has not yet acquired an overseer." A hopeful look bloomed on Dunne's face, but it was quickly dashed with Quin's next statement. "Although I have a potential candidate in mind."

I raised my brows slightly at this.

I hadn't heard anything about a possible new overseer from Quin. After Mr Dunne's failure to arrive at the estate the previous year, there had been only one other candidate I'd been aware of—the man recommended by Sir Spencer several months ago, when Quin had intended to take me to England following Kieran's murder.

My heart gave a sudden thump at the memory. It was his intended interview with the man that had seen Quin leave the estate on the day Doyle had attacked me. Quin's fortuitous return that day had saved my life, but by the time Quin had contacted the potential overseer again some weeks after the missed meeting, he'd already found employment elsewhere. Quin hadn't mentioned he was now actively seeking someone else.

"Oh." Dunne lifted his chin, clearly trying to sound nonchalant at hearing his hopes of finding work at Glaslearg would likely be dashed. "Then I'll not keep

444

you any longer, sir...ma'am." He bowed to Quin and then to me. "I shall count myself satisfied at having appeared before you."

He started turning toward the hallway but was stopped by Quin's voice.

"I didn't say I'd *hired* anyone, Mr Dunne, only that I had a potential candidate."

Dunne turned back toward Quin, looking at him in a mixture of startlement and confusion. "Sir?"

Quin observed the overseer for a moment before responding. "Why have you only come to see me now, Mr Dunne?" he asked suddenly, giving the man a piercing look. "You must have served out your sentence in gaol many months ago and yet, you did not come here immediately. Why?"

Dunne's cheeks reddened at Quin's mention of his arrest and imprisonment, but he met Quin's eyes squarely. "I had a...personal matter to attend to," he said, darting me a brief glance.

"And was this personal matter of a nature similar to that which saw you arrested?"

Dunne shook his head in disbelief at Quin's question. "Are you asking me if it was a matter of violence?"

Quin cocked his head and raised one brow.

"No! It most certainly was not. I am not a violent man." Seeing Quin's sceptical look at this statement, Dunne frowned. "I am not!"

"If that is so, then perhaps you would be kind enough to acquaint us with the circumstances of your arrest?" Quin crossed his arms in front of his chest and looked down his nose at Dunne.

The overseer cleared his throat, looking distinctly uncomfortable. After a moment's silence, though, he began to talk. "It's true, sir, I was arrested for drunken assault.—Although the assault was no more than a single punch thrown in anger! I do admit I was indeed drunk, though. So I suppose it was a fair judgment after all." He compressed his lips briefly at this conclusion but lifted his head as he awaited Quin's response.

Quin eyed the man silently for a minute or two before nodding to himself, as if he'd made up his mind about something.

"Will you be staying in the area a while, Mr Dunne?" he asked, making no reference to the overseer's tale.

"Ah...yes...I suppose I will. I'll likely be staying with a cousin in Ballygawley."

"Constable Ryan, I presume?"

"The same." Dunne looked slightly startled, having evidently forgotten it was Constable Ryan who'd recommended him to Quin in the first place.

"Just so. Would it be agreeable for me to call on you there in a week or so?"

"Yes. Yes, certainly, sir. Does that mean...?" Dunne snapped his mouth shut abruptly.

Quin inclined his head toward the shorter man. "I shall call on you in a week."

"Of course, sir."

"Then I shall wish you a pleasant day," Quin said in obvious dismissal.

"And I wish you the same," Dunne responded rather stiffly. He bobbed a quick bow, and with a muttered "Good day" he was off, before Quin or I had said another word.

I looked after him in some astonishment before turning back to Quin.

"Why did you do that?" I asked him in a mixture of amusement and irritation, coming out from behind the desk as I did so.

"Do what?" Quin looked startled as he turned away from the empty doorway.

"Make the poor man squirm like that."

"The poor man?" Quin repeated, a humorous expression blooming on his face. "You are referring to Mr Dunne, are you not?" I narrowed my eyes at the rhetorical question, making him give a short laugh. "The same Mr Dunne who was arrested for drunken assault and has only recently completed a six-month prison term in punishment for said assault?"

"Yes," I agreed shortly.

"Then that is precisely why I made him squirm, as you describe it.—I was hardly going to welcome him to Glaslearg with open arms."

I could feel myself flush at Quin's words, having had the inclination to do just that when confronted with Dunne's remorseful demeanour.

A slow smile spread across Quin's lips as he watched me. He took a step toward me so he was standing right in front of me. "That's what you would have done, isn't it?"

I shrugged noncommittally but Quin wasn't fooled. "You're more forgiving than I am," he said with a grin.

"You make that sound like a bad thing," I muttered.

Quin laughed and reached out a hand toward me. "It's one of the things I love about you." He pulled me toward him so he could place a gentle kiss on my forehead. "Still, I can't let the man's outward appearance cloud my judgement of him." He gave me a long look, green eyes intent.

I sighed. "I suppose." I lifted one shoulder in some regret. "He just seemed so..."

"Likeable?" Quin suggested.

"Yes. And apologetic."

"And he very well may be those things and more. I just have to be sure of it before hiring him."

"Does that mean you're considering it?"

Quin looked at me thoughtfully for a moment before answering. "I am," he said finally. "I was ready to do so after our first meeting, and if the assault he was arrested for was indeed as slight as he says..." Quin shrugged. "But I do have a few questions about the affair before I make up my mind. If the incident was truly confined to a single blow, as Dunne says, it seems peculiar for him to have been convicted of assault."

I nodded. While drunken brawls and violent behaviour were punishable by law, it wasn't unusual for the odd argument to be settled with the well-placed strike of a fist, an act that would as frequently be laughed off as penalised. I smiled wryly to myself at the thought, shaking my head at the barbaric streak that seemed to run through even many a civilised man.

"What's so amusing?" Quin asked with a suspicious expression on his face, looking so comical I had to laugh out loud. He looked at me in some surprise for a moment before slowly breaking into a broad smile, his eyes softening as they held mine. "It's been a long time since I've heard you laugh," he said, stroking my cheek gently with the back of one hand.

"I suppose it has," I said, suddenly realising I probably hadn't laughed once since Kieran's death. I felt the smile start slipping from my face but made an effort to keep it in place.

Quin chuckled at the grimace that seemed to result. "It's a start," he said in a tender voice, pulling me close.

"I'LL BE LEAVING for Ballygawley after breakfast," Quin said about a week later as we made our way down the stairs to the dining room.

I nodded, aware he'd wanted to visit Mr Dunne that day. "What will you say to Mr Dunne?"

"I haven't decided yet. Much will depend on what *he* has to say."

447

We reached the dining room and Quin pulled out my chair for me, seeing me comfortably seated before settling down himself and continuing his contemplations.

"Dunne's acquaintance swears the man only threw one punch, which would corroborate Dunne's own story.—But the magistrate who convicted him says the victim showed wounds that couldn't possibly have been sustained by a single blow."

"So someone is lying."

"Yes. But who?" Quin raised his brows, giving me a dark green look.

"I don't think it's Mr Dunne," I said with a small shake of the head, remembering the mouse-like man who looked as if he couldn't hurt a fly.

"You like the man," Quin said with a grin.

"I hardly know him. But...I believed him."

Quin was silent for a moment. "So did I." He picked up the teapot and filled my cup. "Let's see what he has to say in his defence."

AFTER QUIN LEFT, I spent the day wandering from one task to the other, tying up some loose ends here and sorting out a few things there. I didn't expect Quin back before early evening and so I was rather surprised to see Rupert, who'd gone with him to Ballygawley, appear at the door as I sat in the study in the middle of the afternoon.

"Rupert, you're back early." I glanced behind him, looking for Quin.

"It's only me, mum," the young valet said, his round cheeks becoming flushed.

"Only you?" A sudden wave of alarm swept over me. "Has something happened?" I croaked as my heart started beating frantically.

"Oh no, mum, nothing's happened," Rupert assured me anxiously. "Mr Williams is quite alright, mum." He nodded vigorously, and I breathed a sigh of relief. "It's only that he's sent me to tell you he'll be staying the night."

"Staying the night? In Ballygawley?" I gaped at Rupert, not understanding. Glaslearg was less than an hour's ride from Ballygawley; it made no sense for Quin to stay overnight.

"Yes, mum."

"I see. Thank you, Rupert." I gave the valet a small smile. "Go ahead and ask Mrs O'Sullivan for something to eat. You must be hungry."

Rupert's face lit up. "Yes, mum. I will, mum." He bobbed his head briefly before disappearing in the direction of the kitchen across the hall.

448

I looked after him in some amusement. At nineteen, Rupert could barely get enough to eat, seeming always ready to accept any food on offer, no matter the time of day.

Thinking about the time of day made me think about Quin and his peculiar decision to spend the night at Ballygawley. I knew he'd wanted to question Mr Dunne once more about the events that had seen the overseer arrested, but I couldn't imagine such an enquiry would require Quin to stay overnight, even if he'd also wanted to speak to somebody else. He'd already had most of the day, after all.

Besides, I knew Quin much preferred to spend the night in his own bed whenever possible, and that he particularly didn't like spending the night away from me. It was unlike him not to take the time to come back when he was so close to home, even if it meant a return trip the following day.

"He'll have his reasons," I muttered to myself eventually, deciding there was no point in speculating. "And he'll tell me all about those tomorrow."

WHEN TOMORROW CAME I started the day ordinarily enough, busying myself with some of the estate's never-ending tasks. But as the clock ticked on in the afternoon, I started getting restless, unable to concentrate on any one thing for longer than a few minutes, my eyes continuously straying to the doorway, hoping for Quin to appear.

Eventually I gave up on the pretence of work, instead sitting down with a book in the drawing room while I waited for Quin to come home.

When he finally did come home in the late afternoon I jerked up in my chair as he entered the room, having nodded off with my book on my lap. He smiled at me as he came toward me, looking a little dishevelled after his ride back. When he reached my chair, he bent down and kissed me softly on the mouth. He smelled of the dust of travel and the sweat of exertion, but I leaned toward him eagerly.

"Quin," I greeted him with a smile of my own when he released me, blinking away my lingering tiredness. "You're back."

He chuckled at the superfluous statement but nodded. "I am."

"What took you so long?"

He didn't respond immediately, instead looking at me speculatively for a moment as the smile disappeared from his face, a thoughtful expression blooming in its place. "I happened upon Constable Ryan at Ballygawley..." he said finally, holding my eyes.

"Yes." I drew out the word into a question while I nodded. He'd gone to see Mr Dunne at Constable Ryan's residence after all, so it was quite conceivable Quin would have encountered the constable himself during the course of his enquiries. "But…"

"We got to talking."

"And this conversation continued throughout the night?" I asked, unable to hide my surprise. Quin and Constable Ryan were hardly more than casual acquaintances, and any chance encounter would unlikely be so long-winded.

Quin cleared his throat. "Well…no…" He narrowed his eyes slightly as he looked at me, as if he were assessing me.

I narrowed my own eyes, starting to get rather irritated with his evasive answers. I raised one brow expectantly, waiting for him to explain himself.

Quin pursed his lips briefly, as if trying to decide what to tell me. "I went to Omagh gaol," he said at last, the words spilling rapidly out of his mouth as he made up his mind to speak.

My heart gave a sudden lurch at the name. Omagh gaol was where Kieran had been imprisoned alongside Martin Doyle. "Why?" I asked slowly in a quiet voice while my heart beat rapidly, a distinct feeling of uneasiness growing inside me.

"I went to see the sheriff, and the warden."

"Why?" I asked again, feeling suddenly like I was struggling to breathe.

Quin's brows drew together in annoyance. "Because I want answers," he said, his voice infused with extreme frustration and a good dose of violence, "about how Martin Doyle came to escape the hangman's noose!"

I got up slowly from my chair and came to stand in front of Quin, who was scowling after his outburst.

"Why?" I asked for the third time, slowly and deliberately, looking Quin in the eye as I did so.

"What do you mean, why?" he exploded, shaking his head in disbelief at my question. "Isn't it obvious?"

"How is anything you may find out going to benefit us?"

He gaped at me. "Don't you want to know who's responsible?" he burst out, his features becoming suffused with rage.

"I already know who's responsible, Quin. And reminding myself Martin Doyle is dead is the only thing that gets me out of bed on some days." I glared at Quin, while he continued to look at me in a mixture of bafflement and anger.

"Somebody arranged Doyle's escape," he said slowly, as if he were talking to a fool. "If that hadn't happened…"

"And if Kieran hadn't gone alone to the barn that day…" I interrupted him, "and if I hadn't gone to the stable after you left for Ballygawley, and if Kieran hadn't gotten mixed up with Doyle in the first place…" I shook my head and took a deep breath. "We can't spend the rest of our lives looking back!"

"I have no intention of doing any such thing, Alannah!" Quin leaned toward me as his eyes bored into mine. "But somebody needs to pay for arranging Doyle's escape! The man murdered your brother and came within an inch of doing you the same favour…all because someone saw fit to have him released when he was already condemned to die for his crimes!"

I flinched at his words but refused to back down. "And is your vengeance going to change the past? Is it going to bring Kieran back?"

"Of course not. But…"

"No but, Quin," I said heatedly. "Doyle is dead. Please…just let it be!"

"I can't!"

"You can't?" I threw his own words back at him, quite unable to be civil by now. "Why? Because you feel like you have to make up for your own imagined failings?"

His nostrils flared angrily. "Is that what you think? That I'm only interested in my own ego?"

"I don't know *what* to think! I thought we were moving forward, that we were putting the whole dreadful affair behind us…"

"We *are* moving forward," he insisted. "That's got nothing to do with it!"

"That's got *everything* to do with it!"

He shook his head, a look of disbelief appearing on his face. "So you're suggesting," he said slowly, his voice strongly tinged with scorn, "that I simply forget the whole thing? That I accept Doyle's death as the end of it…no matter who might have released him or why?"

"You have to, for your own sake…as well as mine."

He stared at me for a moment while I looked back without blinking, neither one of us willing to back down.

"Well I can't, Alannah," he finally said. "Whether it's to make up for my own failings"—he clenched his jaws briefly before going on—"or simply to see justice done. I cannot pretend Doyle's escape was an accident and that his death is the end of it. I can't. And I simply won't! I *will* make sure whoever is responsible for Doyle's escape pays for it, whether I have your support on the matter or not." He gave me a long look but when I didn't respond or make a move toward him, he turned on his heel and disappeared out the door.

I stared after him, standing in the middle of the room, my hands clenched in frustration and anger.

"Stubborn man!" I hissed under my breath.

We had worked so hard to find our way back to each other after Kieran's murder and Doyle's reappearance. Were we to lose each other now, after all?

I sighed and sat back down in my chair. Quin had his reasons for feeling the way he did, of course. I thought he no longer blamed himself for Kieran's death or for what Doyle had done to me, but I knew he did still regret his inability to better protect us from the man. But should I therefore encourage Quin to embark on the path he was set upon?

On the one hand, he was undeniably right. Someone *had* planned Doyle's escape and should be punished for it but on the other...

I had spent weeks after Kieran's death and Doyle's attack on me thinking about what might have been, how things might have been different if only this or that hadn't happened. And it had almost destroyed me. I didn't want Quin to do the same, especially when it was quite possible he would never find out anything, leaving only disappointment and anger in his wake as he tried to find answers to questions that didn't exist.

As for me, I had to look forward.

I could not allow myself to obsess about the circumstances of Doyle's escape or worry about the person responsible. Doyle *had* escaped and all the dreadful events that had followed that fateful day had come to pass—there was nothing anybody could do about it.

Did I want vengeance? Yes, I did. But in my mind, it had already been served. Martin Doyle was dead, killed by Quin's own hands. For me, that was enough.

It had to be.

QUIN STORMED ANGRILY through the entrance hall and out the front door. Not stopping for breath, he continued across the courtyard and up the path past the outbuildings that led to the stream, fuming with rage as his long strides made short work of the distance. He crossed the bridge that led over the small river and continued along the water's edge, until finally, with an explosive expulsion of breath, he came to a stop, sitting down abruptly on the grassy bank as the long rays of the late afternoon sunshine broke through the cloud-streaked sky above.

He pounded his fist onto the ground in frustration, but the spongy grass gave no more than an unsatisfactory soft thump. He grumbled in further annoyance but stayed where he was, looking moodily at the dark water of the stream as it gurgled peacefully past.

"What could there possibly be to disagree with?" he asked himself angrily, his mind flitting through the conversation with Constable Ryan that had sparked his sudden and urgent need for answers. He'd thought about Doyle's escape many times, of course, and had even made a few enquiries before, but his discussion with the constable the previous day had tilted Quin's general interest toward the necessity for immediate action.

"She's just arguing for the sake of arguing," he muttered, finding it impossible to understand how Alannah could have any conceivable objections to finding the person responsible for Doyle's release.

In Quin's mind, it was very simple—whoever had arranged Doyle's escape must be caught and punished. If Doyle had been hanged when he'd meant to, Kieran would never have been murdered and Alannah herself would never have been assaulted. There was nothing complicated about it—it wasn't a series of ifs and buts that needed to be evaluated.

Somebody had seen fit to release a violent criminal, and that somebody needed to be brought to justice. And he, Quin, intended to ensure it was done.

He snorted in irritation. She'd accused him of being preoccupied with the past, of obsessing about what might have been. But should he rather not think about it at all? And let whoever had allowed a condemned man to enact his vengeance get away with it?

"If that's what she expects of me she doesn't know me at all!"

He didn't know, of course, whether the person responsible for Doyle's escape had envisaged what the man might do to them or whether it was simply a matter of seeing Doyle freed out of some allegiance to Doyle himself. But he would be no closer to finding out who or what lay behind Doyle's escape if he simply let the matter rest.

It had nothing to do with obsessing about the past or worrying about what might have been. Nor was it his need to make up for his own imagined failings, as Alannah had so flatteringly put it. He grumbled under his breath, frowning in annoyance, but he had to admit there was some truth to her remark, hurtful though it was—he wasn't sure if he would ever stop thinking he should have been able to do more to protect them from Doyle. But it wasn't even this consideration that had caused him to make up his mind to find the person responsible for the man's escape when his conversation with Constable Ryan had fuelled a thought he'd been suppressing for some time.

Someone had caused them harm—whether intentionally or not—and that person needed to pay for it.

That was all there was to it.

Quin took a deep breath, before blowing it forcefully out of his nose and consciously unclenching his fists. He noticed then a few raindrops had started to fall, stippling the stream's shadowy surface. He looked across at the far side of the water, at the large oak tree that stood there, its leaves rustling softly in the drizzle, and realised suddenly he was sitting in the spot where Alannah and he had had a picnic one beautiful summer's day not so very long ago.

He had been so filled with fascination and admiration that day, for the beautiful black-haired woman who'd come unexpectedly into his life, that he had scarcely been able to contain his joy at being in her presence.

From the start he had wanted her and had wanted to protect her.

He swallowed heavily and clenched his hands into fists once more as a sudden vision of Alannah's beaten and bloodied face came into his mind.

He had wanted to protect her, but he hadn't been able to stop her from coming to harm, nonetheless.

He would not sit by idly now and let those responsible go unpunished.

BY THE TIME he returned to the house it was suppertime, and he was drenched. The rain had picked up rapidly after its gentle start, the water seeping through his outer clothing in a matter of minutes. Quin wasn't bothered, though. Although he was wet, he wasn't cold, and the downpour had helped clear his head.

He made his way cautiously back into the house through the front door and shrugged out of his wet jacket and waistcoat. Finding his shirt and trousers to be only damp, not soaked, he continued on to the dining room in search of Alannah. Discovering this to be empty, he wondered whether she might have gone up to their room. Looking toward the drawing room, though, he saw the door was slightly open. As he got nearer, he could see Alannah, sitting in the same chair she'd been sitting in earlier. He walked slowly toward the door, gathering his thoughts, before pushing his way inside.

Alannah lifted her head as he entered. She looked at him a little uncertainly and didn't say anything, but one corner of her mouth started turning up ever so slightly in a hesitant smile.

A small smile formed on his own lips in response, and he felt a weight lift off his shoulders as he closed the gap between them. He stopped in front of her, raising one brow and cocking his head toward one of the empty chairs. She

454

nodded at him, and he took a seat next to her, forgetting the state of his garments as he lowered himself onto the thick upholstery.

"Alannah," he said gently, deciding to get straight to the point, "I want you to know...that I want us to move forward, just as you do." He took her hand and squeezed it tightly. "But...I have questions that demand answers. And I simply cannot let them be." He looked at her searchingly, wanting her to understand. She blinked and he could see her swallow, but she remained silent. "I want those who have hurt you to be punished. I hope you can understand that."

"I can...truly. It's just that..." She let the comment fade away, her eyes troubled.

"What's done is done," he said firmly, "I know we can't change it. But we can seek justice.—That's all I ask."

Alannah was quiet again for a minute or two, looking down onto her lap. "What did you find out?" she asked finally in a quiet voice, lifting her eyes to his.

"Oh," Quin started, surprised at her question. "Ah...not very much I'm afraid. Neither the sheriff nor the warden, nor several guards I spoke to or even the hangman himself could tell me very much. They had all been under the assumption that Martin Doyle had, in fact, been hanged and only learned of the deceit after he showed up here, alive." Quin compressed his lips at the memory.

"But surely somebody must have noticed something?"

Quin gave an irritable shrug. "Apparently not. Nobody seemed to have realised the hanged prisoner was not Martin Doyle, and nobody missed Doyle after his escape because they had assumed him to have been hanged..."

"But...how is it possible nobody noticed the hanged man was not Martin Doyle?" she protested, voicing a question he'd asked himself a thousand times. "Even if there was a physical resemblance between the two men, surely the man condemned in Doyle's place would have cried out his own innocence on his way to the gallows."

"My point exactly. And even if that had been ignored as the desperate ravings of a dead man, the unknown replacement must assuredly have spent his dying breath denying he was Martin Doyle...whose crimes would have been listed before the sentence was carried out, leaving the unfortunate man in no doubt that the noose around his own neck was meant for somebody else."

"And nobody could tell you anything useful at all?"

"No. One of the guards did grudgingly admit he heard the prisoner attest to his own innocence, but he informed me this was not unusual in those about to meet the hangman's noose." Quin gave Alannah an ironic look. "He therefore paid the man's pleading no mind, or so he said. Just as the hangman himself evidently paid his victim no mind. He told me he performed the duty required of him that

455

day with little thought, and only the barest acknowledgment of who it was he was sending to the beyond." Quin snorted, rather hoping his own demise would be met with a little less indifference.

"But," Alannah started, breaking in on his thoughts, "what about the prisoner who was hanged in Doyle's stead? Even if nobody noticed anything suspicious at the time of the hanging, surely the other prisoner would have been missed after the fact?"

"Well, that's the strange part.—There were no prisoners missing following the hanging."

Alannah looked at him for a moment, confusion plain in her features. "But Doyle...he said..."

"He told you what he was told himself. And the guard who probably told him so, the guard who was to lead Doyle to the gallows that day, has conveniently disappeared..."

"Oh."

They lapsed into silence, Quin mulling over what little he had learned while Alannah's face took on a speculative look.

"Will you try to track him down?" she asked suddenly. "The missing guard, I mean."

Quin nodded slowly, resting his elbows on his knees and steepling his hands. "I would like to do so." He tapped his index fingers together in thought. "I shall have to call on a few acquaintances but...I think it can be done."

"If the man is to be found at all." Alannah lifted one sleek black brow in a meaningful gesture.

"There is that, of course. It hadn't escaped my attention that whoever had Doyle released may have carefully covered his tracks.—Or eliminated them altogether."

Alannah's face took on a carefully blank expression as she made an obvious effort to keep her emotions at bay. "Ah...what about Mr Dunne?"

Quin blinked, having quite forgotten about the man. Seizing the opportunity, though, he leapt onto the change of topic with alacrity. "I've hired him," he announced. "Or should I say, I've *rehired* him." He winked at Alannah, making a small smile come to her lips.

"I'm glad," she said, looking pleased. "What made you decide in his favour?"

"He swore to me on his mother's grave that he only threw a single punch...and that the man deserved it." He chuckled at the memory of the slight man proclaiming his relative innocence.

"But what about the extensive bruising on the victim the magistrate attested to?"

Quin shrugged. "Dunne couldn't tell me anything about that. But it seems there was some long-standing animosity between him and his former employer."

Alannah's eyes went wide. "He assaulted his former employer?"

"He *hit* him...once," Quin corrected with a grin. Seeing her expression, he laughed out loud. "I doubt he's in the habit of doing so. And should he be tempted," he continued cheerfully, "we have agreed he will be summarily dismissed."

"I see. And...did you find out *why* Mr Dunne felt it necessary to hit his employer...at all?"

Quin shook his head. "He was rather close-lipped about it, although I gathered it was something of a personal matter."

"Hm. I suppose he'll tell us about it if ever he wants to."

"I suppose he will," Quin agreed. "In the meantime, I have promised to welcome him to the estate in the new year. There's not much for him to do here before then.—Let us hope my judgement will not prove to be in error."

"It hasn't let you down yet, has it?"

Quin glanced up at Alannah's voice, finding her looking at him with a small smile on her lips.

"No. At least not much."

"You'll be careful, won't you?" she said, her voice soft.

"Of course," Quin responded gently, realising she was no longer talking about Mr Dunne. "I wouldn't knowingly put myself in danger." Alannah gave him a sceptical look. "At least not if I can help it," he amended.

Alannah compressed her lips but didn't comment. "What did Constable Ryan say?" she asked instead. "To make you want to go to Omagh gaol?"

"It wasn't anything in particular." Quin paused, collecting his thoughts. "He enquired about your welfare...whether you had quite recovered from your...shock, as I believe he called it." He frowned slightly at the memory. "We got to talking...about Doyle, his arrest and his escape. Ryan told me he'd looked into the matter himself and had found no leads, only dead ends. And...I suddenly felt...that it was odd."

He gave Alannah a puzzled look.

"Why go to so much trouble to see a brute like Doyle escape?" he asked in the same confusion he'd felt the day before. "And not only escape but leaving everyone else thinking he was dead?—Who was behind it, and why? Who would benefit from the deception?"

"Doyle himself," Alannah suggested. "Do you think...that he was the one who planned it?"

"It seems the obvious answer. With everyone thinking him dead, no one would come looking for him. But...it just..."

"...doesn't fit," Alannah finished the thought for him.

Their eyes met, and Quin's mouth turned up briefly. "Exactly.—How would he have planned such a thing? Who would have helped him?"

"Nobody. He trusted no one."

They were both quiet once more, absorbed with their own thoughts.

"And if he *had* arranged the whole thing himself," Alannah continued suddenly in a quiet voice, "he would have told me."

A cold shiver ran down Quin's back at her words. He held Alannah's eyes, seeing a host of memories flit across her face.

"You're right."

Doyle most certainly would have told Alannah if he'd been the one behind his own escape. In fact, Quin thought with clenched jaws, Doyle wouldn't merely have told her about it, he would have boasted about it, using what he would have thought to be the last few minutes of her life to brag about his own prowess, taunting her with the details of his feat.

Quin breathed out heavily, making an effort to push the thought aside.

"You're right," he said once more, reaching the same conclusion he'd come to the day before. "It wasn't Doyle."

"Then who?"

Quin shrugged. "Somebody who felt some loyalty toward him..."

Alannah shook her head. "Nobody was that loyal to Doyle. At least not according to what Kieran said..."

"But why else arrange his escape? And cover it up so nobody would come looking for him? Who else would benefit from such an undertaking?"

"I don't know."

Quin grumbled in annoyance. "It must have been somebody who had something to do with the blasted man," he muttered. "But who?"

He hadn't really expected an answer to his question, but Alannah's eyes suddenly widened.

"Somebody who had something to do with the man... Somebody like...Herbert Andrews?" She swallowed, looking a little stunned at the thought.

Quin was a little stunned himself, having just about forgotten the man even existed, what with everything else that had happened over the past months. He moved his head slowly from side to side as he contemplated the possibility.

The man must surely be devious enough, he thought, remembering how Andrews had blackmailed Kieran out of his land.

But there was just one problem Quin could see.

"What would Andrews have to gain from Doyle's freedom?"

Alannah looked at him for a moment before answering. "Nothing," she said. "Rather the opposite.—Andrews did see Doyle convicted after all."

Quin snorted at the memory. "A peculiar accomplishment I am still no closer to understanding." He wondered whether they would ever learn what had led Andrews to act as he had.

"Me neither, but I suppose it does rule him out as somebody who would have wanted to see Doyle released."

Quin nodded distractedly, still thinking about Andrews' contradictory actions. Alannah was likely right, though—the man largely responsible for Doyle's conviction would hardly arrange his escape.

Andrews did bear watching, though, Quin reminded himself.

He sighed. "There's little use in speculating, not until we know a little more." He gave Alannah a sideways glance, waiting to see her reaction.

"You said earlier," she started cautiously, "that you would look for answers whether you have my support or not..."

Quin didn't say anything, waiting for her to go on.

"I shall give you my support, if you promise me a few things." She leaned toward him. "Promise me...that you won't let this matter consume you." She gave him a long blue look. "Promise me that you'll hand the matter over to the police if there's any danger. And promise me...that you'll let it go if you find nothing."

Quin looked at her thoughtfully, contemplating what she was asking of him.

"I promise that I won't let this consume me," he said softly, taking hold of her hand. "I am not going to spend the rest of my life looking back. I want to look forward...with you." He gave her hand a gentle squeeze. "But I will seek justice," he went on. "I shall not place myself in danger if I can help it and I'll ask for assistance if I need it but...I will not let it rest."

Alannah compressed her lips but didn't respond.

"There *are* answers to be found, I'm sure of it.—I just have to know where to look."

Alannah lowered her eyes briefly before quickly nodding her head once.

Quin stood up and pulled her out of her chair and into his arms. They held each other for a minute or two, wrapped in silence.

"You're wet," Alannah said suddenly, running her hand down his back and along the waistband of his trousers. While his shirt had mostly dried by now, the thicker fabric of his trousers was still damp.

"Perhaps you would be kind enough to help me out of my wet clothes?" He raised one brow. "Before I catch a cold," he added with a grin.

"Perhaps," she said, gliding her hands over the damp fabric that covered his rump.

"Mmmm." Quin sighed, pressing her hips closer with one hand, the afternoon's argument receding slowly to the back of his mind.

41.

THE PEOPLE OF Glaslearg celebrated the successful harvest at the festival of Samhain. It took place on a beautiful autumn night, the bonfire's flames reaching up into a clear sky as we gave thanks for the land's fruitful bounty and honoured loved ones we had lost. The addition of Kieran's name to the list of those remembered was difficult to bear, as my mind replayed in vivid detail how we had celebrated and danced together at the same festival just one year before.

I knew it would get easier with time, but his absence was no less stark as the months rolled by, as the Christmas celebrations came and went, and as we quietly rang in the New Year in front of the drawing room fireplace. My parents had never been extravagant in their celebrations of such events, but Kieran had always been there—even at times when we'd barely spoken to each other, his presence had been a constant in my life, something I had taken for granted, never expecting its loss.

And it was no less difficult to deal with even a year after his death, although the shock of it had at least subsided.

"Are you ready?" Quin asked gently, laying a hand on my arm.

I nodded silently, and he offered me my coat. I shrugged into it and pulled on my gloves and hat before taking a deep breath. I took Quin's arm and he led me outside, where the carriage was waiting for us under a canopy of thick grey clouds.

We rode mostly in silence, Quin darting the occasional glance in my direction as he held the reins. I turned toward him and tried to smile reassuringly at him, catching his eye briefly before he looked back at the road ahead, one hand clasping mine.

We reached the graveyard without getting wet, although the sky was still leaden and oppressive. We made our way slowly through the headstones, glancing at inscriptions here and there before coming to a stop in front of a simple granite slab engraved with a name I would never forget.

"Kieran," I said softly, my throat feeling suddenly tight.

Quin took my hand as he came up next to me, giving it a gentle squeeze. I leaned toward him, and he wrapped his arm around my shoulders, pulling me close.

The clouds rolled slowly across the sky as we stood together in silence, looking down at the grave, contemplating the life of the man who lay there.

"*Is cuid den saol é an bás.*"

Quin raised his brows while his eyes carefully searched my face.

"Death is part of life," I said with a sigh before kneeling down and placing the heather wreath I'd brought with me in front of the tombstone.

Rising, Quin gave me a hand, pulling me into his embrace. He held me to him and kissed my forehead as I wrapped my arms around him and closed my eyes, leaning against his chest. I could feel the cold stone of Kieran's grave at my back while Quin's heart thumped rhythmically beneath my ear and his breath tickled my cheek, the earthy smell of damp soil caressing my nose. A soft plop announced the opening of the heavens, and I opened my eyes to see numerous wet blotches appearing on the fabric of Quin's coat.

He looked at me with tender eyes and cocked his head. "Shall we?" he asked, seeming not the least bit bothered by the growing rainfall.

I glanced at the raindrops that stippled the surface of the earth, the water trickling slowly down the stark tombstones and into the soil beneath, there to nurture the seeds that lay in wait for spring's return until they could send forth their shoots to heal the scars left behind by the sharp edges of spade and despair.

"We shall," I agreed, lifting my eyes and taking Quin's arm, turning slowly away from Kieran's grave as we headed toward home.

Epilogue

QUIN CONTEMPLATIVELY RUBBED his chin with one hand, while he rhythmically tapped the fingers of the other on the newspaper he had open in front of him. I observed him with interest, wondering what was keeping his mind so occupied.

He stopped suddenly, wrinkling his brow as he turned the page.

"What is it?" I asked, making him look up. The news couldn't be very recent, I decided. The publication appeared to be several months out of date, likely one of the old papers sent to him by his friends in London.

Quin pursed his lips before responding. "Reports of failing potato crops in the Americas...a blight of some kind." He looked back down at the paper briefly before closing it and raising his eyes. "It's not the first I've read about it," he added slowly.

I nodded. I, too, had read the reports, alarming tales of whole fields of potatoes being dug up to reveal nothing but a mass of black, rotten sludge. We looked at each other for a moment in silence.

"It's probably nothing to worry about," Quin said at last, his face resuming its usual expression of good humour. He folded the newspaper into a neat rectangle that he deposited at the edge of the table. "These things usually blow over.— Besides, America is a long way from here. Our own fields are likely to be safe enough." He grinned at me, making me smile at him in reflex.

"Would you like to go for a ride?" he asked suddenly, cocking his head toward the window.

I looked out at the wispy clouds that dotted the blue sky. "Why not?"

Quin rose from his seat and offered me his hand. He pulled me up from my chair and drew me into his arms, holding me close for a fleeting moment before releasing me. I quickly made my way upstairs to change into my riding habit and pin my hat to my hair.

"Ready?" Quin asked when I met him in the entry hall a few minutes later.

I nodded and took his arm as he led me toward the stable, where the horses were already waiting for us.

"Thank you, Bryan," I said to the elderly groom as he handed me the reigns with his gnarled hands, inclining his head in my direction.

"My lady." Quin spoke behind me, and I turned toward him in surprise.

I laughed when I saw him standing on top of the mounting block, holding out a hand toward me. I pulled Milly to a halt beside him and looked up at his beaming face. He reached down, encircled my waist with both hands and, picking me up, placed me gently on Milly's back.

"Mrs Williams," he said softly and pulled me toward him for a lingering kiss, his hands still on my waist.

I leaned into him, reaching out toward him to caress the nape of his neck. Milly pranced impatiently, wanting to get underway, and I reluctantly let go of Quin and opened my eyes. He grinned at me, his green eyes crinkling into triangles as he jumped off the wooden block and mounted Gambit in one smooth move.

We ambled slowly away from the stable, along the path that led down to the stream and into the surrounding hills. We crossed the bubbling water and climbed the rise on the opposite bank, coming to a stop at the top of the hill, the estate spread out below us.

I caught Quin's eye and saw the same memory that had come to my mind flash across his face.

The view that greeted us on this day was a far cry from the one we'd beheld when we'd first stood together on this hill, almost two years before. The neglected and overgrown fields had been replaced with neat potato furrows that adjoined blankets of winter seedlings awakening from their slumber, ready to burst forth with their summer bounty of wheat and oat. The small herd of sheep was grazing peacefully in the distance, looking like small white clouds in an emerald sky on their pasture, wisps of smoke from the tenants' chimneys rising at the horizon beyond.

I looked back at Quin, who was gazing across the land with an expression of contentment. He turned toward me and smiled softly at me, his face suffused with happiness and his eyes filled with love, making my heart soar with joy at thought of the future that awaited us.

THE END

Thank you for reading *Under the Emerald Sky*!

If you enjoyed this book, please consider posting a short review on Amazon or Goodreads. It takes me about two years to write one of these books and a little encouragement from my readers goes a long way toward keeping me motivated! Reviews and telling your friends about the book also help to get the word out. For an independent author, this is vital to the book's success.

Thank you for your help!

The gripping sequel to
Under the Emerald Sky

Beneath the Darkening Clouds

In a land on the brink of ruin, their past can't be outrun.

They've overcome obstacles and endured heartache, but their biggest challenge is yet to come.

It's 1845 and Ireland is plagued with unrest when the unthinkable happens — the potato harvest on which most Irish peasants depend fails, leaving thousands desperate for food. Unease and fear ripple across the land, along with hunger and disease. With the government's response inadequate, it's up to Quin and Alannah to save the people living on their estate.

But all the while, danger lurks from other quarters, as Quin delves into mysteries from his past, incurring the wrath of powerful enemies.

Amid the hardships of the Irish Famine, Beneath the Darkening Clouds sweeps the reader on a heart-wrenching journey of love and loyalty in a myth-shrouded land.

"From the first line, Weber captivates the reader"
THE HISTORICAL FICTION COMPANY

"A sweeping saga with plenty of romantic tension, historical drama, and deeply emotive moments"
READERS' FAVORITE

Acknowledgements

THE AUTHOR WOULD like to thank:

The numerous academics and laypeople who have researched and written about the Great Famine (and unearthed and published historical records), thereby unwittingly helping me write this book by allowing me to delve into the history, politics and social structures of 19th century Ireland; my dear friend Nikola Staab, for reading and rereading everything I wrote, providing me with helpful suggestions and unending support even when I felt like giving up; my parents, for their encouragement when I first told them I would be publishing the book; my sister, for the original cover and help in marketing the book; my brother-in-law, for all sorts of useful information, particularly regarding the use of social media to get my book noticed; my extended family and friends, for their immediate enthusiasm and support when they found out I was publishing a book, when they hadn't even known I was writing one; and finally, my husband, for supporting me throughout, for encouraging me to start writing before I knew when or where the story would take place, and for pointing out that a highborn gentleman wouldn't be traveling alone—"Fine," I said, "he'll have a valet. What should he be called?" "Rupert," came the unlikely answer and thus, Rupert the valet was born.

About the author

JULIANE WEBER IS a scientist turned historical fiction writer, and author of the Irish Fortune Series. Her stories take readers on action-packed romantic adventures amid the captivating scenery and folklore of 19th century Ireland. The first book in the series, *Under the Emerald Sky*, was awarded bronze medals in The Historical Fiction Company 2021 Book of the Year Contest and The Coffee Pot Book Club 2022 Book of the Year Contest. The second book in the series, *Beneath the Darkening Clouds,* was awarded a bronze medal in The Historical Fiction Company 2022 Book the Year Contest.

Juliane spent most of her life in South Africa, but now lives with her husband and two sons in Hamelin, Germany, the town made famous by the story of the Pied Piper.

www.julianeweber.com

https://www.facebook.com/JulianeWeberAuthor

https://twitter.com/Writer_JW

Printed in Great Britain
by Amazon

44910089R00264